P9-DHQ-993

# Institutional Reforms

# Institutional Reforms

## The Case of Colombia

**edited by Alberto Alesina**

The MIT Press
Cambridge, Massachusetts
London, England

© 2005 Massachusetts Institute of Technology

All rights reserved. No part of this book may be reproduced in any form by any electronic or mechanical means (including photocopying, recording, or information storage and retrieval) without permission in writing from the publisher.

MIT Press books may be purchased at special quantity discounts for business or sales promotional use. For information, please email special_sales@mitpress.mit.edu or write to Special Sales Department, The MIT Press, 5 Cambridge Center, Cambridge, MA 02142.

This book was set in Times New Roman on 3B2 by Asco Typesetters, Hong Kong and was printed and bound in the United States of America.

Library of Congress Cataloging-in-Publication Data

Institutional reforms : the case of Colombia / edited by Alberto Alesina.
    p.   cm.
Includes bibliographical references and index.
ISBN 0-262-01214-6 (alk. paper) — ISBN 0-262-51182-7 (pbk. : alk. paper)
1. Constitutional law—Colombia. 2. Law reform—Colombia. 3. Colombia—Politics and government—1974– I. Alesina, Alberto.

KHH2921.I57   2004
342.861—dc22                                                                 200405516

10 9 8 7 6 5 4 3 2 1

# Contents

# Contributors

Olga Lucía Acosta, Fedesarollo

Alberto Alesina, Harvard University

Ulpiano Ayala (late), Fedesarrollo

George J. Borjas, Harvard University

Alberto Carrasquilla, Fedesarrollo and Universidad de los Andes

Juan José Echavarría, Fedesarrollo and Central Bank of Colombia

Maurice Kugler, Southampton University

Steven Levitt, University of Chicago

Roberto Perotti, IGIER–Universita' Bocconi

Gérard Roland, University of California, Berkeley

Howard Rosenthal, Princeton University

Mauricio Rubio, Universidad Carlos III, Spain

Roberto Steiner, Universidad de los Andes

Juan Gonzalo Zapata, Fedesarrollo

# Acknowledgments

This book grew out of an international project to study institutional problems in Colombia. The mission was not just to examine questions and issues but also to suggest possible solutions. Members of the group, and authors of papers, were Olga Acosta, Alberto Alesina, Ulpiano Ayala, George Borjas, Alberto Carrasquilla, Juan Jose Echavarria, Maurice Kugler, Steven Levitt, Roberto Perotti, Gerald Roland, Howard Rosenthal, Mauricio Rubio, Roberto Steiner, and Juan Gonzalo Zapata. These authors teamed up to investigate the problems presented in this book: Maurice Kugler and Howard Rosenthal, "An Assessment of the Institutional Separation of Political Powers in Colombia"; Gérard Roland and Juan Gonzalo Zapata, "Colombia's Electoral and Party System: Possible Paths for Reform"; Steven Levitt and Mauricio Rubio, "Understanding Crime in Colombia and What Can Be Done about It"; Alberto Alesina, Alberto Carrasquilla, and Juan José Echavarría, "Decentralization in Colombia"; Ulpiano Ayala and Roberto Perotti, "The Colombian Budget Process"; Olga Lucia Acosta and George J. Borjas, "Educational Reform in Colombia"; Roberto Perotti, "Public Spending on Social Protection in Colombia: Analysis and Proposals"; and Alberto Alesina, Alberto Carrasquilla, and Roberto Steiner, "Toward a Truly Independent Central Bank in Colombia."

The papers have circulated widely and received both criticism and praise. They are still influencing the debate about institutional reforms in Colombia.

In preparing their papers for publication in this book, authors have expanded their initial work to account for three things. First they have incorporated the debate and criticisms that followed the original presentation of their work. Second they have connected their discussion of Colombia to academic literature on political economics and institutions. Third they have updated their data to reflect current issues. We were happy to see that in some instances the papers had to be revised because the authors' proposals in the original draft were adopted by the Colombian government. To make the urgency of these studies understood by the uninitiate in Colombian affairs, we have added to the book a chapter, chapter 2 by Juan José Echavarría, on the economic and political history of Colombia. It is our hope that the reader will find Colombia's political economy to be an excellent subject for policy analysis.

Many individuals and institutions contributed to the success of this initiative. The project would have not been possible without the full commitment of Fedesarrollo. Juan Jose Echavarria believed in the project from the very beginning and took risks to push it forward. In addition to his contribution as one of the authors, his energy, optimism, and good spirits were essential. Maria Mercedes Carrasquilla is the "hero" of the project. I have never met somebody so efficient, hard working, committed and enthusiastic. She was perfect. She covered an enormous amount of ground, from fund-raising to organizing meetings, to finding data, to helping the authors in any humanly possible way. The entire project would have collapsed without her. Laura Londoño did an excellent job in editing the chapters before publication. Several individuals helped with comments and data in the individual chapters. Dana Andrus did a splendid job of editing the entire manuscript. We are all very grateful to them; their names are acknowledged in the specific chapters.

For financial support we are very grateful to Andean Development Corporation—CAF, Center for International Private Enterprise—CIPE, Central Bank of Colombia, Inter-American Development Bank (Country Division 5—Region 3, RE3/OD5), Italian Individual Consultant Trust Fund of the IDB, Ministry of Mines of Colombia, National Planning Department of Colombia, Trust Fund for Belgian Consultants of the IDB, and The Tinker Foundation.

Finally, as this project was being completed, Ulpiano Ayala suddenly passed away. We will always remember his good humor, hard work, and keen intelligence. This book is dedicated to him.

# 1 Introduction and Summary

Alberto Alesina

## 1.1 Introduction

Colombia faces a critical juncture in its recent history. One road leads to civil war, chaos, and economic collapse. The other leads to peace, reforms, and economic progress.

The need for institutional reforms in Colombia is self-evident. Violence, crime, and terrorism are rampant; the judicial system is incapable of effectively prosecuting crime. The parliament is fragmented; its members code to myriad lobbying pressures, and the economic stability of Colombia is threatened by this institutional shortcoming. Further decentralization has led to large fiscal imbalances and inefficiencies in the central/local government relationship. The budget process is chaotic and nontransparent. Improvements in the development of social services and poverty reduction programs are still lacking because of an inefficient use of limited resources. Monetary and financial stability require a firmer commitment to inflation control.

Although these problems are common to many developing and industrial countries, the combination of them all has led Colombia to the brink of collapse. This is tragic for the people of Colombia. However, for the outside observer and the student of institutional reforms, Colombia offers a fascinating case study of what can go wrong and how to try to fix it. This book can therefore be read with two purposes in mind. One is to learn about Colombia, her problems, struggle, and road to recovery. The other is as a case study to see how political economics can be used in practical circumstances for policy analysis and policy advice.

### 1.1.1 The "New" Political Economics

The common intellectual ground that underlies these essays is the new political economics framework. This is an exciting new area of research that has literally exploded in the last fifteen years at the borderline of economics, political science, and recently sociology. Many economists have started to realize that studying economic policy in a vacuum, without accounting for political constraints and institutions, can produce excellent normative models but not useful "positive" models. They discovered that giving policy advice in an institutional vacuum was rather pointless. Even for international organizations like the IMF or the World Bank, words like "political constants," "governance and corruption," and "institutional failure" have now become part of the common parlance and interest.

Political scientists were for the most part ready to welcome the interaction with economists and provided expertise on institutional issues and details and learned how to think in a more sophisticated way about economic variables. The result of this interaction is an exciting new field that is now in the mainstream of economics and political science. For instance, recent volumes by Alesina, Roubini, and Cohen (1997), Drazen (1999), and Persson and Tabellini (2000) have summarized this field, especially in its relation to the macroeconomic policy sphere.

An important insight that emerges from this body of work is that policy advice based on institution-free models is often irrelevant. For example, how does one advise a country to keep inflation low if its central bank is an agency of the treasury? It is clearly more useful to give advice about central bank independence than specific advice on inflation. This example is simple, but the logic is the same for complex phenomena. The point is that it is not enough to identify policy failures in a country; it is critical to understand *why* these failures occur.

In this respect Colombia is a fascinating case. It shares many common Latin American problems, political instability, corruption, and rural poverty. But in many other ways it is different. Colombia has had relative macroeconomic stability and the least unequally distributed income in the region. Juan Echavarria, in chapter 2, gives a summary of long-run and more recent economic developments in Colombia that deal with these similarities and differences.

From this intellectual base, we can look into the institutional problems of Colombia and aim to find potential solutions. We do not want to produce new theories. We want to be clear about what one can accomplish with institutional reform: individuals, not institutions, make policy decisions. No one should expect that institutional engineering alone can enforce good policies and achieve peace and progress. However, one can ask institutions to avoid creating obstacles for well-intentioned policy makers to achieve the desired good outcomes, and conversely, to create obstacles to corrupt, self-serving, and short-sighted policies.

### 1.1.2 Endogenous Institutions

A goal of this project is to suggest ideas that are politically feasible and require few legislative transaction costs. The formidable obstacles to this goal are the 1991 Colombian Constitution, which is very detailed, and the Constitutional Court, which has been very active in enforcing various constitutional articles. The consequence is that more than in other countries, even relatively small changes of economic institutions, or of economic policy, require a constitutional change.

But why was the Constitution written this way? As becomes clear below, the current Constitution was the result of complex bargaining forces that led to a document containing something for everyone. Further, since some groups did not trust others, extremely detailed prescriptions were added to ensure that the application of the Constitution would be strict.

The case of the 1991 constitution leads to a general observation. Institutions are not randomly assigned to countries; they are chosen by their citizens. Clearly, history matters, and one cannot engineer institutional reform in a laboratory without accounting for why certain institutions that malfunction were chosen. Recent academic research has started to tackle this problem.[1] But it is not the purpose of this volume to describe a history of Colombia and examine why and how this country got to the point where it is now. Nevertheless, some understanding of its history is critical if we are to formulate appropriate solutions.

Some readers may wonder whether issues like decentralization, electoral reforms, and monetary policy even matter in a country on the brink of a civil war and rampant violence. One could argue that until a détente is reached, there can be no talking about anything else. I believe that this is view is incorrect, for two reasons. One is that to the extent that terrorism and narcotraffic are viewed as a special case of crime and violence, how to deal with them is part of an important institutional question. In fact we have devoted chapter 5 to this problem. The second reason is that to the extent that some of the roots of the violence have to do with discontent about governance in Colombia, the pacification process will need to be accompanied by a vision of what will come after.

### 1.2 Organization of This Book

As I noted earlier, chapter 2 sets the stage for what follows with an overview of the recent economic history of Colombia. Unfortunately, this history is very much linked to the evolution of terrorism and the civil war, so much space has to be devoted to these topics.

The next eight chapters are organized in two parts, around political and economic issues. Maurice Kugler and Howard Rosenthal begin, in chapter 3, with a discussion of the role of the judicial system and the separation of powers. Their contribution is followed by Gérard Roland and Juan Gonzalo Zapata's discussion, chapter 4, of the electoral law and structure of parliament. Next, in chapter 5, Steven Levitt and Mauricio Rubio discuss crime prevention and the criminal justice system. With my colleagues Alberto Carrasquilla and Juan José Echavarría, we move to introduce in chapter 6 the issues surrounding economic institutions. We focus on those institutions that have to do with the bureaucracy and provision of social services, and on monetary and fiscal institutions. Ulpiano Ayala and Roberto Perotti, in chapter 7, discuss namely the central bank and the budget process. In chapter 8, George J. Borjas and Olga Lucía Acosta look at the reforms in education, and in chapter 9, Roberto Perotti, at social safety programs in the local/central government relationships. In chapter 10, with my colleagues Alberto Carrasquilla and Roberto Steiner, we raise some pending issues on the functioning of the central bank.

### 1.2.1    Political Institutions

A student of the political institutions of Colombia is immediately struck by several anomalies. Colombia has two parties that are virtually indistinguishable and often share government responsibilities, an extremely fragmented parliament composed of innumerable "lists" of candidates, a conflictual relationship between the executive and the parliament, and constitutional courts that are very active in applying and interpreting a very long, verbose, and interventionist Constitution.

For the most part the current political institutions were born in the 1991 Constitution. This document is very detailed, but it does not preclude interpretation by the courts. A particularly clear example is the article that prescribes "equal treatment" for all. This principle could be seen as a generic statement, but it has often been interpreted by the Court in an interventionist and proactive way that has interfered in economic matters better left for discretionary policy-making. The electoral system has made it easy for "local" lobbies to find a voice in the Parliament, and by a very small number of strategically placed votes to "buy" a seat. Finally, the relatively small ruling class of policy makers and technocrats in administrative positions raises critical issues of separation of power and checks and balances as well as representation.

Some of these institutional features are "old" and explain some "historical" features of Colombia, such as the difficulty in governability.

Others are new, like the 1991 Constitution, and are more directly responsible for the emergence of more recent problems, such as fiscal imbalances.

### 1.2.2 Checks and Balances

As Kugler and Rosenthal show in chapter 3, the 1991 Constitution has vastly changed the Colombian institutional structure. One of the goals of a constitution should be to create a system of institutional checks and balances that allows the executive to govern, while at the same time guaranteeing the rights of the minority and the rule of law. The 1991 Constitution indeed makes progress in this direction, but not enough. Colombia is still governed in a manner that is both unchecked and unbalanced.

The 1991 Constitution grew out of a negotiation to resolve internal conflict. It is a document of rigid micromanagement (e.g., it mandates indexation of pensions and sets specific targets for inflation and the allocation of regional public expenditures) rather than one that establishes basic institutions for democratic decision-making in a dynamic world. In addition the Constitution promises too much to too many citizens, as if Colombia could create the welfare state of an advanced industrial country. For instance, Chapter 2, Article 1, on economic, social and cultural rights creates high expectations for groups in society such as the handicapped, children, and senior citizens. But Colombia, with a per-capita income of less than 3,000 US dollars, cannot possibly emulate Sweden or Canada or even the United States. In contrast, the US Constitution asserts only that it seeks to "promote the general welfare," rather than making specific "promises" to various groups. Likewise an overemphasis on egalitarianism can be counterproductive. For example, Article 58, which permits uncompensated expropriation for reasons of "equity," can be a substantial deterrent to foreign investment.

These declarations about the rights to welfare and equality are not only words on paper. The Constitutional Court has often intervened in these matters with ruling about issues that, in other counties, are left to normal legislation. Furthermore the Constitution gives private individuals standing to contest legislation directly with the highest courts in the land. As a result almost all legislation potentially can be challenged in court. The Constitutional Court is free to pick and choose among the complaints, and often some laws are overturned on procedural grounds.

A second issue concerns the executive–legislative interaction. Often there has been tension between these two institutions. Because of its fragmentation, lack of party structure and clientelism, the legislature has often failed to be a channel of grassroots representation and a "check" on executive power. As discussed by Echavarría in chapter 2, the electoral system has contributed to this situation.

Partly as a result of the poor functioning of the legislature, the executive has enjoyed a large amount of discretion and often bypasses the legislature. This has been achieved by repeated declarations of a "state of emergency," a situation in which policy-making can be very centralized. In other words, the system of checks and balances between the legislature and the government does not work well. A combination of legislative action and court rulings often makes executive action ineffective. On the other hand, sometimes the executive reaction is to infringe on legislative responsibilities, at least temporarily.

Finally, it is worth noting that the institutional structure in Colombia has not been very stable. Since independence in 1810, there have been drastic constitutional changes in 1821, 1848, 1863, 1886, 1910, and 1991. There have been periods of two-party consensus, as in the National Front, as well as winner-take-all arrangements, with widespread redistribution of political control from the losing party to the winning party. Moreover there have been periods of military rule and also one-party dominance.

### Proposals

Successful democracies have adopted very different institutional settings, and the same is true for less successful ones: the "ideal" institutional arrangement does not exist. There is trade-off between alternative goals that can be achieved by different institutions. In addition, it is often hard to predict precisely how these trade-offs may play out in practice in a specific case. Having said that, it is pretty clear that democratic institutions in Colombia do not work well enough and do not provide an appropriate system of checks and balances. The underlying motivation of the following proposals is to suggest improvement in the current system without revolutionizing it.

#### Proposals Concerning the Courts

• Make the hierarchy of decision-making across the three systems of courts (Constitutional Court, Supreme Court, and Council of State) extremely clear, such that decisions can be appealed upward in the hierarchy and that decisions of a higher court in the hierarchy are binding on courts lower in the hierarchy.

• A supermajority vote of seven of its nine members should be required for the Constitutional Court to overturn a law passed with the agreement of the president and Congress.

• Modify Article 253 of the Constitution to make members of the Constitutional Court, the Supreme Court, and the Council of State life appointees.
• Modify Articles 231 and 239 to have judges in the high courts nominated by the executive and confirmed by the Senate.

The motivation for these proposals is to make the constitutional courts more politically independent. At the same time, the second point makes it more difficult for the courts to be excessively proactive in economic matters.

*Proposals Concerning the Executive–Legislative Interaction*
• Modify Articles 154 and 163 to give the president "fast-track" powers to submit unamendable propositions for urgent matters of economic policy to the Congress.
• Eliminate nominal voting in Congress and make compulsory the publication of voting decisions by lawmakers and court magistrates, except on matters relating to organized crime.
• Revise Article 171 such that the size of the Senate is reduced from 102 to 51 members.
• Revise Article 176 such that the size of the Chamber of Representatives does not increase from its present size of 165.

These proposals, coupled with those discussed below on the electoral law, are intended in change the system in two ways. First, they empower the executive with a constitutional guarantee of having a "fast track." This can avoid the unchecked declarations of a "state of emergency." Second, the reduction in size and elimination of secret ballot in the legislature could help reduce the clientelism and fragmentation that is rampant in this institution. Reinforcing the party structure can also help reduce these problems. This is a main objective of the proposals for reforms of the electoral law discussed in the next section.

*Referendum Process*
• Private citizens collecting signatures of 5 percent of the electorate can initiate national referenda on legislation and constitutional changes. (At present, Article 375 allows citizens only to propose changes to Congress.)

### 1.2.3 Electoral Law and the Parliament
As Roland and Zapata show in chapter 4, Colombia's bicameral legislature is characterized by an extreme degree of fragmentation. Although

only two parties exist, different lobby groups compete within each party, and as a result it is often difficult for the legislature to produce laws that pursue the general interest instead of a compromise between competing lobbies. To be fair, many legislatures have this problem, but the Colombian case has some peculiarities. In Colombia, parties do not have control over their party labels, and different lists can compete within the same party. However, the party organization can be made to control and find ways to discipline or control the activities and behavior of party members beholden to lobbists in the legislature.

The proliferation of lists both in the Chamber of Representatives (the House) and in the Senate and the ability of quite small groups to elect a representative follow from the electoral system. Colombia has an LR-(largest remainder) Hare system that works as follows. In each district, seat quotas are calculated by dividing the number of votes by the number of seats. Seats are first allocated to parties according to integer multiples of quotas. The remaining seats are then allocated in order of the largest remainders. In practice, this system has worked in such a way that most seats are allocated by largest remainders, instead of the quota, because of the fragmentation of lists. In fact the larger the number of lists, the lower is the number of votes necessary to win a seat.

The 1991 constitutional reform attempted to threat this problem by instituting a single national electoral district for the Senate. The purpose was (correctly) to encourage candidates to broaden their electoral platform and to rally voters in a nationwide fashion, based on national issues, and to "include" minorities scattered around the country. However, that reform was prone to fail from the start. In the 1991 election in the Senate, the first to be held nationwide, the number of lists decreased only slightly; then over 1994 and 1998 the number of lists steadily increased.

Senators learned quickly that the old clientelistic equilibrium could be replicated in the national district. No representation thresholds were put in place to discourage small lists and the LR-Hare system remains in place, encouraging fragmentation and election by largest remainders. The number of seats allocated by quota has steadily decreased, and in 1998 only 5 out of 100 senators were elected by quota. All the others were elected by remainder. The marginal price of a seat, calculated as the minimum remainder for which a seat was allocated, represents roughly only 40 percent of the number of votes specified by the quota and was lower in 1998 compared to 1991 and 1994. Instead of trying to gather votes across districts as initially intended by the reform, seats are gained mostly by getting regionally concentrated votes.

This fragmentation and the low "price" (in terms of votes) for a candidate to win have had two negative consequences. The first is a loss of legitimacy of many members of the House and of the Senate. The second is the emergence of a strained executive–legislative relationship. Due to the fragmentation in the legislature, the perception is that the only way to govern effectively is to "bypass" the legislature. While a strong executive is essential in a well-functioning democracy, and executive–legislature conflicts are common (even in the United States), the situation in Colombia has vastly deteriorated.

### Proposals

The following proposals aim to reduce fragmentation in the legislature, increase party cohesion, and increase legitimacy. However, when thinking about electoral reforms, it is important to keep in mind "feasibility"—in two senses. One is in terms of transaction costs and history. For example, it would be some task to transform the US system into a parliamentary democracy given its tradition, history, and institutional forms. The second is that existing legislature would have to vote on a reform. Any electoral reform that would make current legislators unlikely to be reelected is likely to be defeated. The following proposals are relatively simple to implement but do have their important consequences.

### Create a Two-Tiered District System

The idea is to keep the current electoral formula (LR-Hare) for the election of the lower chamber (House) but to shift the above-quota residual votes of local district lists to the national arena. Those residual votes would be pooled together by the national party with which the list is associated. National parties would have control over the order of candidates in the upper-tier district. In other words, seats not attributed by local quota would be allocated proportionally to the national district lists. A threshold rule—a percentage of the residuals—would determine what those national parties are.

The threshold limit is important. It is a way to avoid the failure of the 1991 Senate reform. Even relatively low quotas can create a strong incentive for local politicians to "group" and substantially reduce the number of parties represented in the House.

Besides the reform to the electoral system, some other reforms may improve the functioning of Congress and make parties more cohesive.

*Move the Presidential Election before the Legislative Election, but in the Same Month*
This reform should make the newly elected president less dependent on local barons, and allow the newly elected president to create a national "focal point" in the ensuing legislative elections.

*Reduce a Host of Special Privileges to Congress*
This is one of those changes that many legislatures can be expected to oppose, but it should increase legitimacy and voters' participation.

*Introduce Automatic Registration of Voters*
Any measure that increases voters' participation has the potential of reducing the extent of clientelism.

*Better Define the Relationship between the House and the Senate*
Currently the impression is that the two legislative bodies duplicate their functions. An extreme solution to this problem is to move to a unicameral system. This would be complicated, costly, and not likely to pass. An alternative is to define precisely legislative functions and divide the responsibilities.

### 1.2.4   The Judicial System and Crime Prevention
As Levitt and Rubio write in chapter 5, crime is a big problem and likely the major cause of all problems in Colombia. However, contrary to common belief, not every type of crime is uniformly high. Although the number of Colombians victimized by crime is high by international standards, the rate is not out of line compared with other Latin American countries. The important difference is the type of crime. The homicide rates in Colombia are about the highest in the world. It peaked in 1991, when almost one in a thousand Colombians was murdered that year. The homicide rate in Colombia is three times higher than in Brazil or Mexico, and ten times higher than in Argentina, Uruguay, or the United States. Since 1991 the homicide rate has substantially declined. Today the number of people killed every year is about 60 in a 100,000 compared to the 1991 rate. While the homicide rate is high by international standards, property crime rates are not.

What explanation can be found for the exceptionally high homicide rate? The first and obvious is the drug trade. There is overwhelming evidence that the drug trade encourages violence. Participants in the drug market, unable to legally enforce contracts and property rights, turn to violence and intimidation to accomplish these tasks. The illegality of drugs makes traditional forms of industrial competition like advertising and price cutting difficult. In addition the lawlessness of this sector erodes the recourse to law among those marginalized by the drug trade.

The period of sharply increasing homicides in the 1990s matches the time period in which the export market for cocaine rapidly expanded and drug cartels fought for control of markets. The two departments of the country with the highest rates are Valle and Antioquia, in which Cali and Medellin, respectively, are located. The homicide rates in these departments were four times higher than the rate in the median department over the 1990s. Another indication of the link between the drug market and homicides is that much of the drop in homicides since 1991 is due to reductions in Cali and Medellin, as a result of the dismantling of the traditional drug cartels.[2]

The second explanation is the lack of punishment of criminals. Although Colombia has one of the highest homicide rates in the world, it has the lowest punishment rates. In the United States, an arrest is made and the defendant is brought to trial in 65 percent of discovered murders, and a conviction occurs in more than half of these instances. In Colombia, investigations are made in only 38 percent of the homicides, and only 11 percent of these homicides leads to trials. Convictions occur in less than 7 percent of the homicides in Colombia, which is about one-seventh of the rate in the United States. Average sentence length for those convicted of murder in the United States is about twenty years, of which about one-third of the time is usually served. In Colombia, the average sentence length is fourteen years. There is no good information on the fraction of the sentence actually served. If one assumes that the fraction served is about one-third (which may be an overestimate), then combining the information on probability of conviction with average time served yields a calculation of the expected time served behind bars per murder. In the United States, this number is 3.8 years, compared to 0.32 years— less than four months—in Colombia. Thus effective punishment in Colombia seems to be less than one-tenth that of the United States.

The best empirical estimate of the responsiveness of crime to punishment is that a 10 percent increase in punishment lowers crime by 2 percent. If this estimate is correct, then raising Colombian punishment to US levels, which are similar to most European countries, would reduce Colombian crime rates by more than 50 percent. That would mean eliminating over 10,000 murders annually in Colombia.

A third factor often mentioned to explain homicides is the guerrilla activity. Actually the link between guerrilla activities and the homicide rate is weak. Looking across municipalities, areas with a guerrilla presence are no worse than the others, in terms of homicides. Those areas that did not have guerrillas in the early 1990s, but had guerrillas in 1997, have even seen great declines in homicides over the 1990s. Municipalities that never had guerrillas, or those that had guerillas both in early 1990s and in 1997, show smaller declines in homicides. On the contrary, there is, almost by definition, a very strong connection between guerrilla presence and kidnappings, the latter used to finance the former.

An additional explanation often given is that poverty and income inequality foster crime. This is not convincing. Concerning poverty, international evidence suggests that crime is actually higher in richer countries, even though this effect is due to higher reporting rates. As for income inequality, there is indeed a strong relationship between inequality and crime. However, income distribution is not especially unequal in Colombia relative to other Latin American countries. So the exceptionally high homicidal rate in Colombia cannot be explained by income inequality or poverty.

As the previous discussion suggests, the malfunctioning of the criminal justice system has a critical influence on the crime rate in Colombia. There is a large and growing discrepancy between crimes that citizens say they reported and those crimes officially recorded by the police. The number of crimes that citizens say they reported to the police rose substantially between 1985 and 1995, from 941 to 1,296 per 100,000. Official police records, however, show fewer crimes (661 per 100,000 in 1985) than citizens say they report. Moreover the official data actually show a 10 percent decline in crime between 1985 and 1994. There appears to be little relationship between official police records and victimization or citizen claims of reported crime. Police records include fewer than half of the crimes that citizens claim to have reported.

The investigation of crime is also very poor. A striking figure is that the percentage of reported crime investigated is about 40 percent for each type of crime. In most countries this percentage is much higher for more serious crime, like homicide or kidnapping. Colombian authorities shy away from investigating the most serious crimes. Crimes that are easy to solve are investigated; the others are not.

### Proposals

#### Information Gathering
• Take away reporting/statistical duties from the agencies involved in the criminal procedures. This should include the police, the Fiscalia, the Juzgados, and the prisons.

• Maintain regular (every three years) victimization surveys for the whole country, and not just certain urban areas.
• Maintain a log of prison population. It should be possible to accurately determine the composition of prison population by type of crime committed or the actual time served by inmates.

*Fight against Corruption*
• Supervise externally corruption/infiltration investigation in the Fiscalia. Since the Fiscalia are the critical link in bringing criminals to justice, progress in fighting crime cannot be made until improvements are seen here. This is a basic preliminary step toward reducing what, to some people, looks like a Fiscalia-military confrontation.
• Investigate reports of corruption and purge the military of corrupted officials the same as was done with the police a few years ago, with some external supervision.

*Investigation and Persecution*
• Establish a separate task force to thwart kidnapping, made up of an elite group of fiscales who have proved themselves not corruptible. This group would devote 100 percent of their attention to investigating kidnapping incidents.
• Establish an elite task force to investigate every homicide that occurs. For a task force of 1,000 fiscales, there would be roughly 20 cases annually for each fiscal to investigate.
• Establish mandatory sentences for corrupted judges in order to deter judges from collusion with narcos or guerrillas.
• Guarantee the safety of judges and prosecutors. The government should provide twenty-four-hour protection to judges and prosecutors working on cases dealing with narcos or guerrillas. Extremely harsh mandatory sentences should be introduced for intimidation and retaliatory crimes against judges.
• Increase the share of the police, Fiscalia, and prison resources dedicated to violent crime, especially murder and kidnapping, even if this means withdrawing resources from property crime.
• Increase substantially Colombia's prison capacity. It would not be unreasonable to build enough prison cells to hold 100,000 prisoners (compared to the current prison capacity of 28,000 and actual prison population of 40,000). Even with a prison population of 100,000, the number of prisoners per crime committed will still be very low by international and even South American standards.

• Remove control of the prisons from prisoners. Steps must be taken to put the government and not the prisoners in charge.
• Separate prisoners according to the seriousness of their crimes. Guerrilla and paramilitary should be separated from the rest of the prisoners to avoid the rise of conflagration within prisons.

## 1.3  Economic Institutions

By Latin American standards, Colombia has traditionally enjoyed macroeconomic stability, avoiding hyperinflation and the very large deficits common to the region. With long periods of moderate inflation and a relative fiscal balance, Colombia is (or was) considered a model of macroeconomic management for Latin America. Recently, with the much improved macroeconomic situation in the region, Colombia is becoming a "problem case." The appearance of budget deficits and of financial fragility has led to IMF intervention and international concerns.

Macroeconomic stability is only one pillar for economic development. The others are good infrastructures, well-functioning markets, and efficient bureaucracies. In addition economic growth has to benefit the entire population, and not a minority. Poverty reduction and, as much as possible, equal opportunity for all have to be primary policy objectives. In fact income inequality is very high in many Latin American countries, so Colombia is not the worst case in this respect. However, in Colombia poverty reduction and better provision of social services remain a priority. There can be no trade-off between growth, poverty reduction, and macroeconomic stability. They are all part of the same virtuous circle. Growth and poverty reduction are also the critical ingredients to forging a peaceful society. In the next five chapters, we examine the institutional aspects of economic policy-making.

### 1.3.2  Decentralization and Fiscal Federalism
As Alesina, Carrasquilla, and Echavarria show in chapter 6, the interrelationships among the divisions of governments are a hotly debated issue in many countries and international organizations. Colombia has become by some measures the most decentralized Latin American country among the nonfederal types such as Argentina and Brazil. While the process of decentralization had started earlier, the 1991 Constitution has vastly accelerated the process. Tax collection remains centralized but spending is decentralized. This arrangement creates risks of fiscal imbalance, since the level of government that spends does not fully internalize

the costs of its spending. However, in a country at the level of development of Colombia, many localities, especially in rural areas, lack the ability to efficiently collect revenues. Thus centralizing tax collection is a necessity. On the other hand, concentration of spending is rejected because localities should be able to allocate spending in ways closer to the population's needs and preferences. But given how little discretion localities have to allocate spending, it is not clear that this goal of the decentralization process has been reached. For example, about 80 percent of the fiscal allocation to departments and municipalities has to be spent on health and education. In addition teacher's salaries (which are 80 percent of total spending in education) are decided nationally, and localities have very little discretion. A good argument thus in favor of centralization of revenues is that it allows for the redistribution of the tax burden across localities.

The separation of taxation and spending between different levels of government has fueled serious fiscal imbalances. A large fraction of departments and municipalities has accumulated large debts and operating deficits, and as a result the central government has already intervened to bail out localities, with more bailouts to come. Certainly Colombia is not the only country with this problem. The fiscal deficits originating in the localities are an important issue for many industrial and developing countries in general and Latin America in particular. An additional problem stems from the fact that localities can borrow from banks, thus creating dangerous links between fiscal imbalances and the financial stability of the banking system.

Since the bulk of tax revenues is collected by the central government, an important and politically charged issue is the rules for allocation of tax revenues to departments and municipalities. The current rules are relatively complex (especially those for the municipalities). They take into account several parameters and indicators of relative income, the number of users of certain services, the composition of the population, and so on. These allocations leave no room for incentive schemes that can increase the fiscal responsibility of localities and their efficiency in the delivery of public services. In addition it is not clear how equitable these rules are.

Finally, the short horizons of mayors that cannot be reappointed for two consecutive terms make it difficult to implement long-term policies. Mayors have the incentive to spend, knowing that the tax burden is spread over the entire country and will be felt after they leave the office.

## Proposals

The academic literature on fiscal federalism often suggests two general principles for enforcing fiscal responsibility and efficient use of resources by localities. One is to increase the ratio of local spending financed by taxes collected locally. The coincidence of taxation and spending for the same level of government obviously creates the "correct" incentives. The second is to link transfers from a higher level of government to the achievement of certain objectives, in terms of delivery of social services. In theory, these are two impeccable principles. In practice, their implementation in a middle-income country is highly problematic. For a start, many municipalities and departments (especially the poorest ones) lack the technical competence to raise revenues effectively. Second, problems with the measurement of efficiency in the "delivery" of social services are quite difficult, and are likely to foster corruption and arbitrariness.

For these reasons we shy away from making these two rather "radical" proposals, because of difficulties of implementation. Nevertheless, we do think that several significant changes are necessary and feasible.

### Do Not Allow Local Borrowing

Departments and municipalities should not be allowed to borrow, either from the public by issuing bonds or from private or public financial institutions, domestic or foreign. The only way in which a department or municipality should be able to spend, in one year, more than its revenues (local taxes plus transfers from the central government) is to borrow from the following year's transfers from the central government. The government should set a limit (e.g., 5 percent of yearly transfers) for any borrowing against the following year's allocation and should have the right to refuse "lending" even within this limit.

The motivation of this proposal is self-evident. The inevitability of central government bailouts creates incorrect incentives if localities can borrow from the market. An important caveat concerns public investment. Large investment projects may require multi-year financing. If the preceding budget-balance rule left out investment, the main result would be a reclassification of many noninvestment spending items into investment. The discussion (see below) on the budget process makes it clear how that has happened at the central government level, and it is a common phenomenon internationally. Large investment projects, particularly those involving several departments and municipalities, should be financed and controlled by the central government.

*Simplify of Allocation Rules*
Since it is not feasible that localities raise their own revenues, a large fraction of fiscal transfers from the central government to the localities will continue to exist. The allocation rule for these flows must include some system of "weights" for different objectives. We do not want to choose these weights, for that is a political decision to be taken by the government and the legislature. However, we stress that the allocation rule has to be simple and transparent. These two features (clarity and transparency) will make it clear which weights are given to different objectives and will make it more difficult to achieve "political deals" behind the scene.

An ideal rule should achieve three goals: return to the localities a certain fraction of the tax revenues generated by the region (the remaining fraction is kept by the central government), generate some redistributive flow from richer to poorer regions, and allow for some reward for tax collection effort. We propose an allocation rule based on these three principles.

*Allow More Flexibility in Spending Decisions*
If one of the goals of the decentralization process is to make public spending better match the public's needs, increasing the freedom of choice of localities seem reasonable. A cynical observer might argue that the current arrangement allows localities to write "checks" but does not allow them to make any relevant policy decisions.

The increase in flexibility coupled with the balanced budget rule described above should not make the budget of localities less sound. In practice, this proposal implies reducing the shares of the budget allocated by law to certain uses, and increases the "discretionary" share. Even with more discretion, the bulk of local government spending will still be for health and education. See, however, the discussion of social services below (section 1.3.5), which suggests that these two sectors are overextended relative to other social services.

*Clarify Spending Responsibilities*
Spending responsibilities of different government levels of need to be better specified to avoid duplication, waste, mismanagement, and confusion. Lack of clarity often breeds corruption and rewards for individuals with better connections who can "navigate" the system. As we learn in chapter 6, the education sector is a prime example of this confusion. Currently the same school may be financed partly by the central government, partly by a department, and partly by a municipality. This creates confusion,

duplications, and unfair allocation. It is imperative that spending responsibilities be redesigned in a coherent way. More discussion of this issue appears in chapter 8.

*Allow Reelection of Mayors for Two Consecutive Terms of Four Years Each*

The current combination of a very short electoral cycle (three years) and the "one-term" rule gives mayors an exceptionally short horizon. The proposed change is more in line with international standards. It creates a sufficiently long political horizon for mayors and, at the same time, it avoids the excessively long tenures in office that can foster entrenched interests and "local connections."

### 1.3.3   Budget Institutions

Ayala and Perotti deal with the budget process in chapter 7. Budget institutions are all the laws and regulations under which budgets are drafted by the government, approved by the legislature, and then implemented by the bureaucracy. Before proceeding, let us state clearly that there is little defense, procedural or otherwise, against a government that is determined to run a "bad" fiscal policy without opposition from Congress. Nevertheless, a well-structured budget process can fulfill an important role in fiscal policy.

The rules governing the formation and dissemination of information on fiscal policy should achieve as least three goals:

• "Good" fiscal policy run in a transparent manner.
• Fiscal policy that does not get out of control in the presence of shocks of moderate to large dimensions.
• Fiscal policy projections that can be understood by persons with moderate knowledge of economics and accounting and are compared with performance in previous years.

The last condition is the most important. Since there is no enforcement mechanism that can prevent a government from running a "bad" fiscal policy, only the market and public opinion can exert pressure on the government. Thus the public should have a clear and transparent view of the fiscal policy run by the government. In Colombia, however, the preparation, discussion, and implementation of the budget are not transparent. As a result the average citizen, journalist, or trained economist has a hard time understanding the budgetary documents. In recent years, international organizations have put a lot of emphasis on improving transparency, but Colombia has a long way to go.

Several factors contribute to the lack of transparency. The first is the multiplicity of budget documents. Several budget documents could be useful if they had clearly differentiated functions, allowing one to go from one document to the other. Technically, by Article 13 of EOP, the budget must be consistent with the Plan Nacional de Desarrollo, the Plan Nacional de Inversiones, the Plan Financiero, and the Plan Operativo Annual de Inversiones. A careful examination of these documents reveals, however, that the requirement of consistency is often circumvented de facto, and in some places even de iure. The proliferation of documents, which includes multi-year horizons with a very loose enforcement of consistency, makes it fairly easy to find something for everyone in the budget. Therefore, although the Colombian Constitution provides the finance minister with a strong role in the preparation of the budget, the agencies of these documents tend to obfuscate and reduce his role.

The second is the definition and classification of investment spending. Investment is a magic word in the Colombian budget plan (and it becomes even more magical when combined with "social"). This is largely a reflection of the emphasis on planning, of which investment is the key instrument, and of the populist bent of the 1991 Constitution. The assumption underlying all the budget documents is that only investment has any social value—all other expenditures are necessary evils. This, together with the prohibition on cutting the share of social investment spending in the budget, is an open invitation to a very liberal view of investment, one that is at odds with any conventional usage of the term in the macroeconomic and accounting professions. The Manual de Programacion de la Inversion Publica of DNP gives such a loose definition of investment that very little exists that cannot fit into it. Thus the most important process in the budget becomes extremely difficult to interpret.

The third source of lack of transparency is the frequent use of nonstandard accounting practices. Particularly troublesome is the inclusion of gross debt issues (both amortization and new) and of proceeds from asset sales and amortization as a *recurso de captial* (Article 31 of EOP), and hence above the line. That is, the structure of the budget presentation is:

Revenue = Current revenues + New emission of debt
　　　　　　 + Proceeds for asset sales and privatization
　　　　　　 + Other capital spending + Other revenues

Spending = Current spending + Capital spending
              + Interest + Amortization of debt

This classification hides the deficit. The more proper, common definition of the deficit is (see IMF 1999): New emission of debt − Amortization of existing debt + Proceeds from asset sales and privatization (+ Some quasi-fiscal operations of limited size). Without a long and detailed analysis of both the revenue and spending sides of the budget, it is impossible to form an idea of the deficit. Thus it is difficult to assess the budget.

A fourth source of lack of transparency is the incomplete coverage of the budget. Ideally the budget should cover the entire public sector, as prescribed by international standards (e.g., those enforced, by the OECD). This is far from what happens in Colombia. Particularly troublesome is that not even the entire amounts of public pensions are covered in the budget.

A final two sources of confusion have to do with imperfect macroeconomic forecasts and with the intertemporal links between budgets (i.e., arrears). Most governments have a tendency to manipulate forecasts to "predict" the best fiscal outcome with the minimum effort. For instance, GNP growth has been systematically overpredicted in the nineties. The treatment of the "quite large" areas needs to be improved.

Besides the lack of transparency, a second big problem in the Colombian budget process has been the excessive emphasis on planning. The fact that a market economy chooses to name an important and powerful agency the "Planning Department" is quite telling. There are several reasons why the emphasis on planning is counterproductive. First, the Planning Department (DNP) itself is a hodgepodge of good intentions, to which virtually all institutions and interest groups in the country contribute with their own preferred investment projects. According to the Constitution, the DNP is elaborated by the government with the "active participation of the planning authorities, the territorial entities, and the government with the Consejo Superior de la Judicatura." The draft plan must be submitted to the Consejo Nacional de Planeacion, which is formed by "representatives of the territorial entities, and the economic, social, ecological, community, and cultural sectors" (Article 320 of Constitution). In addition one must add the Departmental Consejos de Planeacion, each of which elaborates its own Plan de Desarrollo. The separation of investment from the budget, controlled by the DNP, and the rest of the budget contributes to the budget's decentralization.

*Proposals*

*Reduce the Number and Consolidate Budget Documents*
The entire budgetary process could consist of just one document. At the moment among the documents there are large differences between the semi-accrual figures of the budget and the cash figures imposed by reality (it would not be realistic to impose a move to an exclusively accrual or cash basis). Hence two documents are required: the budget and a finance plan. The two documents should have exactly the same structure and should provide a table of reconciliation. The development plan should be eliminated.

**Adopt Accounting Standards in Line with International Practice, as Prescribed by IMF**
The accounting standards of the budget should be subjected to an "auditing," especially in the transitional period, by internationally respected private firms.

**Broaden the Budget's Coverage as Much as Possible**
The Colombian budget does not provide a complete picture of the central government. It covers only a fraction of public pensions; it should cover them all. Further all the territorial entities should be included as well as the rest of the nonfinancial public sector. There are obvious legal obstacles to overcome.

**Outsource the Government Forecasting Operation to Internationally Reputable Private Companies**

**Extend Budget to Deal with Appropriations That Must Straddle Fiscal Years**
In recent years information on arrears has created considerable problems for the management of fiscal policy. Improvements in accounting may help. The IMF Code of Good Practice on Fiscal Transparency provides accounting procedures that improve transparency and control arrears. Such data do not result from simple cash accounting and must be supplemented with modified accrual statements, such as developed by the International Federation of Accountants, IFAC.

**1.3.4 Bureaucracy, Civil Servants, and Teachers**
As Acosta and Borjas write in chapter 8, public spending in Colombia places a great emphasis on education. Teachers are the largest group

of public employees; currently in Colombia there are about 310,000 teachers, equal to 26 percent of the total number of public employees. The public sector spends about 4.5 percent of GDP on education and about 70 percent of all teachers are in the public sector.

Despite the emphasis of public spending on teachers, several problems negatively influence the outcome of the education sector. The first is the confusion and overlap that exist between different government levels. The reorganization of the education system was developed in the context of a general decentralization of public administration. However, there has been confusion about which level of government is best suited to administer the public education system. Law 29 of 1989 favored the municipalization of public education, but the 1991 Constitution emphasized the role of the departmental level. Similarly Law 60 of 1993, which regulates the system of transfers of central funds to departments and municipalities, enhances the role of municipalities in the administration of public funds for education. In contrast, Law 115 of 1994, the General Education Law, responded to pressure from the teachers' union and assigned a greater role to the departments. As a result there are three types of public school teachers in Colombia: those funded by the central government, those funded by departmental governments, and those funded by municipalities.

The second problem is that teachers, thanks to their powerful union, are an overly protected category that, by and large, receives a very favorable treatment both in terms of salaries and, especially, in terms of pensions. Note that the favorable position of teachers within the public sector is in addition to the favorable treatment (by international standards) of public sector employees. Colombia has the highest public sector wage premium among Latin American countries.

The current regulations of the teaching profession in Colombia originated in an education statute (Estatuto Docente) promulgated in 1979. The statute specifies the norms that regulate the recruitment, labor stability, promotion, and retirement of teachers. The statute, and particularly the way it has been administered, has introduced several inefficiencies into public education:

• *Too much centralization.* Teacher salaries are set by the central government, with little input from the regional government agencies that end up paying the bill.
• *Inefficient appointment process.* The departments and the municipalities can create temporary teaching positions. The provisions of the Estatuto Docente imply that these short-term positions eventually become

permanent positions, putting additional pressure on the central government to increase its monetary transfers.
• *Ineffective disciplinary regime.* The directives (rectors) do not exercise any disciplinary control over the teachers. The Estatuto Docente orders that promotions be determined internally within the magistery, using a set of rules that are not always related to teaching activities.

The pension system of teachers is very generous in comparison with other categories. First, public teachers do not have to contribute to the funding of the system in order to receive a pension. Most nonteachers contribute 25 percent (13.5 percent is obligatory). Second, teachers qualify to receive the special pension (pension de gracia) at 50 years of age. Under the pay-as-you-go system set up by Law 100 of 1993 for nonteachers, the retirement age is 55 for women and 60 for men. Third, a different base salary is used to calculate the pension for teachers and nonteachers. The special pension is based on the basic monthly salary that the teacher had at the time of retirement, including bonuses and other benefits. In addition the teacher's retirement pension is based on the average salary of the last year employed. In contrast, the pension benefits for nonteachers are based on the average salary in the last 10 years of the entire career if more than 1,250 weeks have been contributed. Finally, the pension regime grants teachers the right to receive several of these pensions simultaneously.

A third problem concerns the geographical distribution and allocation of teachers. The centralized setting of wages makes it difficult to let wages adjust to needs. In addition teachers have a very low degree of mobility compared to other workers, in part because they are, on average, an older work force to retrain.

During the 1990s Colombia implemented major reforms in the education sector and substantially increased the amount of resources invested (from 3.1 percent of GDP in 1991 to 4.5 percent in 1997). What has been the outcome in terms of quantity and quality of education? It is still too early for a clear answer: the returns on human capital investment take decades to fully materialize in terms of more productivity and growth. Thus it may be premature to judge this effort, but the initial results are mixed. Enrollment ratios in primary school have increased substantially in the nineties, even though they were increasing before. Enrollment ratios in secondary schools have increased much less.

Measuring the quality of education is very difficult. The available international evidence suggests that Colombia ranks relatively poorly, but not extremely poorly, in terms of test scores, if compared with other countries with a similar level of development. There is some evidence that

Colombia's results on these standardized tests have slightly improved in
the 1990s. Whether or not the large investment in education in the nineties has paid off remains to be seen. However, too much of this effort has
been devoted to increasing the salaries and pensions for teachers, a group
that was already relatively privileged.[3]

Some specific reform initiatives seem to have had much success. One is
the Escuela Nueva Program, adopted in the rural sector. Under this program teachers have much greater flexibility in making their decisions regarding the curriculum. Classroom instruction is also more targeted to
the needs of different students and practical problem solving, so that the
interests of students are more engaged. Parents are encouraged to become
involved through participation in after school activities. It may be useful
to discover if this type of program can be expanded to Colombia's urban
public schools.

### Proposals

*Hiring and Salary Decisions Should Be Made by the Same Government
Jurisdiction*
This simple adjustment would compel those who hire the teacher to pay
attention to the cost of the decision. Also those who set teacher salaries
would have to pay more attention to the factors that determine the number and qualifications of teachers employed.

*Cost of Living Should Figure in Pay Differences across Regions*
In general, the policy of a uniform wage should be abandoned to give
localities flexibility in teacher salaries.

*Generous Teachers' Pensions Should Be Brought in Line with Other
Categories of Workers*
In the context of a broader pension reform, reforming the pension treat-
ment of teachers should receive the highest priority.

*Experiments Like the Escuela Nueva Should Be Supported by Grants*

*Teacher Salaries Should Reflect the Results of Performance Evaluations*
A system of teachers' performance evaluation should be introduced.

### 1.3.5   Provision of Social Services
As Perotti shows in chapter 9, social spending and the delivery of social services should have priority over any other spending. But what is

"social" expenditure? By Article 41 of the Estatuto Organico de Presupuesto, public social spending is "any expenditure whose objective is the satisfaction of unsatisfied basic needs in health, education, environment, drinkable water, housing, and those aiming at the general well-being and the improvement of the quality of life of the population." Thus Colombia combines a very loose definition of social expenditure with a very strong constitutional mandate to protect it. The result inevitably is confusion.

A standard classification of social security services distinguishes among social services (e.g., education and health), social insurance (e.g., old age and invalid pensions and unemployment insurance), and social assistance (e.g., cash transfers to the poor, family assistance benefits, maternity benefits, in kind transfers, and employment generating programs). Most industrialized countries have built their social protection systems around social insurance, leaving social assistance to pick up the uninsured individuals who fall through the cracks and to subsidize large families and maternal leaves.

There are three reasons why Latin American countries cannot aspire to the same structure of social protection. First, they can rely only on much smaller revenues. Second, because of the widespread rates of informal work and other technical problems, it is difficult to keep track of the work and contributory history of individuals; in any case, few workers would have unbroken records of contributions. Third, for many poor individuals, it makes sense to stay out of an insurance system, even if subsidized: poor individuals have much shorter life expectancies, and they put a high premium on liquidity. On the other hand, the experience of industrialized and developing countries alike has shown that universal, untargeted social assistance programs can quickly become very costly, and thus they are too costly for Colombia.

This leaves two more options: targeted social assistance, or social service spending. So far Colombia has clearly chosen the latter, devoting a large fraction of its efforts to health and education.[4]

One of the main arguments of chapter 9 is that given Colombia's limited fiscal resources, the emphasis on health and education has left out large pockets of extreme rural poverty. Since it is hard to think of social objectives that do not include the welfare of the extremely poor, this calls for a restructuring of social spending. More effort should be devoted to targetcd social assistance programs.

As for the question of how to target, several considerations are important. The same objectives in terms of poverty reduction are achieved more cheaply: (1) by targeting the very poor, (2) by reducing overlaps between programs, (3) by achieving organizational simplicity, and (4) by a proper account of long-run sustainability (the long-run costs of a program may be much higher than the initial costs, as membership increases toward a steady state).

Finally, a word on "community involvement" as a targeting device. This approach has been very influential in Colombia and in other Latin American countries. It has taken various forms, wherein local residents initiate and even control the implementation of certain local services (e.g., child care centers in Colombia), they present the menu of projects for employment and housing programs, and they help locate the beneficiaries of targeted programs. Unfortunately, programs relying heavily on community involvement rarely reach the very poor. The very poor are exactly those that, for a variety of reasons, do not have the ability or the incentives to participate in the community initiatives. For instance, they do not have the financial means and the technical skills required to develop projects for local public employment programs, nor do they have the human capital to participate effectively in local debates and assemblies.

How effective has social spending been in Colombia? Most statistical sources about poverty agree that poverty has been declining in the 1990s, after a peak in 1991 to 1992. Some sources (probably the most reliable) indicate that poverty reduction is only an urban phenomenon, and that rural poverty is increasing. According to these sources, Colombia has one of the most skewed urban–rural poverty distributions of Latin America. Other sources indicate a more uniform distribution of poverty. However, even with these imperfect data, it is almost certain that better results in poverty reduction can be achieved by more targeting of the rural areas.

### Proposals
The task of examining shortcomings and making proposals for the entire social service sector is enormous. Nevertheless, in chapter 9 Perotti manages to touch a remarkable number of issues with great care. This summary only touches briefly on some of the issues he addresses.

### Policies for the Elderly and the Disabled
The distributional flows implied by the current system are very generous but have a very low coverage rate. Only about 2 percent of the population receives a pension, or 30 percent of the population over 60. The average pensions are very high, about twice the GDP per capita. The pension system is based on three pillars: The first is the state-run defined benefit pension scheme (or Prima Media). The second is the private sec-

tor, defined contribution system of AFP's, Chilean-style. In contrast to other countries, like Argentina, these two pillars are mutually exclusive for an individual. Together they make up the "social insurance" component of the policies for the elderly. The third pillar is a purely redistributive scheme for the elderly poor that are not entitled to a social insurance pension. At present, this pillar is represented by a small program, Revivir, and by many small programs run by municipalities. This is the "social assistance" component of the policies for the elderly.

The Prima Media has implied redistributive flows toward the relatively well-off workers in the formal sector. Also many benefits are redistributed to civil servants (especially to teachers, as discussed above). The system includes very little targeting of the very poor. Within the pension system, two programs target the very poor: the minimum pension guarantee and the Fondo de Solidaridad Pensional. Both are quite small and suffer from problems of low membership, especially in rural areas. Administrative problems also have vastly undermined the efficacy of the system and even the collection of information about the system. Outside of the main pension system, the Revivir program established in 1993 is directed toward the indigent elderly, as identified by municipalities. Once again, very low membership and administrative shortcomings are serious problems.

In summary, the key problem of the current pension system is clear: it spends too much on too few people. Resources should be moved away from relatively privileged groups (civil servants, relatively well off elderly members of the formal labor market) to the very poor, including those teachers in rural areas.

*Policies for Families and Children*
At present, policies for families and children are run mostly by ICBF, a central government agency with a total 1998 budget equal to about 0.5 percent of GDP (0.6 percent with municipal participation) and funded with the proceeds of a 3 percent payroll tax. A few programs are run by the RED de Solidaridad Social, often in coordination with ICBF. The present system contains elements of several different programs:

• Day care
• Food distribution and nutrition help
• Feeding children at school
• Help for mothers who are heads of families
• Preventive and health care

• In-kind support for children of school age
• Various programs for adolescents and minors

As for child care, there are three programs: CAIP, the older one; HCB; and Jardines Comunitarios de Bienestar. In 1997 CAIP represented 12.5 percent of all spending by ICBF, HCB 41 percent, and Jardines Comunitarios a small 0.1 percent.

One distinctive feature of the HCBs is the community involvement. A "community mother" (a person with no special qualification) is chosen by the community to be a child care provider. Because existing data are poor, it is very difficult to evaluate the cost effectiveness of the two HCB programs. The available, imperfect, information shows that HCBs are heavily used in rural areas where there are also indications of high unmet demand. The educational functions of HCB are extremely limited, and the quality of care provided is inferior to that of CAIP. There are concerns about the effectiveness of ICBF programs for children aged 0 to 2. It seems that the HCBs are more costly and, therefore, the policy of promoting HCDs over CAIP may be misguided.

*Employment and Unemployment Policies*
Colombia does not have formal unemployment insurance. Because of the high rate of informal employment and the difficulties in keeping individual work-history records, a formal, well working unemployment insurance system is virtually impossible in a country like Colombia. In fact few Latin American countries have unemployment insurance, and where one exists it is almost invariably limited to very few individuals (e.g., to little more than 100,000 in Argentina).

Unemployment in Colombia is highly concentrated among youth: the unemployment rate among individuals in the 18 to 24 age group is 25.7 percent, compared to 6 percent in the 50 to 59 group. Training programs tend to be most effective in situations where there is a high rate of youth unemployment. The training of displaced adult workers rarely provides them with the skills necessary to return to the labor market, while short training programs might be adequate to provide young adults entering the labor force with job search skills.

Training in Colombia is the realm of SENA, the state training agencies patterned after Brazil's SENAI. SENA is a large organization, with a 1998 budget equal to about 0.3 percent of GDP. It provides training both for youths entering the labor force and for displaced workers. The available evidence on this program raises serious questions. The SENA training is highly geared toward the upper quintiles. This is not just a reflection of the fact that it is mostly an urban program: even among urban individuals, the poor enroll in SENA less frequently than the nonpoor. There is also a growing consensus that SENA, like most training agencies in Latin America, is a highly rigid institution, very reluctant to change and to adapt to the changing labor market.

Colombia has had a limited experience with employment generation programs in the recent past, in the form of two programs administered by the RED: one for urban areas and one for rural areas. The urban employment program (*Empleo Urbano*)[5] is one of the few RED programs that has been the object of some quantitative evaluation. A striking characteristic of this program is the extremely high wages it paid: in infrastructure projects, on average in 1997 it paid about 170 percent of the wage offered in the private construction sector; in services, it was about 150 percent of the wage offered in the "communal service" sector.

### 1.3.6  The Central Bank

As Alesina, Carrasquilla, and Steiner show in chapter 10, a widely accepted view in both the OECD and developing countries is that an independent central bank is conducive to a stable monetary policy. If a government (and in particular, a treasury) has day-to-day influence over monetary policy, the temptation will be strong to use monetary instruments to finance government deficits and overstimulate the economy for short-term benefits (or to be "weak" in inflation fighting) at the cost of long-term stability and growth. Central bank independence is insured by an arm's-length relationship between government officers and central bankers, appropriate appointment procedures for officers of the central bank, and a clear mandate for the central bank.

The Constitution of 1991 included sweeping reform of Colombia's central bank law. However, while the degree of Central Bank independence was increased relative to the previous arrangement, it was a compromise between two views: one that favored unconditionally the idea of central bank independence, and one that supported government intervention and control, especially in exchange rate policy. While some of the wording of the law indicates a strong stance for independence, certain aspects of the central bank law are at odds with the same idea of independence. For example, the fact that the treasury minister is not only a voting member of the central bank board but also is its president is extremely unusual by international standards. Also, as testified to by various Constitutional Court rulings, a fair amount of institutional confusion remains regarding the objectives of monetary policy and of the central bank. In fact the 1991 Constitution attempted to delegate to the central bank the goal of inflation control. But various Constitutional Court rulings do not make it clear who has precedence if the Plan de Desarrollo and the Central Bank have different inflation targets.

The 1991 Constitution was especially concerned about keeping the government involved in the choice of exchange rate policies and exchange rate regimes. However, for a small open economy like Colombia's the exchange rate is a tool that cannot be detached from an inflation control policy package. If the government is part of the exchange rate management "team," it means that the government is involved in monetary policy. The unclear position of the central bank, originating in the 1991 Constitution, has shown its consequences on a couple of occasions. In 1997 an overexpansion of monetary policy in response to a downturn in 1996 contributed to monetary and financial turbulence in the ensuing year. In early 1997 the Samper government had the opportunity to appoint three new members of the board—all of them recruited within the ranks of government. Recent interventions in the banking sector have led to a coordinated government–central bank effort to bail out banks that have gone beyond a temporary provision of liquidity.

In summary, the gist of our proposals is to eliminate the "confusion" surrounding the institutional position of the central bank and its mandate. The purpose is to reform the central bank law in order to make the central bank an institution to which the government delegates the goal of keeping inflation under control and supervising the financial stability of the country. It is important to stress that a truly independent central bank does not contradict the principles of democracy. Delegation and democracy are not incompatible. The "people" may democratically decide that a certain function (e.g., monetary policy) should be delegated to an institution appointed by the people but retaining independence in the administration of its duty—in the interest of the people itself.

### Proposals

#### Composition of the Board
• Remove any member of the executive branch from the board of the central bank
• Reduce the board from the current five members to three, plus a chairman, who must cast the tie-breaking vote

The aim is to make the board small but strong without government participation.

*Appointment Procedures*
· Lengthen the term of office of all members of the board to seven years
· Introduce a staggered system of appointments so that no single administration has the prerogative of appointing a large fraction of the board
· Restrict who can be appointed in the board—current members of the administration or those who have served in the previous two years should not be allowed to be appointed chairman or members of the board

The aim is to maintain a stable central bank board that cannot be frequently changed or influenced by a single government. Restrictions on who can be appointed should also reduce direct government intervention.

*Goals of Monetary Policy*
· The central bank should set the inflation target; if in the central bank's judgment a particular Plan de Desarrollo threatens the medium-run goal of inflation control, the central bank's goal of inflation control should have precedence.

This legislation should clarify the confusion that exists in the Constitution about who really should set the inflation target.

*Supervision of the Financial System*
· The central bank should take this control from the treasury. The current situation ignores the conflict of interest between the goal of financial solidity and the goal of financing government spending.

*Disclosure and Secrecy*
· The central bank should adopt clear and binding procedures about the source and timing of official statements of the bank. Specific rules about disclosures of board minutes and announcements to the markets should be adopted and closely followed.

The aim is of course to give some transparency to the markets and to remove uncertainty and speculation.

## 1.4   Conclusions

With this book we aim to provide the reader with a good understanding of the economic and institutional problems facing Colombia today as well as a possible road to reform. We offer an example of how the tools developed in the new political economics framework can be used for policy analysis and policy advice.

Many of the institutional problems of Colombia—misguided social spending programs, ineffectual decentralization, disagreements between executive and legislative, branches, just to name a few—are quite common in developing countries. The experience of Colombia can help shed light on these problems in other countries.

## Notes

1. See, for example, Aghion, Alesina, and Trebbi (2002).

2. The evolution of violence in Bogotá is harder to explain. Even though public officials optimistically claim the various policies since 1994 to be successful, a careful analysis of weekly data shows this not to be the case. See Paz Publica, "Homicidios en al Ciudad de Bogotá," forthcoming.

3. See the appendix to the chapter 6, for the different measures undertaken to improve the quality of education in the 1990s.

4. See also the discussion of this issue in chapter 6.

5. *Empleo Urbano* has three components: employment generation proper, training, and support for micro enterprises. The last was extremely small—less than 1 percent of the budget, covering only 56 projects in 26 municipalities—so it will be ignored. Training received about 13 percent of the budget in 1996 as was discussed in section 1.4.3. The remaining 86 percent of the budget was spent on employment creation programs.

## References

Aghion, P., A. Alesina, and F. Trebbi. 2002. Endogenous political institutions. NBER Working Paper.

Alesina, A., N. Roubini, and G. Cohen. 1997. *Political Cycles and the Macroeconomy*. Cambridge: MIT Press.

Drazen, A. 1999. *Poltical Economics and Macroeconomics*. Princeton: Princeton University Press.

Persson, T., and G. Tabellini. 2001. *Political Economics*. Cambridge: MIT Press.

# 2 Recent Economic History of Colombia

Juan José Echavarría, Maria Angelica Arbeláez and Alejandro Gaviria

The average Colombian politician firmly believes that the blame [for poor economic growth] lies with the neo-liberal policies introduced in the early 1990s.—
*The Economist*, Survey: Colombia, April 19, 2001

While no estimate of the effect of such recurrent violence on Colombia's economy is possible, it probably has quite a lot to do with Colombia's poverty today.— Easterly (2001)

## 2.1 Introduction

Colombia and Brazil are the only Latin American countries whose GDP from 1960 to 1995 grew faster than that of the world overall, although both growth rates were relatively modest if compared with those of Asia in the same period. Suddenly, after decades of continual expansion, Colombia stopped growing. Income per capita fell in 1995 to 2000 for the first time in a hundred years and future prospects for a healthy growth appear slim.

The Colombian experience in the 1990s was actually much more complex than that of Brazil. As in the rest of Latin America, Colombia had introduced pro-market reforms that created large inflows (1990–1997) and outflows (1997–2000) of capital, but other factors were present. The Constitution adopted in 1991, in part, encouraged large expansions in government expenditure, and violence was allowed to escalated out of control. It is not easy to disentangle the separate effects of the reforms, large economic shocks, and new rules of the politics brought by the new Constitution.

As we show in section 2.2, a basic feature of the long Colombian period of growth was that for decades, particularly during the 1980s (the "lost decade" in the Latin American region), growth was cheap (mostly based on technical change) and the size of government was small.

While it is not easy to account for the fall in growth after 1995, the factors that certainly played a big role are the explosive rise of government spending and a drastic fall of investment. Also contributing were the dismantling of the coffee industry and the burst of a large land-housing bubble that developed in 1990 to 1995.

In section 2.3 we describe the main economic reforms undertaken in the first part of the 1990s and evaluate their impact on total factor productivity (TFP) and on capital accumulation in manufacturing. Reforms were conducive to growth: TFP increased quickly between 1989 and 1997, particularly in open, labor-intensive, and recently created firms. Credit affected capital accumulation more than TFP, and variable sociopolitical conditions and violence affected the country's productivity.

In section 2.4 we consider the impact of violence on economic growth. We survey previous studies and complement the database constructed by Barro and Lee (1994) to analyze cross-country evidence on the impacts of violence and war. We discuss the drug-trafficking channels and law enforcement mechanisms operating in Colombia and attempt to quantify their impact on growth.

It is, of course, too early to judge whether the recent crisis is just a transitory phenomenon related to capital outflows and to the burst of the land-housing bubble, or whether much more is at stake. Have the new institutions brought about by the Constitution of 1991 and the escalation of violence permanently altered the successful growth of the past? Conflict, institutions, and economic policy are interconnected in recent Colombian history. The Constitution of 1991 adopted under President Gaviria's administration (1990–1994) attempted to provide a mechanism to incorporate guerrilla interests in the political process. Subsequently it was almost impossible for the Samper government (1994–1998) to pass reforms while the whole country was obsessed with the impeachment of the president. Later the peace settlement attempts with the guerrilla delayed fiscal and structural reforms during the Pastrana administration (1998–2002).

## 2.2   Colombian Growth, Reforms, and the Crisis of 1995 to 2000

### 2.2.1   Colombian Past Growth and Productivity

At least five different periods have been identified in the growth of the Colombian economy after World War II. From 1950 to 1979 Colombia followed the standard Latin American import substitution strategy with moderate to low protection. During the 1980s, the lost decade in the

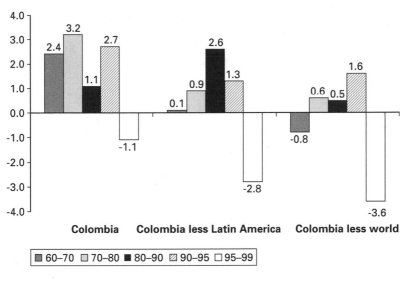

**Figure 2.1**
Colombian per capita growth (From De Gregorio and Lee 2001 for 1960 to 1995; World
Bank indicators for 1995 to 1999)

region, Colombian growth slowed down, but it was much higher than
that of the rest of Latin America.[1] Important liberalization reforms were
introduced in 1990 to 1995, a period of high growth when foreign capital
flooded the country and land prices quickly rose. In 1995 to 2000, growth
per capita began to fall for the first time in decades, foreign capital left
the country, and the real estate bubble burst.

Figure 2.1 compares per capita growth in Colombia with that of Latin
America as a whole and that of the world in different periods. After 1995
production increased less than population for the first time in recent
Colombian history, whereas in the rest of Latin America and in the world
growth increased. Figure 2.2 shows quarterly GDP growth. Note the
volatility in the economy after 1994, with low average growth occurring
in 2000.

We also know that growth has been historically low in Colombia, although productivity has been high by Latin American standards (figure
2.3). The contribution of total factor productivity to growth was 2.3, 2.0,
and −0.2 percent in Colombia during the 1960s, 1970s, and 1980s, and
much lower in Latin America (1.9, 0.7, and −2.0 percent). The contribution of capital accumulation was 1.6, 2.0, and 1.8 percent in the same
periods, compared to 2.0, 2.5, and 1.2 percent in Latin America.

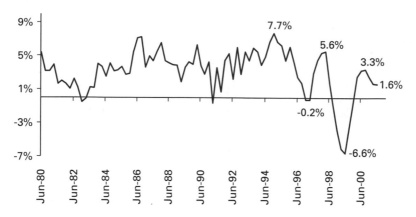

**Figure 2.2**
GDP quarterly growth in Colombia, 1995 to 2000 (From DANE, National Accounts)

### 2.2.2   Growth "Fundamentals"

Shown in figure 2.4 are the factors contributing to the growth differences between Latin America and Asia, and between Colombia and Latin America according to De Gregorio and Lee (2001). The independent variables are trade,[2] inflation, government consumption, law and order, education, democracy, investment, initial income, health, and the terms of trade. Note that the regional growth was annually 3.5 points below Asia from 1960 to 1995. About 50 percent of the difference is explained by lower trade levels (0.9) and hyperinflations (0.7); other contributing factors were large government consumption and low education expenditures. The main factors behind Colombia's large relative growth were low government consumption and democractic institutions, partially countered by the general lawlessness.

Why was per capita growth in 1995 to 1999 negative, and the lowest in Colombian economic history, at a time when healthy growth was observed in Latin America and elsewhere in the world? On the positive side, the economy was applied, and the inflation rate dropped from 22 percent in 1985–1995 to 13 percent in 1995–1999. Investment remained relatively high in 1995 to 2000, but it took a drastic fall after 1997–1998.[3]

The negative side of the period, first and foremost, has to do with the escalated violence, and the indexes reflecting brazen disregard of "rule of law." Its effect on the Colombian economy will be explored later in this chapter. Next, government expenditures doubled from 1985 to 1995 (6.77 percent) and from 1995 to 1998 (13.04 percent). Colombia's main growth advantage was its relatively small government before the

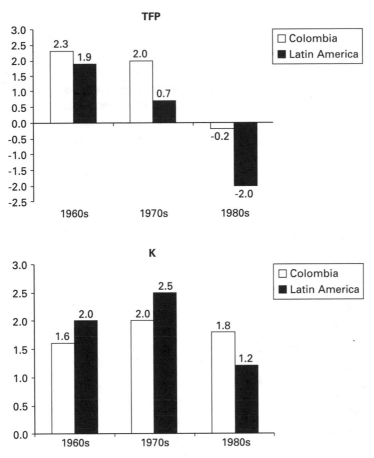

**Figure 2.3**
Contribution of K and TFP to growth, 1960 to 1990 (From De Gregorio and Lee 2001)

1990s.[4] Another negative impact on the economy came from the deterioration of the terms of trade, although the deterioration in 1995 to 2000 was mild compared to that in 1985 to 1995. Finally, as table 2.1 shows, Colombia has been slipping from its initial advantage in secondary and tertiary education.[5]

### 2.2.3 Poverty and Income Distribution

There is wide disagreement over the impact of income distribution on economic growth. Forbes (2000) challenged Alesina and Rodrik's (1994) claim that income inequality has a negative effect,[6] and Barro (1999) did not find any strong relation, except in the case of very poor (positive

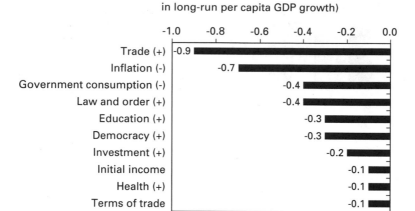

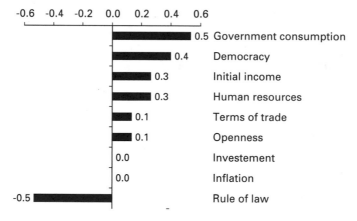

**Figure 2.4**
Growth differences of Latin America, Asia, and Colombia (From De Gregorio and Lee 2000, 2001)

**Table 2.1**
Growth fundamentals in Colombia and Latin America

|  | Colombia | | | | Latin America | | | |
|---|---|---|---|---|---|---|---|---|
|  | 1965–75 | 1975–85 | 1985–95 | 1995–99 | 1965–75 | 1975–85 | 1985–95 | 1995–99 |
| A. Pro-growth |  |  |  |  |  |  |  |  |
| Openness (Sachs-Werner) | 0.00 | 0.00 | 0.88 | — | 0.00 | 0.00 | 0.38 | 0.38 |
| Inflation | 12.95 | 20.97 | 22.20 | 13.00 |  |  |  |  |
| Democracy | 0.71 | 0.83 | 0.83 | 0.83 | 0.67 | 0.50 | 0.83 | 0.83 |
| Investment/GDP | 15.97 | 16.12 | 13.98 | 17.14 | 16.79 | 17.49 | 13.99 | 15.51 |
| B. Against growth |  |  |  |  |  |  |  |  |
| Rule of law |  | 0.33 |  | — |  | 0.43 |  |  |
| Government consumption | 7.46 | 7.71 | 6.77 | 13.04 | 8.49 | 10.36 | 8.37 | 9.11 |
| Terms-of-trade change | 0.21 | 1.30 | −4.31 | −1.54 | −1.05 | −2.41 | −1.88 | 0.91 |
| Secondary education | 0.64 | 1.12 | 1.03 | 1.01 | 0.44 | 0.74 | 1.05 | 1.21 |
| Tertiary education | 0.10 | 0.16 | 0.25 | 0.29 | 0.09 | 0.17 | 0.25 | 0.34 |

Sources: De Gregorio and Lee (2001), World Development Indicators, and author calculations.

effect) or very rich (negative effect) countries.[7] The regressions appear to be highly sensitive to the fertility rate.

In figure 2.5 the "poverty," "extreme poverty," and the Gini coefficient are compared in Colombia over the 1978 to 1999 period, and Gini coefficient for households from 1978 to 1995. Big efforts were made to reduce poverty between 1978 and 1995 but were stopped in 1995 to 1999. Income distribution, on the other hand, remained relatively constant in 1978 to 1988 (and even improved slightly for workers) but deteriorated in 1990 to 1995.

According to Cárdenas and Bernal (2000), 37 percent of the decline in the urban income levels during the 1990s can be explained by differences in education. Another important change was in the complementarity between physical capital and skilled labor during the large investment boom that took place in the first part of the 1990s.

There are conflicting opinions on how income distribution, poverty, and violence are related. Levit and Rubio (chapter 5 in this volume) compare the top decile with the bottom decile in the income levels of different countries and conclude that the income distribution in Colombia is fairly similar to that of other Latin American countries. While Colombia does have substantial income inequality relative to many countries worldwide, the income is more equally distributed than it is in Brazil, Chile, and Puerto Rico. The authors argue that while the large disparities

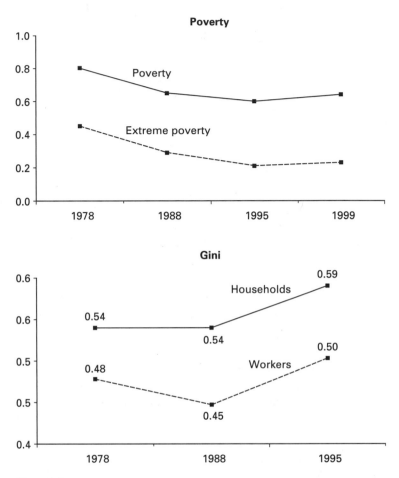

**Figure 2.5**
Poverty and income inequality in Colombia, 1978 to 1999 (From Giugale et al. 1999, 2003)

of income may contribute to the high crime rates in Latin America, poverty does not explain why the Colombian crime rate is so much higher than that of other Latin American countries.

The issue of income distribution remains a sensitive area, and one that cannot be easily settled. A good reason is that 4 percent of the citizentry controls more than 50 percent of the land in Colombia (Ocampo 1987). Lorente, Salazar, and Gallo (1984) show that land concentration increased during the 1960s but remained relatively constant between 1970 and 1984.[8]

## 2.2.4 Coffee and Shocks[9]

From 1970 to 1992 Colombia's economy was the least volatile in Latin American (Inter-American Development Bank 1997), with stable economic policies. This was, in part, due to successful stabilization schemes in the coffee sector and to orthodox fiscal management mentioned above. The coffee industry was largely dismantled in the 1990s.

### *Coffee, the National Coffee Fund, and Stabilization*[10]

Some authors have suggested that before the "age of coffee" there was no Colombian nation. Coffee production utilized previously unemployed resources and did not require large amounts of capital. It could be cultivated efficiently in almost all the mountainous regions of the country, and could coexist with other agricultural products. It allowed permanent cultivation of land that otherwise could be only partially cultivated during the year, and it promoted the clearing of more land for agriculture.

Coffee has also had a profound influence in shaping the culture of the country. It gave rise to a Colombian obsession with merits of the small property ownership, and to high risk aversion and "conservatism" in economic policy. Important institutions developed around coffee. The National Federation of Coffee Growers (NFC; Federacion Nacional de Cafeteros) has been considered by some as a "state within a state," and coffee producers and exporters have been successful in guaranteeing that coffee proceedings be returned directly to them, or be reinvested in the coffee sector.[11] The NFC has been able to control parliamentary discussion over coffee policy. Producers' representatives at all levels are elected by direct vote, and when negotiating with the NFC, governments have been aware that the coffee constituency can account for a tenth of Colombia's population.

Coffee remained the main source of exports until recently, comprising nearly 60 percent of total exports some decades ago. Exports of gold were relatively important at the start of the twentieth century, and again during the 1930s, but became marginal in other periods. Oil production and exports began in the 1920s, with participation close to 20 percent throughout that time. Manufactured exports started in the 1960s and 1970s, and they represent one-third of total exports today.

It is no wonder, then, that Fernández and Gonzáles (2002) find much similarity in the economic cycles of Colombia, Brazil, and Costa Rica as the coffee sector figures largely in these economies. While coffee

**Figure 2.6**
Domestic and international real coffee prices (From National Federation of Coffee Growers)

prices were more volatile than those of most other commodities in the international commodities' "lottery" (determined mainly by weather conditions in Brazil), stabilization policies and imaginative policy tools were able to smooth the effects of external shocks. This is why the GDP and consumption in Colombia have been relatively more stable than in other coffee-producing countries.

The effects of coffee exports on the state's revenues were actually indirect. They allowed imports, and tariff revenues were the main source of government revenue. The National Coffee Fund served as an important internal price stabilizer,[12] stimulating savings and easing the immediate pressures on internal demand. It provided credit to coffee producers and removed the pressure on the Central Bank to grant credit.

Figure 2.6 shows the evolution of international and domestic real coffee prices from 1930 to 2002. There were two large coffee *bonanzas* in the mid-1950s and in 1975 to 1978, but international coffee prices have been falling markedly in recent decades; today prices are the lowest observed in more than seventy years. The figure shows the effects of the successful stabilization scheme implemented through the coffee institutions in Colombia. Note that the volatility of coffee prices was relatively low in the 1990s.

## The "Good" Old Days, 1970 to 1989

The Economist (August 26, 1978, pp. 74–75) summarized well the situation at the end of 1978, when President López (1974–1978) left power and Julio Cesar Turbay (1978–1982) started his presidency:

Luckily for President Turbay, his predecessor, Mr. Alfonso Lopez Michelsen has left him a healthier legacy than Latin American presidents usually get. Mr. Lopez came to office with one of the largest majorities in Colombian history. He left unsung, largely because he resisted the temptation (to which Colombia's oil-rich neighbour, Venezuela, has succumbed) of using a commodity price jump as a springboard for unsustainable economic growth. He tried to prevent the flood in coffee earnings (supplemented by a handy illegal income from marijuana-growing and cocaine-processing, reckoned to add up to $1 billion–3 billion) from launching domestic inflation or sucking in disproportionate imports. President Lopez clamped on bank lending curbs, allowed government spending to grow no faster than inflation, held down overseas borrowing and kept the budget balanced. He also took steps to control the inflow of legal and illegal dollars.... And Colombia has been depreciating the peso gradually in spite of a surplus on the current account....

But Colombia is Latin America's forgotten country—the country's businessmen usually spell wrongly with a u.

Conservative macroeconomic policies and successful economic performances characterized the 1970s. The economy grew at an annual rate of 6.1 percent, inflation was below 10 percent, and fiscal deficits oscillated around 2 percent of GDP. Exports were growing fast, with a decreasing current account deficit, growing international reserves, and low debt.

Unlike other countries in the region Colombia was successful in its countercyclical management of the mid-1970s coffee boom (figure 2.6). On the fiscal front, the public deficit was reduced, and both public and private external debt fell from 27 percent of GDP in 1975 to 17 percent of GDP in 1978. As private consumption was much less volatile than the external sector, the country was able to maintain a competitive real exchange rate with a crawling peg regime.

## The "Lost Decade" of the 1980s

In his recent study on Latin American growth Loayza et al. (2002) shows that the benefits of relatively modest structural reforms during the 1980s were fully overshadowed by the deterioration in stabilization policies, with disastrous consequences in some countries like Peru. External factors, convergence, and cyclical reversion in the region resulted in a "lost decade" of growth. Colombia fared better than the rest of the region because of the government's prudent management of the external debt and stabilization policies.

To deal with the imbalances that appeared at the beginning of the 1980s, a new Development Plan was adopted in 1982. It proposed large increases in externally financed public investment (and spending), which increased the fiscal deficit and debt levels and caused revaluation of the exchange rate and inflation. The fiscal deficit reached 7.4 percent of GDP by 1982, and the financial sector was in deep trouble for domestic and international reasons.

The measures taken in 1982 initially focused on recouping the financial losses.[13] A classic package was adopted with strict fiscal spending adjustments, tax reform, reduction of credit to the private sector, and currency devaluation. In addition the Coffee Fund's surplus was partly used for the reduction of the coffee sector's external debt and invested in national savings bonds used to aid growers in areas hit by some natural disaster (i.e., by eruptions from *Nevado del Ruiz*). The national government took control of 33 percent of the Coffee Fund surplus in order to pre-pay external debt. Two years were enough to adjust the fiscal and external accounts.

### The 1990s Bubbles: Oil, Credit, and Land

*Oil: The Expected Oil Boom That Never Materialized*
The consequences of oil volatility are not as great in Colombia and Peru as in Venezuela, Ecuador, or Bolivia (Cárdenas et al. 1998), but they are large nevertheless. The "virtual" shock of the 1990s was not well managed and produced real effects. Very optimistic projections were made at the beginning of the 1990s on the likely evolution of oil discoveries. Estimates indicated that the discovery of *Cusiana* and *Cupiagua* would provide in 1995 to 2000 resources equivalent to 25 percent of 1993 GDP, and that oil would allow GDP to be 5 percent larger in 2000. The participation of oil should be close to 1.8 percent of GDP at the beginning of the 1990s and rise to 3.5 to 4 perent of GDP in the following years.

But it was always apparent that the boom at the time was transitory. Contractionary fiscal and monetary policies had to be adopted to compensate for any eventual "Dutch disease," so the oil revenues were partially retained in an oil fund. The Oil Stabilization Fund (FAEP—*Fondo de Ahorro y Estabilización Petrolera*) was created in 1995 to stabilize the large amounts of foreign resources that would enter the economy, to diversify investment out of the oil sector, and to avoid the inflationary pressures brought by the monetization of the new resources available.

Yet the expected oil boom never materialized. Production did not increase at the expected rates and international prices fell.[14] The main effect was to increase government current expenditures against future public resources and to revaluate the real exchange rate. The government projected a 6 percent annual increase in public spending in 1994 but the ex post increase was 17.6 percent, a trend that continued through the 1990s.

*Credit and Land Bubbles*
Empirical evidence of the relation between recent credit crunch episodes and "exogenous" capital outflows is provided by De la Torre et al. (2002) for Latin American countries, and by Tenjo and López (2002) for Colombia. Possible channels are detailed in Calvo (1998). The volatility of capital flows in Colombia during the 1990s was not as high as in other countries of the region[15] but had a large impact on the evolution of credit and on the land-housing bubble that burst after 1995.

The first part of figure 2.7 shows the close relation between the evolution of the capital account and domestic credit during the 1980s and 1990s, and the second part shows the evolution of "size" (assets/GDP) and "activity" (stock of credit to the private sector/GDP) in the financial sector. Both of the last variables remained relatively constant until 1991, increased markedly between 1991 and 1997 (size tripled and activity doubled), and fell again in 1998 to 2000 to levels close to those in the 1990s. The construction and the financial sectors grew very fast from 1990 to 1995 and fell markedly when the credit and land bubbles burst in 1995 to 2000. Other nontradables like government consumption and commerce also grew slowly after 1995. Colombia's land bubble was partially due to the expansion of credit. As shown in figure 2.8, the price of land more than doubled from 1990 to 1995 and then fell drastically, starting in 1995.

## 2.3 Pro-market Reforms of the 1990s, and Their Impact on Productivity and Investment

### 2.3.1 Reforms
The Colombian economy experienced several structural reforms during the 1990s. They were bold compared to previous reforms in the country's history but mild by Latin American standards (Lora and Barrera 1997). At the macro level the Constitution of 1991 created a fully independent Central Bank and decentralized most government spending.

Other important reforms were implemented during the first part of the 1990s. Quantitative restrictions were dismantled and average import

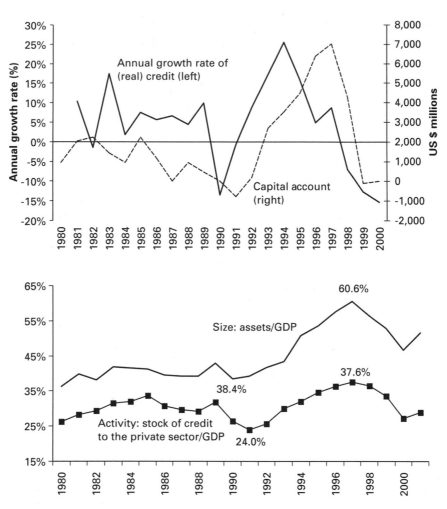

**Figure 2.7**
Capital flows and domestic credit (From IMF, Superintendencia Bancaria, Arbeláez and Echavarría, and author calculations)

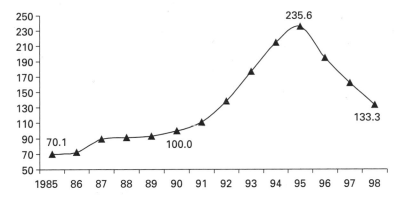

**Figure 2.8**
Price of urban property in Colombia (From Lonja de Propiedad Raíz, arithmetic average for Bogotá, Medellín, and Cali)

**Table 2.2**
Economic growth in Colombia by sector, 1925 to 2000

|  | Participation (%) | Annual growth rates (%) | | |
|---|---|---|---|---|
|  | 1990–99 | 1980–90 | 1990–95 | 1995–00 |
| Construction | 2.6 | 4.0 | 9.5 | −9.7 |
| Government | 7.9 | 4.8 | 4.4 | −1.4 |
| Commerce | 11.0 | 2.7 | 5.2 | −1.1 |
| Manufacturing | 17.7 | 2.8 | 2.1 | −0.9 |
| Finances | 15.9 | 3.6 | 7.0 | 0.2 |
| Agriculture | 19.3 | 2.7 | 2.1 | 0.9 |
| Transport and communications | 9.3 | 2.5 | 4.7 | 2.6 |
| Minning | 5.0 | 19.1 | 3.1 | 4.6 |
| Others | 11.2 | 0.6 | −6.0 | 9.6 |

Sources: Central bank and author calculations.

tariffs drastically reduced. Trade integration agreements were signed with Venezuela, Mexico, Chile, and CARICOM between 1991 and 1994. Restrictions on the capital account were lifted in 1993, and major changes in labor legislation took place in 1990 and in the social security system in 1993. Reforms were introduced to attract foreign investment and to deregulate the financial sector and the exchange rate market in 1991. Finally, changes were introduced in the health and pension system in 1993 and in the area of privatization and "concessions" in 1991, 1994, and in the following years.

The new Constitution of 1991 authorized large transfers of resources to the country's regions for use in education and health, and this led to huge government expenditures. The central government did not contract in either of these two areas, partially because public wages increased dramatically during the 1990s. These rises in government expenditures and large capital inflows during the first part of the 1990s brought a real revaluation of the exchange rate of more than 20 percent between 1992 and 1998.

Tax revenues were never enough, and the fiscal deficit increased markedly after 1994. Four tax reforms were introduced during the 1990s, and another was approved at the end of 2000. The result is a skewed tax structure faced by Colombians today (Fiscal Mission 2003).

Regarding monetary policy, the constitutional reform of 1991 increased the autonomy of the Central Bank (Alesina et al. 2000). A broad-based package of reforms was implemented in the financial sector during the early 1990s, aimed at enhancing competition, allowing the operation of foreign banks in the country, increasing the reliance on market instruments,[16] and reducing government and monetary authorities' intervention in the financial system. The cornerstone in the area was the financial reform introduced by Law 45 of 1990, followed by Law 35 of 1993.

Tariff rates were reduced from 40 percent in 1985 to 11 percent in 1990 to 1993. Imports covered by quotas moved from 73.8 percent in 1988 to 1990 to just 1.7 percent in 1991 to 1993 (Edwards 1995). The importance of export taxes was minimal in Colombia and the black market exchange rate premium strongly decreased in 1985 to 1995 (Cárdenas 1997). Important protection measures remained in the agricultural sector, however, with the implementation of *price bands* in 1993 by the Andean Group (Torres and Osorio 1998). Imports increased (manufacturing imports increased even faster), but exports decreased during the 1990s. The combined weight of exports and imports is still today one of the lowest in the Latin American region.

### 2.3.2   TFP and the Capital Stock in Manufacturing

*TFP*

Did reforms contribute to the decline in growth rates as suggested by most politicians in the country? Did they have adverse effects on total factor productivity and capital accumulation? The first panel of figure 2.9 shows the TFP curve (unweighted) from 1983 to 1999 based on a Cobb-Douglas production function for two types of measures: the semi-parametric estimators (Olley and Pakes (1996); Levinsohn and Petrin

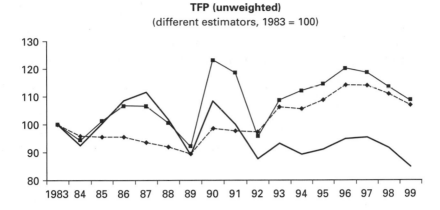

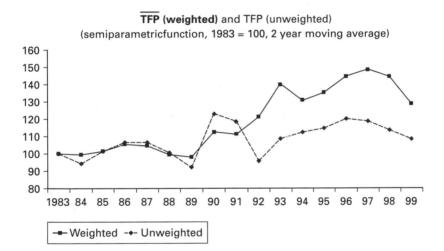

**Figure 2.9**
Evolution of total factor productivity in manufacturing (From DANE and author calculations)

(2000)) and simple OLS estimators. The second panel compares TFP weighted with $\overline{TFP}$ unweighted for the semiparametric function. The larger this difference, the higher the share of output that goes to the more productive firms. The shapes of $\overline{TFP}$ and TFP are fairly close, although $\overline{TFP}$ is more volatile.

The second panel of the figure shows that TFP productivity was relatively stagnant during the 1980s and resource shifts were small compared to the 1990s. All this means both that important changes took place inside the firms and that resources were transferred to more productive activities after the reforms of the 1990s.

### Investment

Average investment/GDP in 1995 to 2000 was higher in Colombia than in the rest of Latin America (figure 2.10), but the comparison of averages conceal the recent deterioration in Colombia investment. Note also the small contribution of the Colombian private sector to investment.

Figure 2.11 shows the evolution of different types of investment. In 1995 investment in construction and housing started falling; investment in machinery and equipment did not fall until after 1998.

### 2.3.3   Factors behind TFP and the Evolution of the Capital Stock

In this section we show that the liberalizing reforms introduced during the 1990s greatly contributed to growth. Total factor productivity increased faster in open, labor-intensive, and newly created firms. Also, contrary to the view of Beck et al. (2000), we find that credit affected capital accumulation much more than TFP. The sociopolitical conditions appear to be closely related to TFP growth. We do not find more innovation in multinational firms nor important effects of tax exemptions.

We use the semiparametric production function in our analysis, and we focus on the reform period of 1989 to 1996. The dependent variables we use are annual TFP growth and K growth. The independent variables we consider are openness (exports, imports and foreign direct investment (FDI)) in table 2.3, credit and taxes in table 2.4, and sociopolitical conditions in table 2.5. We include dummy variables for the economic sector (isic 4 digits) and the region (Colombian department).

The dependent variables appear in separate panels: TFP growth (top panel) and K growth (botton panel). As independent variables we use dummies for exports (d_X/Q), with 1 for firms with the relation between exports and production exceeding the median value.

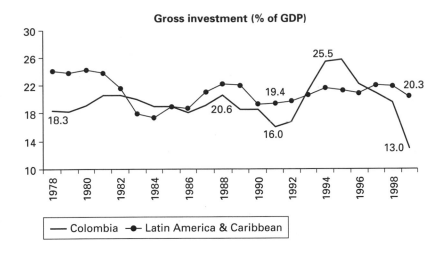

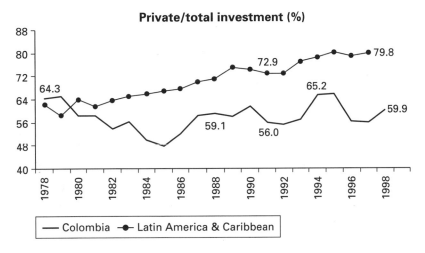

**Figure 2.10**
Investment in Colombia and in Latin America (From World Bank, World Development Indicators)

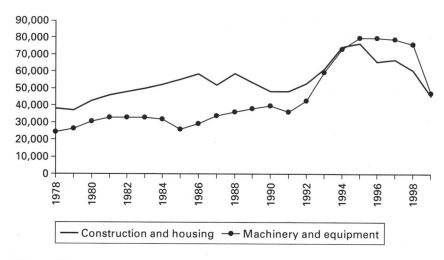

**Figure 2.11**
Investment in housing, construction, and in machinery and equipment (From Banco de la República, DANE, and author calculations)

The results of the first panel of table 2.3 suggests that "open" firms were more innovative, both in $X/Q$ and in $M/Q$ (thus also in $X + M/Q$). A comparison of columns 1 and 2 reveals that the results are due to differences across sectors. The coefficients of columns 5 and 6 indicate that multinational firms innovated less than the local firms, probably because they produce mainly for the domestic market, which is still very closed. The second panel of the table suggest that investment is not different for open or closed firms, nor for the other categories used in the regressions (age, size, etc.). The expansion of credit positively affected investment but not productivity,[17] and tax preferences did not affect either investment or productivity (table 2.4). This means that the increasingly distortionary tax reforms introduced during the 1990s were costly and worthless.

We have aggregate information on the impact of violence, a topic we cover in more depth in section 2.4. The variables consist of homicides, robbery, and kidnappings, all of which are common to most plants. Starting in 1988, we decided to introduce micro evidence of violence from the quarterly survey produced by Fedesarrollo on economic and sociopolitical conditions of investment at a plant level. The survey covers close to 400 plants of major firms in the four main municipalities of the country. Respondents were asked to use the scale 1 for "favorable conditions," 2 for "neutral," and 3 for "unfavorable conditions." We averaged the

**Table 2.3**
Openness, TFP, and investment

| | Openness | | | | FDI | |
|---|---|---|---|---|---|---|
| | d_X/Q 1991 | d_X/Q 1991 | d_M/Q 1991 | d_(X + M)/Q 1991 | d_DFI 1987.1994 | d_DFI |
| | (1) | (2) | (3) | (4) | (5) | (6) |
| **A. TFP growth, 1989–1996** | | | | | | |
| | 0.02 | 0.03 | 0.03 | 0.04 | −0.04 | −0.05 |
| | (1.5) | (5.0)*** | (3.4)*** | (6.2)*** | (−2.7)*** | (−8.7)*** |
| d_isic_4 | × | × | × | × | × | × |
| d_department | × | 0.00 | 0.00 | 0.00 | × | × |
| age | 0.00 | 0.00 | 0.00 | 0.00 | 0.00 | 0.00 |
| | (−4.4)*** | (−9.2)*** | (−8.8)*** | (−8.7)*** | (−4.4)*** | (−6.8)*** |
| size-employment | 2.E-07 | −1.E-06 | −1.E-06 | −4.E-06 | 1.E-05 | 1.E-05 |
| | (0.1) | (−0.3) | (−0.4) | (−1.0) | (1.8)* | (3.7)*** |
| # observations | 3,661 | 3,661 | 3,661 | 3,661 | 3,661 | 3,661 |
| $R^2$ | 0.25 | 0.14 | 0.14 | 0.15 | 0.25 | 0.15 |
| **B. K growth** | | | | | | |
| | 5.07 | −0.09 | 0.99 | 1.02 | 0.36 | 0.37 |
| | (1.5) | (−0.1) | (0.7) | (1.0) | (0.2) | (0.2) |
| d_isic_4 | × | × | × | × | × | × |
| d_department | × | × | × | × | × | × |
| age | −0.01 | −0.03 | −0.04 | −0.03 | −0.01 | −0.04 |
| | (−0.2) | (−0.8) | (−0.7) | (−0.5) | (−0.3) | (−0.8) |
| size-employment | 5.E-04 | 7.E-04 | 6.E-04 | 6.E-04 | 3.E-04 | 6.E-04 |
| | (0.4) | (0.8) | (0.6) | (0.5) | (0.2) | (0.4) |
| # observations | 3,954 | 3,954 | 3,954 | 3,954 | 3,954 | 3,954 |
| $R^2$ | 0.13 | 0.005 | 0.005 | 0.00 | 0.13 | 0.00 |

Notes: d_: dummy variables (1 for high and 0 for low, etc.); d_isic_4: 91 dummies for the 92 isic 4 digits sectors; d_department: 22 dummies for 23 Colombian departments. Also ***, **, *: significant at 1, 5, or 10 percent respectively; constant not reported; heteroscedasticity consistent t values in brackets.

**Table 2.4**
Credit, taxes, TFP, and investment

| | Independent variable | | | | | |
| --- | --- | --- | --- | --- | --- | --- |
| | Credit | | | | Taxes | |
| | d_debt^ 1989–96 | | d_debt/sales, 1989 | | d_tax/profits, 1989 | |
| | (1) | (2) | (3) | (4) | (5) | (6) |
| **A. TFP growth, 1989–1996** | | | | | | |
| | 2.E-03 (0.8) | -2.E-02 (-4.5)*** | 2.E-03 (0.8) | 8.E-03 (1.2) | 1.E-03 (0.4) | 2.E-02 (1.7)* |
| d_isic_4 | × | × | | × | × | × |
| d_department | × | | × | | × | × |
| age | -1.E-03 (-4.6)*** | -2.E-03 (-10.0)*** | -1.E-03 (-4.6)*** | -2.E-03 (-9.2)*** | -1.E-03 (-4.6)*** | -2.E-03 (-8.7)*** |
| size-employment | 5.64E-07 (0.1) | 2.E-06 (0.6) | 5.26E-07 (0.1) | 2.E-06 (0.5) | 0.0000107 (1.7)* | 1.E-05 (2.5)*** |
| # observations | 3,383 | 3,383 | 3,383 | 3,383 | 2,847 | 2,847 |
| $R^2$ | 0.21 | 0.16 | 0.2126 | 0.16 | 0.21 | 0.17 |
| **B. K growth** | | | | | | |
| | 0.30 (0.9) | 1.73 (1.7)* | 0.81 (2.5)*** | 0.78 (0.8) | 1.38 (1.5) | 0.08 (0.1) |
| d_isic4 | × | × | × | × | × | × |
| d_department | × | | × | | × | |
| age | 2.E-03 (0.1) | -7.E-02 (-1.3) | 2.E-03 (0.1) | -7.E-02 (-1.2) | -1.E-02 (-0.2) | -6.E-02 (-0.9) |
| size-employment | 1.E-03 (0.8) | 2.E-03 (2.1)** | 1.E-03 (0.8) | 2.E-03 (1.9)** | 2.E-03 (1.3) | 2.E-03 (1.7)* |
| # observations | 3,648 | 3,648 | 3,648 | 3,648 | 2,995 | 2,995 |
| $R^2$ | 0.04 | 0.01 | 0.04 | 0.01 | 0.03 | 0.01 |

Notes: d_: dummy variables (1 for high and 0 for low, etc.); d_department, etc.); d_isic 4: 91 dummies for the 92 isic 4 digits sectors; d_department: 22 dummies for 23 Colombian departments. Also ***, **, *: significant at 1, 5, or 10 percent respectively; constant not reported; heteroskedatsiticy consistent t values in brackets.

**Table 2.5**
Economic and sociopolitical perceptions, TFP, and investment

| | Independent variables: Economic and socio political conditions (survey) | | | |
| --- | --- | --- | --- | --- |
| | Economic | | Socio political | |
| | (1) | (2) | (3) | (4) |
| **A. TFP growth, 1989–1996** | | | | |
| | −3.E-03 | 2.E-03 | −1.E-02 | −9.E-03 |
| | (−0.6) | (0.5) | (−2.4)*** | (−1.7)* |
| d_isic4 | × | | × | |
| d_department | × | × | × | × |
| age | −1.E-03 | −1.E-03 | −1.E-03 | −1.E-03 |
| | (−4.6)*** | (−6.8)*** | (−4.4)*** | (−6.7)*** |
| size-employment | −3.E-06 | 6.E-06 | −6.E-06 | 4.E-06 |
| | (−0.5) | (1.7)* | (−1.0) | (1.1) |
| # observations | 518 | 518 | 518 | 518 |
| $R^2$ | 0.47 | 0.16 | 0.48 | 0.17 |
| **B. K growth** | | | | |
| | −1.45 | −2.15 | −1.12 | −1.99 |
| | (−1.3) | (−1.6)* | (−0.8) | (−1.6)* |
| d_isic4 | × | | × | |
| d_department | × | × | × | × |
| age | 9.E-02 | 2.E-02 | 9.E-02 | 2.E-02 |
| | (1.7)* | (0.5) | (1.7)* | (0.5) |
| size-employment | −6.E-04 | −2.E-03 | −5.E-04 | −2.E-03 |
| | (−0.6) | (−3.3)*** | (−0.5) | (−3.1)*** |
| # observations | 538 | 538 | 538 | 538 |
| $R^2$ | 0.36 | 0.10 | 0.36 | 0.10 |

Notes: d_: dummy variables (1 for high and 0 for low, etc.); d_isic_4: dummies for the 92 isic 4 digits sectors; d_department: 22 dummies for 23 Colombian departments. Also ***, **, *: significant at 1, 5, or 10 percent respectively; constant not reported; heteroskedatsiticy consistent $t$ values in brackets.

answers from the plants obtained in 1990 to 1995; the larger averages in table 2.5 reflect where the worst conditions were perceived. The results suggest that poor sociopolitical conditions negatively affected TFP and poor economic conditions negatively affected investment and TFP. This is a good first indication of the negative effects of violence on economic growth. The aggregate results of this survey are interpreted in the next section.

From the data in the three previous tables it should be clear that newly created firms innovated more despite no significant differences on the pattern of investment. The same may be true for large firms, but the evidence is less conclusive here.

## 2.4    Violence

We showed in the previous sections that the reforms introduced in the early 1990s had a positive effect on productivity and investment, and that a healthy flow of innovation was led by labor-intensive and newly created firms. A similar point is made in a recent paper by Loayza et al. (2002) on the stabilization and structural reforms introduced in Latin America during the 1990s, which they show had a favorable effect on growth and productivity.

Why, then, did Colombian growth stagnate in the late 1990s? In earlier sections we considered some major potential contributing factors to be large external shocks and the burst of the land bubble. Indeed, the worse hit sectors in 1995 to 1999 were some nontradables like the construction industry, which started to experience declines in investment in housing soon after 1994, and government services.

Recent research suggests a much worse scenario developing. Already the recession has lasted much longer than at any time in the past. Violence, civil unrest, and corruption within institutions of government are becoming the norm (Cárdenas 2002). Coincidently it appears that the only countries where reforms did not produce entirely positive growth effects in Latin America were El Salvador, Honduras, and Nicaragua during the 1980s and Colombia and Haiti during the 1990s (Loayza et al. 2002). Although industrial productivity is high compared to previous decades, violence has negatively affected TFP. Besides its negative impact on TFP and investment, violence has spread to the rural areas, and some sectors like tourism have been badly hit.

### 2.4.1   The Evolution of Violent Crime in Colombia
The magnitude of violent crime in Colombia is staggering. The homicide rate is three times higher than in Brazil or Mexico, and ten times higher than in Argentina or the United States. Even compared to other Latin American countries, where violent crime has been increasing steadily for years, violence in Colombia has shown disproportionate growth. Only El Salvador and Jamaica have comparable homicide rates, but no other country in Latin America (or in the world, for that matter) has comparable kidnapping rates.

However, Colombia has not always been a violent country. In the early 1970s our homicide rate was not very different from that of its neighboring countries. Starting in the late 1970s, the homicide rate escalated dramatically and by the early 1990s had more than tripled. At its peak in the early 1990s, the homicide rate reached epidemic proportions in some cities. About five of every thousand individuals were murdered in Medellín in 1991. Other metropolitan areas, notably Cali and Bogotá, experienced comparable levels of violence during the same period.

Since the mid-1990s the homicide rate has been falling in the main metropolitan areas of the country but increasing in rural areas and small municipalities. Kidnappings have been escalating dramatically. Recent statistics from the Colombian National Police show that kidnapping rates have grown at an annual rate of almost 25 percent since 1995. It is often said that 60 percent of all kidnappings in the world take place in Colombia. About half of the kidnappings are attributed to leftist guerrillas, and this proportion may be much higher.

Figure 2.12 shows the increase of kidnappings, robbery, homicides, and their combined growth. Kidnappings rose dramatically between 1980 (0.12) and 1999 (7.3), increasing at 36 times the rate with a temporary break from 1992 to 1995. Homicides more than tripled between 1968 and 1992 but have started to fall in the last few years. There is no clear pattern to the robbery continually plaguing the country. Overall all three components of violence were low from 1962 to 1977, and from 1992 to 1995 all three slowed to a temporary break.

Most studies looking at the causes behind the escalation of violent crime in Colombia underscore the role played by drug trafficking. Two different mechanisms are mentioned in this respect. First, the inherently murderous nature of the fight over the control of drug markets is a major cause of the increase in the homicide rate. Second, the rise of drug trafficking has congested law enforcement institutions. The dissemination of criminal know-how has amplified the initial effect and catapulted the level of violence to the staggering rates recorded at the start of the 1990s.[18]

Drug trafficking, and in particular, the shift of the bulk of coca production from Bolivia and Peru to Colombia, has also been linked to the increasing power and influence of leftist guerrillas and paramilitary groups. Since the early 1990s these organizations have profited from drug trafficking, mainly through the taxation of coca production. Recently, and coinciding with the demise of the main drug cartels, some rebel groups have begun to actively process and export drugs. These activities have improved their financial situation, allowing them to update their weaponry and recruit more people. As a result both the guerrillas and the paramilitary have adopted a more aggressive and proactive stance, turning sleepy guerrilla warfare into an outright civil war. Figure 2.13

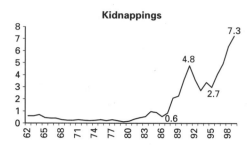

**Kidnappings**

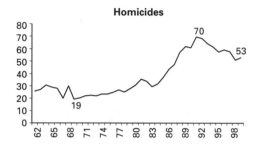

**Homicides**

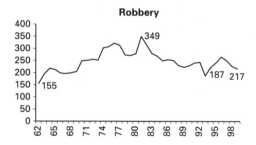

**Robbery**

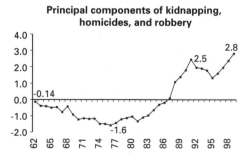

**Principal components of kidnapping, homicides, and robbery**

**Figure 2.12**
Violence in Colombia (From Fajnzylber et al. 1998; Buvinic and Morrison 1999)

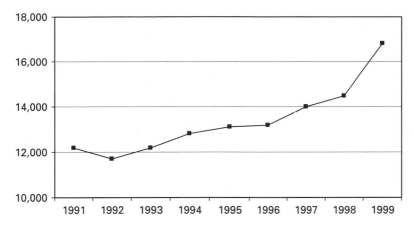

**Figure 2.13**
Number of guerrilleros in Colombia 1991 to 1999

shows the increase in the number of rebels—*guerrilleros*—that took place in the last decade.

Data limitations not withstanding, most analysts agree that the homicides that can be linked, directly or indirectly, to guerrilla warfare have increased dramatically in recent years. Besides, the increase of kidnappings, many of which involved random victims taken from motor vehicles on the main Colombian highways, have caused many people to avoid extensive road travel altogether. As a consequence Colombia has become a country of loosely connected cities, whose inhabitants of small towns live at the mercy of armed groups and inhabitants of large cities live in fear of straying away from their safe, if precarious, hideaways.

When did Colombia's civil war actually start? Guerrilla warfare in Colombia has dragged for over forty years—a long time indeed.[19] In all these years the social conflict (a new euphemism for it) has changed its nature and intensity several times. At the beginning the conflict was concentrated in a few areas of the country, the rebels were mostly landless peasants, and their fight was mainly over land reclamations. Later the conflict came to the cities, disgruntled middle-class youths joined the fight, and social justice and civil liberties became the issues of the day. Ultimately the conflict spread over most of country, poor underpaid peasants have joined the rebel forces in masses, and the rents of coca production have become the reason and fuel of the fight.

When did Colombia pass the threshold from guerrilla warfare to a civil war? If we adopt the definition proposed by Singer and Small (1994), who

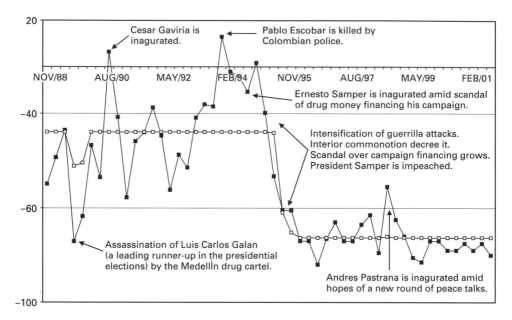

**Figure 2.14**
Changes in opinions about the sociopolitical conditions of Colombia

define civil war in terms of violence rather than in terms of the goals of the protagonists and set a limit of one thousand deaths a year, civil war started in Colombia in mid-1980s.[20] If we adopt a looser definition, the beginning of the war could be moved back to the early 1970s or even to the 1960s.[21] But more than the opinion of scholars and academics, the opinion that matters here is that of the people of Colombia who have to ponder about the implications of the war before making personal or financial decisions. In their opinion the actual state of war has appeared only recently.

Figure 2.14 presents the results of a public survey that tracks the opinion of the Colombian managers and entrepreneurs. The survey has been conducted annually by *Fedesarrollo* since the late 1980s. About 400 firms are surveyed, and together they represent close to 30 percent of the industrial production of the country. Every quarter since 1988, the participants are questioned about changes in the sociopolitical conditions. They are asked specifically whether the political and social conditions were favorable, unfavorable, or neutral for their investment decisions. The figure shows the difference between the fractions of respondents who answered that the conditions were favorable and those who answered that they were unfavorable.

Note the clear shift in the graph around 1995.[22] Before 1995 the opinions were divided and varied widely, mainly in response to salient political events (assassinations, presidential inaugurations, etc.). After 1995, however, the large majority of respondents have consistently found the sociopolitical conditions to be unfavorable to investment decisions. Moreover opinions no longer ranged but were locked into a war mood, literally and metaphorically. Again, before 1995 Colombian managers and entrepreneurs felt that they could, by and large, deal with the high levels of violence that plagued the country since the mid-1970s, but after that year things changed so fundamentally that the seriousness of the situation became apparent to just about all the respondents.

To sum up, we can distinguish two periods of escalating violence in Colombia. From 1975 to 1995, violent urban crimes skyrocketed, as drug cartels engaged in a direct confrontation with the state, murdering some of Colombia's leading politicians, judges, and journalists and waged a bloody campaign of bombings. From 1995 to the present, urban violence has declined, the confrontation between drug traffickers and the state has subsided, but rebel activity has soared. Kidnappings, for example, have increased threefold and guerrilla attacks have become a staple of Colombian newscasts. As a result few still doubt that the country is at war. The principal components of figure 2.12 escalate year after year after 1977 and reach the highest levels today after a temporary fall in 1992 to 1995.

### 2.4.2 Repercussions of Civil War and Violence

The destruction of productive assets is the obvious channel through which civil war affects an economy. As a consequence of warfare, public and private infrastructures are often destroyed or damaged. But accompanying the losses of physical capital are, of course, losses of human capital as many of the labor force are killed or maimed. Moreover the lost capital is not likely to be replaced any time soon. As civil war creates temporary uncertainty about the future returns to local assets, thus raising the premium on liquid assets, new investments are likely to be postponed.[23]

Civil war further causes capital to flee to safer and more secure countries. Primarily this concerns financial capital, but it does include human capital—and even physical capital. Thus, where local resources flee, foreign assets stampede, thereby reducing FDI in the host country. This not only affects factor accumulation but may also affect productivity, at least insofar as FDI generates knowledge spillovers—a frequent argument in the literature.[24] With the flight of capital, the supplies of human and physical capital will contract relative to land, buildings, and unskilled labor, and this will cause those sectors that are relatively intensive in capital to contract. Since these sectors are less likely to innovate, this may add to the deleterious effects of war on productivity mentioned above.

### Previous Studies

While many empirical studies have attempted to estimate the effects of political instability on economic growth, few have tried to measure the effects of civil war (or social disorder) on the same variable.[25] Political instability, understood as the propensity of government to collapse, is one of the likely manifestations of civil war, but it cannot be equated, in all circumstances, to civil war. Moreover political instability is just one of many channels through which civil war can affect growth, but its effect on growth should be considerably lower than that of civil war in the same variable. A similar argument applies to the effect of military spending on growth.

Table 2.6 presents a summary of the main findings of representative studies on the relationship between civil warfare and economic growth. Three studies use cross-country data and the rest examine the experiences of countries and regions. One study focuses on the effects of political instability, another on the effects of military spending, and the rest on the general effects of civil warfare. Although no definitive conclusions can be drawn from these studies, some general trends are apparent.

First and foremost, civil warfare appears to reduce growth rates substantially—two percentage points annually according to the most reliable estimates. Second, this result cannot be explained by the effect of military spending on civil war, as shown by the much more modest impact of this variable on growth. Nor can it be explained by the effect of civil war on political instability—as shown by the weak effect of political assassinations on growth. Finally individual country studies confirm the adverse consequences of civil war in terms of growth, though the results cannot be extrapolated because of the specific circumstances of the countries under scrutiny.

The previous results can be used to estimate the extent to which the recent increase of military spending and political assassinations has adversely affected the rate of economic growth in Colombia. Military spending in Colombia increased from 2.6 percent of GDP in the first half of the 1990s to 4.5 percent in the second half. According to the results of Knight et al. (1996), this would reduce growth rates by at most 0.1 percentage points a year. On the other hand, political assassinations in Colombia

**Table 2.6**
Civil war and growth: Empirical evidence

| Author(s) | Sample | Indicator of civil war | Conclusion |
|---|---|---|---|
| Collier (1998) | 79 countries 1960–90 Panel data | Months of civil war in a decade from Small and Singer (1994) | Civil war reduces growth rates by 2.2 percentage points a year |
| Easterly and Levine (1997) | 96 countries 1960–90 Panel data | Political assassinations from Banks (1994) | In a country of 30 million inhabitants, five political assassinations per year during a decade reduces annual growth by 0.4 percentage points |
| Knight, Loayza, and Villanueva (1996) | 124 countries 1972–90 Panel data | Military spending from Hewitt (1993) | Increase in military spending over GDP of 10 percentage points reduces annual growth by 0.3 percentage points |
| Rubio (1995) | Colombia 1960–93 Time series | Homicides per 100 thousand from Colombian national police | Increase of the homicide rate in Colombia from 20 in the 1970s to 80 in the 1990s reduces annual growth by at least 2 percentage points |
| Abadie and Gardeazabal (2001) | Basque country 1975–2000 time series | Homicides linked to ETA terrorists attacks | Over two decades, terrorism reduced per-capita GDP in the Basque country by at least 15 percentage points |

shifted from 2.5 a year in the second half of the 1980s to 5.0 a year in the first half of the 1990s. According to results of Easterly and Levine (1997), this change would reduce growth rates in at most 0.2 percentage points per year. Even if lumped together, these effects explain only a marginally fraction of the effect of civil war on growth as predicted by Collier (1999) and Rubio (1995), which confirms our presumption that the effects of civil war on growth go well beyond the effects of greater political instability and higher military spending.

### New Results

The evidence presented thus far indicates that political instability and resource diversion via higher military spending are little more than small (if interesting) subplots of a more complicated story. We tackle this question using a cross-country regression approach. Our dependent variable is the real growth of GDP per capita over three different periods (1965–1974, 1975–1984, and 1985–1994) and 83 countries.[26] The independent variables include in the regressions, among others, measures of human capital, terms of trade, and policy outcomes.

In table 2.7 are the main results of the regressions. As in most of the literature, it is evident that a low initial level of economic activity, an educated labor force, and favorable terms of trade have a positive impact on economic growth. However, civil wars (measured by Singer and Small's correlates of war) also have a negative impact on growth. On average, a ten-year civil war reduces annual growth by 1.7 percentage points—a similar result to that obtained by Collier (1999).

The first regression deliberately omits the policy variables because, as we argued earlier, some of the effects of civil war work through policies.[27] In this respect the coefficient on civil war can be seen to shrink considerably and lose its significance completely once the analysis controls for policy variables—government spending, inflation, and the black market premium in this case. This result suggests that *civil wars affect growth rates mainly by causing a relative deterioration of macroeconomic policies.* However, the exact mechanisms by which war affects policies remain unclear, and they are likely to differ substantially from country to country.

The second panel of the table examines the effects of violence, measured by the number of homicides per hundred thousand residents, on growth rates.[28] As in civil war, violence adversely affects growth rates. An increase of the homicide rate from 20 to 80 reduces yearly growth by 1.4 percentage points. In contrast to the previous case, however, the effect of violence on growth doesn't work through policies. Quite on the con-

Table 2.7
Growth, civil war, violence, and political instability

| | (1) | | (2) | | (3) | |
|---|---|---|---|---|---|---|
| Log of initial income | −0.019 | −0.045 | −0.052 | −0.099 | −0.009 | −0.041 |
| | (1.40) | (2.55) | (2.43) | (4.52) | (0.55) | (2.29) |
| Secondary education[a] | 0.007 | 0.004 | 0.006 | 0.004 | 0.006 | 0.003 |
| | (3.12) | (2.07) | (2.33) | (1.69) | (2.47) | (1.52) |
| Terms of trade | 0.145 | 0.109 | 0.138 | 0.0921 | 0.136 | 0.0971 |
| | (3.53) | (2.81) | (2.90) | (2.11) | (3.27) | (2.50) |
| Civil war[b] | −0.0017 | −0.0007 | | | | |
| | (2.06) | (0.86) | | | | |
| Homicide rate[c] | | | −0.00023 | −0.00024 | | |
| | | | (1.38) | (1.56) | | |
| Assassinations[d] | | | | | −0.00434 | −0.00400 |
| | | | | | (2.00) | (1.98) |
| Policy variables | No | Yes | No | Yes | No | Yes |
| N observed | 285 | 285 | 166 | 166 | 290 | 284 |
| $R^{2e}$ | 0.09 | 0.24 | 0.09 | 0.24 | 0.08 | 0.24 |

a. Secondary education refers to the secondary years of schooling of males over 25.
b. Civil war index is from Singer and Small (1994).
c. Homicide rate is United Nations. See Ledderman and Loyza (1999).
d. Assassinations is from Banks (1994). See Easterly and Levine (1997).
e. All regressions were estimates using OLS. Sur estimation yields almost identical results.

trary, the coefficient on the homicide rate increases slightly once the policy variables are added to the specification.

The third panel examines the effects of political instability—measured by the yearly average of political assassinations. Again, there is a negative association between the variables in question: in a decade one more political assassination a year reduces growth by 0.5 percentage points.[29] As in circumstances of violence, the assassinations have no effect on policies, a result consistent with the findings of Alesina et al. (1996).

In sum, the available international evidence suggests, first, that civil war have a sizable impact on growth (about two percentage points a year), and second, that this impact is transmitted through bad policies. On the other hand, violence (political or otherwise) also appears to have a sizable impact on growth, but bad policies do not appear to be the main mechanism of transmission in this case.

Civil war can affect the level of economic activity through several channels. In general, these channels can be divided in two groups: those that reduce output directly by diminishing factor productivity and those that reduce output indirectly by reducing or impeding factor accumulation. Whether or not these channels also affect the steady state growth rate depends on the model one has in mind. Nonetheless, the growth rate would fall in the short run as the economy moves from the initial steady state to the new one.

### 2.4.3　Civil War and the Recent Growth Collapse

Growth of GDP per head went from 2.3 percent in 1985 to 1994 to −1.5 percent in 1995 to 1999. The drop in the terms of trade explains 6 percent of the growth reduction. The intensification of war explains 45 percent of the growth collapse—or 1.7 percentage points. For its part, the increase of government spending explains 16 percent of the growth decline, but some of this effect is already captured by the intensification of war.

What can be recognized from these growth figures is that policy attempts to stem the escalation of the conflict and narco-traffic in Colombia are too recent to provide definite results. A casual view of the events of the 1990s, however, tends to support our contention; that conflict and war lead to bad economic policy. This leads us back to the Constitution of 1991, which partially promoted and adopted a mechanism to incorporate the guerrilla in the political process.[30] The 1991 Constitution had many virtues, as some of its advocates mention, but it has not facilitated growth. There is also no doubt that the peace negotiations with the guerrilla undertaken under President Pastrana (1998–2002) have made it almost impossible for the administration to adopt fiscal reforms and make adjustments in government expenditures (table 2.8). Complicit institutions and bad economic policies are clearly interconnected.

### 2.5　Conclusions

Colombia and Brazil were the fastest growing Latin American countries from 1960 to 1995, though their growth rates were modest compared to those of some Asian countries. But after decades of continual expansion Colombia stopped growing. Income per capita fell in 1995 to 2000 for the first time in a century and future prospects now appear slim.

Despite popular beliefs to the contrary, our evidence suggests that the economic reforms introduced during the 1990s had a healthy effect on growth. Financial liberalization expanded and rationalized credit and had a large impact on investment; the opening of the economy increased productivity and technological change. The firms that innovated were new, and operated in open and labor-intensive sectors. These results are consistent with Loayza et al. (2002) findings, showing that the liberalizing

**Table 2.8**
Civil war and the growth collapse in Colombia

|  | 1985–94 | 1995–99 | Difference |
|---|---|---|---|
| Growth of GDP per capita | 2.30% | −1.50% | −3.80% |
| Secondary schooling | 1.05 | 1.01 | 0.00% |
| Terms of trade | −0.04 | −1.53 | −0.22% |
| Civil war | 0 | 1 | −1.70% |
| Government expenditure over GDP | 6.7% | 13.0% | −0.63% |

reforms undertaken in Latin America during the 1980s and 1990s had important positive effects on growth.

What, then, caused the recent collapse of growth in Colombia after 1995? The volatility of capital flows is a good candidate, though we show in the chapter that this volatility was much larger in other Latin American countries. The burst of the land-housing bubble in 1995 may be an important factor, although the participation of the construction sector in the economy was close to just 3 percent. Coffee prices are very low today compared to the last decades, the participation of coffee in the economy is much lower today than in the past, and the instability of coffee prices was low during the 1990s.

It is too early to evaluate if the recent crisis is just a transitory phenomenon. Much is at stake, and we are compelled to say that the new institutions brought about by the Constitution of 1991 and the escalation of violence appear to have permanently altered the successful Colombian growth record of the past.

The recent downturn has lasted much longer than in any previous cycle, and it can be no coincidence that the only countries in the region where reforms did not produced the strong expected growth results in Loayza (2002) were El Salvador, Honduras, and Nicaragua in the 1980s and Colombia and Haiti in the 1990s, all regions with intensifications of conflict.

In the long run the intensification of guerrilla warfare will surely play a detrimental role. The increase of kidnappings, the worsening of perceptions and the growing constraints in spatial mobility, may account for almost half of the observed decline of economic growth. The policy advice should be relatively similar despite the different scenarios. The Colombian government should concentrate on the design of good institutions, the reduction of public expenditure, the deepening of the economic reforms introduced in the first part of the 1990s and the reduction of violence.

## Notes

This paper draws heavily on Arbeláez, Echavarría, and Gaviria (2003).

1. During the 1980s Colombia grew at 1.1 percent and Latin America at −1.5 percent according to the figures provided by De Gregorio and Lee (2001).

2. See *Coyuntura Económica*, September, 1998.

3. The authors use the Sachs-Werner index, calculated as the fraction of years that the country was considered to be open to trade. The evaluation of the country's openness is made on the basis of the four dimensions of trade policy: average tariff rates, quotas and licensing, export taxes, and black market exchange rate premium. Rodríguez and Rodrik (2000) have forcefully questioned the use of this index as a measure of openness. The debate is hot and will continue. See, for example, the recent work by Wacziarg (2001), who shows that the estimated effects of the trade-to-GDP ratio are almost identical when the ratio is instrumented by Sachs-Werner index as when it is instrumented by other policy indicators such as average tariffs and the nontariff barrier coverage ratio. See Lederman and Maloney (2002).

4. There is a wide discussion on the impact of moderate inflation (Fischer 1993). Investment has been considered as an endogenous variable by Barro (1997), another unsettled issue.

5. See also Echavarría (2000b).

6. The average years of secondary schooling (male population over 25) was higher in Colombia than in Latin America in the first two decades considered in the table, but lower after 1985. Something similar happened to tertiary education, which shows a small lead at the beginning and a growing lag after 1985.

7. Using a new (and improved) data set and a panel estimation that allows to control for country-specific effects, Forbes shows that an increase in a country's level of income inequality has a significant positive relationship with economic growth, at least in the short and medium term. Many doubts remain, however, as to the robustness of the results to alternative measures of inequality and as to the specific mechanisms whereby inequality can affect growth rates.

8. Barro does find a strong positve relation if fertility is excluded, a questionable course considering the strong theoretical and empirical emphasis given to this variable in the literature.

9. Large farms expanded and small ónes united in the 1960s, but in 1970 to 1984 both large and small farms split up into smaller units. More recent information on this crucial development is not available.

10. This section is based on Echavarría (2000b), Arbeláez and Echavarría (2001), and Vélez et al. (1999).

11. The following paragraphs are based on Echavarría (2000a).

12. A tax on coffee exports was created in 1927. New "taxes" were imposed in the 1930s and 1940s, but all such revenues went back to the sector, and were reinvested in coffee cultivation, stabilization, and technology programs. Export taxes represented more than 20 percent of taxes on foreign trade in Bolivia, Chile, Ecuador, and Paraguay but were practically nonexistent for Colombia.

13. The large surpluses generated during the period of high world prices were used to acquire exchangeable bonds of the Central Bank to prevent the monetization of the foreign currency then entering the country. Since the Fund was not allowing the increase in the external coffee price to be totally transferred to the internal prices, the national coffee producers were granted a "bonus" in the form of Coffee Savings Bonds (TAC—*Título de Ahorro Cafetero*).

14. The solvency crisis was treated directly with measures to improve the profitability of the financial entities and indirectly with aid to the corporate sector. The government was empowered to nationalize any entity undergoing a severe crisis without compensating those

responsible for its failure. So certain elements were introduced that opened the way for future financial sector reform.

15. The Fund's resources could be used to buy Colombian external debt bonds, which countered its stabilization goal, and nothing could prevent *Ecopetrol*, one of the Fund's largest members, from acquiring a huge external debt. For the Fund to adequately accomplish its stabilizing goal in the exchange rate, it would have had to save 81 percent of the public oil income, and not the 30 percent the law had established.

16. Volatility is apparent in the behavior of several variables, and particularly, in gross capital flows, net private capital flows, and foreign direct investment, based on their standard deviations and differences between maximum and minimum values.

17. The package included tax reform (Law 75 of 1986), foreign investment reform (Law 9 of 1991), labor reform (Law 50 of 1990), and social security reform (Law 100 of 1993).

18. The result is contrary to Beck et al. (2000) but consistent with additional empirical work by Arbeláez and Echavarría (2001).

19. See Gaviria (2000) for a detailed analysis of violence in Colombia.

20. The long duration of the Colombian conflict has given the world that rare individual: the aging guerrillero. Rebel leaders were supposed to die young (Guevara), take over power and hold onto it (Castro), or retire and fade into oblivion (Pastora). None of this has happened in Colombia, where at least one rebel leader (Marulanda) has completed 40 years of irresolute fighting.

21. According to Singer and Small (1994), civil war in Colombia began in 1984. Singer and Small's index was later used by Collier (1999).

22. According to Sivard (1993), civil war in Colombia began at some point before 1960. Sivard's index is frequently used in the economic literature. See, for example, Easterly and Levine (1997).

23. Formally, one could compute the transition between the two regimes—war and peace—using Hamilton's (1992) methodology.

24. See Dixit and Pindyck (1994) for the relationship between investment and uncertainty.

25. See, for example, Romer (1994).

26. See Barro and Lee (1994).

27. For a thorough description of the variables and sources, see De Gregorio and Lee (1999).

28. Obviously, violence is greater in countries entrenched in civil war, such as Colombia where the yearly average homicide rate is 14.1 compared to 6.8 in countries at peace.

29. This rate is not in terms of number of assassinations per inhabitants, as is done, for example, in Easterly and Levine (1997).

30. See Cepeda (2001).

# References

Alesina, A., A. Carrasquilla, and R. Steiner. 2000. The Central Bank in Colombia. Working Paper 13. Fedesarrollo.

Alesina, A., and D. Rodrik. 1994. Distributive politics and economic growth. *Quaterly Journal of Economics* 109: 465–90.

Arbeláez, M. A., and J. J. Echavarría. 2001. Financial liberalization, credit and investment in the Colombian manufacturing sector. Mimeo. Prepared for the Research Network of the IDB. Fedesarrollo.

Barro, R. J. 1997. *Determinants of Economic Growth: A Cross-country Empirical Study.* Cambridge: MIT Press.

Barro, R. J. 1999. Inequality, growth, and investment. NBER Working Paper 7038.

Barro, R. J., and J. Lee. 1994. Sources of economic growth. *Carnegie-Rochester Conference Series on Public Policy* 40: 1–46.

Beck, T., R. Levine, and N. Loayza. 2000. Finance and the sources of growth. *Journal of Financial Economics* 58: 261–300.

Calvo, G. 1998. Capital flows and capital market crises: The simple economics of sudden stop. *Journal of Applied Economics* 1: 35–51.

Cárdenas, M. 1997. *La Tasa de Cambio en Colombia, Cuadernos.* Santafé de Bogotá: Tercer Mundo Editorei.

Cárdenas, M. 2002. Economic growth in Colombia: A reversal of fortune? CID Working Paper 83. *Center for International Development.*

Cárdenas, M., and R. Bernal. 2000. Changes in the distribution of income and the new economic model in Colombia. Mimeo. CEPAL, Santiago, Chile.

Cárdenas, M., R. Correa, J. J. Echavarría, and C. J. Rodríguez. 1998. Exchange rates and macroeconomic interdependence among the Andean countries. Mimeo. Fedesarrollo.

Cepeda, M. J. 2001. Cómo se hizo la Asamblea Constituyente? In R. Pardo, ed., *El Siglo Pasado. Colombia: Economía, Política y Sociedad.* Colpatria-CEREC, pp. 459–91.

Collier, P. 1999. On the economic consequences of civil war. *Oxford Economic Papers* 51: 168–83.

De Gregorio, J., and J.-W. Lee. 2001. Economic growth in Latin America: Sources and prospects. Mimeo. Paper presented for the Global Development Network.

*Coyuntura Económica,* Fedesarrollo (various issues).

De la Torre, A., A. Leipziger, and M. Gasha. 2002. Behind credit fluctuations in Latin America: Old and new suspects. Washington: World Bank.

Dixit, A. K., and R. S. Pindyck. 1994. *Investment under Uncertainty.* Princeton: Princeton University Press.

Easterly, W. 2001. *The Elusive Quest for Growth: Economist's Adventures and Misadventures in the Tropics.* Cambridge: MIT Press.

Echavarría, J. J. 1999. Hacia la devaluación real, adiós bandas cambiarias. *Coyuntura Económica* 29: 87–105.

Echavarría, J. J. 2000a. *Crisis e Industrialización. Las Lecciones de los 30s.* Tercer Mundo, Fedesarrollo y Banco de la República.

Echavarría, J. J. 2000b. Colombia en la década de los 90s: neoliberalismo y reformas estructurales en el trópico. *Coyuntura Económica* 30: 121–48.

Edwards, S. 1995. *Crisis and Reform in Latin America: From Despair to Hope.* Washington: World Bank.

Fernández, C., and A. Gonzáles. 2002. Integración y vulnerabilidad externa en Colombia. Mimeo.

Fiscal Mission. 2002. *Proposals for Tax Reform in Colombia.* Mimeo. Fedesarrollo.

Fischer, S. 1993. The role of macroeconomic factors in growth. NBER Working Paper 4565.

Forbes, K. J. 2000. A reassessment of the relationship between inequality and growth. *American Economic Review* 90: 869–88.

Gaviria, A. 2000. Increasing returns and the evolution of violent crime: the case of Colombia. *Journal of Development Economics* 61: 1–25.

Giugale, M. M., O. Lafourcade, and C. Luff. 2003. *Colombia: The Economic Foundation of Peace.* Washington: World Bank.

Inter-American Development Bank. 1997. América Latina tras una década de reformas. *Progreso económico y social de América Latina.*

Knight, M., N. Loayza, and D. Villanueva. 1996. The peace dividend: Military spending cuts and economic growth. *International Monetary Fund Staff Papers* 43: 1–37.

Lederman, D., and W. Maloney. 2002. Trade structure and growth. Mimeo. World Bank. Office of the Chief Economist for Latin America and the Caribbean.

Levinsohn, J., and A. Petrin. 2000. When industries become more productive, do firms? Investigating productivity dynamics. NBER Working Paper 6893.

Loayza, N., P. Fajnzylber, and C. Calderón. 2002. Economic growth in Latin America and the Caribbean: Stylized facts, explanations and forecasts. Mimeo. World Bank.

Lora, E., and F. Barrera. 1997. A decade of structural reform in Latin America: Measurement and growth effects. *Policy Discussion Paper, Inter-American Development Bank* (Special issue 1998, pp. 55–86).

Lorente, L., A. Salazar, and A. Gallo. 1984. *Distribución de la Propiedad Rural en Colombia, 1960–1984*. Ministerio de Agricultura-CEGA, Bogotá.

Medina, P., M. Melendez, and K. Seim. 2002. Productivity dynamics of the Colombian manufacturing sector. Mimeo. A Report to the Inter-American Development Bank.

Ocampo, J. A. 1987. La consolidación del capitalismo moderno. *Historia Económica de Colombia*. Siglo XXI Editores-Fedesarrollo.

Olley, S., and A. Pakes. 1996. The dynamics of productivity in the telecommunications equipment industry. *Econometrica* 64: 1263–97.

Rodríguez, F., and D. Rodrik. 2000. Trade policy and economic growth: A skeptic's guide to cross-national evidence. In B. Bernanke and K. Rogoff, eds., *NBER Macroeconomics Annual* 15: 261–325.

Rubio, M. 1995. Crimen y crecimiento en Colombia. *Coyuntura Económica* 25: 102–25.

Sivard, R. 1993. *World Military and Social Expenditures*. Washington: World Priorities.

Tenjo, F., and E. López. 2002. Burbuja y Estancamiento del Crédito en Colombia. *Coyuntura Económica* 32.

Torres, L. A., and H. Osorio. 1998. Sistema andino de franjas de precios: Evaluación e implicaciones para Colombia. CEDE, Universidad de los Andes.

Vélez, C. E., A. Kugler, and C. Buillón. 1999. The reversal of inequality gains in urban Colombia, 1978–1995: A combination of persistent and fluctuating forces. Mimeo. World Bank.

Wacziarg, R. 2001. Measuring the dynamic gains from growth. *The World Bank Economic Review* 15: 393–429.

# I Political Institutions

# 3 Checks and Balances: An Assessment of the Institutional Separation of Political Powers in Colombia

Maurice Kugler and Howard Rosenthal

## 3.1 Introduction

In this chapter we evaluate the institutional and judicial structure of the Colombian government. Specifically, we analyze the performance of arrangements for the separation of powers, with particular reference to the legal system and the role of courts. We explore how potential reforms of current institutional checks and balances can be designed to promote the rule of law, preserve property rights, and stimulate economic growth. A new institutional structure must acquire broad popular legitimacy, and be conducive to widespread human capital formation and participation in the benefits of growth, to be sustainable in the long run. To further these objectives, we advocate, on the basis of the analysis below, the policy recommendations set forth above.

The 1991 Constitution indeed makes commendable commitments to these objectives. Yet, due to its constitutional structure, Colombia is governed in a manner that is both unchecked and unbalanced. Here are some examples:

• Articles 356 and 357 of the Constitution of 1991 commit the central government to a rigid schedule of increasing redistribution of tax revenues to regional entities. This schedule cannot, in principle, be checked by events. The functions of national defense and internal security may require the central government to have a higher share of revenues in a recession—or experience; other functions with cross-regional externalities, such as environmental regulation, might be better pursued by the central government. At the same time the Constitution does not provide for balances that lead the regional governments to fiscal responsibility. The regional governments can have unbalanced budgets and run fiscal deficits with the implicit expectation of a bailout by the central government.

• The Constitution, partly out of an unbalanced commitment to equality of results rather than equality of opportunities, has permitted the Constitutional Court to act in an activist manner in which it regularly overturns legislation passed with the assent of the President and the Congress. For example, the Court has blocked the deindexation of wages for public employees simply because pensions were indexed (by Article 53 of the Constitution). The Constitutional Court has also ruled against the government's policies relating to reform of bureaucracy, to the structure of interest payments on mortgages, and to differential taxes on consumer banking as opposed to interbank transactions.[1] In all cases the rulings can be deemed to have caused significant macroeconomic damage. More generally, the Court has stepped beyond the normal check known as "judicial review" by overturning several governmental initiatives, unduly controlling the normal executive and legislative direction of economic policy.
• The Constitution gives private individuals standing to contest legislation directly with the highest courts in the land. As a result a considerable amount of legislation is contested. Often legislation is overturned on narrow procedural grounds. The Court and the legislature are not evenly balanced because in part details of the internal organization of the legislature—such as requirements for debate—are incorporated into the Constitution. Unlike most other nations, where internal organization is left to the discretion of the legislature, the inclusion of details about how laws are passed in the Colombian Constitution has contributed to extensive intervention by the Court. It has become difficult for the government to anticipate which legislative acts will be sustained.

The Constitution of 1991 was negotiated as a means of ending internal strife. The former revolutionary group M-19, which turned into a populist party with overarching redistributive goals, had a major success in the popular elections for the Constitutional Assembly and received one of the three main chairs at the table. In fact their party, Alianza Democrática, had the highest proportion of delegates compared to any of the competing lists emanating from the fragmented traditional political parties. The result was an enormously long document that attempted to reassure all sides that the future would be to their liking by introducing article after article with explicit provisions for all, many of which unfortunately, the state has been unable to fulfill.[2] The Constitution attempts to be a document of rigid micromanagement (such as mandating indexation of pensions, setting targets for inflation and the allocation of regional public expenditures) rather than one that establishes basic institutions for democratic decision-making in a dynamic world. Moreover, written at the time when many nations in the world were emerging from state socialism and moving to market capitalism, the Constitution commits and creates expectations of a welfare state. Such emphasis runs orthogonal to the market-oriented economic reforms introduced the same year by the government. Specifically, chapter II, Article I, "Economic, Social and Cultural Rights," creates expectations for subgroups in the society such as the handicapped, children, and senior citizens. But a middle-income country like Colombia, with an annual per capita income under US$3,000, cannot possibly emulate the type of welfare state system of Sweden and Canada. In contrast, such text is not found in the Canadian Constitution.[3] Meanwhile the US Constitution asserts only that it seeks to "promote the general welfare." Worse, an overemphasis on egalitarianism can lead to widespread misery. For example, Article 58, which permits uncompensated expropriation for reasons of "equity," might be a substantial deterrent to investment and economic growth.

Our examination of the Constitution of 1991 sounds a warning about the process of national conciliation. The nation's long-run economic health may be seriously impaired if peace is bought at the price of widespread concessions with regard to either the process of decision-making about the economy or to the content of future government economic policies. One may buy transitory tranquility, which may not translate into lasting peace, at the price of long-term instability and turmoil. The implied trade-off may be most undesirable.

In section 3.2 we provide a theoretical discussion of how government can be structured to provide checks and balances. Then, in section 3.3, we discuss the major problems of Colombia and how our policy recommendations are designed to meet these problems. In section 3.4 we explore the issue of institutional instability and in particular the nature of the executive-legislative relation. In section 3.5 we follow up with an assessment of the balance of powers among the three branches of government and the operation of institutional checks. After that in section 3.6 we deal with the problem of concentration of power and the implications for the electoral system. We close with conclusions, and ponder further issues, in section 3.6.

## 3.2  Advantages of Checks and Balances

Democracy can lead, as Alexis de Tocqueville noted in *Democracy in America* (1835), to a "tyranny of the majority" in which minority rights and preferences are given short shrift. For example, citizens can have short-run perspectives and use majority rule for redistribution. Too much redistribution not only can harm some individuals in the short run but also seriously affect the incentives necessary to promote long-run growth. Moreover, in any political system, self-interested politicians will seek to extract rents. That is, any political system can offer plenty of opportunity for corruption. This is particularly present in Colombia where politics has traditionally been organized along clientelist lines, where the loyalties of politicians are to narrow interest groups, such as teachers' unions or localities, rather than being organized into broad coalitions formed around "ideological" parties.[4] In this section we discuss the theory behind the separation of powers as well as some crucial general considerations.

### 3.2.1  Theory of Separation of Powers

The doctrine of the separation of powers is a basic principle within the liberal constitutionalist tradition. Some political philosophers have enshrined the separation of executive, legislative, and judicial powers as an important institution in order to prevent the abuse of political power by officeholders.[5] While elections are a disciplining device, various political systems have different degrees of balance of power among the citizenry and the branches of government. The general presumption is that the separation of powers gives voters in liberal democracies a greater degree of control to discipline elected officials. If there is competition by division of powers among government agencies, say, along geographical lines, agents not only can voice their opinion in the next elections but also exercise an exit option should they be dissatisfied.[6]

Recent political economy literature has assessed the impact of the separation of powers on the well-being of citizens. Some have taken a skeptical stance with respect to the presumption that the separation of powers is an optimal arrangement. Brennan and Hamlin (1994, 2000) argue that in some instances the separation of powers may be detrimental in that a common pool problem may be induced, leading to negative externalities between various branches or hierarchies of the state. Hence checks and balances may cause a failure by the government to deliver to the citizens due to distributional conflict. Chari, Jones, and Marimon (1997) explore this theme further by analyzing split ticket voting among federal and decentralized agencies, in a static model with endogenous policy formation. In general, separation of the executive and the legislature will not guarantee an optimal outcome.

Alesina and Rosenthal (1996, 2000) show in a dynamic framework that bicameralism, federalism, presidentialism, and other forms of separation of powers are beneficial as voters have more possible choices spanning the political spectrum. The voters can thereby obtain moderate policies even when the political parties are polarized. It is implicit that the judiciary recognize that the bargaining process between the executive and the legislature is legitimate and within the rules of the game. Also Persson, Roland, and Tabellini (1997a,b) show that the separation of powers eliminates political rents accruing from information asymmetry and abuse of power. In both cases it is assumed that an independent and benevolent judiciary is capable of enforcing the constitutional rules, which provide checks through mutual agreement requirements and balances by distributing agenda control.

The assumption that the judiciary will perform its function without distortions is one that may not be appropriate in general and especially with reference to the Colombian case. One of the main contributions of modern political economy has been the introduction of strategic behavior by politicians. Here we explore also the consequences of strategic behavior by judges, who may be politically and economically motivated. A politically and economically motivated judiciary could result in a bad form of policy gridlock.[7] Although gridlock can occur even when the judiciary does not intervene, this can happen *only* when there is not a large popular majority for policy change (Krehbiel 1998; Brady and Volden 1998). While Montesquieu in *Spirit of the Laws* (1748) extols the virtues of the independent English courts, in contrast to French legal centralization, judges with political agendas of their own can be damaging by fostering myopic decisions to win constituencies. The bad scenario would be where a narrowly representative judiciary blocks policy change that has been approved by the executive and legislative branch reflecting broad consensus. Moreover distortions leading to allocation of resources by the judiciary toward legislative challenges further weaken enforcement capacity in ordinary justice.

### 3.2.2   General Considerations

#### *Constitutional versus Civil Courts*
Whereas it has been noted that judicial power in constitutional matters has increased, the courts' effectiveness to rule on administrative and criminal matters remains weak and impunity is rampant. Indeed, the worst-case scenario is where courts fail at their basic functions of enforcing human rights and property rights but overly intervene at the highest level of policy-making.

However, a strong Constitutional Court can have positive effects since a judiciary weak in constitutional matters can leave the door open for covert collusion, through the exchange of favors, between the executive and the legislature.[8] For example, the court has halted in many instances the passage of laws that have not been duly deliberated in Congress. The problem is when the court decisions are beyond the realm of ruling about the legality of the dealings of governmental agencies and impinge more directly on the viability of policy implementation. Since citizens are entitled to challenge the laws passed in Congress and any decisions taken by the Executive, the Court has received a deluge of challenges, only a fraction of which actually can be processed directly. While the Court has to rule according to the Constitution, it has ample discretion as to which cases it selects to process. Unfortunately, since its inception in 1991, the Constitutional Court seems to have spent a lot of resources upholding challenges to laws and policies, with an egalitarian bias inducing significant economic inefficiency and ultimately welfare losses. This outcome is partly due to a combination of the Colombian legal tradition rooted in civil law and the multiple articles in the Constitution explicitly dictating equality of outcomes, compounded by the populist bias induced by the incentives faced by judges in Latin America, who often run for office after short tenures.

### How Much Change Is Needed?

Clearly, there is need for change in the political system of Colombia in order to reduce pressures for short-run redistribution, corruption, and clientelism. A central question concerns the extent of change required. It is doubtful that solely incremental change within the current system can achieve the desired goals. On the contrary, it is likely that fundamentally different institutions are required to attain political stability and economic prosperity. A closely related question concerns whether the changes can be limited to the formal governmental structure. Change in executive-legislative relations and in the structure of courts cannot be meaningful without addressing the fact that Colombia is faced with very significant extra-legal activity. In particular, those segments of Colombian society that identify with the insurgent political groups, both left-wing and paramilitary, must be included in the democratic process in order to achieve long-term stability. Also we must consider the fact that the extensive extra-legal activity itself could be related to distributive conflicts stemming from limits to meritocracy, which are perpetuated by how clientelist interests shape political outcomes, and which are claimed to be at the heart of the origins of political violence.

### *There Is No "One Best Way"*

We approach our task with a large measure of humility. Numerous nations have by now attained a high level of economic development and a relatively high level of personal freedom and physical security for their citizens. The institutions of government vary widely across these nations. In some, at best only recently have the executive and legislative branches of government been "checked" by an independent judiciary. In many, cabinet government prevails, and individual legislators are allowed little initiative in the policy process. In others, legislative dominance has been asserted. Similarly there is variation in the independence of central banks and other agencies of economic regulation.[9]

These observations suggest there is unlikely to be "one best way," even for a given country. Even if there were "a best way," feasible change will be highly path-dependent. For example, the presumption that the separation of powers in government is the best way to achieve political accountability relies on the enforcement capacity and impartiality of the judicial branch. Indeed, this last element seems to be the essential one. Parliamentary democracies perform well without separation between executive and legislative powers and achieve balance through bicameralism. In contrast, presidential democracies without independent courts can lead to dismal outcomes when the executive power can coerce the legislatures. Generally, many institutions designed to provide a check may fail to work in the manner intended.[10]

### *Governmental Institutions and Separation of Powers*

Checks and balances institutions that address the problems induced by simple majority voting include executive vetoes, bicameral legislatures, requirements for supermajority votes in some areas, and judicial review. All of these institutions induce bias toward maintaining the status quo over that found in majority rule. These institutions can also be used to design incentive systems that improve the accountability of politicians.

In general, if electoral control is imperfect, mutual agreement requirements and the agenda-setting structure may be used to mitigate the concentration of political power. For example, accountability might be improved by allowing one set of political actors to decide on the size of a budget (level of taxation) and another to decide on how the budget is to be allocated across programs.[11] In practice, the separation of powers needs to be complemented by a division of powers. The latter establishes the distribution of political power among government agencies above and beyond the allocation of functions among the various branches of government furnished by the separation of powers.[12]

### Electoral Institutions and Political Parties

Accountability is also impaired by clientilist politics. Healthy political systems in Europe, North America, Australia, and New Zealand aggregate these interests not directly in the legislature but first in broad-based parties that are coalitions of interests. The legislative goals of these parties then represent packages of national policies. The parties become effective advocates for the interests of large groups in the public. At the same time, the institutional framework effectively checks extra-legal activity related to interest-group activity.

A cost of a party system is that the parties tend to become advocates for relatively extreme interests. In the United States (Britain), the Democrats (Labour) can be seen as advocating policies too favorable to labor and the Republicans (Conservatives) are too favorable to capital. But checks and balances can be and have been incorporated in the electoral system that allow voters to obtain more moderate compromises by creating divided government or by signaling, in by-elections, disapproval of current government policy. Such opportunities appear to be effectively used in the United States,[13] France,[14] Canada,[15] and Germany.[16] Colombia itself currently has divided government. President Uribe does not have a majority in either the lower or the upper house of the legislature. In fact, only 29 of the 102 senators are bona fide "Uribistas." The problem is that the two parties have failed to articulate the interests of broader publics by aggregating interests to align policy.

### Referenda and Initiatives

When either legislative accountability or legislative responsiveness is weak, it may be desirable to counterbalance representative democracy with elements of direct democracy. The advantages of referenda are that the executive or legislature can leave difficult decisions to the public and that the result, having been decided by the public, will have greater legitimacy than a legislative action. The disadvantage is in the opportunity to frame the proposal in a manipulative manner. Initiatives are direct popular proposals. The advantage is that they enable majorities to go "over the head" of legislatures. A disadvantage is represented by our earlier critique of the "tyranny of the majority." Making it relatively costly—in terms of required signatures, for example—to place an initiative on the ballot can mitigate this disadvantage.

## 3.3   Colombia's Major Problems and Proposals for Institutional Change

In this section we list the basic problems of the Colombian political system and discuss how our proposals aim to address them. These problems are the lack of security, the lack of transparent decision-making, and a nonrepresentative political system.

### 3.3.1   Lack of Security

Because of the threats to physical security, lasting several decades, from the high criminal activity spread throughout the territories and the violence of armed guerilla and paramilitary units, the military has been endowed with a considerable political influence. Traditionally there had been an absence of civilian pressure on the military at least until the mid-1980s. The military's ability to obtain relatively large budgets in recent years may be paradoxically due to narco-trafficking. Trade in narcotics has not only resulted in the government delegating more autonomy and resources to the military but also in direct benefits to the military from links with paramilitary organizations. Thus the military has no strong incentives to deal with the problem of physical security.

### 3.3.2   Lack of Transparency

Tackling the security problem is outside our assigned task. We do note, however, that this problem has been an important factor in the lack of transparency in political decision-making. For example, the Congress has justified nominal voting in response to physical threats to its members. Nominal voting removes the transparency of political decision-making by reducing accountability of the legislature. It enables the politician to engage in ex post facto credit claiming for decisions that turn out to be popular and to avoid unpopular actions. Our proposal is to eliminate nominal voting in areas that do not pose threats to physical security. Also, if there is lack of disclosure about individual voting decisions and only overall outcomes are reported, voting becomes de facto nominal. For example, most sentences of the Constitutional Court do not provide information about the votes of individual magistrates, although they are free to express dissent or approval. The benefit of public over nominal voting is that individuals become accountable to their constituencies through their track records; unverifiable claims by decision makers seeking further terms in office are not feasible.

### 3.3.3 Nonrepresentative Politics

At present, Congress is clientelist in its orientation. As a result it tends toward "pork barrel" politics, so policies are inefficient and rents are distributed to special interests. Executive proposals to improve efficiency and promote growth are either rejected outright or modified to promote inefficient redistribution. Alternatively, the executive is forced to make pork barrel concessions to members of the legislature. The electoral reform proposals[17] to change the electoral system from the largest remainder to a proportional representation and our proposals to reduce the size of the legislature are also designed to attack the problem of clientelism. In addition our proposal for popular initiative is designed to promote citizen action when the legislature is highly unresponsive.

Even when the executive and legislature agree on legislation, the legislation is often struck down by the judicial branch. Unwarranted judicial activism is produced, in part, by the overly egalitarian expectations created by the Constitution and, in part, by the tendency to populism in the judiciary throughout Latin America.[18] Institutionally, activism is promoted by the absence of a hierarchical structure within the judicial system. Activism can be attacked both by establishing a hierarchical structure and by requiring supermajority decisions. Our first proposal confronts this problem. Analogous to jury trials, where unanimity can be required to convict, supermajorities of judges would be needed to overrule legislation. In other words, the executive and legislature are "innocent until proved guilty." Our third proposal, life tenure for judges, would reduce the political incentives to populism. Similarly executive and legislative appointment of judges in the highest courts would eliminate pressures for populism induced by self-recruitment in the judiciary.

Finally, the Colombian elite is perceived as relatively narrowly based. For example, there appears to be a strong element of family heredity in the presidency (e.g., three pairs of close relatives who were presidents: two Pastranas, two Lopez's, two Lleras's). The top levels of the government have a strong technocratic element. At the same time, as stated by the *Economist Intelligence Unit*, "ideological differences between the parties have all but vanished as both now support economic liberalism and some degree of federalism." In this situation there is clearly a need for change such that the Congress can better represent the mass public.

### 3.4    Institutional Instability and Executive–Legislative Relations

In this section we explore the roots of institutional instability and consider how the relationship between the president and Congress has been affected. Colombia appears to have experimented with a very wide range of institutional structures. Since independence in 1810 there have been drastic constitutional changes in 1821, 1848, 1863, 1886, 1910, and 1991. In more modern times, besides the Constitutional Assembly of 1991, there were important modifications in the constitutional reform of 1936 and Article 120 in 1968. Important changes were also made in the degree of decentralization of political power.

There have been periods of two-party consensus, as in the National Front, as well as winner take all arrangements, with widespread redistribution of political control from the losing party to the winning party. Moreover there were periods of military rule and also one-party dominance, namely the Liberal era from 1930 through La Violencia period and ending with the military dictatorship from 1953 to 1957. Clearly, the periods of military rule were not democratic, but during other periods consensus was based on power-sharing among narrow groups. Because of these varying allocations of power, little has been achieved in fostering and strengthening grassroots democracy.

### 3.4.1    The Roots of Instability

We observe that the executive has since 1948 enjoyed great discretionary power and has repeatedly bypassed the formal system of checks and balances, by assuming special powers during states of emergency.[19] One possible explanation is that the political attempts necessary to reform this institution have been stymied by either localism or Liberal party dominance in the Congress, and thus instability in the coalition formation within the legislature that could have corrected this executive exercise of discretion. However, the most common justification given historically for the declaration of states of emergency by the president has been to restore the rule of law and order, rather than to override Congress.

The violence endemic to contemporary Colombia has been perpetuated to a point where it has become a political and economic asset and provides a strong incentive for some institutions to abandon established democratic processes. Hence the institutional instability is a salient feature in this environment that enables both the concentration of political power and political violence to persist.

With the suspension of normal functioning of the judicial and legislative branches of government, as dictated by the frequent declaration of states of emergency, there is ample means for the executive branch and the military to exercise political control. During emergency periods, politics are run in extremely centralized fashion with neither checks nor balances. Over time substantial increases in the defense budget were justified on the ground that the country was nearing civil war. Interestingly, both the threat of rebel takeover and the end of political violence have always been remote possibilities. Until the last decade, before the alliance of the guerrillas with drug cartels raised the stakes, the political violence had persisted in sustainable equilibrium. The end of the guerrilla movement would have eliminated the call for states of emergency and thereby would have deprived the executive of the benefits of concentrated political power, and the military would have lost substantial resources as well.

In the 1990s the armed left-wing political movements remained strong despite both a secular decline in income inequality and increased real growth. The guerrillas became allies of illegal drug cartels.[20] These cartels have co-opted remote areas where they were able to operate with local logistical support and protection. This development has resulted in a guerrilla arsenal that is sufficiently strong to take over half of the municipalities in the country. They are aided by illegal paramilitary groups that also provide services to illegal drug cartels. The stock of arms held by these illegal groups is a big political asset. In particular, it is the power of coercion alone that makes the guerrilla a political player to be reckoned with.

For the last decade the government's inability to contain left-wing insurgent groups has made it turn a tolerant, and some say even sympathetic, blind eye toward illegal paramilitary groups supported by the victims of guerrilla violence. The adoption of either military rule or emergency powers as an easy response to violence appears to have been successfully addressed by the 1991 Constitution. Colombia has had civilian rule, but it has come at a cost that has made it nearly impossible to legislate reforms.

### 3.4.2 The Tension between Congress and the President

Can the balance of power between the executive and the legislature be redressed to prevent the dictatorial situation of executive emergency power? With respect to the operation of legislature, we suggest that secret voting in Congress be eliminated as it hampers monitoring of representatives by voters. This is a way to break up the political gridlock and not involve a messy collision at one extreme or a complete suspension of judicial and legislative powers at the other. We further suggest (also as we noted in section 3.2) that the executive be allowed "fast track" agenda-setting powers to pass urgent legislation quickly, without additions or modifications. Both are ways to limit the extent to which members of Congress force the executive into negotiations that result in the introduction of clientelistic clauses in unrelated laws.

Our recommendations are in line with changes elsewhere in the last half of the twentieth century, particularly in the United States and France. The French system goes much further than the US system in reinforcing executive powers through "fast track" procedures. However, there is substantial oversight and investigative power given the legislature in the United States.

Although both the French and US governments grant large power to their executive branches, in comparison to pure parliamentary systems, they provide for the voter's voice in balancing the office of president by the creation of divided government in the United States or cohabitation in France. Persson and Tabellini (1998) show that this balancing of presidential systems favors smaller governments with fewer political rents and less redistribution. Alesina and Rosenthal (1995, 2000) show that this balancing leads to more moderate policies than in pure presidential systems.

An important feature of the separation of government is that opposing policy viewpoints and public debate are possible. If, on the other hand, the divisions of government simply return to nontransparent negotiated settlements, as in the National Front era, the divided government is not desirable. Political competition, which is the sine qua non for the separation of powers, presents the voter with well-defined political choices. For the system to work, it requires stronger political parties and fewer candidates.

## 3.5   The Three Branches of Government

In this section, we discuss areas where change is desirable. The separation of power stipulates that the different branches of government be controlled by different agents. However, these agents may represent narrow interests if they all belong to the same party. Indeed, this is a likely outcome in democracies with one dominant party.

### 3.5.1   Executive Branch

In Colombia there has been a move from traditional bureaucracies to modern technocracies. But it is not clear whether this development has been accompanied by a sufficiently widespread rise in meritocracy. In particular, the cabinet is being increasingly composed of professionals educated abroad. The presence of "technocrats" in the cabinet may reflect the resulting barriers to entry faced by less well-off segments of the population. Alternative modes of recruitment could give better representation in the cabinet to individuals who have previously had substantial experience in elective office.

All politics begin at the local level. The need is for Colombia to build policy consensus as much from the grassroots up as from the top down. Therefore technocratic trends in the executive should be viewed cautiously.[21] Apart from the cabinet, government officials should be well-established locally. This is the practice, for example, in the United States with regard to regional federal reserve banks and with the appointments of federal district judges, bankruptcy judges, appeals court judges, and district attorneys from local or regional bars.

Recent attempts were made by the executive to introduce reforms to limit the scope for corruption in public office. The proposed measures of state reform aimed to incorporate transparency and accountability in the public management of resources. This legislative initiative was blocked in Congress, with the endorsement of the Constitutional Court. Also called into question was the constitutionality of the special powers granted to the executive to draft laws in this direction. This is another instance of recent rulings by the Constitutional Court that have overturned executive policy. We could interpret this as a backlash against the historically observed unfettered self-attribution of special prerogatives by newly elected presidents. Yet there is a clear present need for fast-track provisions that endow the executive with agenda-setting powers to avoid undue gridlock.

### 3.5.2 Legislature

The Congress is bicameral with senators elected in a nationwide ballot and representatives to the Chamber elected in multi-member districts, both for four-year terms. In addition the largest remainder system is used as the method of proportional representation. The system as a whole permits the election of members who have either narrow geographic bases, in the case of the Chamber, or narrow special interest bases, in the case of both the Senate and the Chamber. The result is the adverse "pork barrel" consequences of local politics without the positive "grassroots" connotations. Changes should be made to improve the representative basis of the legislature.

There are many reforms to consider that would lead to more productive interactions between the executive and the legislature. First, although we favor stronger agenda control powers for the president, it would be desirable to increase the oversight and information gathering capacity of the legislature in a way that permits the legislature to make constructive recommendations on legislation. Second, with regard to the general theme of corruption, legislators should be insulated from illegal influences through campaign finance reform. Third, there should be a reduction in the size of the Senate, which is the largest upper house in the Western Hemisphere (Culver 1999, p. 14). Large legislatures have been seen as simply a source of employment for party fund-raisers (see Culver 1999, p. 6).[22] There should be a limit to the size of the legislature and safeguards against tinkering with the electoral system[23] to correct the extensive corruption, since the 1990s in both the Senate and the Chamber of Representatives. Fourth, provision should be made to limit the expansion of the Chamber of Representatives rather than, as in the current Constitution, allowing for expansion with population increases.

A recent episode with regard to a misuse of funds in Congress, shows the benefit of improving the oversight of the legislature. The problem was contextualized by the attorney general Carlos Ossa Escobar, who said (on March 25, 2000): "[I]n general, there are three types of responsibility: disciplinary, penal and political. Oftentimes it is more important to enforce political rather than penal responsibility. It is the lack of political control that facilitates corruption because timely political control can avoid dozens of penal processes." While this may sound like an argument to bring self-policing to the legislature, it is remarkable that President Andrés Pastrana himself had to call for resignations of senior members of Congress. The evidence was so overwhelming that legislators had to bow to the order of the executive. Even more remarkable was the threat of recall of the whole Congress, but its members fulfilled their duty of oversight and uncovered inappropriate conduct by its top officials, who then resigned.

With the Congress undermined by corruption at the top, the executive then questioned the integrity of the whole Congress, and in particular proposed that the terms of all lawmakers be revoked. The Congress fended this off by proposing that the President's term be revoked on exactly the same grounds, and provided evidence of questionable practices by members of his cabinet.

This scandal indicates the extent to which the problem of impunity may be driven by lack of incentive to bring out information about corruption rather than lack of efficiency in the part of those who should discover such information, especially when the incentives in the branches of government are closely matched.

### 3.5.3   Courts

The introduction of the Constitutional Court in 1991 has triggered a long struggle within the judiciary against both the highest criminal court and administrative court, namely the Supreme Court and the Council of State. Since 1992, the Constitutional Court has repealed many rulings by the other high courts. One of the roles of this Court is to identify collusion between the executive and legislative branches, or constitutional mistakes, in the enactment of laws. Colombia also has activist courts that intervene frequently in the legislative process. These independent courts are part of a worldwide trend of courts assuming the responsibility to intervene and oppose certain government policies.

Unfortunately, activist courts often make decisions that do not reflect widespread consensus and thereby they can engender long-standing conflicts.[24] Activist courts also encourage the use of lawsuits to produce policy changes that politically disadvantaged groups cannot accomplish via the usual legislative process. There is a trade-off between activism to protect minority rights but going against majority opinion. One negative consequence of activism is an increase in uncertainty, which in turn acts as a disincentive to investment.

Sometimes the courts should have purely negative impacts on government policy, thus leading to more status quo bias. Other times they attempt to actively legislate. In Colombia the activism of these courts has pushed the entire judicial system into a precarious state. Resources are being devoted to overturn economic policies on dubious constitutional grounds. A judiciary that should be active in enforcing existing laws on crime and corruption, is wrapped in the process of lawmaking.

In Colombia, the way in which the higher courts are organized, and the magistrates chosen, suggests that the magistrates face much the same incentives as politicians. The magistrates are selected by peers and by the executive for relatively short periods of eight years and without the possibility of reappointment. This limits the scope for the members of the higher court to be chosen in the context of their career development. After having served in the higher courts, where they cannot be reappointed, magistrates cannot hold public office for one year. The short career span of a high court judge thus makes them prone to render short-term populist decisions. The populist character of the high courts is reinforced by the lower court judiciary from which it is recruited.

The way in which the Constitution is written gives the Constitutional Court ample leeway to interpret laws. The diversity in the elected Constitutional Assembly that drafted the 1991 Constitution did not lead to an agreement on rules and procedures, with the view that lawmaking would reflect the preferences of citizens without infringing on the rights of minorities. The Assembly indeed failed to agree on general principles to facilitate political and economic decision-making. Instead of resolving differences, all sorts of interests were protected in hundreds of articles, which made unrealistic promises to all groups in society. This has meant that any group that loses out can challenge a law as unconstitutional. As the actions of individual magistrates are in the public domain, incentives are clearly biased toward populist decisions as a magistrate's term nears its end.

Changes to the general structure of the higher courts will require constitutional amendments. Some modifications that do not call for structural changes concern the number of members of the Constitutional Court as well as the nature of the majority vote required. Law sets the number of magistrates. Lowering this number may induce status quo bias in the sense that, given the odd number of magistrates, a majority for a decision would require a higher proportion of supporters in the Court. Also this would generate a concentration of power within the Court. Another way to limit the influence of the Constitutional Court in getting overly involved in influencing the lawmaking process is to require supermajorities in declaring laws unconstitutional, as we recommend in proposal 2. In this case support for a decision would also require a higher proportion of supporters than before.

The main changes to the judiciary that would enhance the operation of checks and balances involve constitutional amendments. Article 233 of the Constitution stipulates that the members of the Constitutional Court be chosen, for a fixed eight year term without reelection, by the Senate on the basis of lists of three candidates provided respectively by the executive, the Supreme Court and the Council of State. The myopia that this induces distorts the magistrates' decision-making adversely. Since toward the end of their relatively short terms, there will arise clear populist bias, due to the prospect of a political career, we propose that the term for magistrates be lengthened. While longer terms would be desirable, we recommend life appointments, as we indicate in section 3.2. If the term should remain fixed for any reason, one possibility would be to allow magistrates renewable terms.

Another source of inefficiency in the judiciary is the lack of a hierarchical structure among the higher courts as well as an ambiguous division of labor among them. It should be clearly established which is the highest court in the land. The Constitution says that the Council of State may rule on some constitutional matters, but it does not spell out which. Also there is no explicit rule to resolve conflict in the decisions of the various higher courts. In principle, the Council of State should deal with administrative law and the Supreme Court with civil law matters. This is a valid division of tasks. But it would be desirable to have a hierarchy among the courts that induces a clear process, as we recommend in section 3.2. At present any citizen can challenge a law on the basis of constitutionality and the court has to look at every complaint. Hence any law can be challenged immediately and overturned if the majority of magistrates deem it unconstitutional. A process would be desirable in which the Constitutional Court is the last instance of decision-making within the judiciary.

One role of the courts is to check the executive for arbitrary or capricious actions, and the legislature for unconstitutional legislation. Another, though much debated, is to act as a balance and assume a legislative role when legislatures fail to act.[25] Legislatures, of course, can check the courts by passing legislation that overrides court actions. Again, we need to think about appropriate hurdles. If we consider the possibility of strategic behavior by the judiciary, the picture gets substantially more complex. We want to prevent the control from degenerating into tit-for-tat games. This has started to happen not only among branches of government but also within the judiciary. For example, as already pointed out, the Constitutional Court and the other high courts have been in a gridlock over some decisions. Beyond the separation of power among branches clearer decision processes within branches are needed. The manipulation of administrative procedures can have adverse consequences (McCubbins et al. 1987; Spiller 1990). Our proposals aim to limit the adverse consequences of strategic behavior by judges through the elimination of short terms and the introduction of a clear hierarchy among courts.

We also recommend limiting the Constitutional Court's jurisdiction over economic matters that are of national importance and professional training for judges dealing with economic matters. Expertise in lower courts might reduce deleterious interference by the high courts, which may assume a populist political stance having very adverse effects on incentives.[26]

## 3.6   The Concentration of Political Power and the Electoral System

In any liberal democracy elections are one of the most important discipline devices for voters to avoid abuse of power by policy makers. Checks and balances cannot be conceived in isolation of electoral institutions. In this section, we discuss direct democracy and electoral competition as ways of controlling politicians. Political competition provides further incentives for politicians to look out for the welfare of the citizenry and limit personal ambitions. Generally, we should view the separation of powers and electoral competition as complements rather than substitutes. In Colombia, during the 1958 to 1974 period of the National Front, collusion induced de facto concentration of political power, although different agents performed separate governmental functions. Persson and Tabellini (1998) show that majoritarian, rather than proportional, elections increase competition among parties by focusing on key marginal districts. The outcome yields fewer rents to politicians and more redistribution but larger government.

### 3.6.1 Direct Democracy: Referendum, Initiative, and Recall
The referendum typically used to establish popular support for a particular policy or constitutional change. The initiative is a form of popular democracy on demand, where a policy vote is called on the initiative of private citizens. Recall is an initiative used to remove an elected or appointed official, including judges, from office.

There is wide variance in which all three forms are used throughout the world. For example, Italy permits use of the initiative to repeal laws but not to pass new laws. The motivation for referendum is that it allows governments to legitimate contested policies or to "pass the buck" to the voters. The motivation for an initiative is to check the influence of special interest groups on government. Colombia allows for some direct initiative in presenting bills to the Congress, but this is different from allowing the voters to "go over the heads" of the legislature.

In Colombia, where the claim is that the government is responsive to a relatively small elite, some forms of such direct democracy might make particular sense. However, direct democracy dependents on very small details. For example, the number of signatures that are required for an initiative is a crucial variable in determining the performance of this mechanism. It is also important to decide whether separate elections will be held or whether such issues will be voted on during general elections.

While details merit careful attention, Colombia, given the poor results from its current institutions, might do well to make more use of direct democracy institutions that are widely used in other nations. National referenda are used frequently in Europe. Although there is no provision for direct democracy in the US constitution (because it was a deliberately elitist eighteenth-century document), referendum and initiative became popular at the state level in the United States with the Progressive Movement at the end of the nineteenth century. In Switzerland, almost everything gets done by referendum, and major changes require not just a majority of the voters but also a majority of the cantons. This form of a "double majority" might be a way to give some guarantees to the groups, some of them illegal, that have regional support.

### 3.6.2   Political Competition

Political competition itself may be the most important check in a political system. The standard prescription of economists is for a political system that has the rule of law, maintains property rights, allows minimal government intervention in the economy, and has economic policy-making, particularly with regard to central banks, that is "independent" of political influence. We need to specify in this framework the relevance of the principle: one citizen, one vote.

Political competition is essential for several reasons. First, it may solve agency problems and reduce rent seeking and corruption that would be present in an unchecked political, even if technocratic, monopoly. Second, weighting citizens equally rather than by wealth creates advocacy for redistribution. Some redistributive policies may promote growth. Such policies would include investment in education that increases human capital formation among children from poor families, investment in health and nutrition for the same purpose, and bankruptcy policies that allow for fresh starts from economic failures. Third, when there are redistributive excesses, political competition creates advocacy for reforms that increase economic incentives. Colombia may need reform with respect to political competition.

Several facts hint that political competition is lacking. First, since the end of the military dictatorship in 1957, the Liberals have held the presidency for all but fourteen years, and the Liberals now hold twice as many seats as the Conservatives in both houses of Congress. Second, as indicated earlier, more broadly, there should be incentives to create new representative political parties to enter the political competition. Finally, many observers have noted a narrowing of policy differences between the two major parties. There are therefore some open questions: Is there a redistributive conflict? If not, the entire system may lack legitimacy. Is there adequate advocacy? In the Colombian context there is a need to promote political competition, not only through checks and balances but other institutions as well, that serves the objectives of monitoring and advocacy in a way that aggregates conflict into consensus on policies.

## 3.7 Conclusion

Our analysis and recommendations rest on the maintained assumption that Colombia both retains a presidential system, with the separation of executive and legislative powers, and remains in the legal tradition of civil law, with a specific code that does not depend on prior case experience. It is not obvious a priori that such structure should be preserved. For one, Hayek (1973) notes that:

The freedom of the British which in the 18th century the rest of Europe came so much to admire was thus not, as the British themselves were among the first to believe and as Montesquieu later taught the world, originally the product of the separation of powers between legislature and executive, but rather a result of the fact that the law that governed the decisions of the courts was the common law, a law existing independently of anyone's will and at the same time binding upon and developed by the independent courts; a law with which parliament only rarely interfered with and, when it did, mainly only to clear up doubtful points within a given body of law. One might even say that a sort of separation of powers had grown up on England, not because the "legislature" alone made law, but because it did not; because the law was determined by courts independent of the power which organized and directed government, the power namely of what was misleadingly called "the legislature."

While the interpretation of civil law ultimately rests with the legislature, the interpretation of common law rests with the judiciary. Hence checks and balances can be achieved without the complete separation of powers advocated by James Hamilton as long as the judiciary can sustain the division of political power, where judges are endowed with incentives distinct from those faced by politicians. Hayek (1960) thus distinguishes the independence of English judges in the administration of justice from the American system in which judges constrain lawmaking through constitutional review. La Porta et al. (2002) empirically test the consequences of this institutional difference. Reported results indicate that the English independent judicial system predicts relatively better economic freedom, and less well political freedom, while the American institutions of checks and balances strongly predicts political freedom. Furthermore, the greater economic freedom identified in common law countries (e.g., La Porta et al. 1998) is found to be explained greatly by judicial independence.

It would then seem that the key to effective checks and balances is a judiciary with the power to interpret and change the law. In a system of common law, judges exercise this power in different ways to check and balance democratically elected sovereign powers. In the case of Colombia we suggest that the powers of the Constitutional Court need to be limited. The reasons for this are the short-term nature of the incentives faced by magistrates and the civil law tradition that dictates application of the code in the ill-conceived Constitution without much scope for interpretation. Therefore it could be proposed that not only the Constitution is overhauled but also that Colombia move to a system of common law. However, we have steered away from those options. We propose changes to articles in the Constitution but in the present environment of persistent turmoil to draft a new one may prove politically unfeasible. With respect to common law, as Glaeser and Shleifer (2002) point out, its origin indicates that the emergence of trials by independent juries was made possible in England in the thirteenth century due to the relatively peaceful environment. In contrast, civil law developed in less peaceful France where the protection of law enforcers from coercion through violence and bribes dictated the protection and control of judges, who were controlled by the state. The current situation in Colombia would not make common law viable.

Since at present the Colombian system of civil law cannot be replaced by common law, a parliamentary system cannot be advocated in place of a presidential one. Without an independent judiciary, which can affect the evolution of the law, a parliamentary system would induce the tyranny that James Hamilton warns about when he advocates the separation of powers. Under civil law, checks and balances cannot be achieved just by the division of powers of bicameralism, they require the separation of executive and legislative powers of presidentialism. Hence the proposals that we make incorporate as constraints the existing division of the branches of government and the legal structure.

We have documented a need for the political system in Colombia to become both more competitive and more balanced. The competition should take place between broadly based coalitions rather than politicians with narrow clienteles. A more competitive system will probably require a broadening of governmental representativeness. At the same time the judiciary needs to redirect its emphasis from populist rejection of government proposals on misguided norms of equality or equity, with short-run benefits for the disadvantaged but inflicting long-run damage, to enforcement of legislation dealing with crime and corruption.

Colombia clearly has major problems connected to violence, guerilla insurgency, and military-civilian relations. Those problems are outside the purview of this chapter, but they affect the functioning of institutions.

For example, the threat of violence has affected voting in Congress and also the functioning of the judiciary. More generally, the severe deterioration of law and order has fed back into institutional paralysis and has served to reinforce negative trends in relationships among the branches of government.

In the executive–legislative interaction we observe a pattern that swings back and forth between extremely close cooperation and complete gridlock, with attempts by the executive to invoke extraconstitutional powers. With respect to the role of the judiciary in providing checks and balances, the presence of the Constitutional Court since 1991 has reduced the scope for potential covert collusion in lawmaking and for the declaration of states of emergency by the executive. On the other hand, the Court has introduced very costly distortions by intervening in the legislative process. This is due to the incentives and feasibility for the magistrates to make populist decisions.

Nonetheless, even with a background of violence, we believe that Colombia can benefit from institutional change. The most important changes concern the judicial system. A clear hierarchy of decision-making needs to be established, including courts specializing in economic matters. Judges need to be made independent by receiving lifetime tenure. At the same time the judiciary needs to be checked by making appointments independent of the judicial system. Finally, the tendency of the courts to almost automatically override the executive and the legislature needs to be checked by requiring a supermajority of court judges to reject legislation.

Other essential changes concern the legislature. On most matters nominal voting should be eliminated. Clientelism needs to be curbed by reducing the size of the legislature and by changes in the electoral system. Clientelism and pork barrel bargaining can also be limited by giving the executive fast-track powers to make unamendable proposals. Finally, the legislature (and the executive) could be checked by popular initiative.

While well intentioned, the Constitution of 1991 has left Colombian institutions with a diminished capacity to govern in a manner that promotes economic efficiency and growth. In the present crisis the changes we have recommended merit serious consideration.

### Appendix: Policy Recommendations

1. Establish a clear *hierarchy* of decision-making across the three systems of courts (Constitutional Court, Supreme Court, and Council of State) such that decisions may be appealed upwards in the hierarchy and such

that decisions of a higher court in the hierarchy are binding on courts lower in the hierarchy.

2. For the Constitutional Court to overturn a law passed with the agreement of the President and Congress should require a *supermajority* vote of 7 of the 9 members.

3. Modify article 253 of the Constitution to make members of the Constitutional Court, the Supreme Court, and the Council of State *life appointees*.

4. Modify Articles 231 and 239 to have *judges* in the high courts *nominated by the executive and confirmed by the Senate*.

5. Modify Articles 154 and 163 to give the president *fast-track* powers to submit *unamendable* propositions for urgent matters of economic policy to the Congress.

6. Eliminate nominal voting in Congress and make compulsory the publication of voting decisions by lawmakers and court magistrates, except on matters relating to organized crime.

7. Revise Article 171 such that *the size of the Senate is reduced* from 102 to 51 members.

8. Revise Article 176 such that *the size of the Chamber of Representatives does not increase* from its present size of 165.

9. Private citizens collecting signatures of 5 percent of the electorate can *initiate national referenda* on legislation and constitutional changes. (At present, Article 375 allows citizens only to propose changes to Congress.)

## Notes

We are grateful to George Borjas, Alberto Carrasquilla, Ignacio Donoso, Alan Hamlin, Bernardo Kugler, Steve Levitt, Roberto Perotti, Pablo Spiller, Roberto Steiner, Gerard Roland, and especially Alberto Alesina for very valuable comments. We also thank Carlos Amaya, Ethan Cohen-Cole, and Gerardo Ruiz Morales for research assistance and suggestions.

1. Low taxation of interbank transactions allows a smooth flow of money in the economy, since any friction in the systems of payments could bring the economy to a grinding halt by causing a liquidity crisis.

2. This is an extreme instance of a general trend. Mueller (1996, ch. 21) found that constitutions drafted in recent years have not produced the governmental structure and rules of the political system best suited to the welfare of the state over the long term, rather they have been geared to the short-term interests of the politicians who convened the constitutional conventions. This is consistent with the findings of Shuggart (1998), who modeled cases of political reform with the result that in equilibrium the constituencies of incumbents are favored.

3. The most that the Canadian Constitution has is a provision for affirmative action programs under certain circumstances (see Article 15, Constitution Act, 1982, below). On the general powers of the federal parliament, Article 91, Constitution Act of 1867, states: "It shall be lawful for the Queen, by and with the Advice and Consent of the Senate and House of Commons, to make Laws for the Peace, Order, and good Government of Canada, in re-

lation to all Matters not coming within the Classes of Subjects by this Act assigned exclusively to the Legislatures of the Provinces."

In the Constitution Act of 1982, Article 15 states: "(1) Every individual is equal before and under the law and has the right to the equal protection and equal benefit of the law without discrimination and, in particular, without discrimination based on race, national or ethnic origin, colour, religion, sex, age or mental or physical disability. (2) Subsection (1) does not preclude any law, program or activity that has as its object the amelioration of conditions of disadvantaged individuals or groups including those that are disadvantaged because of race, national or ethnic origin, colour, religion, sex, age or mental or physical disability."

4. A big problem is where to draw the line between clientelist systems and interest group politics. On the one hand, interest group politics occurs in a framework of organized competition among many effective interest groups, thereby resulting in politicians' representation of varied interests. And, where extra-legal means are used, existing political institutions check such extra-legal means. On the other hand, clientelist politics is marked by politicians' expression of a limited number of interests based on legal and extra-legal means of influence, and without checks or balances.

5. James Madison asserts in *The Federalist* (1788), 47, that "the accumulation of all powers, legislative, executive, and judiciary, in the same hands, ... may justly be pronounced the very definition of tyranny." To see the limits of this doctrine, consider that the United Kingdom is a successful democracy without separation of powers between the executive and the legislative, and without a formal Constitution for that matter. The Magna Carta is not a declaration that fully specifies the political system. On the other hand, separation of powers makes more sense in the United States largely because of the federal system. The legislature provides regional interests with a vehicle for checking the executive. The same seems to have been attempted in Colombia, but it has not gone far enough.

6. Brennan and Hamlin (2000) take these two types of responses introduced by Hirshman (1970) and analyze the separation of powers.

7. Spiller (1990), Gely and Spiller (1992), Spiller and Spitzer (1995), and Spiller and Tiller (1996) model how judges might engage in strategic behavior if they are politically and economically motivated.

8. Hartlyn (1988) discusses various kinds of political coalitions in Colombia, including collusion.

9. For example, there are large differences between bankruptcy law and procedures in the United Kingdom and in the United States, even though both countries have similar legal traditions and both are electoral democracies. See Franks and Sussman (1998).

10. Here are two examples.

• The constitution of the French Fifth Republic provided for indirect election of the President of the Republic. The intent of the framers, principally Michel Debré, was to provide a conservative bias to the procedure. In fact the members of the Electoral College had a conservative bias but were anti-Gaullist. Provision for direct election was made in 1962 through a referendum that amended the constitution.

• The bicameral US system was designed so that an indirectly elected Senate can balance a popularly elected House of Representatives. The House was to be elected every two years; the framers believed it would be too sensitive to swings in public opinion. The Senate was indirectly elected with staggered six-year terms. Each state had two senators. This feature allowed the small states to "balance" the representation of the large states in the House. Indirect election was entirely abolished in 1912. The framers had failed to anticipate a process of democratization that first involved removal of property restrictions on voting and later removal of racial and gender restrictions.

Constituency service is in fact a major feature of the modern political system (e.g., see Fiorina 1989) by which the House incumbents can maintain a virtual lock on reelection. In contrast, Senate seats are less secure. The obvious explanation is that senators run in statewide constituencies, making television marketing more cost-effective. It is easier for challengers to become visible and get their message across. For these reasons we recommend that the size of the Senate be reduced. Moreover the Senate cannot be apportioned to provide seats for incumbents.

11. See Persson, Roland, and Tabellini (1997a).

12. See Brennan and Hamlin (2000).

13. See Alesina and Rosenthal (1995), Scheve and Tomz (1999), and Mebane (2000).

14. See Alesina and Rosenthal (1995).

15. See Erikson and Filipov (1996).

16. See Lohmann, Brady, and Rivers (1997).

17. This may involve a change to Article 263 of the Constitution by which the largest-remainder electoral system was established for choosing who is voted into office in multiple representative districts.

18. The populist decisions of Latin American courts is noted in a set of IADB country studies on credit markets in Pagano (2001).

19. The French system is perhaps instructive here. Special powers were frequent in the 4th Republic, where the Parliament dominated and the Cabinet had weak or no agenda control powers. In the Fifth Republic, the Council of Ministers/President has taken over much decision-making power from "the governing princes" (to use Debré's term) and government has been both smoother and more legitimate at the price of being less open to initiatives by individual members of the legislature.

20. The clear exceptions are the peace pact signed by the government with M-19 and the temporary peace settlement in 1983 with FARC, which created the political party Union Patriotica. The M-19 pact pardoned the members of their previous illegal activity. However, in the case of FARC, widespread assassinations began of those who sought legitimacy by gaining elected office, and the assassinations sparked the return to insurgency.

21. We live, of course, in a world with rising expectations about democratization. Citizens of nations are becoming skeptical of meritocracies such as the "ENArques" in France.

22. When given the choice, as in Illinois in 1953, voters have chosen to reduce the size of legislatures.

23. A classic example of the "employment" motive is the enlargement of the French lower house and a shift from single-member districts to proportional representation by the French Socialists just prior to their certain loss in the 1986 elections. It appears that the electoral system is best fixed in the Constitution to remove the incentive for an outgoing legislature to adjust the system for a short-sighted political advantage.

24. Two examples from the United States are court-ordered busing to aid school integration and court-ordered equalization of spending on public schools. In some states, voter recall is a check on activist courts.

25. An outrageous example of this is the Constitutional Court's attempt to dictate the monetary policy of Banco de la República.

26. Kalmanovitz (2000) has documented decisions by the Constitutional Court on mortgage interest accrual and the provision of public services that fly in the face of economic logic. Basically in its focus on fairness and citizens' rights, it has attempted to impose actions that are inconsistent with budgetary concerns not only of the central government but also private sector banks.

# References

Alesina, A., and H. Rosenthal. 1995. *Partisan Politics, Divided Government, and the Economy*. New York: Cambridge University Press.

Alesina, A., and H. Rosenthal. 1996. A theory of divided government. *Econometrica* 64: 1311–41.

Alesina, A., and H. Rosenthal. 2000. Polarized platforms and moderate policies with checks and balances. *Journal of Public Economics* 75: 1–20.

Brady, D., and C. Volden. 1998. *Revolving Gridlock: Politics and Policy from Carter to Clinton*. Boulder: Westview Press.

Brennan, G., and A. Hamlin. 1994. A revisionist view of the separation of powers. *Journal of Theoretical Politics* 6: 345–68.

Brennan, G., and A. Hamlin. 2000. *Democratic Devices and Desires*. Cambridge: Cambridge University Press.

Bushnell, D. 1993. *The Making of Modern Colombia*. Berkeley: University of California Press.

Chari, V., L. Jones, and R. Marimon. 1997. The economics of split-ticket voting in representative democracies. *American Economic Review* 87: 957–76.

Culver, W. 1996. Legislatures in Latin America. Working Paper. SUNY-Stony Brook.

Erikson, R., and M. Filipov. 1996. Ideological balancing in elections: The case of Canada. Working Paper. California Institute of Technology.

Fiorina, M. 1989. *Congress: Keystone of the Washington Establishment*. New Haven: Yale University Press.

Franks, J., and O. Sussman. 1998. Financial Innovations and Corporate Insolvency. Working Paper. London Business School.

Gely, R., and P. Spiller. 1992. The political economy of Supreme Court constitutional decisions: The case of Roosevelt's court-packing plan. *International Review of Law and Economics* 12: 45–67.

Glaeser, F., and A. Shleifer. 2002. Legal origins. *Quarterly Journal of Economics* 117: 1193–1230.

Glaeser, E., S. Johnson, and A. Shleifer. 2001. Coase versus the Coasians. *Quarterly Journal of Economics* 116: 853–900.

Hartlyn, J. 1988. *The Politics of Coalition Rule in Colombia*. Cambridge: Cambridge University Press.

Hartlyn, J. 1994. Presidentialism and Colombian politics. In J. Linz and A. Valenzuela, eds., *The Failure of Presidential Democracy*: The Case of Latin America, vol. 2. Baltimore: Johns Hopkins University Press.

Hayek, F. A. von. 1960. *The Constitution of Liberty*. Chicago: University of Chicago Press.

Hayek, F. A. von. 1973. *Law, Legislation, and Liberty*. Chicago: University of Chicago Press.

Ingberman, D., and H. Rosenthal. 1996. Median voter theorems for divisible governments. Fondazione ENI Enrico Mattei Note di Lavoro 42/96.

Kalmanovitz, S. 2000. Los efectos económicos de la Corte Constitucional. Working Paper. Banco de la República, Santafé de Bogotá, Colombia.

Krehbiel, K. 1998. *Pivotal Politics: A Theory of U.S. Lawmaking*. Chicago: University of Chicago Press.

La Porta, R., F. López-de-Silanes, C. Pop-Eleches, and A. Shleifer. 2002. The guarantees of freedom. NBER Working Paper 8759. Cambridge, MA.

Lohmann, S. 1992. Optimal commitment in monetary policy: Credibility versus flexibility. *American Economic Review* 82: 273–86.

Lohmann, S., D. Brady, and R. Douglas Rivers. 1997. Party identification, retrospective voting, and moderating elections in a federal system: West Germany, 1961–1989. *Comparative Political Studies* 30: 420–49.

McCubbins, M., R. Noll, and B. Weingast. 1987. Administrative Procedures as Instruments of Political Control. *Journal of Law, Economics, and Organization* 3: 243–77.

Mainwaring, S., and M. Shugart. 1997. *Presidentialism and Democracy in Latin America.* New York: Cambridge University Press.

Mebane, W. 2000. Coordination, Moderation, and Institutional Balancing in American Presidential and House Elections. *American Political Science Review* 94: 37–57.

Mueller, D. 1996. *Constitutional Democracy.* New York: Oxford University Press.

Pagano, Marco, ed. 2001. *Defusing Default.* Baltimore: Johns Hopkins University Press.

Persson, T., G. Roland, and G. Tabellini. 1997a. Separation of powers and political accountability. *Quarterly Journal of Economics* 112: 1163–1202.

Persson, T., G. Roland, and G. Tabellini. 1997b. Comparative politics and public finance. CEPR Discussion Paper 1737.

Persson, T., and G. Tabellini. 1999. The size and scope of government: Comparative politics with rational politicians. *European Economic Review* 43: 699–735.

Poole, K., and H. Rosenthal. 1996. Are legislators ideologues or the agents of constituents? *European Economic Review* 40: 707–17.

Scheve, K., and M. Tomz. 1999. Electoral surprise and the midterm loss in US congressional elections. *British Journal of Political Science* 29: 507–21.

Shuggart, M. 1998. The inverse relationship between party strength and executive strength: A theory of politicians' constitutional choices. *British Journal of Political Science* 28: 1–29.

Spiller, P. 1990. Politicians, interest groups and regulators: A multiple principals agency theory of regulation (or let them be bribed). *Journal of Law and Economics* 33: 65–101.

Spiller, P., and M. Spitzer. 1995. Where is the sin in sincere: Sophisticated voting in the courts. *Journal of Law, Economics and Organization* 11: 32–63.

Spiller, P., and E. Tiller. 1997. Decision costs and the strategic design of judicial review and administrative processes. *Journal of Legal Studies* 26: 347–70.

# 4 Colombia's Electoral and Party System: Possible Paths for Reform

Gérard Roland and Juan Gonzalo Zapata

## 4.1 Introduction

An increasing body of research has been analyzing the impact of institutions, and in particular, political institutions on economic outcomes and performances. Research on political economics, namely the interface between political processes and economic outcomes has developed very fast in the last few years, and it is not a coincidence that three new and important textbooks (Drazen 2000; Persson and Tabellini 2000; Grossman and Helpman 2001) cover this new field of research.

The innovation of political economics is that it goes beyond debates economists have been having for more than 200 years about the nature of government: in the main, whether government behaves like a "benevolent planner," seeking to maximize welfare, or like a malevolent "Leviathan," pursuing only the interests of politicians in power. Neither view corresponds to the real world. Government does not behave like a benevolent planner because, as we have learned from the public choice school, political agents are utility maximizers, just like economic agents. On the other hand, the view of malevolent government, while not inaccurate in many cases, suffers from major weaknesses. The basic assumption is that there is a malevolent ruler concentrating all government powers in its own hand, ruthlessly using the monopoly of violence to pursue its own interest.

This view is wrong, at least from two perspectives. First of all, under democratic governments, the power of the executive is severely constrained and subject to various checks and balances (separation of powers, party systems, etc.). The combination of these constraints on the use of power, together with the incentives to be reelected, serves the purpose of aligning the interest of incumbent politicians with those of their electoral constituencies. Second, government cannot be accurately described as a "representative agent." Government institutions are composed of multiple agencies, often with conflicting interests. The multiple interests that confront each other in the process of legislative and executive activities of government may, as stated above, serve as systems of checks and balances. They may also lead to forms of free-riding like the common pool problem in budgetary processes and they may lead to different forms of coordination failures.

Methodologically, political economics analyzes government-related economic outcomes (the size and composition of budgets, deficits, the quality of legal systems and their effect on investment, etc.) as equilibria of extensive form games in which various political agents follow their own interests within the constraints imposed on them by constitutions. The nature of the interaction of political agents also depends on the constitution. Specific political institutions thus determine to what extent the interests of politicians are aligned with that of the population, how the diversity of preferences of different groups within the population are represented within government, and how the interaction between various political agents determines the economic outcomes of the political process. Such a methodology automatically leads one to compare the economic outcomes generated by different political systems.

This way of thinking can be very useful to understanding the needs for political reforms in particular countries. Colombia can serve as a useful example. Its flawed electoral system, which we analyze in this chapter, encourages the proliferation of hundreds of different electoral lists and discourages the formation of any serious party system. This leads to a system where legislators can be elected with a very small number of votes. Such a system creates in turn an incentive to cater to very narrow clientelistic interests instead of broad interests of the population. This is one explanation for the difficulty that elected presidents have had in trying to solve the very serious problem of civil war and the spiraling increases in criminal activity over the last few years.

What does political economics, and in particular, the comparative analysis of political institutions, have to say about how to reform inefficient institutions like those of Colombia? Here caution is strongly needed. The knowledge of the superiority of other existing systems should *not* lead to automatic recommendations of importing "best practice institutions." Such recommendations (e.g., "adopt the US or the German political institutions") may prove very disruptive, or at best sterile. The political economy of reforms is an object of study itself that has been very much inspired by the failures and successes of the transition process in former socialist countries (for a survey, see Roland 2000). This field of research shows that there is great value in trying to think about efficiency-enhancing reforms that are based on the existing conditions of a country. The reason is that our knowledge of the complementarities between institutions remains relatively limited and large-scale institutional change fraught with unexpected consequences.

The tabula rasa approach to destroy inefficient institutions and to replace them by importing institutions that were successful elsewhere is thus very risky. By building on existing institutions, one minimizes the disruption, builds on local knowledge and practice, making reforms easier to understand and to support. It is such an approach that we have advocated in the case of Colombia. We recommend minimal changes to the existing electoral system but these small changes are expected to bring deep changes in the behavior of political agents, and therefore in the political process, hopefully leading to more efficient economic outcomes.

In section 4.2, we give background information about Colombia's electoral and party system. In section 4.3, we analyze what we think are the main weakness of Colombia's political institutions. In section 4.4, we discuss various possible paths to reform the electoral and party system, discussing their pros and cons in the particular conditions of Colombia. Our proposal for reform is discussed in section 4.5. Section 4.6 concludes.

## 4.2   Colombia's Electoral and Party System

### 4.2.1   Presidential Elections

The president in Colombia is chosen by popular and direct election. Prior to 1991 the president was elected by plurality rule, and since 1991 he must gain more than 50 percent of the votes. The latter feature has ensured greater popular participation and enhanced the legitimacy of the presidency. The president cannot be reelected after his four-year mandate.

### 4.2.2   Congressional Elections

Colombia has a two chamber system (the Senate and the House of Representatives). Since the 1991 reform, senators are elected in a nationwide senatorial district, and the representatives to the House in territorial districts and special districts for ethnical and political minorities. In the last forty years the same formula has been used in order to establish the composition of the Senate. It is the LR (largest-remainders)-Hare system.

The LR-Hare system works as follows: In each district, seat quotas are calculated by dividing the number of votes by the number of seats. Seats

**Table 4.1**
Illustration of the LR-Hare system

| Lists | Total votes | Seats allocated by quota | Seats allocated by remainders |
|---|---|---|---|
| Liberal Cuenca | 34,840 | | 2 |
| Liberal Triana | 33,996 | | 3 |
| Liberal Mosquera | 22,942 | | 5 |
| Conservative Cabrera | 38,512 | 1 | |
| Conservative Caicedo | 26,745 | | 4 |
| MNC | 20,239 | | |

Source: Cox and Shugart (1995).
Note: District magnitude 5. Total votes: 182,507. Quota: 36,501.

are first allocated to lists according to integer multiples of quotas. The remaining seats are then allocated in order of the largest remainders. Table 4.1 illustrates the functioning of the LR-Hare system.

### 4.2.3    Regional Elections
Since 1986 mayors of municipalities have been directly elected and governors since 1991. Governors and mayors have the right to a single four-year mandate. Re-election is possible but not immediately.

*Party System*
Colombia has mainly had two parties in most of its history, the Liberal and the Conservative party. The latter has always been more representative of rural districts and their big landlords, while the Liberal party's natural constituencies are urban. As urbanization increased, the Liberals increased their share of seats in Congress. The two parties maintained a balance between the 1960s and the 1970s, with a slight Liberal majority. The Liberal party consolidated its lead in the 1980s, achieving an average representation of 55 percent in Congress, while the Conservatives averaged about 25 percent, and the remaining 20 percent went to other political forces (see table 4.2).

The former President Pastrana was Conservative but benefited from the support of several Liberal factions. In the 1991 Constituent Assembly, AD M-19, the political arm of the former guerilla movement M-19 played an important role. They received 26.8 percent of the votes and had 19 seats (against 25 to the Liberals, 9 to the Conservatives, and 17 to other lists). They got 13 seats in the House and 9 in the Senate in the 1991 elections but lost most of the votes and seats in subsequent elections. The

**Table 4.2**
Seats obtained by political party: Lower chamber

|  | 1991 | 1994 | 1998 |
|---|---|---|---|
| Liberal | 87 | 88 | 87 |
| % | 54.04 | 54.66 | 54.04 |
| Conservative | 42 | 49 | 38 |
| % | 26.09 | 30.43 | 23.60 |
| Others | 32 | 24 | 36 |
| % | 19.88 | 14.91 | 22.36 |

Source: F. Gutiérrez, "Rescate por un elefante: Congreso, sistema y reforma política," in A. Bejarano and A. Dávila, "Elecciones y democracia en Colombia 1997–1998." Uniandes, Fundación Social, Veeduría a la elección presidencial, 1997, pp. 232–334.

**Table 4.3**
Number of parties and lists to the senate

|  | Number | | | | Growth (%) | | |
|---|---|---|---|---|---|---|---|
|  | 1990 | 1991 | 1994 | 1998 | 1990–91 | 1991–94 | 1994–98 |
| Registered parties or movements | 8 | 21 | 54 | 80 | 163 | 157 | 48 |
| Registered lists | 213 | 141 | 245 | 319 | −34 | 74 | 27 |

Source: Senate data base: Juan Carlos Rodríguez Raga; calculations by Miguel García.

national parties do not control party labels in elections and there is a proliferation of party lists. Even after the 1991 institution of the single nationwide district for the Senate, this proliferation has not stopped. This list fragmentation and the associated lack of party cohesion and discipline constitute one of the main problems of the current Colombian system.

## The Legislative System

According to Zambrano et al. (2000), legislative initiatives originate mainly in Congress, followed in importance by the executive's initiatives, and practically no law has come about by popular initiative. However, the projects presented by the executive tend to have a greater success probability and are the ones that generate more debate. In 1998, as shown in table 4.3, 45 percent of the Senate's projects were unsuccessful in the first stages of the legislative process. Also it is worth noting that the projects coming out of the Senate and the Lower Chamber have a greater regional focus than a national one, which is in line with the interests of the constituencies that elected them to their posts. Finally, there is no major difference between the work performed by the two chambers.

Congress works in full-sessions (*plenarias*) and commissions (seven) that debate budget issues as well as other issues of national interest. The election of the presidents of these commissions is quite complex because the parties and movements within Congress participate and the executive increasingly meddles in the process. The system is designed in such a way that the commissions elect the presidents among themselves, but in practice the executive negotiates congressional support in order to favor certain political forces that are in the presidential coalition. Of course, this conduct has high budget costs associated with it since support must be bought by promises of legislation favoring local political clienteles of congressmen.

### 4.3    Problems with Colombia's Electoral and Party System

The main problem we identify in Colombia's political system is a lack of effectiveness of Congress in legislating on the provision of necessary national public goods. Law and order and the problem of violence are main concerns of Colombian citizens. Various important reforms are needed in important domains such as land and pension reform, and other reforms that are considered important items of the national political agenda. There is a wide consensus among the public on the necessity of land reform. However, there is strong resistance to any land reform within Congress. Attempts to broaden the coverage of social security and to target it less to privileged groups have failed. For the peace process itself, Congress has shown an incredible amount of inertia despite the urgency of the situation.

This observed inertia of Congress is directly related to the institutional features of the Colombian political system. The president who is elected nationally is the main advocate for the provision of such national public goods, and it is fair to say that all elected presidents in the last decades have tried hard to push reforms that would enhance the provision of national public goods. However, Congress has generally blocked such reforms and presidents have had to use extraordinary or emergency powers to make progress in reforms:

1. President López Michelsen (1974–1978) wanted to reform public administration and attack the important problem of income inequality. Most of his program was defeated in Congress. He attempted to turn around the legislature by getting government reforms passed via a constitutional as-

sembly, but the Supreme Court nullified his effort. He was, however, able to pass by decree a more progressive income tax.

2. President Turbay Ayala (1978–1982) tried again to push reforms, including a more ambitious program of reforming the judiciary, the banking system, and economic management. Congress voted against his reforms, and an attempt to circumvent the Congress was declared unconstitutional.

3. President Betancur (1982–1986) tried an even broader reform program and attempted to reach a peace plan with the guerilla. Congress rejected his reforms, and an attempt to introduce a major tax reform by emergency decree was declared unconstitutional.

4. President Barco Vargas (1986–1990) tried to build in Congress a broad coalition for the failed reforms of his predecessors, but the coalition collapsed and the reform package could not be passed. Eventually he proposed the creation of an unconstitutional constituent assembly. Public opinion created such large pressures for reform that the Supreme Court approved the constitutional assembly, despite its illegality. This led to the 1991 constitutional reform. As we will see below, that reform did not deal satisfactorily with the main problems of the Colombian political system.

5. Even after the 1991 reform, Presidents Gaviria, Samper, and Pastrana have taken the lead in legislative initiatives, and Congress has generally had a passive attitude in generating proposals for issues related to national public good provision or have had a tendency to block legislative proposals coming from the presidency. However, it must be mentioned that during the Gaviria administration a considerable legislative activity took place. In contrast, during the last two administrations, Congress, thus maintaining the status quo and the party and electoral systems, has blocked the two political reform initiatives. The previous proposal by President Pastrana to hold a popular referendum on constitutional reforms is in line with the pattern of behavior of former presidents.

Why do we observe this regular pattern of presidents pushing for reforms leading to more and better provision of public goods and Congress blocking? This is related to the different incentives of the president and legislators. A nationwide electorate elects the president whereas legislators are accountable only to a small and narrow group of local voters on which their reelection depends. The policy interest of congressmen in the last decades has been dominated by clientelistic interests catering to their narrow group of voters.

The prevalence of clientelistic interests of congressmen not only can be explained by the fact that they are elected in local districts. In many electoral systems legislators are elected in local districts and they have a national policy focus. The best example of this is the United Kingdom where all members of Parliament are elected in local districts and nevertheless vote in a disciplined way on national policy issues. Electoral campaigns also turn around national policy issues. The dominance of clientelistic interests in the Colombian Congress relates to other factors. First of all, parties do not have control over their party label. Therefore it is possible to have electoral lists in the same district with the same party label but a different faction. Party leaders thus do not have means to discipline the congressmen of their party by exercising control over the electoral lists. The existence of different lists with the same party label, a phenomenon quite unique to Colombia (and also to neighboring Ecuador), creates *intraparty* competition instead of *interparty* competition. It is this intraparty competition that leads to clientelism since heads of different lists try to differentiate themselves by targeting narrow local interest groups instead of trying to rally voters on party platforms.

The incentives for the proliferation of lists under the same label, known as the *operación avispa* are directly related to the LR-Hare electoral rule. Table 4.1 shows this very well. Fragmentation of lists allows gaining seats on the basis of the largest remainders instead of the quota. In table 4.1, the electoral quota attributes only one seat. The largest remainders attribute the other four. Fragmentation of lists thus allows seats to be gained on the basis of the largest remainders instead of the quota, thereby reducing the "price" of one seat in terms of the number of voters. The more lists there are the "cheaper" "price" of a seat. Congressmen are thus elected by a relatively narrow group of local voters, and they cater to the clientelistic interests of the latter. In the current system they have no incentive to deviate from this clientelistic behavior.

The 1991 constitutional reform tried to tackle the problem of the Colombian Congress by instituting a single national electoral district for the Senate. The purpose was correctly to encourage candidates to broaden their electoral platform and to rally voters nationwide on the basis of national issues. However, that reform has failed. Table 4.3 shows that the 1991 election in the Senate, the first to be held on the basis of the nationwide district, brought a decrease in the number of lists. This decrease was only slight, and the number of lists steadily increased in 1994 and 1998.

The reform has failed because senators learned quickly that the old clientelistic equilibrium could be replicated in the national district. Indeed, no representation thresholds were put in place to discourage small lists and the LR-Hare system remained in place encouraging fragmentation and election by largest remainders. As shown in table 4.4, the number of seats allocated by quota has steadily decreased and in 1998, only 5 out of 100 senators were elected by quota, all the others by remainder. The marginal price of a seat, calculated as the minimum remainder for which a seat was allocated, represents roughly only 40 percent of the number of votes specified by the quota and was lower in 1998 compared to 1991 and 1994.

Instead of trying to gather votes across districts as initially intended by the reform, seats are gained mostly by getting regionally concentrated votes. As shown by the regional concentration index, more than two-thirds of votes are, on average, regionally concentrated. Note also that the turnover of senators has decreased between 1994 and 1998. Whereas in 1994, 59 percent of the seats were renewed, in 1998 only 39 percent were. Moreover the turnover takes mostly place among the independent senators. Besides, many of the new senators have often been elected in the past.

The increased fragmentation of lists has led to an important loss of legitimacy. Table 4.5 shows that participation rates in Senate elections have been low. They declined between 1990 and 1994. They increased in the 1998 election but remained at only 44 percent. This low participation rate in the Senate is a general phenomenon and can be observed across regions.

The latter evolution is worrying. Shugart and Carey's (1992) analysis of presidential systems, mostly situated in Latin America, shows two clusters of presidential regimes depending on measures of party strength and presidential strength. One cluster has strong parties with weaker presidents and the other has strong presidents with weak parties. Countries with the latter regime have had less stable democracies and higher tendencies to evolve toward dictatorships. The recent evolution of other Andean countries like Perú and Venezuela seems to confirm such a view. Colombia has had a very long experience with democracy, compared to many other Latin American countries. It is, however, important to note that the relationships between the executive and the legislature of the last decades, with Congress blocking presidential initiatives and the latter trying systematically to bypass Congress, is not normal for a healthy democracy. A stable democracy requires an improvement of the relationship between the executive and the legislature via an urgent reform of Congress. The status quo cannot be maintained indefinitely, especially

**Table 4.4**
Elections to the Colombian Senate, 1991 to 1998

| Year | Number of lists | Votes for Senate | Positions by quota | Minimum quota | Minimum remainder | Minimum remainder as a % of votes | Regional concentration index |
|------|-----------------|------------------|--------------------|---------------|-------------------|-----------------------------------|------------------------------|
| 1991 | 143 | 5,241,938 | 19 | 52,419 | 21,064 | 0.41% | 62.4% |
| 1994 | 251 | 5,170,300 | 13 | 51,703 | 21,961 | 0.42% | 70.3% |
| 1998 | 319 | 9,461,328 | 5 | 94,613 | 37,294 | 0.39% | 67.4% |

Sources: Botero (1999); Ministry of the Interior.

Table 4.5
Voting participation to the Senate election, 1990 to 1998

|  | 1990 | 1991 | 1994 | 1998 |
| --- | --- | --- | --- | --- |
| Electorate | 13,779,188 | 15,037,526 | 17,028,961 | 20,767,388 |
| Votes | 7,653,710 | 5,512,897 | 5,467,535 | 9,073,254 |
| Participation | 56% | 37% | 32% | 44% |

Source: Senate data base: Juan Carlos Rodríguez Raga.

Table 4.6
Status of the projects presented by the lower chamber in 1998 by origin of the legislative initiative

|  | Lower chamber | Senate | Rest of the government |
| --- | --- | --- | --- |
| Publication approved | 52 | 13 | 1 |
| In first debate | 22 | 17 | 1 |
| In second debate | 19 | 28 | 2 |
| In third debate |  | 2 |  |
| Commission suspended its study | 2 | 0 |  |
| Filed | 27 | 65 |  |
| Returned | 3 | 4 |  |
| Withdrawn | 13 | 4 |  |
| Pending ratification | 4 | 6 | 1 |
| Law | 0 | 0 |  |
| Constitutional revision | 1 | 0 |  |
| Without information | 6 | 21 | 68 |
| Total | 149 | 160 | 73 |

Source: L. Zambrano, F. Botero, and F. Quiroz, *Qué hace funcional al Congreso?*

with the continuation of the guerilla movement and the big problem of violence and the influence of the narco-traffic in Colombian society.

## 4.4  Proposals for Reform

The main objectives for electoral and political reform in Colombia should be the following:

1. Create incentives for legislative cohesion, as a stable majority discipline in Congress can better promote the provision of national public goods. A prerequisite for stable majority discipline is party discipline in Congress, which is currently nonexistent.
2. The history of violence and civil war in Colombia makes it important to encourage popular participation and allow the entry of new parties

reflecting social and political movements that have been excluded from the political process. Despite the integration of M-19 in the country's political life with its participation in the Constituent Assembly of 1991, guerrilla activity has not been reduced but has increased. Without improving political participation, the objective of civil peace may not be reached and the country may be dragged into a full war and even split apart. Reforms aimed at popular participation must recognize the aspirations of regional movements and other new political movements that have been expressed recently. While the two-party system under majoritarian electoral rule has worked quite well for a long time in the United States, United Kingdom and elsewhere, the very low political participation in Colombia is related to the civil war. The entry of new parties should serve to encourage the disengaged to participate. We have in mind a nonfragmented party system where not more than four or five parties would be represented in the legislature and would shape the dynamics of majority coalition and opposition.

3. Political feasibility of the reform must be assessed carefully. It must gain sufficient support from key players: the president, congressmen, local politicians (governors and mayors), and other political players. Political feasibility in the end is a matter of judgment by the actors of the reform process and many solutions are, in principle, be possible. Therefore we think it is our task to provide a menu of possible reform packages, indicating each time the complementary reforms that are needed to achieve the efficiency objectives while at the same time aiming to achieve political feasibility.

We first discuss various alternatives weighing their costs and benefits and point out the scenario's for electoral reform that seem to be the most promising in view of the above objectives. We then outline several complementary reforms that are necessary and desirable.

### 4.4.1   Give Parties Full Control Rights over Party Labels?

This measure seems, at first sight, to be the obvious policy response to the problem of list fragmentation. We think that calling for party control over political labels, whatever the exact legal form, would not be effective in itself and would in all likelihood not be enforced without a change in the electoral law. Party labels represent little more than vehicles for presidential elections. Presidential candidates need the support of various factions within their parties in presidential campaigns. Local faction chiefs do not depend on the party leadership, whereas party leaders need the support of faction chiefs when running as presidential candidates. Congressional elections are basically races between various dispersed lists in order to maximize the number of seats given the electoral system. In the current system the party leadership would lose more than gain from refusing the party label of given lists. We thus have doubts that party leaders would be able to enforce a law giving them monopoly rights over party labels. Even if it would try to enforce such a measure, or if unity of party labels like "liberal" or "conservative" were determined and enforced by law without leaving enforcement to the party leadership, one would surely face the emergence of other parties. Indeed, the cost for lists of coming up with a new label would probably be outweighed by the electoral advantage of fragmentation. All in all, a candidate may prefer to come up with his own list and win a seat with a small number of votes rather than being on a party list without the freedom to cater to his own narrow constituency. The fragmentation of parties would thus still be a problem. Moreover the fragmentation of parties may make it more difficult to build coalitions for the presidential campaign. We thus have doubts that such a measure can be enforced in the current context without important other complementary reforms, involving a change of the electoral system for Congress.

### 4.4.2 Introducing Single-Member Districts with Plurality Rule?

The plurality rule in single-member districts means that one seat is attributed per district and is allocated to the candidate with the most votes. This system exists in 23 countries including the United States, the United Kingdom, Canada, India, New Zealand, and in many former British colonies.

Undoubtedly, such a reform would bring a quick end to fragmentation, since it would give to various lists an incentive to regroup in order to maximize the number of votes. Elections in single-member districts generally lead to the formation of two major lists per district between which the real political competition takes place. This is known as *Duverger's law*, on which there is a vast literature, both theoretical and empirical in political science. Other lists either withdraw or abstain from entering because of the low likelihood of winning the seat. Moreover voters strategically abstain from voting for small lists, even when they are the closest to their preference because they do not want to waste their vote on losing lists.

However, it must be noted that such a reform does not automatically lead either to some version of Duverger's law at the national level (see

Cox 1997), nor does it lead *per se* to strong legislative cohesion in Congress, a necessary condition to provide more national public goods. To see this, one can contrast easily the situation of the United Kingdom and the United States, both of which use plurality rule for the election of legislators. The British Parliament is one of the most disciplined in the world whereas the US Congress is not very cohesive and actually shares some of the features of the Colombian Congress, even though in a much less pronounced form. Congressmen, unlike British members of Parliament, are very focused on the interests of their local constituencies and have less interest and cohesion on nationwide issues. Much of the pork-barrel politics in Congress relates to coalition-building for bills where given congressmen agree to support a given bill in exchange for support on other bills that favor their local constituency. The US Congress is thus more focused than the British Parliament on local issues and less focused on national issues. It is very difficult for the president who typically has a national agenda to build stable coalitions for his legislative initiatives. Even when the majority in Congress belongs to the same party as the president, the latter cannot count on disciplined support from the congressmen of his party. Coalitions are built issue by issue through individual negotiations with pivotal congressmen to catch their vote. Similarly US lobbyists target individual congressmen to influence their vote, a move that makes less sense in the British context where the party leadership determines how to vote. British lobbyists target party leaders and influence activities toward individual congressmen aims at influencing the party leadership.

The reason for the higher discipline in the British Parliament and the bigger focus on national issues compared to local issues relates directly to the difference between a parliamentary and a presidential democracy (Diermeier and Feddersen 1998; Persson, Roland, and Tabellini 2000). Parliamentary democracies tend to favor more legislative cohesion because the executive arises from a majority coalition in Parliament and because the executive can at any moment in time be voted down by a vote of confidence in Parliament. Since the majority coalition forming the cabinet enjoys important powers, including agenda-setting powers, from being in the executive and would be hurt by a government crisis following a vote of confidence, the possibility to associate a vote on a bill with a vote of confidence for the cabinet generates legislative cohesion: representatives from the majority coalition vote in a disciplined way on proposals from the cabinet. In contrast, in presidential democracies, the executive is independently elected by a popular vote and cannot be voted down by Congress. There are thus fewer incentives for cohesion.

This discussion shows that it is important to understand that legislative cohesion depends not only on the electoral rule but also on the institutions of legislative bargaining. While the difference between the United States and the United Kingdom highlights the difference between a parliamentary and a presidential democracy, one must also acknowledge that not all presidential democracies exhibit the same degree of legislative cohesion. Following Shugart and Carey (1992), one could say that presidential systems with less power for the president and more power to the legislature also exhibit stronger voting discipline in Congress.

We do not think it would be politically feasible to transform Colombia into a parliamentary democracy. We do not think it would be necessary either. For example, the French political regime has both an elected president and a strong legislative cohesion because of the institution of the vote of confidence in the government. It is not necessary to go all the way to the French system, but it is important to emphasize that some mechanisms strengthening the powers of the legislature are necessary in order to achieve the objective of stronger party and legislative cohesion.

These remarks on the importance of reform of Congress, in association with electoral reform, are valid for some other electoral reforms we will discuss. We will return later to possible ways of strengthening voting discipline in Congress.

Coming back to the issue of replacing the current electoral system by the single member district system, note that the latter is not well suited for the objective of enhancing political participation since it creates important barriers to entry for new nonestablished parties. We think this objection is important enough in the Colombian context. This requires us to stick to some form of proportional representation.

### 4.4.3  Replace the LR-Hare System with the D'Hondt Electoral Formula?

The D'Hondt rule for seat allocation is the most frequently used in systems with proportional representation. It is used in most European countries and in Argentina, Brazil, Chile, and Uruguay. Its introduction was proposed in the proposal for constitutional change (*proyecto de acto legislativo No 018 de 1998 Senado No 088 de 1998 Cámara*) that was recently rejected in the Senate. It is well known that the D'Hondt formula favors less fragmentation as seats are allocated according to a divisor method

**Table 4.7**
Hypothetical illustration of the D'Hondt rule

|         | Total votes | Divisor (= 2) | Divisor (= 3) | Divisor (= 4) | Divisor (= 5) |
|---------|-------------|---------------|---------------|---------------|---------------|
| Party 1 | 74,000 (1)  | 37,000 (2)    | 24,667 (3)    | 18,500 (4)    | 14,800 (5)    |
| Party 2 | 14,000      | 7,000         | —             | —             | —             |
| Party 3 | 12,000      | —             | —             | —             | —             |

**Table 4.8**
Allocation of seats with the D'Hondt formula

| Lists                | Total votes | (divisor = 2) | (divisor = 3) |
|----------------------|-------------|---------------|---------------|
| Liberal Cuenca       | 34,840 (2)  | 17,420        |               |
| Liberal Triana       | 33,996 (3)  | 16,998        |               |
| Liberal Mosquera     | 22,942 (5)  | 11,471        |               |
| Conservative Cabrera | 38,512 (1)  | 19,256        |               |
| Conservative Caicedo | 26,745 (4)  | 13,373        |               |
| MNC                  | 20,239      | 10,120        |               |
| Liberal              | 91,778 (1)  | 45,889 (3)    | 30,593 (5)    |
| Conservative         | 65,257 (2)  | 32,628 (4)    | 21,752        |
| MNC                  | 20,239      |               |               |

Note: District magnitude 5.

and remainders play no role. It is also known to be the least favorable to smaller parties.

With the D'Hondt rule, votes for each list are divided by 1, 2, 3, and so on. The first seat is allocated to the largest number among the numbers calculated with the first divisor (here the number of votes). The next seat is allocated to the next highest number across all divisors and so forth. Table 4.7 illustrates this with a simple example, assuming that there are 5 seats, 100,000 votes, and three parties that get, respectively, 74, 14, and 12 percent of the votes. One sees that party 1 gains all the seats since the fifth divisor 14,800 is higher than the number of votes for party 2. For party 2 to win at least one seat, it would have to have more than a fifth of the votes of party 1. If parties 2 and 3 formed a joint list, they would get one seat together. The D'Hondt system is proportional but since seats are integer numbers, it tends to favor the bigger lists.

To illustrate how the D'Hondt system works and to compare it with the LR-Hare system, we take the votes from table 4.1 and allocate seats according to the former method. This is shown in table 4.8. As can be seen, nothing is changed in the allocation of seats under separate lists but also nothing changes with regrouping of lists. The liberals still get three seats and the conservatives two. This is, of course, only a hypothetical case. We doubt that the introduction of the D'Hondt rule alone can reduce fragmentation. It favors bigger lists when they exist. However, in the absence of big parties and in the presence of a large number of fragmented lists, the D'Hondt rule tends to maintain the status quo and thus only gives weak incentives to regroup existing lists.

Introducing the D'Hondt formula would have an advantage over single-member districts in that the system would be more proportional and would favor more easily entry by new parties. However, just as would be the case for single-member districts, it would not alone be conducive to more party cohesion in Congress nor lead to more focus on national public good provision.

### 4.4.4   Closed List PR Systems?

Orthogonal to the issue of the electoral formula (LR-Hare or D'Hondt, district magnitude) is the issue of party control on the list order of candidates. This is a fundamental tool used to obtain party discipline since reelection to Congress is dependent on the party leadership. Some form of closed list PR is used in most European parliamentary systems, usually combined with the D'Hondt rule. In Central and Latin America, it has been used in Argentina, Bolivia, Costa Rica, Ecuador, El Salvador, Honduras, Nicaragua, Uruguay, and in pre-Chavez Venezuela. In Bolivia, Costa Rica, and Honduras, closed list systems are associated with LR-Hare. Brazil has the D'Hondt rule but candidates are elected by preference votes and its Congress is quite fragmented. Moreover, according to a law called *candidato nato*, elected candidates have the right to continue to have a place on party lists in the future independently of the will of the party leadership.

Introducing closed list PR would quickly create a party system and party discipline as party candidates could be punished for deviating from party objectives by removing them from eligible places on the party lists. At the same time proportional representation would allow for relatively easy entry for disciplined parties.

However, while closed list PR systems do promote party discipline, which can contribute to cohesion, there are important costs to consider. Most important is that the accountability of individual candidates to voters is lost. Elected representatives are characterized by party loyalty but not necessarily by their charisma or popularity with a constituency.

There is thus a danger of too large a distance between the population and the political elites. This is said to have been the main reason behind the loss of legitimacy of the Venezuelan Congress.

Such a reform may moreover lead to the other excess of promoting only national issues and neglecting local concerns and interests. While local issues are best managed at the local level, it is useful for voters to be in touch with their representatives in Congress and to make them accountable. From the past history of the Colombian system, however, we do not think that this will receive much political attention.

### 4.4.5  Single Transferable Vote?

The system of single transferable vote, in operation in Ireland and Malta, allows voters to rank their preferred candidates. It works this way. The candidates are listed on the ballot. If there are five seats, and thus five candidates, voters are asked to number them in order of preference. The first seat is allocated to the candidate who has the highest number of first-placement votes exceeding the electoral quota. The next seats are allocated in subsequent order in proportion to the preferences expressed, weighted by rank. If no quota is reached, the weakest candidate is eliminated and his votes are shifted up to the winner of the next level of preferences expressed on the ballot, and so on.

The system can get rather complex, but the counting allows voters to give more information on preferences and also to choose candidates across party lines. However, because of the latter feature, the system does not provide for party cohesion. Also, for operational purposes, the districts must have a small enough number of seats. As the number of seats increases, so does the complexity for voters.

### 4.4.6  German-Style PR with Combination of Single-Member Districts and List Voting?

There is yet an interesting change that might be obtained in Colombia by the introduction of an electoral system used in Germany. This system combines single-member district and preference vote with closed list voting. Citizens receive two votes: one for a local candidate based on a preference vote and one for a party list. This allows voters to cast a vote for a local candidate who does not necessarily belong to the party for whom their list vote is cast. Local candidates compete in single-member districts determining half of the seats in the Lower Chamber (*Bundestag*) while the party list vote determines the other half so as to achieve proportionality of seats between parties. There is, however, a threshold for representation: 5 percent of the party lists or three single-member district seats.

Such a system combines several advantages over other systems. For example, the single-member district system rewards politicians who represent well the interests of local constituencies, so it promotes the accountability of politicians. Because there is an incentive to attend to the interests of local constituencies and compete for their votes, the representatives must stay close to their constituencies. As in the STV system, voters can express their preferences in a more detailed way than if they were to cast their vote for a single candidate or list. As in proportional systems, the presence of party-controlled national lists promotes party cohesion and keeps the barriers low to entry by new parties while maintaining barriers high enough to prevent proliferation of small lists. Easy entry would be a big help in the Colombian situation, and it may even allow fast accommodation of critical new issues and cleavages. In some European countries with proportional representation, ecological parties that represent a new cleavage after the "nineteenth-century" cleavage (rural conservative religious–urban progressive tolerant) and the "twentieth-century" (left–right) cleavage are now part of various government coalitions (Germany, France, and Belgium). One could claim that participation in government has given ecologists bargaining power in these countries with majoritarian systems where ecologists can penetrate or lobby the existing two-party system to influence policy.

## 4.5   Our Proposal: A Two-Tier District PR System

Our favorite proposal shares many of the features of the German system but has the advantage that it can be obtained by a small departure form the existing system and thus may be politically more feasible. This apparently minor change would, in our view, lead to important changes in political practices and lead both to halt the fragmentation of lists and to enhance party cohesion.

Our proposal is to keep the current electoral formula (LR-Hare) for the election of the Lower Chamber (House) but to transfer the above-quota residual votes of local district lists to a national district. The residual votes could be pooled together and allocated to the national party with which the list is associated. National parties would then have control over the order of candidates in the upper-tier district. A threshold rule (as a percentage of the residuals) would determine what those national

**Table 4.9**
Two-tier district with transfer of above quota residuals to a national district

| Lists | Total votes | Seats allocated by quota | |
|---|---|---|---|
| Liberal Cuenca | 34,840 | | |
| Liberal Triana | 33,996 | | |
| Liberal Mosquera | 22,942 | | |
| Total liberal | 91,778 | If united list, 2 seats and 18,776 remainders | 91,778 remainders |
| Conservative Cabrera | 38,512 | Number 1 | |
| Conservative Caicedo | 26,745 | | |
| | | If united list, 1 seat and 28,756 remainders | 28,756 remainders |
| MNC | 20,239 | | |

Note: District magnitude 5. Total votes: 182,507. Quota: 36,501.

parties are. Without such a threshold rule, a failure similar to that of the 1991 Senate reform would occur, resulting in as many upper-district lists as in the lower districts. Seats not attributed by local quotas would be allocated proportionally to the national district lists according to the D'Hondt formula, which leaves no remainders. Some other allocation rule for the national district can also be envisaged.

By this reform, local candidates should have an incentive to join their lists and pool their votes within the district in order to maximize the number of district-allocated votes and to give away remainders to the national party lists. This way fragmentation can be reduced at the local level. We think that such a change will be very rapid and that the visible outcome will be in the reduced fragmentation. We think that national parties will then have more power because the largest remainder seats will be allocated to the national level.

Although it works to strengthen Congress, this reform will not require many changes in the current situation. Because there will be more party cohesion, the smaller number of lists will encourage voter participation. Because the PR will be combined with the allocation of seats via the upper-tier district, there will be new party entries with sufficient national support. This effect is illustrated in table 4.9, using the same district votes as in the other examples.

Note that in table 4.9 the number of lists and the votes cast on those lists are unchanged, as only one seat is allocated by quota to the first conservative candidate. All other votes are pooled nationally. The national liberal list receives 91,778 votes from that district, whereas the conservative party receives the above-quota votes of the elected conser-

**Table 4.10**
Summary of election results for the lower chamber 1998

| | |
|---|---|
| Total votes | 8,916,731 |
| Total number of lists | 666 |
| Number of seats | 162 (Quota: 5; residual: 157) |
| Lists without seats | 157 (3,433,000 votes not represented) |

vative candidate plus those of the other candidate, totaling 28,756 remainders. If the liberal and conservative lists are joined to maximize the number of quota seats, then the liberals get two seats and the 18,776 remainders are transferred to the national liberal party.

### 4.5.1 Possible Scenarios

In order to indicate better the impact of the reform, we take all districts in the elections of 1998 and examine various scenarios. Table 4.10 shows the main results of the elections for the Lower Chamber in 1998. There is a proliferation of lists, with 666 lists in total for 162 seats. Only 5 of the 162 seats were assigned by quota, and the remaining 157 by residual. Also note that the number of parties and independent movements increased notably, which finally resulted in the following Lower Chamber composition: 87 liberals, 38 conservatives, and 36 independents.

Simulations were made with the objective of measuring the impact of our proposal. We used two basic scenarios. The first scenario, shown in table 4.11, assumes that parties do not regroup at the local level and that all residual votes (after allocating quota seats) are regrouped by national parties with different thresholds for the residuals. The choice of regrouping lists in national parties was not easy. We put all liberal lists together, all conservative lists, and well-identified parties. Coalitions were regrouped on a working assumption that they would regroup at the national level.

A first thing to notice is that a threshold of only 1.5 percent of the residuals reduces the number of "national" parties to 4 with the liberals getting an absolute majority with 96 seats. Our initial count of parties is 58. Without thresholds for the residual votes, 42 seats go to other parties than the Liberals and the Conservatives and 24 seats are dispersed to very small parties.

We then assume that because of the incentives to regroup locally, local lists of the same label will regroup to gain quota seats. The important expected effect of our proposal is that politicians will have incentives to

**Table 4.11**
Simulation of 1993 election with assumption of no regrouping

| Parties | Departmental quota seats | Total seats | | | |
|---|---|---|---|---|---|
| | | With no threshold | With 1% threshold | With 1.5% (or 2%) threshold | With 5% threshold |
| Liberal | 4 | 76 | 92 | 95 | 102 |
| Conservador | — | 43 | 53 | 55 | 59 |
| ADM19 | — | 7 | 6 | 6 | — |
| Cristianos | — | 3 | 5 | 5 | — |
| Laicos por Colombia | — | 2 | 2 | — | — |
| Coaliciones | — | 2 | — | — | — |
| UP | — | 2 | — | — | — |
| Unitario metapol. | — | 2 | — | — | — |
| All others | — | 24 | 3 | — | — |
| Total | 4 | 161 | 161 | 161 | 161 |

**Table 4.12**
Simulation of 1993 election with assumption of local regrouping

| Parties | Departmental quota seats | Total seats | | | |
|---|---|---|---|---|---|
| | | With no threshold | With 1.5% threshold | With 2% threshold | With 5% threshold |
| Liberal | 61 | 84 | 87 | 89 | 91 |
| Conservador | 21 | 48 | 53 | 55 | 56 |
| ADM19 | — | 7 | 7 | 8 | 8 |
| Cristianos | — | 6 | 6 | 6 | 6 |
| Laicos por Colombia | — | 3 | 3 | 3 | — |
| Coaliciones | — | 2 | 2 | — | — |
| UP | — | 2 | 2 | — | — |
| Unitario metapol. | — | 1 | 1 | — | — |
| All others | — | 8 | — | — | — |
| Total | 82 | 161 | 161 | 161 | 161 |

unite in the local constituencies in order to avoid transferring their votes to the national lists of parties and movements. The results are shown in table 4.12.

Note that now 82 instead of 4 seats are allocated by quota, and thus only half of the seats get allocated residually. Note also that now a 5 percent threshold is needed in order to get only 4 parties represented. Nevertheless, with a 2 percent threshold, we still only get 5. The scenario with local regrouping is probably the most realistic scenario. By these simulations it should be clear that even a small threshold of 2 percent is politically feasible to reduce the fragmentation of parties.

While our suggestion for electoral reform is novel with regard to Colombia's problem of list fragmentation, it is based on the two-tier district systems widely used for vote-pooling in many countries. Austria, Belgium, Denmark, Iceland, and Sweden, and most Central European countries have some form of two-tier district system. After the fall of communism, the Czech Republic, Poland, Slovakia, and Slovenia, in adopting democracy, introduced two-tier districts that differ in many details as the second tier can be national or subnational. Rules for aggregating lists also differ. Aggregation can be, for example, within parties or across parties. For Colombia we suggest that the number of seats allocated at the national level be endogenous. In countries where the number of seats are allocated exogenously, in two-tier district systems, voters have only one vote, but the vote can be used in the primary or in the secondary district, or in both. It is especially interesting that emerging democracies in Eastern Europe have adopted either a version of the German electoral system or a version of a two-tier district system. Either system (the German system or the two-tier system) can achieve a good balance between party cohesion and political participation. We do not think that outcomes will be very different, so we do not recommend one over the other. The two-tier system is just easier to introduce politically.

### 4.5.2 Complementary Reforms

Besides the objective of party cohesion, a reformed electoral system should incorporate some other reforms. The most important secondary reform, as discussed above, is to give more legislative power to Congress relative to the president. There are several ways of doing this. One example is to have the Congress organized in "groups" that can be in terms of parties or sub-parties. These groups would then choose a party "whip." The whip would have certain powers, such as appoint commissions, and commission chairs. Although a party whip would be chosen by the members of the party, in groups with coalitions of small lists, the choice would be negotiable. Party whips could be given the right to exclude group members from commissions, for example, to enforce discipline. Responsibility for negotiations with the president to create coalitions could be given to the whip, and so forth. Congress would acquire more power because the coalitions would decide on the commission appointments and on a legislative program. Commissions should be given much more resources (staff, library, etc.) to prepare legislative proposals. Most discipline could be obtained if Congress were given the right to a vote of confidence on the composition of the commissions overall, as agenda-setting rights are allotted to the group leaders, in possible collaboration with the president.

Such a reform would go in the direction of creating legislative cohesion while maintaining the presidential system and the powers of the president.

We also propose other reforms:

• The presidential election should take place some months before the election of Congress and not after or jointly as is currently the case. The current system causes the president to be dependent on the support of local barons. The way congressional elections are presently held after presidential elections, the electoral campaign can turn around support for, or opposition to, the newly elected president and push national issues to the forefront. After elections, parties have to deliver on the national issues they raised in the campaigns. Thus there is the incentive to be disciplined along party lines. Voters can use the congressional elections to strengthen the mandate of the president or to override it by introducing a divided form of government.

• The law on party formation should be revised to facilitate entry of new parties. This would avoid the existing practice of building factional lists within existing party labels and reduce the confusion of trade-offs in the process of choosing between parties, which has dampened political participation. Although proposals for election thresholds have met with strong resistance, thresholds are helpful in reducing electable parties to a manageable number. The additional parties must be able to compete and at an early stage exceed the thresholds for eligibility. A 5 percent (or three district seats) rule is, for example, a lower than effective threshold for single-member district elections.

• There must be a reform of campaign financing. A certain amount of public financing of parties should be allocated to newly entering parties and allocated to existing parties only on the basis of past performance. Party financing is an issue in all democracies, and there are no perfect solutions. A case for public financing can be made on several grounds. First, a legal cap on campaign financing would avoid cases where the financing is channeled only to making more flashy use of media than that of competitors. All around this escalates to campaign expenditure. Second, public financing reduces a candidate's dependence on lobbies and nontransparent gifts from interest groups. European countries are moving in the direction of public financing despite the scandals still appearing from time to time due to public financing (e.g., in Germany), especially where there is no legal cap on campaign contributions.

• Reforms within Congress must make its members more accountable and withdraw some of the rent: First, and most important, is the abolition of the secret vote and registration of individual votes of congressmen. No democracy can function properly without this transparency. Secret votes were disastrous in the postwar Italian system. Registration of votes enhances accountability to party members and to voters. Second, unpopular privileges of congressmen, such huge pensions, should be reduced and rules revised on the use of substitutes by elected representatives. Third, the reform on the election of Congress should be accompanied by reforms on the election of mayors and governors who have a stronger electoral base than congressional representatives and much larger voter turnout rates.

Fourth, the restriction of one-term mandate for mayors and governors should be lifted and extend to two terms or more. Longer mandates create accountability via the motive of reelection and thus provide an incentive to invest in long-term projects.

Fifth, to control clientelism, there should be introduced automatic registration of voters. Larger voter participation increases the costs of clientelism as it requires extending patronage to a broader group of voters.

Last, within the bicameral legislature it would be useful to have different sectors of the population represented in the lower and upper Houses. In many countries, the upper House is more representative of regional interests (US Senate, German Bundesrat). We think that the lower House could be reformed to have more seats for minorities to complement our suggested electoral reform for the Congress and to enfranchise broad regional interests. Presently there is the impression that the two Houses of legislature are duplicates and that bicameralism is not necessary. We are against all proposals for a unicameral system. The main justification for bicameralism is the separation of power that ensures checks and balances in legislation so that the interests of greater number of the population can be taken into account.

## 4.6 Conclusion

Many possible packages can be put together that foster more legislative cohesion, more public good provision, and more political participation. However, one must keep in mind the complementarity of the proposed packages to the political circumstances. Change of some detail of a proposed reform can kill its effectiveness. The 1991 reform of the Senate could have had positive results if it were tied to an electoral threshold. We recognize that this holds true for the proposals we make in this chapter. Electoral reform is necessary but not strong enough alone if the objective is legislative cohesion in Congress. The reform of Congress is equally crucial.

## Notes

We thank Miguel Garcia, Alejandra Corchuelo, and Xavier May for excellent research assistance and are grateful to Alberto Alesina, Ana Maria Bejarano, Moritz Kraemer, Maurice Kugler, Javier Leon, Eduardo Lora and Howard Rosenthal, and participants at the Cartagena workshop for their comments on the first draft.

## References

Alesina, A., and H. Rosenthal. 1995. *Partisan Politics, Divided Government, and the Economy*. Cambridge: Cambridge University Press.

Archer, R. P. 1995. Party strength and weakness in Colombia's besieged democracy: In S. Mainwaring and T. Scully, eds., *Building Democratic Institutions: Party System in Latin America*. Stanford: Stanford University Press.

Archer, R., and M. S. Shugart. 1997. The unrealized potential of presidential dominance in Colombia. In S. Mainwaring and M. S. Shugart, eds., *Presidentialism and Democracy in Latin América*. Cambridge: Cambridge University Press.

Botero, F. 1998. El Senado que nunca fue. La circunscripción nacional después de tres elecciones. In *Elecciones y democracia en Colombia 1997–1998*. Bogotá: Universidad de los Andes.

Botero, F. 1999. Circunscripción nacional y prácticas electorales. Los esperados, inesperados e inciertos efectos de un intento de cambio en el sistema electoral colombiano. Mimeo. Universidad de los Andes–Colciencias.

Botero, F., et. al., En busca de lo nacional y lo regional en el congreso. Una aproximación inicial. Mimeo, primera versión. Bogotá.

Bejarano, A. M. 1998. La Constitución de 1991: Un proyecto de construcción institucional. Mimeo. Universidad de los Andes, Bogotá.

Bendel, P. 1995. Democracia y partidos políticos en América Central. In D. Nohlen, ed., *Democracia y neocrítica en América Latina*, Madrid: Iberoamericana.

Bushnell, D. 1993. *The Making of Modern Colombia: A Nation in Spite of Itself*. Los Angeles: University of California Press.

Cepeda Espinosa, M. 1996. Derecho, política y control institucional. Facultad de Derecho. Universidad de Los Andes, Bogotá, D.E.

Cox, G. 1997. *Making Votes Count. Strategic Coordination in the World's Electoral Systems*. Cambridge: Cambridge University Press.

Cox, G., and M. S. Shugart. 1999. In the absence of vote pooling: Nomination and vote allocation errors in Colombia. *Electoral Studies* (14) 4: 441–60.

Dávila Ladrón de Guevara, A. 1999. Anotaciones sobre la crisis, fragmentación y pulverización de los partidos en Colombia. Mimeo. Universidad de los Andes.

Diermeier, D., and T. Feddersen. 1998. Cohesion in legislatures and the vote of confidence procedure. *American Political Science Review* (92) 3: 611–21.

Drazen, A. 2000. *Macroeconomics and Politics*. Princeton: Princeton University Press.

García S., M. 1999. La elección popular de alcaldes y las terceras fuerzas. Un análisis del sistema de partidos colombiano en el ámbito municipal, 1988–1997. Mimeo. IEPRI, Bogotá.

Gargarella, R. 1997. Recientes reformas consitucionales en América Latina: Un primera aproximación. *Desarrollo Económico* 36 (144).

Grossman, G., and Helpman. 2001. *Special Interest Politics.* Cambridge: MIT Press.

Gutiérrez, F. 1997. Rescate por un elefante. Congreso, sistema y reforma política. In A. Bejarano and A. Dávila, eds., *Elecciones y democracia en Colombia 1997–1998.* Uniandes, Fundación Social, Veeduría a la elección presidencial, pp. 232–334.

Gutierez, F. 1999. La reforma política: una evaluación crítica. In *Análisis Político, 1999.*

Hartlyin, J. 1999. El presidencialismo y la politica colombiana. In *La crisis del presidencialismo—el caso de Latinoamérica.* Madrid: Alianza Universidad.

Kline, H. F., and H. J. Wiarda. 1996. *Latin American Politics and Development,* 4th ed. Boulder, CO: Westview Press Harper Collins Publishers.

Londoño, J. F. 1999. Sistema de partidos y régimen electoral. La gobernabilidad contra la democracia en la propuesta de reforma política. *Análisis Político, 1999.*

Martz, J. 1997. *The Politics of Clientelism: Democracy and the State in Colombia.* Somerset, NJ: Transaction Publishers.

Ministerio del Interior. 1997. Comisión para el estudio de la reforma de los partidos políticos—Memoria de Trabajo. Secretaria Técnica. Bogotá.

Ministerio del Interior. 1999. Reforma Política: Un Propósito de Nacion—Memorias. Serie documentos 17. Bogotá. November.

Navas Carbo, X. 1995. El financiamiento de los partidos políticos en América Latina. In D. Nohlen, ed., *Democracia y neocrítica en América Latina.* Madrid: Iberoamericana.

Persson, T., G. Roland, and G. Tabellini. 2000. Comparative politics and public finance. *Journal of Political Economy* 108 (6): 1121–61.

Persson, T., and G. Tabellini. 2000. *Political Economics.* Cambridge: MIT Press.

Rodríguez, R. J. C. 1999. Posibilidades y riesgos de la actual reforma electoral en Colombia. Un anaálisis del sistema electoral colombiano. *Análisis Político, 1999.*

Roland, G. 2000. *Transition and Economics: Politics, Markets and Firms.* Cambridge: MIT Press.

Ruiz, G., and E. Ungar. 1998. Hacia la recuperación del congreso. In *Elecciones y democracia en Colombia 1997–1998.* Universidad de los Andes, Bogotá.

Sartori, G. 1999. Ni presidencialismo ni parlamentarismo. In *Las crisis del presidencialismo.* Madrid: Alianza Universidad.

Shugart, M. S., and J. M. Carey. 1992. *Presidents and Assemblies: Constitutional Design and Electoral Dynamics.* Cambridge: Cambridge University Press.

Uribe, R. 1990. La quiebra de los partidos. *Escuela de estudios políticos.* Bogotá: Rafael Uribe Universidad.

Valenzuela, A., et al., 1999. Sobre la Reforma política en Colombia. In Ministerio del Interior, *Reforma Política un propósito de Nación—Memorias.* Serie documentos 17, November.

Woldenberg, J. 1996. Para que sirven las instituciones? Rev. *Reformas electorales,* México. November.

Zambrano, L., F. Botero, and F. Quiroz. 2000. *Qué hace funcional al Congreso?* Mimeo.

# 5 Understanding Crime in Colombia and What Can Be Done about It

Steven Levitt and Mauricio Rubio

## 5.1 Introduction

Homicide rates in Colombia are among the highest in the world. It peaked in 1991 when almost one in a thousand Colombians was murdered that year. The homicide rate in Colombia has remained three times higher than in Brazil or Mexico, and ten times higher than in Argentina, Uruguay, or the United States. High homicide rates, however, do not tell the full story of Colombian crime. There is enormous variation across the country in crime rates. In the area of property crime, Colombia does not look exceptional compared to other Latin American countries. In recent years homicide rates have begun to fall in the most violent areas of Colombia.

In this chapter we attempt to better understand Colombia's crime situation. It is our belief that high rates of homicide in Colombia can largely be explained by the breakdown of the criminal justice system and the prevalence of the illegal drug trade. Guerrilla activity appears to be systematically related to the kidnapping epidemic. Despite the enormous attention to poverty and income inequality received as explanations for Colombia's crime problem, we find little empirical evidence to support that point of view. Nor does there seem to be any evidence that Colombians (for whatever reason) have a particular propensity toward violence that is greater than other countries residents. We feel that the best way to lower crime in Colombia is to fix the beleaguered and overburdened criminal justice system.

## 5.2 The Facts about Colombian Crime

### 5.2.1 Homicide Rates
After the period of political violence known as La Violencia, homicide rates in Colombia remained almost stable for nearly two decades at

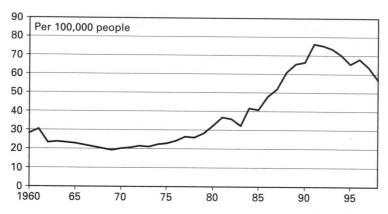

**Figure 5.1**
Homicide rate 1990 to 1998

nearly 20 homicides per 100,000 residents annually.[1] In the late 1970s a sharp increase began, reaching a peak at about 80 per 100,000 in 1991. Afterward the aggregate number of homicides began to fall significantly but not as rapidly as it had previously grew (figure 5.1).

Even by Latin American standards, where rampant violence during the 1990s has been a major concern, Colombian violence looks unusually high. Only El Salvador, another country with a long civil conflict, surpassed Colombia in terms of homicide rates in the last decade (figure 5.2).

### 5.2.2 Crime Rates

Official data on other crimes are much less reliable than for homicides, for two reasons. First, only a fraction of the committed crimes are reported by the victims to the police. Second, it seems that not all reported crimes are registered in the police statistics. Victimization surveys provide an alternative source of data to official records, but only two such surveys are available for Colombia.[2] The official data and the victimization surveys tell a very different story. Police statistics show a continuous decline in crime rates from the beginning of the 1980s, whereas victimization surveys show a small increase (less than 7 percent) in the overall crime rate between 1985 and 1995 and a sharp increase in violent crime (violent property crime grew 106 percent in that decade). There is even an inconsistency between the official figures (crime reports) and what the victims said they reported to the police in the victimization surveys (figure 5.3).

This notable and increasing discrepancy between official records and victimization figures (42 percent in 1985 and 111 percent in 1995) can be explained by a perverse tendency of the Colombian criminal justice system to focus only on crime where offenders have been identified by the victims at the expense of unsolved crime. Cases with an unidentified criminal have been progressively left out, even from the statistical records. It is not a matter of coincidence that there exists a strong association between crime rates as reported by the police and the number of apprehended offenders (figure 5.4).

Although under reporting of crime and low quality police statistics make international comparisons difficult, Colombia's crime and reporting rates can be brought into a Latin American context with two alternative sources of data on victimization. The first one is the Latinobarometer, a public opinion survey with a criminal incidence module,[3] and the second one is the International Crime Victim Survey (ICVS), now available for six Latin American countries.[4]

Overall, what these surveys show is that Colombia is not exceptional in terms of general criminal incidence. According to Latinobarometer, Colombia shows a very high level of average victimization: more than 35 percent of households were victimized during the year before the survey. But this is not unusual for Latin American countries. Higher rates were observed in 11 of the 17 countries included in the sample. The highest rate, in Guatemala, is almost 15 percentage points higher than the rate for Colombia (figure 5.5). Colombia also fits the continental pattern of positive connection between socioeconomic status and victimization rates.[5]

ICVS results corroborate the impression that Colombia is not anomalous among Latin America countries in terms of overall criminal incidence. At the moment ICVS results are available only for a small sample of Latin American countries: Colombia, Paraguay, Bolivia, Argentina, Brazil, and Costa Rica. None of the countries with the highest overall victimization rates according to Latinobarometer, however, are included in the ICVS sample. Even so, Colombia does not stand as the leader in any of the criminal incidents individually considered in the ICVS results (figure 5.6). Colombia's highest ranking, after Brazil and not far above Bolivia and Argentina, is for assault with force.

Nor does Colombia appear to be an outlier in the ICVS with respect to reporting rates to the police (figure 5.7), avoiding certain places after dark, general fear of crime, subjective likelihood of burglary, or gun ownership for crime prevention purposes. The latter feature is higher in Costa Rica, Argentina, and Paraguay.[6]

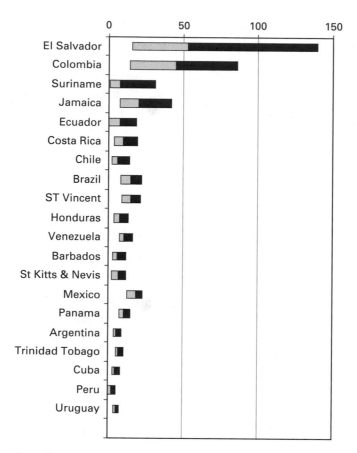

**Figure 5.2**
Homicide rates in Latin America

### 5.2.3  Drop in Homicide Rate

Since 1991 the homicide rate in Colombia has fallen more than 20 percent. As figure 5.8 shows, the national decline is attributable to a fall in homicides in Bogotá, Medellín, and Cali. At the peak in violence in 1991, homicides in these three main cities accounted for 38 percent of the national total. That year, the Medellín figure began to fall. Homicides in Bogotá reached their maximum level in 1993, while the break in Cali came one year later. The average homicide rate in these three cities fell from 120 per 100,000 in 1991 to less than 80 in 1997; their share of the total number of murders decreased to about 30 percent. The homicide rate for the rest of the country remained practically constant at 60 per 100,000 between 1991 and 1997 (figure 5.8).

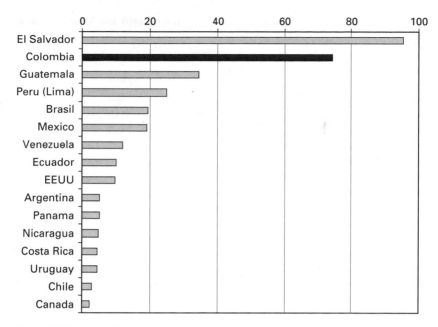

**Figure 5.2** (continued)

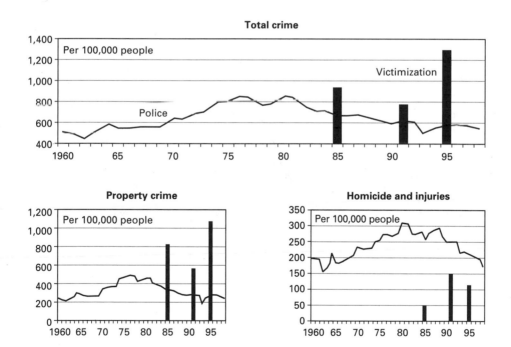

**Figure 5.3**
Crime rates. Reports of the national police and victimization surveys (From Policía Nacional, Revista Criminalidad; DANE, ENH)

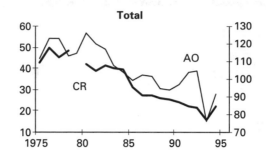

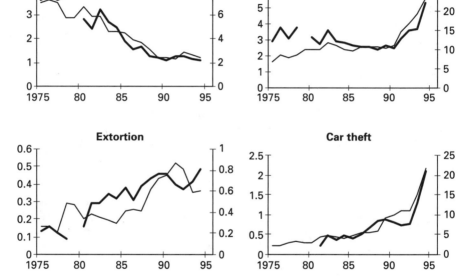

**Figure 5.4**
Police crime statistics. Crime reports (CR) and apprehended offenders (AO) 1975 to 1994
(From Policía Nacional)

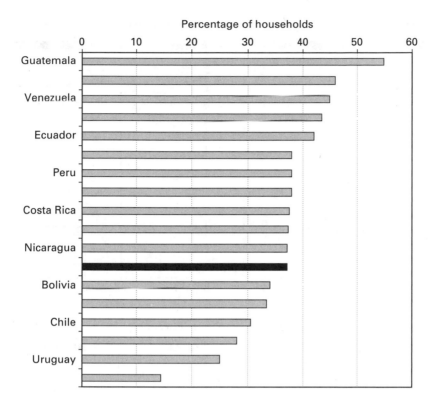

**Figure 5.5**
Victimization rates in Latin America (From Gaviria y Pagés 1999)

A close look at the rate of change of homicides in the other munici-palities shows that the aggregate stability is not the result of any homo-geneous evolution but, rather, that the falling rates in some places were compensated by rising rates in other municipalities. Between 1990 and 1997, one-fourth of municipalities showed a decrease in homicides rates between 0 percent and 10 percent, while another third suffered a similar increase. In 12 percent of the municipalities, homicide rates fell between 10 percent and 20 percent, but in a similar proportion of localities homi-cides rose by the same amount (figure 5.9).

Furthermore the changes in homicide rates appear to be negatively associated with the levels of violence in 1990. In the 200 most violent[7] municipalities, homicides reached a peak of 220 per 100,000 in 1991 and then dropped to less than 140 in 1997. On the other hand, in the 200 most peaceful localities, homicide rates remained almost stable between 1990

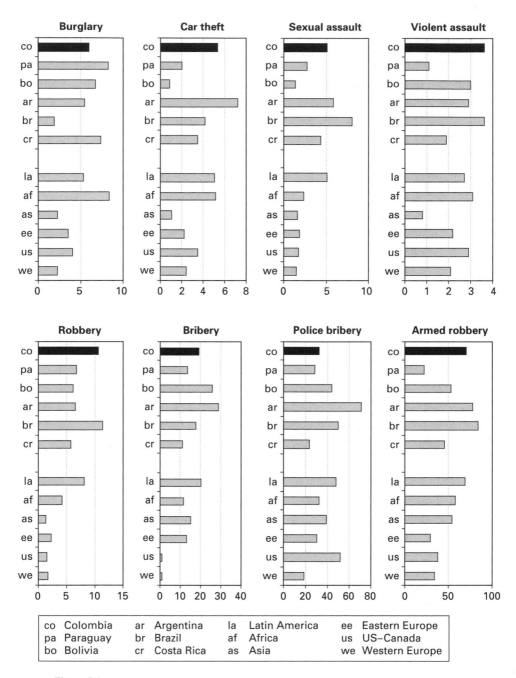

**Figure 5.6**
Victimization rates in Latin America and the world (International crime victim surveys from Alvazzi 1998)

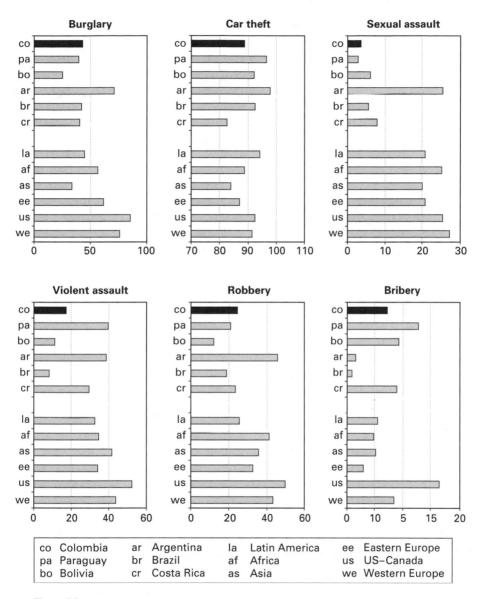

**Figure 5.7**
Reporting rates in Latin America and the world (International crime victim surveys from Alvazzi 1998)

**Medellín, Bogotá, and Cali**

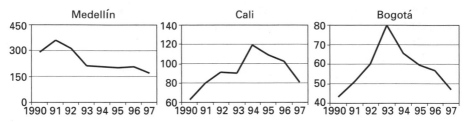

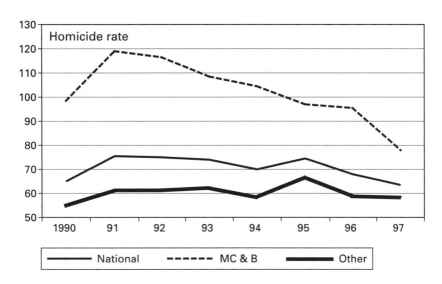

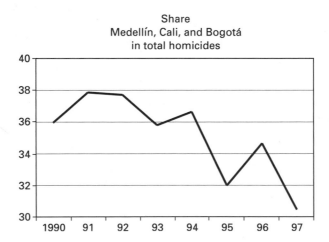

**Figure 5.8**
Falling homicide rates in the 1990s

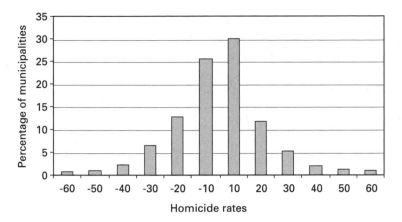

**Figure 5.9**
The 1990 to 1997 change in homicide rates was not even. Distribution of average growth, homicide rate in 1990 to 1997

and 1994 but suddenly increased from 7 per 100,000 to almost 14 after 1995 (figure 5.10).

Another way of looking at this kind of convergence in homicide rates is to compare the distribution of homicides across municipalities at different points in time. In 1990, 35 percent of the municipalities had a rate less than 10 per 100,000, while in 1997, only 20 percent showed such a low level. On the other hand, in 1990, 30 percent of towns had a homicide rate between 10 and 50. By 1997, 42 percent of localities were in such a range (figure 5.11).

A third way of demonstrating the progressive spread of violence during the 1990s is by computing a Lorenz curve. This curve shows what proportion of the population is responsible for what proportion of homicides and how this distribution changed between 1990 and 1997. In 1990, the 20 percent of the population in the least violent municipalities committed less than 5 percent of the homicides. By 1997 this figure reached almost 10 percent. It is clear that between 1990 and 1997 the distribution of violence across the population became much more even (figure 5.12).

## 5.3 Costs of Crime in Colombia

In this section we offer an overview of the literature on costs of crime in Colombia. We concentrate on work attempting to analyze the impact of crime on the allocation of resources and efficiency.

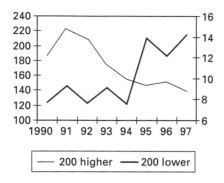

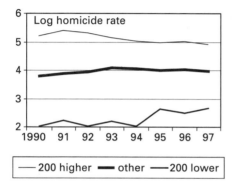

**Figure 5.10**
Homicide rates. Drop in 200 most violent municipalities and rise in 200 least violent municipalities

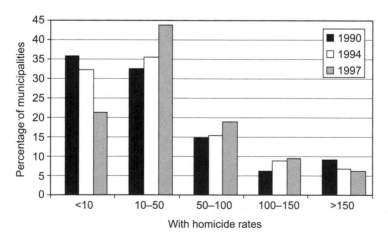

**Figure 5.11**
Distribution of homicide rates in municipalities, 1990 to 1997

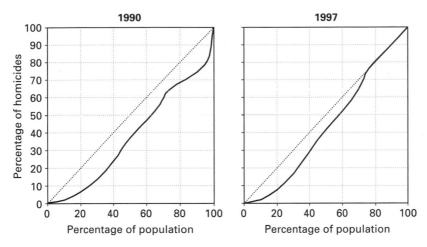

**Figure 5.12**
Lorenz curve of population and homicides, 1990 to 1997

Three categories of "efficiency studies" can be mentioned. First, there are some papers about public and private expenditures to prevent and control crime. Second are studies that deal with the impact of violence on physical capital (environment, infrastructure) and on human capital. Third, a Colombian specialty, are papers that analyze the impact of crime on aggregate investment and productivity growth.

### 5.3.1 Expenditures to Prevent and Control Crime
The interest of public health professionals in violence has lead to emphasis in the calculation of the financial burden of violence on medical assistance to the victims. For Latin America, health is probably the sector where cost accounting methodology[8] and detailed case studies[9] are most developed.

In sharp contrast with this interest in public health, detailed cost studies of prisons, the judiciary, the police, and the military are hard to find. Papers dealing with the aggregate evolution of military or judiciary expenditures are recent. The methodology is still quite simple: analysis of budget trends and correlation with aggregate variables. This type of study faces serious difficulties in getting even basic data. Some analysts argue that military expenditure records are completely unreliable.[10] Leal (1995) offers a descriptive analysis of the evolution of military expenses since the 1950s, and finds these costs increasingly embedded in overall public expenditures. Granada and Prada (1997) model the "demand" for military expenditures as a function of GDP, total public expenditure, homicide rate, and number of guerrilla members. They conclude that (1) there is a long-term and stable correlation between military expenditure and guerrilla growth, (2) there is a strong inertia, and (3) homicide rates do not help to explain the dependent variable. Recent works show[11] that public expenditures in security and justice are now around 5 percent of GDP, with a rise of nearly 2 percent during the 1990s.

As for private expenditures in security and protection, information is scarce. There is some data about the labor force involved in these activities but only for the legal and regulated firms. These data show that the increase in private security guards has been faster than for police officers: in 1980 there were 2.5 police officers for each private guard. In 1995 this ratio had been reduced to 1.[12]

Information about the evolution of other armed private guards, informal or illegal, is nonexistent. For paramilitary groups there is no agreement about the number of combatants. One can assume that their evolution has been similar to that of the guerrilla. Journalistic estimates of the paramilitary are around 10.000 men with a per-capita monthly cost of around US$500.

Ethnographic work[13] suggests that in popular neighborhoods gangs offer private protection and private justice services.[14] Some surveys corroborate these findings: in Bogotá, Cali, and Medellín, 22 percent of the households reported an influence in their neighborhood of armed groups different from guerrillas.[15]

The social impact of private protection gangs goes beyond efficiency considerations. For Medellín, Jaramillo (1993) and Corporación Región (1997) show that when private protection schemes become generalized, and there are links with organized crime, there is a progressive concentration of criminal activities, a reduction in petty crime, and high homicide rates. The 1995 victimization survey corroborates this for Medellín: low overall victimization and high homicide rates.[16]

Information about household expenditures on protection and security is scarce too. Rubio (1997), based on a survey for Bogotá, Cali, and Medellín, estimates this figure around 1.4 percent of GDP.

### 5.3.2  Destruction and Damage of Capital

Londoño (1998) estimates that human capital lost cause by violent death amount to around 4 percent of GDP each year.[17] Trujillo and Badel (1998), with a quite rigorous methodology, calculate this cost at around 1 percent of GDP. In these two papers, loss of human life is converted to money terms. Other studies[18] estimate the figures in "AVISA."[19] A detailed inventory of the demographic impact of violence is given in INS-CELADE (1991) and Romero (1997).

Much attention has been given to the problem of the "desplazados" or internally displaced people.[20] The Defensoría del Pueblo estimates around 200,000 people, the yearly flow of "desplazados," 50 percent of whom are infants.

A second dimension of the destruction of capital deals with the damage to infrastructure—petroleum, electricity, roads, and airports—and to the environment. Cost estimation has normally been limited to repairs. Even with such under estimation, costs have been calculated around 1 percent of GDP.[21]

### 5.3.3 Impact on Investment

Some effort has been done to show how crime has an impact on human capital investment. First, there is the effect of organized crime recruiting young people[22] and the impact that the armed conflict is having on children.[23] On the other hand, a national survey estimates that 14 percent of night schools students quit for security reasons and that night shift jobs for young people have been reduced by almost 30 percent.[24] Knaul (1997), with data for Bogotá, measures the impact of violence in school enrollment.

Bejarano (1988) may be the first paper showing how violence negatively affects investment and production decisions in agriculture. Thoumi (1990) offers a similar argument. Several recent econometric studies corroborate these early insights. Rubio (1995) proposed that violence had an effect on investment and productivity growth. Statistical evidence with aggregate data corroborates such an impact. It is found that the compound impact on GDP growth could have been as high as 2 percent in some years. Bonell et al. (1996) re-estimated three previously published (between 1976 and 1990) investment models introducing the homicide rate as an additional independent variable. They found a negative and statistically significant effect. Parra (1997) also estimates several investment functions using the homicide rate as a right hand side variable and finds a negative, significant effect. She finds that the impact on investment could have been as high as 40 percent in some years. Cross-sectional growth models for Latin America that include the homicide rate as an explanatory variable corroborate these findings.[25] Plazas (1997), using time series data for departments, finds that kidnapping, more than homicide, has an impact on productivity growth.

Chica (1996) reviews the results of econometric work done in the National Study on the Determinants of Productivity Growth. Two of these models included violence as an explanatory variable and found a robust influence. Sánchez, Rodríguez, and Núñez (1996) also use econometric work to compute an effect of violence on productivity growth.[26]

## 5.4   Explanations for Colombia's High Crime Rate

The reasons for Colombia's crime problem are undoubtedly complex. Disentangling the causes of the situation is an inherently difficult task that is made even harder by serious data limitations. Because of these data restrictions, we focus the analysis that follows almost exclusively on homicide, the crime for which the data are most available. We devote this section of the chapter to the leading explanations for why crime is so high in Colombia. The five explanations we consider are (1) the illegal drug trade, (2) the lack of punishment of criminals, (3) the presence of extra-governmental groups (guerrillas and paramilitaries) that have taken over traditional governmental roles in parts of the country, (4) poverty and income inequality, and (5) the possibility that Colombia's decades of internal strife has created a populous that is simply more innately violence prone. For each of these five causes we consider their theoretical justifications, the international evidence, and whatever else Colombian information is available. We address each argument in turn.

### 5.4.1   The Drug Trade
There has never been anything approaching agreement among Colombian analysts about the size of drug exports or production activities, much less about the country's share in the world trade.[27] L'Observatoire Geopolitique des Drogues[28] argues that during the 1980s there was a spreading of influence from Colombian drug cartels to neighboring countries through the imports of chemicals and money laundering. But it was in 1989, after the murder of presidential candidate Luis Carlos Galán and the subsequent war against the Medellín cartel, that the Colombian drug lords rapidly spread their activities all over the continent. By the mid 1990s there was "no single country in Latin America or in the anglophone Caribbean islands that is not involved, in one way or another, in the production and trade of drugs."[29]

Colombia is still considered the leader in the cocaine export business. Most of the coca is now cultivated in the country but there are still imports from Peru and Bolivia.[30] Although the DEA argues that 75 percent of the cocaine reaching the United States originates in Colombia, there seems to be consensus that nowadays Mexico is the number one route for drugs entering the United States.[31] Since getting the drug into the consumers market has been long recognized as the lion's share of the business,[32] this new scenario suggests a decreasing share of Colombian profits in the Latin American drug trade.

Estimates of the revenues of the drug trade in Colombia show high variance but, for the late 1980s, run as high as US$5,500 million, whereas minimum estimates were around US$1,200 million (Thoumi 1994 and Steiner 1998 review this literature). This range in the value of cocaine exports is equivalent to between 3 and 14 percent of Colombian GDP.

There is overwhelming evidence that the drug trade encourages violence. From a theoretical perspective, drug distribution fosters violence because participants, unable to legally enforce contracts and property rights, turn to violence and intimidation to accomplish these tasks. The illegality of drugs makes traditional forms of industrial competition like advertising and price-cutting more difficult. Instead, violence is the primary means of establishing market dominance. It has also been argued that the continuing presence of this lawless sector erodes respect for the law among those outside the drug trade, as well as diverting limited criminal justice budgets from the enforcement of everyday crime to breaking the drug cartels.

Empirically both international and Colombian data unambiguously suggest a causal link between the drug trade and high levels of violence. The experience of the United States is particularly telling.[33] Figure 5.13 presents the homicide rates per capita in the United States over roughly the last 100 years. There are two periods where the number of homicides is exceptionally high: the Prohibition years (1920–1933) when the sale of alcohol was outlawed, and from the early 1980s to the early 1990s when the sale of powder cocaine, and later crack cocaine, flourished in the United States. In their day the legendary mobsters of the US Prohibition years (with names like Al Capone and Bugsy Malone) were as ruthless as Pablo Escobar. When the Prohibition was ended, the homicidal rates quickly reverted to typical levels. The later crack cocaine epidemic is likewise clearly connected to a spike in violence. Black street gangs, overwhelmingly youths, controlled the distribution of crack cocaine in inner-city ghettos. Between 1985 and 1991, homicide rates for Black males aged 18 to 24 more than tripled, according to the Bureau of Justice Statistics. Kennedy et al. (1996) and Levitt and Venkatesh (2000) demonstrate how these homicides were heavily concentrated among those

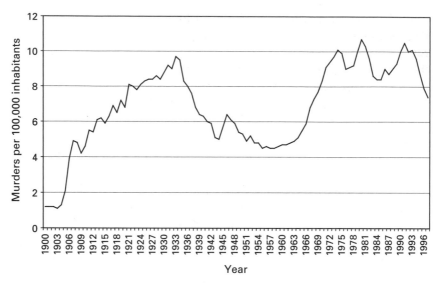

**Figure 5.13**
Murder rate in the United States, 1900 to 1997 (From National Center for Health Statistics, Vital Statistics)

engaging in drug distribution. Almost every other segment of the US population experienced *declining* homicide rates during this time, including older Black males.

The Colombian experience of drug production is similar in its relationship to violence. The period of sharply increasing homicides in figure 5.1 matches the time period where the export market for cocaine was rapidly expanding and drug cartels were vying for control of the markets. The two departments of the country with the highest homicide rates were Valle and Antioquia, in which Cali and Medellín are, respectively, located. The homicidal rates in these departments were four times higher than in the median department over the 1990s. Furthermore much of the drop in homicides since 1991 is due to reductions in Cali and Medellín, and has been attributed to the dismantling of the traditional drug cartels.[34]

### 5.4.2 Lack of Punishment of Criminals
Punishing criminals by locking them up reduces crime in two ways. First, when criminals are behind bars they are physically unable to continue committing crimes. This is termed the "incapacitation" effect. Second, the threat of punishment may *deter* potential criminals from entry into a career of crime.[35]

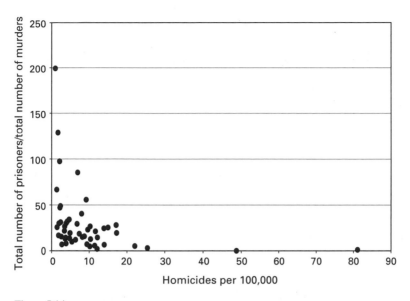

**Figure 5.14**
Cross-county crime and punishment, 1990 to 1994 (From United Nations Survey of Crime
Trends and Operations of Criminal Justice Systems, various years)

The data from the United States has been used in many studies to demonstrate the strong connection between increases in punishment and lower
crime rates. Among the deterrents studied are increases is sentence severity
(Kessler and Levitt 1998), higher arrest rates (Levitt 1997), and larger
prison populations (Levitt 1996; Marvell and Moody 1994; Spelman
1994). The best estimates from this large literature suggest that a 10 percent increase in the expected punishment lowers crime by about 2 percent.

The poor quality of international data makes it difficult to construct
reliable cross-country comparisons of expected punishments. In figure
5.14 we attempt a crude comparison along these lines. We compare the
number of prisoners (for all crimes) and the number of homicides in a
country, using the most recent data available for the country in question.
Clearly, this measure of punishment is imperfect because most prisoners
are incarcerated for crimes other than murder. Nonetheless, we hope that
it captures to a first approximation the extent to which a country punishes
its criminals. Figure 5.14 makes two important points. First, only countries with low punishment rates (the points to the left of the figure) have
high crime. Colombia has both the highest homicide rates in the sample
and the lowest punishment rate. Second, all high punishment nations
(these include, among others, the United States, Singapore, England,
Bermuda, and Madagascar) have low homicide rates.

**Table 5.1**
Criminal justice treatment of murderers in Colombia and the United States

| Country | Probability of an investigation if a murder occurs | Probability of an arrest and trial if a murder occurs | Probability of conviction if a murder occurs | Expected time served if convicted of murder | Expected years in prison if I commit a murder |
|---|---|---|---|---|---|
| Colombia | 38% | 11% | 7% | 4.5 years | 0.32 years |
| United States | 100% | 65% | 58% | 6.5 years | 3.8 years |

Sources: Values in the table are authors' estimates based on a variety of published data sources. For the United States, estimates are based on information published in *Sourcebook of Criminal Justice Statistics*, published annually by the Bureau of Justice Statistics. For Colombia, estimates are based on DANE—Estadísticas Judiciales and Consejo Superior de la Judicatura.

It is instructive to compare Colombia to the United States, which has a high punishment rate, in order to understand why the expected punishments in these two countries differ so much. We present this analysis in table 5.1. In the United States an arrest is made and the defendant is brought to trial in 65 percent of murders, and a conviction occurs in more than half of all homicides. In Colombia, investigations are done in only 38 percent of homicides, and only 11 percent of homicides lead to trials. Convictions occur in less than 7 percent of homicides in Colombia, only one-seventh the rate in the United States. Average sentence length for those convicted of murder in the United States is about 20 years, of which perhaps one-third of the time will actually be served. In Colombia, average sentence length is 14 years. Although we do not have good information on the fraction of the sentence actually served, we estimate that value to be one-third, which is probably an overstatement. Combining the information on probability of conviction with average time served yields the last column of the table, which is the expected time served behind bars per murder. In the United States, this number is 3.8 years, compared to 0.32 years—less than four months—in Colombia. Thus effective punishment in Colombia is less than one-tenth of that in the United States. If one is to connect a murder, Colombia is a much better place to do it.

We noted early in this section that the best empirical estimate of the responsiveness of crime to punishment is that a 10 percent increase in punishment lowers crime by 2 percent. If this estimate is correct, then raising Colombian punishment to US levels (which are close to those of most European countries) will cause Colombian crime rates to fall by more than 50 percent. That means that over 10,000 murders will be eliminated annually in Colombia.

We need to stress at this point that we are not advocating any particular policy but merely attempt to demonstrate the factors that make Colombia an international outlier with respect to homicide. To make policy recommendations, it is necessary to balance the benefits of greater punishment (lower crime) with the costs (the expense of catching criminals and locking them up, and any issues of civil liberty that may arise). There also may be important institutional barriers to effectively increase punishment, such as corruption on the part of police and judges. In sections 5.5 and 5.6 we return to these issues in much greater detail.

### 5.4.3 Guerrillas

An important difference between Colombia's crime problem and what is happening in the rest of Latin America is the prevalence of conflict, the increasing guerrilla/paramilitary presence, and their threatening activities.

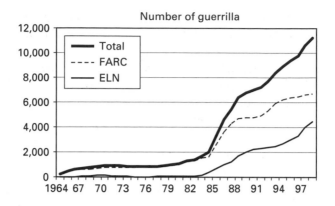

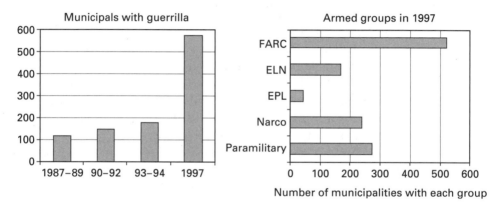

**Figure 5.15**
Guerrilla and armed groups

The origin of Fuerzas Armadas Revolucionarias de Colombia (FARC) can be traced back to the period of La Violencia. The second major group, Ejército de Liberación Nacional (ELN), was created by a crew of students that came back from Cuba in the aftermath of Fidel Castro's revolution. From their beginning, both groups had a slow but continuous growth. It was not until the mid-1980s, after an aborted peace process, that their real strengthening began. From less than 2,000 armed men at that time, by the end of the 1990s they had reached almost 12,000 active combatants (figure 5.15). In terms of their regional influence, the number of municipalities (out of 1,075) with guerrilla presence went from a little more than a hundred in the late 1980s to almost 600 in 1997.

The link of guerrillas, paramilitary, and other armed groups with crime can be analyzed from two dimensions. The first, and most straightforward, is through the performance of the criminal justice system: a weak judiciary encourages both crime and the consolidation of armed groups—or, the other way around, armed groups that weaken the judiciary indirectly encourage other types of crime.

The second dimension comes from considering armed groups as suppliers of private protection services (see Gambetta 1993). In this sense the association with violence, or crime, is rather complex. Successful protection providers need credibility, which means a stock of violence reputation. So it is clear that *past* violence is positively associated with armed groups. However, eventually these groups may reduce their effective use of violence and—more effectively—employ threats. On the other hand, high crime and a poor judiciary are good incentives for buying private protection services. Effective protection providers would tend to reduce crime but not as much as to completely eliminate demand for their services. So, in theory, the connection between armed groups and crime, from third parties, is ambiguous. Third, if some armed groups engage in illegal production or trade activities with self-protection schemes, there may be as well some division of labor in illegal markets; illegal producers may contract private protection services. In any event, illegal activities are always positively associated with the presence of armed groups. Last, private armies may need to finance their military activities, and may also provide protection against themselves. This normally means high levels of kidnapping and extortion.

There is some evidence that from their beginning, guerrilla groups provided protection against cattle theft in rural municipalities (Rangel 1999). Rapid growth of ELN in the 1980s is associated with extortion to oil companies. Most paramilitary groups, even a strong one financed by drug lords—known as MAS (Muerte a Secuestradores: Death to Kidnappers)—were created as a response to kidnapping by guerrillas (Thoumi 1994; Cubides 1999). There is ample controversy in Colombia about the association between ordinary crime, violence, and guerrillas (Echandía 1999).

During the 1990s the empirical evidence on a link between homicide and guerrilla activity is very weak. Across municipalities, areas with a guerrilla presence appear no worse than other areas (using the 1997 assessment of the Inteligencia Militar as to guerrilla presence in a municipality). Consejeria para la Paz reports information about guerrilla presence in the period 1990 to 1992. Municipalities that did not have guerrillas in the early 1990s, but had guerrillas in 1997, actually show the greatest declines in homicide over the 1990s. Municipalities that never

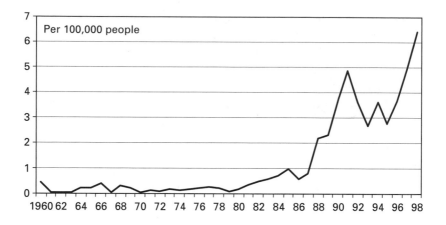

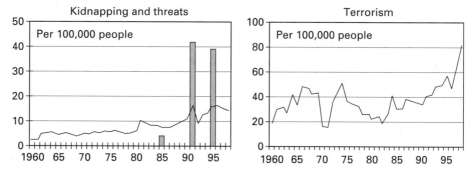

**Figure 5.16**
Kidnapping and terrorism (From Policía Nacional; DANE, ENH)

have had guerrillas, or municipalities that had guerillas both in the early 1990s and in 1997, show smaller declines in homicide.

A parallel analysis to that of the preceding paragraph can be made for kidnapping. Its rise suggests a strong causal link between the kidnapping rate and the scope of guerrilla activity. Moreover the rise in the number of active combatants and the spreading of guerrilla presence across municipalities is associated with a significant increase in criminal activities traditionally associated with guerrilla: terrorism and kidnapping.

Terrorist actions reported by the police have been steadily increasing since the 1980s from less than 500 in 1985 to more than 1,700 in 1997 (figure 5.16). Reported kidnappings to the police show two periods of extraordinary rise. During the first rise, from 1986 to 1991, the kidnapping rate (per capita) grew at more than 40 percent a year. The second rise, from 1995 to the present, in kidnapping reports per capita is at an annual rate of almost 25 percent.[36]

Some further indicators corroborate the link between guerrillas and kidnapping. First, more than half of the kidnappings reported to the police between 1991 and 1999 are attributed, by the victims, to guerrilla groups.[37] The other half of kidnappings was attributed to "common criminals."[38] It is not unusual, however, that this latter group would buy protection from or "sell" their hostages[39] to the guerrillas. Second, for the period 1991 to 1995 it has been estimated that kidnapping ransoms accounted for 22 percent of the guerrilla income.[40] Average ransom paid within this period can be calculated at around US$100,000.[41] During 1997 ransoms in the million-dollar range seemed to be frequent.[42] Third, criminal cases against kidnappers have been continuously falling since the early 1980s. Arrest rates felt from 11 percent in 1980 to 2 percent in 1994, while conviction rates dropped from 4.4 percent in 1978 to 1.8 percent in 1994.[43] On top of this, in prosecuting kidnappers there seems to be a bias of the criminal justice system against "common criminals" and in favor of guerrillas, and within the latter against low-ranking agents in favor of group leaders.[44] In 1996, while guerrillas committed 43 percent of reported kidnappings, only 29 percent of apprehended offenders belonged to these groups.[45]

### 5.4.4  Poverty and Income Inequality

Among many leading Colombian thinkers the leading explanation for Colombia's crime problem is the country's poverty and low "social justice" (Comisión de Estudios Sobre la Violencia 1987). From the data there is little evidence to support this view.

There is a large academic literature that studies the cross-country correlation between crime and poverty/inequality.[46] There is no systematic evidence of a link between a country's poverty and its crime rate. Indeed, many studies (summarized in Soares 2000) find that richer countries experience *more* crime, although Soares demonstrates that this surprising result is due only to more rigorous reporting of crime in rich countries— victimization surveys show no relationship whatsoever between a country's GDP per capita and crime.

Income inequality, on the other hand, does appear to be causally linked to crime in cross-country studies (Fajnzylber et al. 1998; Soares 2000).[47] Soares (2000) finds that increasing the ratio of GDP of the top 20 percent to GDP of the bottom 20 percent by one, increases crime between five and ten depending on the crime category.

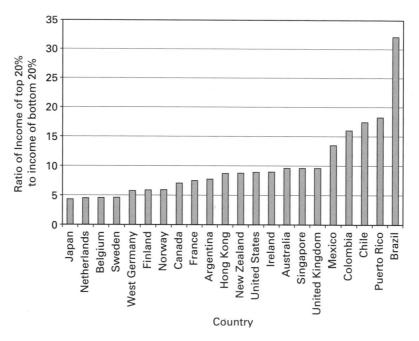

**Figure 5.17**
Cross-country inequality (From United Nations Development Programme)

It is important to note, however, that the income distribution in Co-lombia is not particularly unequal compared to other Latin American countries. Figure 5.17 presents the ratio of income in the top 20 percent relative to the bottom 20 percent, in the income distribution for a range of countries. Colombia has substantial income inequality relative to many other countries, but income is more equally distributed than in Brazil or Chile. Thus, while a high degree of income inequality may help to explain generally high crime rates in Latin America, it does not provide a reason why Colombian crime is so much higher than other Latin American countries.

A comparison of Colombian municipalities further calls into question poverty and income inequality as explanations for high crime rates. Fig-ure 5.18 plots average homicide rates per capita over the period 1990 to 1998 by municipality against the fraction of municipality's households that are below the poverty threshold for unmet basic needs according to the 1993 Census-DANE. Included in the figure is the fitted regression line summarizing the estimated relationship between the two variables. The data reveal no relationship: areas with high levels of poverty are actually

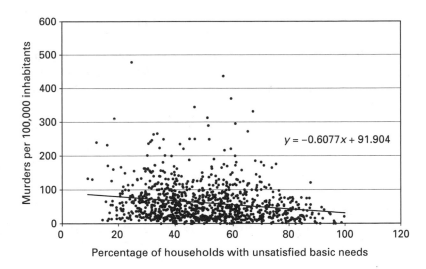

**Figure 5.18**
Poverty and average murder rate, 1990 to 1998 (From DANE, Consejería para la Paz, Policía Nacional)

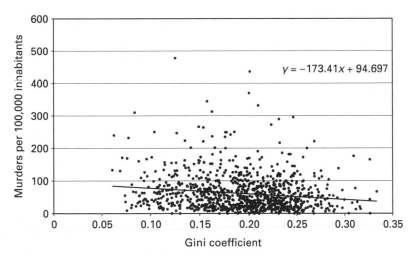

**Figure 5.19**
Inequality and average murder rate, 1990 to 1998 (From Sarmiento 1993, Consejería para la Paz, Policía Nacional)

*less* likely to experience high homicide rates than areas with a low incidence of poverty.

Figure 5.19 is similar to Figure 5.18, but the income inequality in a municipality is measured by a Gini index from 1993 (Sarmiento 1998). Note the very weak relationship between income inequality and homicide across Colombian municipalities.

From these analyses we are led to conclude that neither poverty nor income inequality can explain Colombia's high crime rate. While redistribution of income to the poor may be desirable for many reasons, lowering crime is certainly *not* foremost among these reasons.

### 5.4.5   Do Colombians Have a Unique Propensity to Violence?

Among many Colombian analysts, there is an idea that Colombia has a long history of violence (Gaitan 1994; Monetengro y Posada 1995 review the literature on how Colombians have become inherently more violent than residents of other countries). It is also argued that most violence in Colombia is not drug or conflict related but rather comes from generalized violence among ordinary citizens (Comisión de Estudios Sobre la Violencia 1987).

We offer two different kinds of evidence against this conjecture. First, crime in Bogotá is similar to that of Rio de Janeiro, São Paulo, Caracas, San Salvador, and Guatemala City.[48] Our second counterargument is that for other manifestations of violence that are unrelated to the drug trade, Colombia is not an outlier; the situation did not get worse during the 1980s when homicide rates significantly rose. In terms of domestic violence, for example, Colombia looks quite similar to Chile, or Costa Rica, and falls behind Perú, Nicaragua, and Mexico (Buvinic and Morrison 1999). Thus there is little need for a claim that Colombians are simply more violent than others by nature.

### 5.5   The Colombian Criminal Justice System

The analysis of the preceding section suggests that the absence of an effective Colombian criminal justice system is a major contributor to Colombia's crime problem. While this is by no means the only cause of high crime rates, we feel that reforming the criminal justice system is the most direct and feasible way to lessen the burden of crime felt by Colombian citizens in the short run. In this section we document each step of the criminal justice process, providing empirical evidence wherever possible. We attempt to isolate the steps in the process where the greatest breakdowns occur. In section 5.6, where we make policy recommendations, many of our suggestions will be related with the reforming of the criminal justice system to remove these bottlenecks.

### 5.5.1  Reporting Crime to the Police

The first step in the process is the willingness of victims to come forward and report crimes to the police. Without this action there is no hope that a crime can be solved and a criminal be brought to justice, except through vigilantism. As noted earlier, Colombian reporting rates are not unusual for a Latin American country (Alvazzi 1998).

We also noted earlier that there is a large and growing discrepancy between crimes that citizens say they reported and those crimes officially recorded by the police. The number of crimes that citizens say they reported to the police rose substantially between 1985 and 1995, from 941 to 1,296 per 100,000. Official police records, however, show fewer crimes (661 per 100,000 in 1985) than citizens say they report. Moreover the official data actually shows a 10 percent *decline* in crime between 1985 and 1994.

There appears to be little relationship between official police records and either victimization or citizen claims of reported crime. Police records include less than half of the crimes that citizens claim to have reported. The discrepancy between official data and victimization data—in both the levels and trends—causes us great concern as to the reliability of the official data. In fact, as we argue below, beginning in the mid-1970s, official crime statistics do not only reflect crime but also a propensity to not record crimes unless an offender was identified, making these data useless for tracking crime trends.

### 5.5.2  Criminal Investigations

Once a crime is reported, the first step to solve a case is an investigation. In Colombian data there are two types of investigations: preliminary and *sumario*. Police conduct the preliminary investigations, which involve basic fact checking in cases where no offender is identified. *Fiscales*—powerful prosecutors—are in control of sumarios that involve preparation for bringing a case to trial. Figure 5.20 presents the fraction of reported crimes in which an investigation is conducted and the fraction of those investigations that result in a trial, by type of crime in 1995. In cases involving homicide and personal injury, roughly 40 percent are investigated. For property crime, roughly the same proportions hold. For kidnapping, investigations are slightly less frequent. Across all three crime

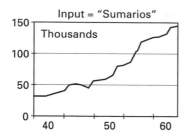

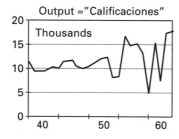

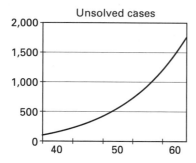

**Figure 5.20**
Congestion 1940 to 1964

categories, the percentage of investigations that lead to a trial is similar: about 30 percent. The results in the figure are both surprising and disturbing. It is surprising that the fraction of cases investigated and the fraction of successful investigations (i.e., investigations resulting in a trial) is similar across crime categories as different as homicide and personal injuries, kidnapping, and property crime. In most countries, investigations are much more likely in serious crimes such as kidnapping and murder than in property crime. Moreover the rate of solving crimes in other countries, such as the United States, is proportional to the seriousness of the offense. For instance, in the United States, roughly 65 percent

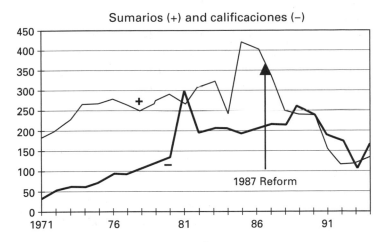

**Figure 5.21**
Efforts against congestion from 1971

**Table 5.2**
Judiciary performance, 1995

|  | All crimes | Property | Homicide and injuries | Sexual assault | Kidnap-ping | Other |
|---|---|---|---|---|---|---|
| Crime | 100.0 | 100.0 | 100.0 | 100.0 | 100.0 | 100.0 |
| Reports | 14.9 | 7.4 | 96.8 | 27.7 | 21.7 | 76.5 |
| Investigations | 9.9 | 3.3 | 37.9 | 57.3 | 8.6 | 178.8 |
| Trials | 2.8 | 1.0 | 11.2 | 17.2 | 2.5 | 49.8 |
| Sentences | 1.7 | 0.6 | 6.8 | 10.4 | 1.5 | 30.2 |

Sources: Policía Nacional—DANE: ENH and Estadísticas de Justicia.

of murderers are brought to trial (or plead guilty prior to a trial), whereas for burglaries reported to the police, the same percentage is less than 10 percent. But in Colombia, the percentage of reported crimes that eventually lead to a trial is between 10 and 15 percent across all of the crime categories, suggesting that a great deal of effort is devoted to solving minor crimes in Colombia while the more serious and socially costly crimes go unpunished.[49] The roots of this investigative crisis go back many decades. Beginning in the 1940s, when official data first became available, the number of sumarios, or formal investigations, grew by 6 to 7 percent per year (see figure 5.21). In contrast, however, table 5.2 shows that the number of cases actually appearing before judges rose only 1 to 2 percent annually. Consequently a huge and growing backlog of unsolved cases emerged. In response, a specialized judge (*juez de instrucción*) was first introduced in 1971. Their priority was to solve the backlog problem, rather than to fight crime per se. In the decade following their introduction, the number of sumarios rose from 35,000 annually to 300,000. Yet this increase in investigations appears to have been at the expense of toughness. In 1971, almost 30 percent of sumarios went to trial, but by 1981 the proportion had fallen to only 9 percent. The introduction of the jueces de instrucción institutionalized the policy that persists to this day: hopelessly overloaded, the criminal justice system focuses its meager resources on crimes that are easily solved, even if such crimes are minor and murderers and kidnapers go free. Furthermore a legislative decree adopted in 1987 virtually ensures that difficult cases will not be solved. In response to the crime backlog, it was legislated that a sumario only be initiated if the offender was identified, and if after 60 days of the crime the offender is not identified, then the case is closed. In essence, the law said that fiscales can only investigate those crimes in which there is little need for investigation! Although Ley 81 of 1993 formally eliminated this time limit, this approach to investigation continues to be prevalent. In the most recent data 90 percent of the investigations are concluded within two months. Thus the fiscales have proved to be quite efficient in carrying out the tasks that they have historically been pressured into focusing on, although in our opinion these are not the activities that have the greatest social benefits.

### 5.5.3   Criminal Trials, Sentencing, and Time Served in Prison

The final stage of the criminal justice system is the trial, sentencing, and punishment of criminals. Of cases that go to trial or for which there is *sentencia anticipada* (a plea bargain), guilty sentences are obtained roughly 90 percent of the time overall, and 76 percent of the time for homicide. Thus the primary bottleneck in achieving more convictions does not appear to lie with the judiciary but, rather, with the fiscalía bringing only a limited number of cases.

Once convictions occur, the sentences handed down by the courts are in line with sentences in other countries. For instance, as noted earlier, the average sentence for a convicted murderer in Colombia is 14 years although there is enormous variation in this number: 25 percent of convicted killers got 2 years or less, and 25 percent got 25 years or more.

Although we do not have reliable information on the actual time served, it is much less than the sentence handed down by courts. As in other countries, sentences are reduced for good behavior in prison. In addition it is estimated that approximately 2 percent of prisoners escape every year.[50]

A high rate of prison escapes is just one dimension along which the Colombian prison system performs poorly. There are currently 40,000 prisoners in Colombia held in facilities designed to hold only 28,000 inmates. This overcrowding, without doubt, contributes to prisoner escapes, as well as to violent conditions within the prisons. On average, 150 prisoners are killed in prison each year—in Bogotá earlier this year 23 prisoners died on a single day in one prison. Some of this prison violence is attributable to conflicts between paramilitaries and guerrillas housed within the same prisons. Moreover it is claimed that crime, especially kidnapping, is actually done by prison inmates who bribe guards in order to temporarily leave the prison grounds to conduct their crimes.

## 5.6 Recommendations

In this chapter we have attempted to provide a careful analysis of Colombia's crime situation, as well as the reasons why Colombia suffers a level of violence that is among the highest in the world. We conclude the chapter with a series of recommendations for policy makers in Colombia. Although we have given some thought to political feasibility in crafting our suggestions, effectiveness—not politics—is the primary factor that has determined our recommendations. Consequently some of our ideas may be difficult to implement in the current political environment. Nonetheless, we feel it is useful for these politically challenging policies to be added to the public debate. We have, however, limited ourselves for the most part to policy changes that do not require changes to the existing Constitution.

Our policy recommendations are divided into four categories: information/statistics, lessening corruption in the criminal justice system, micro-priorities, and macro-priorities. For each category we provide a brief overview of the rationale underlying the suggestions, and then present specific policy recommendations in a bullet-point format.

### 5.6.1 Information/Statistics

Our first set of recommendations has little to do with the direct activities of fighting crime. Rather, it is our belief that access to better statistics and information on crime and criminal justice would be useful to policy makers. These first suggestions are generally not expensive to implement and are unlikely to be as politically charged as our later recommendations.

Our specific recommendations are as follows:

• As police reports show, when an agency is evaluated using its own reports there is a high risk of a low-quality statistical output. We suggest that reporting/statistical duties be taken away from the agencies involved in the criminal procedures. This will include (1) not only the police but also (2) the fiscalía, (3) the juzgados, and (4) the prisons. In fact, with the creation of the fiscalia, and of the Consejo Superior de la Judicatura (the administrative branch of the judiciary) official figures got worse than they were when judiciary statistics were under the sole responsibility of DANE.

• Homicide statistics, which are currently of relatively high quality, should be "protected" because they may also deteriorate. The statistical duties of Medicina Legal should be broaden to cover all municipalities and be separated from judicial investigations.

• Based on the existing academic research which points out that reported crime rates are not reliable indicators of underlying crime victimization, we recommend the creation of a regular (every three years) victimization survey representing the whole country, not just some urban areas. Especially important in these victimization surveys is detailed information about the influence of armed groups and drug cartels in the crimes that are occurring.

• Much more information is needed about prisons. It is currently not possible to accurately determine the composition of the prisons by type of crime committed or the actual time served by inmates. We suggest that a prison census be conducted every three years. This census will help policy makers understand how prison resources are being allocated (e.g., between violent and non-violent offenders). Such a census will also provide the basis for determining how much prison capacity is required to house the existing and projected prisoner population.

### 5.6.2  Corruption of Agencies

It is clear that corruption and/or intimidation on the part of drug cartels and armed groups currently interfere with effective enforcement of the law. While recognizing the difficulties involved with reducing such corruption, we nonetheless feel that the benefits of doing so are so immense that an investment in this area is likely to prove extremely cost effective.

Reductions in corruption among the police in recent years provide an excellent example of how successful such programs can be.

Specific recommendations:

• An externally supervised corruption/infiltration investigation in the fiscalía. Since the fiscalía is the critical link in bringing criminals to justice, progress in fighting crime cannot be made until improvements are seen here. Moreover this is a basic preliminary step for reducing what, for some people, looks like a fiscalía-military confrontation. The legitimacy of fiscalía is also crucial for making progress investigating human rights issues.
• Anticorruption investigation/purge of the military like there was of the police a few years ago. Some external supervision would also be useful. Any links between military and paramilitary or narcos have to be left behind if some progress is to be made against guerrillas. For investigating paramilitary activity fiscalía has recently said that it felt unsafe. This is another issue for which coordination between noncorrupt fiscales and noncorrupt military is important.

### 5.6.3 Micro-priorities

By micro-priorities, we mean legal or institutional changes that can be quickly implemented or done on a small scale that may nonetheless have an enormous impact on the safety and well-being of Colombians. These recommendations are likely to provide the greatest benefits relative to their costs of the various suggestions that we make. Thus, we feel that these may be the most important recommendations we make.

Specific recommendations:

• The establishment of a separate antikidnapping task force. This task force would be made up of an elite group of fiscales who have proved themselves effective and noncorrupt. This group would devote 100 percent of their attention to investigating kidnapping incidents. Our estimate is that less than 100 dedicated fiscales could dramatically reduce kidnapping in a short amount of time. Such a program in Brazil has already proved very effective.
• The establishment of an elite antihomicide task force, similar to that proposed for kidnapping. This task force would be responsible in carrying out a serious investigation of every homicide that occurs. If the task force contained 1,000 fiscales, then there would be roughly 20 cases annually for each fiscal to investigate.

• Kidnapping and homicide task forces, whatever their size, should be completely isolated from congestion in other areas.

• Establish mandatory sentences to lessen the scope for corruption of judges and also to lessen the ability of judges to be intimidated by narcos or guerrillas.

• The safety of judges and prosecutors must be guaranteed. An unacceptable number of judges and prosecutors are murdered in Colombia. We recommend that the government provide twenty-four hour a day protection to judges and prosecutors working on cases dealing with narcos or guerrillas.

• Violent crime, especially murder and kidnapping, should receive an increased share of the police, fiscalía, and prison resources, even if this means devoting less resources to property crime. The social costs of violent crime far outweigh those of property crime.

• A substantial increase in Colombia's prison capacity. It would not be unreasonable to build enough prison cells to hold 100,000 prisoners (compared to the current prison capacity of 28,000, and actual prison population of 40,000). Even with a prison population of 100,000, the number of prisoners per crime committed will still be very low by international and even South American standards.

• Steps must be taken to put the government—not the prisoners—in control of the prisons. This will have two impacts: the first is to safeguard the human rights of prisoners; the second is to safeguard the citizens outside prisons from frequent escapes.

• Prisoners should be separated according to the seriousness of the crimes. Especially, guerrilla and paramilitary should be separated from the rest of the prisoners to avoid the spreading of conflict within prisons.

### 5.6.4 Macro-Priorities

Unlike the micro-priorities described above, our last set of recommendations relates to fundamental political issues, rather than to easily implemented stand-alone policy recommendations.

Specific recommendations:

• Take the political decision to fight kidnapping/extortion, even from guerrillas. We would go as far as to recommend giving some tax money to guerrillas to replace what they are getting from kidnapping activities. This has already been discussed with ELN. This will have the duel advantages of lessening kidnapping and lowering the incentives for *new* paramilitary activity. Most important, this would define kidnapping fighting as a public issue and undermine the private protection schemes (with both paramilitary and guerrilla).

• In Plan Colombia it appears that kidnapping, which we consider one of the most important issues, has not been defined as a priority. The only references to kidnapping in Plan Colombia call for social participation and political pressure on guerrillas to end this practice. Clearly, this is not sound criminal policy.

• Plan Colombia intends to invest a great deal of resources in high-conflict areas. What we would recommend, instead, is that resources should be channeled to very poor, but *nonviolent*, regions. By distributing resources to nonviolent areas, this eliminates the perverse incentives of formerly nonviolent areas attracting guerrillas. Moreover this encourages local authorities to aggressively fight crime to protect the flow of funds from the central government. (There is an historical argument in favor of this. In thirteenth-century England high-crime areas were taxed more heavily than low-crime areas. Also an incentive to investigate homicides was that the crown got the murderers' property.)

• Drug policy should focus on trading, money laundering, and prosecuting drug lords, not farmers. There are many, and strong arguments against fumigation of coca plantations, and public opinion opponents to this can be found all over the political spectrum.

## Notes

1. Throughout the chapter, we will report homicide rates in terms of homicides per 100,000 residents per year.

2. See Rubio (1999) for the problems with the 1991 survey.

3. See Gaviria and Pagés (1999).

4. See Alvazzi del Frate (1998). Data for Colombia in the ICVS comes from a survey done in Bogotá in 1997.

5. Gaviria and Pagés (1999, p. 3).

6. Alvazzi del Frate (1998, p. 132).

7. In terms of the average 1990 to 1997 homicide rate.

8. See Bobadilla et al. (1995).

9. Studies for Río de Janeiro, São Paulo, Kingston, México, and Perú can be found in Domínguez et al. For Colombia there is some work in Ministerio de Salud (1995) and Trujillo y Badel (1998).

10. Leal (1994) or IEPRI (1997).

11. Comisión de Racionalización del Gasto y de las Finanzas Públicas (1996), "Defensa, Seguridad Ciudadana y Gasto Público" y "El Sistema Judicial y el Gasto Público," Mimeo–Bogotá.

12. Ospina (1996).

13. Jaramillo (1993), Corporación Región (1997), and Salazar (1994).

14. For Medellín, there is such a proliferation of *bandas* and *milicias* that it has been estimated that every popular neighborhood has its own private army (Corporación Región 1997).

15. Rubio (1997).

16. Rubio (1996).

17. There is no detailed explanation of the methodology.

18. INS (1994) or Echeverri et al. (1997).

19. "Años de Vida Saludable Perdidos."

20. A review of the literature up to 1995 in Conferencia Episcopal de Colombia (1995). See also Murillo y Herrera (1991), Giraldo, Abad y Pérez (1997), and Morrison y Pérez (1994).

21. Trujillo y Badel (1998).

22. Corporación Región (1997), Jaramillo (1993, 1994), Salazar y Jaramillo (1992), and Salazar (1994).

23. Defensoría del Pueblo (1996).

24. Cuéllar (1997).

25. Corbo (1996).

26. All this work has been done with aggregate data. The impact at the micro level has only been analyzed for agriculture. See Bejarano (1996) or Escobar (1994).

27. See Thoumi (1994) or Steiner (1998) for "size of the industry" estimates and comparisons.

28. Koutozis (1996).

29. Koutozis (1996, p. 82).

30. Rufin (1999).

31. See for example, Uncle Sam's war on drugs, *The Economist*, February 20, 1999, p. 59.

32. Thoumi (1994) or Rocha (1997).

33. Much of the international evidence in this chapter will be from US data. This is partly because the United States has some of the most reliable crime statistics available, and thus has been the focus of a great deal of research, but also because one of the chapter's authors has a particular expertise in US crime.

34. The evolution of violence in Bogotá is harder to explain. Even though public officials optimistically explain this fall with various "successful policies" that were undertaken from 1994, a careful time series analysis of weekly data suggests that this is not the case. See Paz Publica, "Homicidios en la Ciudad de Bogotá," forthcoming.

35. This does not require that criminals be "rational," but rather merely that they respond to incentives. Decades of research by psychologists, sociologists, and economists demonstrate that people respond to incentives (as do rats, dogs, and pigeons).

36. País Libre—a private nonprofit organization that was set up by a former kidnapping victim in 1991 to support victims, gather information, and lobby for legal reform against kidnapping—argues that the 1993 to 1995 drop in rates can partially be explained by a harsh antikidnap law that was approved in 1993. Although this legal initiative was almost dismantled by a Constitutional Court decision, it might have had an effect on reporting rates.

37. Paramilitary kidnapping apparently did not begun until 1998 and is still below 4 percent of the total figure (País Libre).

38. The so-called "delincuencia común."

39. Trujillo (1997).

40. Echandía (1999, p. 135).

41. Global figure in Echandía (1999) divided by average kidnapping reports for the same period.

42. Trujillo (1997, p. 51).

43. Gómez (1996). See also section 5.5.

44. Santos (1997).

45. País Libre.

46. Fajnzylber et al. (1999).

47. There are competing explanations as to why crime and inequality are linked. Sociologists suggest that exposure to the rich raises the aspirations of the poor, but when the poor's ability to achieve their materialistic aims is frustrated, their frustration is manifested in criminal acts (cites). An alternative theory comes from evolutionary psychology. The essence of the argument is that competition for resources among young men becomes violent when there is also a lack of equilibrium in the mating market. Poor young men will kill fellow young men when competing for resources only if mating opportunities are scarce and the lack of resources can jeopardize reproductive success. (Daly and Wilson 1989). This type of reasoning also addresses one of the most general and well-known facts about violence: strong and almost universal gender differences.

48. Mexico City is unusually low, less than 20.

49. An alternative explanation for this pattern is that minor crimes are simply not officially recorded in many cases if a suspect is not identified, so the reported crimes dramatically understate the true number of crimes. Under this interpretation it is not that the fiscales spend too much time investigating minor crimes, but rather, that they are equally ineffective in solving both violent and property crime.

50. For purposes of comparison, approximately 1 in 1,000 prisoners escapes each year from US prisons, and virtually all of these escapes are from low- or minimum-security facilities.

# References

Alvazzi del Frate, A. 1998. *Victims of Crime in the Developing World*. Publication 57. Rome: UNICRI.

Bejarano, J. A. 1996. Inseguridad y violencia: sus efectos económicos en el sector agropecuario. *Revista Nacional de Agricultura*, pp. 914–15.

Bejarano, J. A. 1988. Efectos de la violencia en la producción agropecuaria. *Coyuntura Económica*, vol. 18 (September).

Bohadilla, J. L., V. Cárdenas, B. Coutolenc, R. Guerrero, and M. A. Remenyi. 1995. *Medición de los costos de la Violencia*. OPS.

Bonell, A., P. Gómez, and F. Moreno. 1996. Efectos del aumento en la criminalidad sobre la inversión industrial en Colombia. *Trabajo de Grado no publicado*. Bogotá: Universidad Javeriana.

Buvinic, M., and A. Morrison. 1999. *Notas Técnicas. Prevención de la Violencia*. Washington: BID.

Chica, R. 1996. *El Crecimiento de la Productividad en Colombia—Resumen de los resultados del Estudio Nacional sobre Determinantes del Crecimiento de la Productividad*. Bogotá: DNP, Colciencias, DANE.

Conferencia Episcopal de Colombia. 1995. *Derechos Humanos. Desplazados por Violencia en Colombia*. Bogotá: Conferencia Episcopal.

Comisión de Estudios Sobre la Violencia. 1987. *Colombia: Violencia y Democracia*. Bogotá: IEPRI, Universidad Nacional, Colciencias. 4a Edición.

Corbo, V. 1996. *Modelo de crecimiento para América Latina*. Bogotá: Seminario CEDE.

Corporación Región. 1997. Una aproximación a la Conflictividad Urbana en Medellín. Mimeo. Medellín.

Cubides, F. 1999. Los paramilitares y su estrategia. In M. Deas and M. V. Llorente, eds., *Reconocer la Guerra para Construir la Paz*. Bogotá: Uniandes, CEREC, Norma.

Cuéllar de Martínez, M. M. 1997. *Valores y Capital Social en Colombia*. Bogotá: Corporación Porvenir y Universidad Externado de Colombia.

Daly, M., and M. Wilson. 1988. *Homicide*. Paris: Aldine de Gruyter.

Deas, M., and M. V. Llorente, eds. 1999. *Reconocer la Guerra para Construir la Paz*. Bogotá: Uniandes, CEREC, Norma.

Defensoría del Pueblo. 1996. El conflicto armado en Colombia y los menores de edad. *Boletín 2*, Bogotá.

Echandía, C. 1999. Expansión territorial de las guerrillas colombianas. In M. Deas and M. V. Llorente, eds., *Reconocer la Guerra para Contruir la Paz*. Bogotá: Uniandes, CEREC, Norma.

Escobar, S. 1994. Estudio del impacto de la violencia en la producción agropecuaria. *Documento de Trabajo*. Bogotá: Oficina del Alto Comisionado para la Paz. Observatorio de violencia.

Fajnzylber, P., D. Lederman, and N. Loayza. 1998. *Determinants of Crime Rates in Latin America and the World: An Empirical Assesment*. Washington: World Bank Latin America and Caribbean Studies.

Gaitán, F. 1994. Un ensayo sobre la violencia en Colombia. In M. Deas and F. Gaitán, eds., *Dos Ensayos Especulativos sobre la Violencia en Colombia*. Bogotá: Tercer Mundo.

Gambetta, D. 1993. *The Sicilian Mafia: The Business of Private Protection*. Cambridge: Harvard University Press.

Gaviria, A., and C. Pagés. 1999. Patterns of crime victimization in Latin America. Mimeo. IADB, Washington.

Giraldo, C. A., J. A. Colorado, and D. Pérez. 1997. *Relatos e Imágenes. El desplazamiento en Colombia*. Bogotá: CINEP.

Gómez, O. 1996. Causas Económicas del Secuestro en Colombia. Departamento de Economía, Universidad Javeriana, Bogotá.

IEPRI. 1997. *La paz es rentable. Balance de los Estudios*. Proyecto de consultoría al DNP.

INS.CELADE. 1991. *Accidentes y muertes violentas en Colombia. Un estudio sobre las características y consecuencias demográficas 1965–1988*. San José, Costa Rica.

Jaramillo, A. M. 1993. Milicias Populares en Medellín, entre lo privado y lo público. *Revista Foro 22*. November.

Jaramillo, A. M. 1994. *Entre la Guerra y la Paz*. Palabras Más, Corporación Región, Medellín.

Kennedy, D., A. Piehl, and A. Braga. 1996. Youth violence in Boston: Gun markets, serious youth offenders, and a use-reduction strategy. *Law and Contemporary Problems* 59: 147–83.

Kessler, D., and S. Levitt. 1999. Using sentence enhancements to distinguish between deterrence and incapacitation. *Journal of Law and Economics* 17(April): 343–64.

Knaul, F. 1997. *The importance of family and community social capital in the creation of human capital in urban Colombia*. Bogotá: LACEA.

Koutouzis, M. 1996. *Atlas Mondial des Drogues*. Paris: Presses Universitaires de France.

Leal, F. 1994. Defensa y Seguridad Nacional, 1958–1993. In F. Leal and J. Tokatlián, eds., *Orden Mundial y seguridad. Nuevos desafíos para Colombia y América Latina*. Bogotá: IEPRI-SID-FESCOL.

Levitt, S. 1997. Using electoral cycles in police hiring to estimate the effect of police on crime. *American Economic Review* 87(3): 270–90.

Levitt, S., and S. Venkatesh. 2000. An economic analysis of a drug-selling gangs finances. *Quarterly Journal of Economics*, forthcoming.

Londoño, J. L. 1998. *Epidemiología económica de la Violencia.* Ponencia ante la Asamblea del BID. Cartagena.

Marvell, T., and C. Moody. 1994. Prison population growth and crime reduction. *Journal of Quantitative Criminology* 10: 109–40.

Ministerio de Salud. 1995. Evaluación de la demanda de atención y costos ocasionados por las lesiones de causa externa en un hospital de Bucaramanga, entre el 1 de Enero y el 31 de Diciembre de 1994. Mimeo.

Montenegro, A., and C. E. Posada. 1995. Criminalidad en Colombia. *Coyuntura Económica*, vol. 25(1).

Morrison, A., and M. Pérez. 1994. Elites, guerrillas and narcotraficantes: Violence and internal migration in Colombia. *Canadian Journal of Latin American and Caribbean Studies* 19: 37–38.

Murillo, G., and M. Herrera. 1991. *Violence and Migration in Colombia.* Washington: Center for Immigration Policy and Refugee Assistance, Georgetown University.

Ospina, P. 1996. *Gasto Público y Privado en Seguridad.* Trabajo de Grado no publicado. Bogotá: Universidad Javeriana.

Parra, C. E. 1997. Determinantes de la Inversión en Colombia: Nueva evidencia sobre el Capital Humano y la Violencia. Bogotá: Programa de Economía para Graduados, Universidad de los Andes.

Plazas, A. 1997. Impacto de la violencia sobre la productividad departamental en Colombia. Departamento de Economía. Universidad Javeriana, Bogotá.

Rangel, A. 1999. Las FARC-EP una mirada actual. In M. Deas and M. V. Llorente, eds., *Reconocer la Guerra para Construir la Paz.* Bogotá: Uniandes, CEREC, Norma.

Rocha, R. 1997. Aspectos Económicos de las Drogas Ilegales. In PNUD-DNE, *Drogas ilícitas en Colombia. Su impacto económico, político y social.* Bogotá: Ariel Ciencia Política.

Romero, G. 1997. Demografía de la violencia en Colombia. Mimeo. Universidad de los Andes CCRP, Bogotá.

Rubio, M. 1995. Crimen y Crecimiento en Colombia. *Coyuntura Económica*, vol. 25(1).

Rubio, M. 1996. Inseguridad y Conflicto en las ciudades colombianas. *Documento CEDE*, 96–09. Bogotá: Universidad de los Andes.

Rubio, M. 1997. *Percepciones Ciudadanas sobre la Justicia—Informe final de Investigación.* Bogotá: Ministerio de Justicia, Cijus-Universidad de Los Andes.

Rubio, M. 1999. *Crimen e Impunidad. Precisiones sobre la Violencia.* Bogotá: CEDE-Tercer Mundo.

Rufin, J. C. 1999. *Mondes rebelles: Guerres civiles et violences politiques.* Paris: Editions Michalon.

Salazar, A. 1994. *No Nacimos pa Semilla.* Bogotá: CINEP.

Salazar, A., and A. M. Jaramillo. 1992. *Las Subculturas del Narcotráfico.* Bogotá: CINEP.

Sánchez, F., J. I. Rodríguez, and J. Nuñez. 1996. Evolución y determinantes de la productividad en Colombia: Un análisis global y sectorial. Archivos de Macroeconomía—DNP UAM.

Santos, F. 1997. Legislación anti-secuestro. Qué sirve y que no. *Memorias Seminario Internacional de Violencia, Secuestro y Terrorismo.* Bogotá: Universidad de Los Andes.

Sarmiento, A. 1998. La Violencia y las variables sociales. In DNP, *La Paz: El desafío para el desarrollo.* Bogotá: TM Editores, Departamento Nacional de Planeación.

Soares, R. 2000. Development, crime and punishment: Accounting for the international differences in crime rates. Mimeo. Department of Economics, University of Chicago.

Spelman, W. 1994. *Criminal Incapacitation*. New York: Plenum.

Steiner, R. 1998. Colombia's income from the drug trade. *World Development* 26(6): 1013–31.

Thoumi, F. 1990. Algunas implicaciones del crecimiento de la economía subterránea en Colombia. In J. Tokatlián and B. Bagley, eds., *Economía y Política del Narcotráfico*. Bogotá: Ediciones Uniandes-CEREC, pp. 87–107.

Thoumi, F. 1994. *Economía Política y Narcotráfico*. Bogotá: Tercer Mundo.

Trujillo, I. 1997. Secuestro y Violencia en Colombia. *Memorias Seminario Internacional de Violencia, Secuestro y Terrorismo*. Bogotá: Universidad de Los Andes.

Trujillo, E., and M. Badel. 1998. *Los costos económicos de la criminalidad y la violencia en Colombia: 1991–1996*. Documento 76. Archivos de Macroeconomía. Bogotá: DNP.

# II Economic Institutions

# 6 Decentralization in Colombia

Alberto Alesina, Alberto Carrasquilla, and Juan José Echavarría

## 6.1 Introduction

The allocation of responsibilities between central and local governments and their fiscal relationships are the most important and complex issues of public finance. The general tendency in the last decade all over the world was toward more decentralization. The main motivation is that local governments are supposed to be closer to the people, and therefore to have better information on how to choose policies that fit citizen needs.[1] Whether this process has been a success remains to be seen.

Decentralization, in practice, can take many different forms. A particularly important distinction arises from the degree of correspondence between the revenues raised at each level of government, on the one hand, and their weight in total spending decisions, on the other. While in a centralized system all revenues are raised by the national authorities and all spending decisions are made by the central government, in decentralized countries one has to think of polar cases. At one extreme are systems in which all revenues are collected nationally, they are transferred to the regional governments, and all spending decisions are taken locally. At the opposite extreme are systems where a large fraction of revenues are collected locally and local governments can exercise expenditure decisions, only to the extent that they are able to obtain revenues.

Another important difference concerns whether or not local governments can run deficits and borrow freely in the financial markets. The main potential problem of local borrowing is moral hazard: local governments have frequently been bailed out by the central government, and this possibility can seriously distort incentives. Banks will be willing to finance unreasonable projects, knowing that the central government will eventually step in. Local governments will borrow even at high rates, knowing that the central government will bail them out. A challenging problem is how to avoid this distortion of incentives without curtailing too much flexibility of local budgets and the financing of long-term investment projects.

Critics of decentralization have argued that delegation of fiscal responsibilities to local governments often results in fiscal problems at the local level or, more often, transmitted from the local to the national level.[2] That is, a lack of fiscal discipline at the local level can generate large national deficits and debts even when central governments were running tight finances at the national level. Two important examples of this phenomenon in Latin America are Brazil and Argentina.[3] While it is not a necessary feature of decentralization to create national deficits, if the design of the fiscal relationship between central and local governments is not carefully controlled, decentralization can become a major source of fiscal imbalance.

By the Constitutional reform of 1991, most of Colombian public finances became decentralized, sharply accelerating a decentralization program that was initiated somewhat earlier. In terms of public spending allocated by subnational governments, Colombia in 2001 ranked first after the two federal countries in the region, namely Argentina and Brazil. In Colombia, over 40 percent of total government spending is allocated by subnational governments, against an average of 15 percent in Latin America. The bulk of tax revenues (over 80 percent) is collected at the national level and, along with other minor collected revenues, is transferred to the regional governments in accord with the current set of rules. The local governments receiving these transfers must spend them in rather tightly defined ways. However, local governments are allowed to run deficits and issue debt.

We argue below that these features of decentralization systems fail to impose tight budget constraints at the regional levels, and the regional fiscal imbalances are apt to be transmitted to the central government. In fact the fiscal stability of Colombia was jeopardized soon after the 1991 reform, largely as the result of problems with the decentralization process. Furthermore, given the rigidity about the allocation of government spending at the local level, it is not clear to what extent the fiscal decentralization of 1991 has reached the goal of tailoring spending to local needs and improving efficiency in the delivery of social services. (In chapter 9 Perotti argues that in fact the excessive imbalance of social spending on health and education has interfered with an efficient use of resources to reduce poverty.)

**Table 6.1**
Central government finances in Colombia (GDP ratios)

|      | Revenue | Expenditure | Surplus | Total debt | Interest |
|------|---------|-------------|---------|------------|----------|
| 1990 | 8.9%    | 9.7%        | −0.8%   | 14.9%      | 1.1%     |
| 1991 | 10.4%   | 10.6%       | −0.2%   | 12.9%      | 1.2%     |
| 1992 | 10.8%   | 12.5%       | −1.7%   | 13.6%      | 1.0%     |
| 1993 | 11.6%   | 12.3%       | −0.7%   | 13.4%      | 1.1%     |
| 1994 | 11.4%   | 12.8%       | −1.4%   | 12.0%      | 1.2%     |
| 1995 | 11.3%   | 13.6%       | −2.3%   | 13.2%      | 1.2%     |
| 1996 | 12.0%   | 15.7%       | −3.7%   | 13.9%      | 1.9%     |
| 1997 | 12.6%   | 16.3%       | −3.7%   | 17.5%      | 2.0%     |
| 1998 | 11.9%   | 16.8%       | −4.9%   | 21.6%      | 2.9%     |
| 1999 | 13.4%   | 19.3%       | −5.9%   | 29.6%      | 3.3%     |

Source: Ministry of Finance.

## 6.2 Fiscal Decentralization in Colombia

### 6.2.1 Introduction

In sharp contrast to the historical record until the 1990s, recent fiscal performance in Colombia has been troublesome. For the first time ever, Colombia signed a formal agreement with the IMF, late in 1999, in an attempt to halt erosion of domestic and international confidence, which permeated markets in 1998 and 1999. This deterioration was largely due to fiscal unbalances that originated in local and central government relationships.

While the share of central government expenditure in GDP increased by 9 percentage points, the share revenue increased by only 4. Consequently, in terms of GDP, the stock of debt doubled and interest payments tripled (see table 6.1).

With unchanged legislation, public finances appeared in even worse shape in the long run, given the expected evolution of the social security system and of the projected public intervention in the financial sector.[4] Furthermore the tax code was frequently changed (nine tax law reforms in just the last six years), seriously compromising the stability of the system and thus the incentives to invest.

Many observers agree that a permanent resolution of the increasing fiscal imbalance in Colombia requires a revision of the arrangement between the central government and the local governments. In fact, an increasing share of central government outlays is in the form of transfers to the regional governments (departments and municipalities), as mandated by the 1991 Constitution. In 1999, for instance, transfers to the regions amounted to over 27 percent of total central government expenditures.

### 6.2.2  Current Rules

The 1991 Constitution established the three important guides to decentralization as it currently functions in Colombia:

1. The central government retains its prominence in terms of taxation and is mandated to transfer a significant share of these resources to the regional governments (Article 356). Law 60 (1993) develops this mandate and introduces the specific mechanisms now in operation, as discussed below.
2. The aim of decentralization is to make social expenditures (mostly health and education) more efficient. Specifically, it establishes that health and education expenditures should account for the bulk of the transferred resources. Local governments, however, have little discretion regarding the allocation of the transferred funds. Colombia has the highest conditionality of this type among decentralized countries in Latin America.[5]
3. It establishes a general, albeit very vague, mandate (Article 364) wherein local governments may not "spend beyond their means." Only six years later, through Law 358 (1997), were specific parameters introduced.

*Specific Arrangements: Local Taxes*

Departmental taxes are levied mostly on consumption of liquor, beer, and tobacco. The sum of these three taxes is about 70 percent of the total. Of the remaining 30 percent, 20 is a tax on motor vehicles, and the rest are small taxes. Figure 6.1 displays the compositions of taxes for departments.

As for municipalities, they are concentrated on property, industry, and commerce, basically sale taxes. Figure 6.2 shows the composition of municipal tax revenues.

Local taxes, as mentioned, account for about 19 percent of total taxes in the country. The projections for 2000 are shown in table 6.2. Regional authorities do, in fact, have instruments available that can be used to enhance their current revenues, and there are many examples in which this has occurred since the 1991 Constitution. In Medellín, for example, the ratio of transfers to total current income decreased from 43 percent in

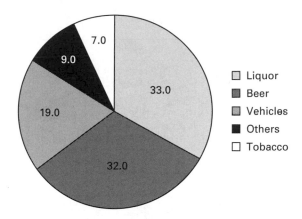

**Figure 6.1**
Participation of taxes, departments, 1997

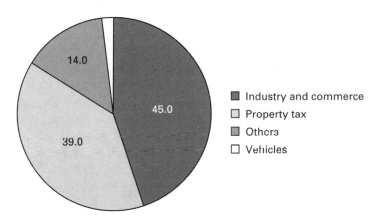

**Figure 6.2**
Participation of taxes, municipalities, 1996

**Table 6.2**
Distribution of taxes: Projected values, 2000

|          | Amount (billion pesos) | Share |
|----------|------------------------|-------|
| Local    | 4,682                  | 19.8% |
| National | 18,933                 | 80.2% |
| Total    | 23,615                 | 100%  |

Source: Ministry of Finance.

**Table 6.3**
Rules as of 2001

|                       | Departments                                                              | Municipalities                                                     |
| --------------------- | ------------------------------------------------------------------------ | ----------------------------------------------------------------- |
| How much is transferred? | 24.5% of current central government revenue                           | 20% of current central government revenue                         |
| With what criteria?   | Formula with 4 components (per-capita expenditure 82%; equal share 15%)   | Formula with 10 components (15% fixed, 31% poor, 15% UBN)          |
| To what purpose?      | 60% education 20% health                                                 | 30% education 25% health 45% other social expenditure             |

Source: Ministry of Finance.

1997 to 22 percent in 1999, reflecting sharp fiscal effort implemented locally, while in Barranquilla it has increased from 43.4 to 48.7 percent in the same period.

### Specific Arrangements: Transfers

The basic workings of decentralization, with respect to the transfer of resources from the central to the regional governments, are contained in Law 60 (1993).[6] There are three types of regional governments: departments (32), special districts (3), and municipalities (1,080). Transfers are defined as a function of the central government's current revenues and allotted according to the nature of each regional government. According to Articles 356 and 357 of the Constitution, and to Law 60, transfers must increase from 26 percent in 1990 to 46 percent in 2002. However, see below for proposed changes to this rule. Transfers are divided into three categories (see table 6.3):

1. Situado Fiscal (SF), which is transferred to the 32 departments and the 3 special districts. The SF has risen from 13.8 percent of current central government revenue in 1990 to 24.5 percent at present.
2. Municipal participation (MP), which has its origin in the transfer of the value-added tax. MP outlays have risen from 12.2 percent of current revenue in 1990 to 21 percent at present and 22 percent in 2001.
3. Transfer of royalties (R), levied by the central government, which are paid by mineral producing companies (oil and coal account for the bulk of resources). According to Law 141 (1994), which implements Articles 360 and 361 in the Constitution, the revenue from royalties is divided as follows: 47.5 percent is transferred to the departments where the minerals

are produced, 12.5 percent to the producing municipalities, 8 percent to municipalities where ports operate, and 32 percent to the National Royalty Fund (FNR). The total amount of royalties distributed in 1999 represents about 7 percent of current revenues.

## How Are the Resources Allocated?

### The Situado Fiscal (SF)

The SF (transfers to departments and special districts) is divided into two parts. The first part (15 percent) is transferred by equal shares to each of the 32 departments and three special districts. The second part (85 percent) is allocated according to the following rules:

1. Each departmental and special district receives a share, which is a function of the "current" targeted population (i.e., the number of students in public education and the number of patients in the health care system). This accounts for 82.8 percent of the total SF resources transferred.
2. Local governments additionally receive resources according to "potential" users of the education and health care systems (i.e., school-age population lacking school and population not in the social security system). These resources account for 2.2 percent of total SF transfers.
3. Local governments receive some resources as a function of their "fiscal effort," roughly defined as their ability to raise revenue locally. This accounts for a tiny 0.02 percent of total SF transfers.

### Municipal Participation (MP)

In the case of the MP transfers to municipalities, the rules are very complex. First, the total amount that is to be transferred (22 percent of total central government revenue in 2002) is divided into two portions. The first portion is called "special allotments" and encompasses about 6.7 percent of the total. These resources are transferred on a special basis to small municipalities (4.2 percent), Indian reserves (1.3 percent), and other minor components. The remaining portion of total transfers are transferred according to the following components:

1. Forty percent of this total is transferred as a function of population living under "unsatisfied basic needs."
2. An additional 20 percent is transferred according to the municipalities' relative standing (vis-à-vis national averages) with respect to poverty.

**Table 6.4**
Composition of transfers, 1995 to 1999 (billion pesos)

|                | MP  | SF  | R   |
| -------------- | --- | --- | --- |
| 1995           | 1.2 | 1.7 | 0.4 |
| 1996           | 1.6 | 2.3 | 0.6 |
| 1997           | 2   | 2.7 | 0.9 |
| 1998           | 2.6 | 3.3 | 1   |
| 1999           | 3   | 3.6 | 1   |
| Average growth | 17% | 21% | 27% |

Source: J. J. Echavarría, C. Rentería, and R. Steiner (2000).

3. Another 22 percent is allocated according to population size.
4. The last 18 percent of this portion of MP transfers (16.5 percent of total) is a complex mix of several components that attempt to introduce efficiency criteria. One-third is allotted according to "fiscal" progress (per capita taxation), one-third to "administrative" progress and one-third to "performance" in generating gains in quality of life.

*The Royalties (R)*
The central government imposes a tax on the production of oil and coal and then transfers the receipts to the regions. Royalties are divided in four parts: (1) 47.5 percent go to the departments that produce the mineral (oil and coal account for well over 95 percent of the total), (2) 12.5 percent to the municipalities that produce it, (3) 8 percent to the municipalities that act as ports, and (4) 32 percent to the National Royalty Fund (FNR). The total amount of royalties represent around 1 percent of GDP.

There is an important qualification, however. In an attempt to make a more equitable distribution of the resources derived from "extraordinary" outputs of oil, these rules apply only up to certain ceilings in production levels. From then on, the share of resources that are transferred diminish substantially. In the case of transfers to the oil-producing departments, transfers are the established 47.5 percent when production does not exceed 180 thousand barrels per day. After that, transfers fall to 10 percent (for production levels that reach 600 thousand) and to 5 percent after that. In the case of transfers to municipalities, on the other hand, transfers fall from 12.5 to 10 percent for production levels in excess of 100 thousand barrels per day. The residual is allotted to the FNR (65 percent) and to nonproducing departments in the same region (in the case of transfers to departments). In the case of municipalities, 60 percent of the residual goes

**Table 6.5**
Allocation of public expenditure decisions

| Public service | Amount | Structure | Execution | Supervision |
|---|---|---|---|---|
| National defense | N | N | N | N |
| Natural resources (oil) | N | N | | N |
| Education | | | | |
| Elementary | N, D, M | N, D | N, D, M | N |
| High School | N, D | N, D | N, D | N |
| Universities | N | N | N | N |
| Health | N, D, M | D, M | N, D, M | N |
| Housing | N, M | N, D, M | M | M |
| Hospitals | N, D, M | N, D, M | N, D | N |
| Water service and sewerage | M | M | M | N |
| Public transportation | M | M | M | M |
| Streets | M | M | M | M |
| Waste disposal and cleaning | M | M | M | N |
| Public lighting | N, M | N | N, M | N |
| Highways | N, D | N, D | N, D | N, D |
| Telecommunications | N, M | N, M | N, M | N |
| Ports | N, M | N, M | N, M | N |

Source: J. J. Echavarría, C. Rentería, and R. Steiner (2000). N: national; D: departmental; M: municipalities.

to the FNR and the rest to nonproducing municipalities in the same department. Table 6.4 shows the current amounts of the three types of transfers.

### How Are the Resources Spent?

Rigid rules establish how localities can spend the transfers received by the central government. In the case of SF, 60 percent of transfers must be spent on education, 20 percent on health and the remaining 20 percent is discretionary. For municipalities, 30 percent of the MP resources must be spent on education, 25 percent in health, 20 percent on water and sewage projects, and the remaining 25 percent on other projects that Law 60 contemplates (see table 6.3).

Finally, in the case of R, the basic issue is the allotment of the resources that are transferred to the (nonmineral producing) regional governments by the FNR. The law is quite "loose" on this front, the important point being given by the idea that these resources should be spent in investment projects. There is no specific rule such as those that govern expenditures of the other types of transfers. Overall, about 80 percent of all transfers are allocated by rules to education and health expenditures.

A related problem concerns the confusing division of labor between levels of government on spending programs. Table 6.5, reproduced from

Echavarría, Rentería, and Steiner (1999), highlights the complex web of responsibilities of different levels of governments. In health and education (where most of the money goes) the three levels of government interact in ways in which are far from clear and transparent. Although the 1991 Constitution implies that health and education spending are to be delegated to localities, the central government retains much responsibility in this area as well.

The confusing allotment of expenditure responsibilities has been highlighted as a substantial problem by several authors.[7] On the one hand, educational and health institutions receive their funding from too many sources, and on the other, there is no clear way to make anyone really accountable for quality. In the case of education, the process is the following:

• The central government transfers resources to the regional governments.
• The departmental government spends the educational portion of this money paying some of the teachers and transferring the rest to the school.
• The municipal government spends this money paying another group of teachers, building infrastructure, and transferring the rest to the schools.
• The school then receives money from two different sources and has little say in the hiring, firing and salaries of its teachers.

In the case of health, matters are even more complex:

• The central government transfers resources to the departments and municipalities.
• The departmental government spends the health component of these resources (tightly defined, as discussed above) in two ways. First, a share goes to the hospitals directly; second, another share goes to institutions that manage demand-based expenditures.
• The municipal government spends the money in the same manner: some goes to hospitals directly, the rest to the EPS (Empresa Promotora de Salud) that manage demand.
• The central government spends additional money on the hospitals.
• Any given hospital, at any particular time, receives funds from two different sources: the regional government and the EPS. The EPS, on the other hand, gets its money from three sources: the central, departmental, and municipal governments.

**Table 6.6**
"Warning" rules

| Variable | Green light | Yellow light | Red light |
|---|---|---|---|
| Interest/operational savings | <40% | 40 < 60% | >60% |
| Stock of debt/current income | <80% | <80% | >80% |

Source: Law 358 of 1997, Ministry of Finance.

Clearly, this system leads to frictions and duplicating functions, low accountability, and waste of resources.

### Debt and Deficits at the Regional Level

Regional governments in Colombia may (and actually have) run large budget deficits. The regional governments ran a deficit of 0.7 percent of GDP in 2000, up from 0.4 percent in 1999, which was equal to 26 percent of total local taxes. This number does not fully reflect the decentralization of the fiscal imbalances, since much of the central government budget deficit was due to the increasing transfers to localities. The stock of debt grew rapidly since 1992, in the context of a more general credit boom, which doubled the size of the banking sector balance sheet (in real terms) between 1992 and 1997 (see table 6.1). A rule, established in 1986, stated that regional governments are creditworthy when debt service does not exceed 30 percent of current income. The constraint was made much softer as the decentralization process proceeded.

Law 358 of 1997 defines the concept of operational savings as the difference between current income and current expenditures, net of interest payments. It then defines three types of circumstances in which a particular regional government may find itself, according to the ratio of interest payments to operational savings (see table 6.6). The first, when the ratio of interest payments over operational savings $(i/OS)$ is less than 40 percent, while at the same time the stock of debt is less than 80 percent of current income. Under these circumstances the regional government is allowed to borrow without any central government intervention or monitoring. This is called *green light* status. The second scenario is when the $i/OS$ ratio lies somewhere between 40 and 60 percent while at the same time the stock of debt is less than 80 percent of current income. Under these circumstances—dubbed *yellow light* status—the regional government can autonomously negotiate debt contracts but must obtain authorization from the Ministry of Finance or from the governor of the department, in the case of municipalities in order to do so. The third and

**Table 6.7**
Interest payments as a fraction of current savings

| Type | 1997 | 1998 | 1999 |
|---|---|---|---|
| Departments | 84.7% | 147% | −50% |
| Municipalities | 49.2% | 45.7% | 56.5% |

Source: Ministry of Finance.

last possibility is that the $i/OS$ ratio is greater than 60 percent, and the stock of debt exceeds 80 percent of current income. Under these conditions the regional government cannot autonomously negotiate debt contracts and must submit an adjustment program to the central government. This circumstance is dubbed *red light* status.

Overall, this system of warning lights is relatively relaxed, since the red light status is reached only when the fiscal situation is in rather critical shape. One may argue that while the stock of existing debt is a good indicator of the state of local public finances, the ratio of interest payments over savings may be too volatile as an indicator. Short-run (perhaps cyclical) fluctuations in the denominator may generate large swings in this indicator. Table 6.7 shows the relationship between interest payments and operational savings between 1997 and 1999.

Decree 2187 of 1997 establishes that in terms of risk weights, banks must value all regional government debt at 100 percent if it is in green light status and at 130 percent if in either yellow or red light status. In 1998, in the midst of financial turbulence affecting many regional entities, the central government took a step back and set the weight at 100 percent for regional governments in yellow or red light status, provided they had a "program" of adjustment spelled out. Furthermore, in the case of loans that are guaranteed by the central government, the 1998 decree stipulates that the guarantee may be written off the relevant weight.

The results are worrisome. As of 1997, out of 27 departments for which data is known at this writing, 18 (67 percent) are in red light status and a further 8 are in yellow light status. A total of 56.2 percent of departmental debt, as of 1998, is in red light status. In the case of municipal debt, 28.7 percent (0.4 percent of GDP) was in this situation.

The central government has bailed out regional governments and, at least, a portion of the regional government debt that is in red light status may well be subject to bail out, furthering the moral hazard problem. Indeed, the central government has a program, with a capital totaling

US$72 million granted by multilateral agencies, known as the PASFFIET (loosely translated, it is the "program for the support of fiscal enhancement and institutional strengthening of regional entities") which was activated in 1993 in the bail out of two departments under severe financial stress. Since then the central government has received a continuous flow of requests for bailouts.

The exposure of the financial system to the territorial entities is one important factor explaining the precarious situation of the financial system. The participation of regional loans (in the total loans of the Colombian financial system) increased from 14.3 percent in 1995 to 20.8 percent in 2001; the increase was equally shared by "other" regional entities (1.8 additional points), the departments (2.4 points) and the municipalities (2.2 points). The quality of regional loans has been deteriorating fast and it is a cause of great concern. Thus, the relation between nonperforming loans and total loans jumped from 11.2 percent in 1998 to 60.6 percent in 2000 for the departments, and from 11 to 50 percent for the municipalities. A regional default could certainly hit the Colombian financial system. Nonperforming loans for the whole country moved from 13.1 percent in 1998 to 16.8 percent in 2000.[8]

### 6.2.3  Efficiency in the Provision of Public Services

A very important point in the discussion of the decentralization process in Colombia is whether the provision of social services (especially in health and education) has improved with decentralization. A thorough examination of the efficiency level in the delivery of health and education would require an entire volume in itself. We cannot even begin to provide a complete treatment of this matter.

Perotti in chapter 9 argues that the almost exclusive concentration of spending in health and education has failed to tackle problems of extreme poverty. Welfare spending for the very poor is chaotic and broken down in myriad of small uncoordinated programs. Spending on education is almost exclusively used to pay salaries (and pensions) for teachers. This is relatively normal, but the regional distribution of teachers and their productivity has been widely questioned (as Borjas and Acosta make clear in chapter 8). In other words, it would seem that due to the limited resources to combat extreme poverty, the marginal benefit of a tax dollar spent on education is not always higher than the benefits of other programs. However, the rigidity of the parameters setting nationwide standards for salaries and pensions of teacher, combined with rules about spending shares of transfers to local governments, make it very difficult to alter the composition of local spending.

### 6.2.4   Recent Developments[9]

The debt situation of the Colombian Territorial Entities (TEs) has improved in the last two or three years, partially because banks simply stopped lending during the crisis of 1998 to 2000 (Arbeláez-Echavarría 2002). But recent measures have also had a favorable impact. Some of them were motivated by the knowledge that a TE default with a private bank would end up being paid by the central government (CG). There have been important cuts in regional expenditures, increases in taxes, debt control measures, and more fiscal responsibility in some of the reforms adopted in 2000 to 2002. In fact, oil and the fiscal adjustment of the TEs has allowed Colombia to reach the fiscal goals agreed with the IMF. As important, Colombia accepted the idea that regions are different, and they should have different relations with the CG during a "transition period."

Zapata and Acosta (2001) present a detailed review of some of the most important recent legislation in the area, and we will only introduce here a brief summary of them:

Law 549 of 1999, creation of FONPET (national fund to cover the liabilities of the TEs) provides additional money from the CG and from the TEs to cover the pension system liabilities at the regional level. Most of the increase in transfers to the regions between 2000 and 2002, 20 percent of national royalties, and the resources from potential future privatizations will go to this Fund.

Law 617 of 2000 creates limits to the current expenditures of the TEs and defines seven different categories of departments and municipalities. The small poor municipalities and departments can spend 80 percent of their current income on operational expenditures (wages, interests, and general expenditures), 50 percent for the large rich TEs. Some public wages (mayor, Assembly, etc.) vary among the seven categories, and there are limits to the size and growth of public wages in the TE.

The Legislative Act 012 of 2001 modified Articles 356 and 357 of the Constitution of 1991 created the *General System of Participations* (*Sistema General de Participaciones*), which subsumes the old *Situado Fiscal* (*SF*), the *Fondo de Compensación Educativa (FEC)*, and the *Municipal Participations* (*MP*). It also delinks regional transfers from CG's current income until year 2008.[10]

Law 715 of 2001 improves the criteria used in Law 60 for regional expenditures in education and health. Thus, for example, transfers are now assigned according to the number of children enrolled at the schools for each TE, instead of the complicated previous rules for SF, or the obscure or nonexistent rules of FEC. It was a politically sensitive issue opposed by FECODE, the powerful teacher's union. It is clearly better to assign money for education based on the number of children covered than by the value of total wages for education in each TE.

The recent measures imply a return to the old principal–agent model, however, where the CG (the principal) designs policies, and local governments (the agent) execute them. Greater fiscal discipline is assured, but efficiency would suffer without accountability and autonomy at the local level. The debate will continue, of course, and in this chapter we argue for a strong movement in the opposite direction: regions should be totally free to choose the type of expenditures required; regional debt should be prohibited.

### 6.2.5  Summary
• Decentralization, a process that was occurring gradually since at least the early 1980s, is accelerated notably by the 1991 Constitution.
• Decentralization is set up within the framework of centralized taxation (80 percent of all tax revenues are national) and then a system of transfers, currently encompassing well over 42 percent of all central government current income.
• Transfers are governed by a tight set of rules that heavily underweight incentive schemes.
• Expenditure of these resources, which currently represent about 5.4 percent of GDP, is governed by a tight set of rules that seek to enhance the quality of social spending (education and health). It is highly questionable whether these rules, and more generally, the process of decentralization has increased efficiency.
• Regional governments have run large deficits and have accumulated substantial amounts of debt. Issues of bailouts are at the forefront of the discussion.

### 6.3  Fiscal Federalism: Issues and Problems

A vast literature has studied the optimal arrangement concerning the fiscal relationships between levels of governments. In what follows in this section, we highlight a few points that are especially relevant for Colombia.

### 6.3.1   Which Level of Governments Should Do What?

Consider a country subdivided into several regions. A few public functions clearly belong to the central government. One is the redistributive function across regions, which can be achieved in a variety of ways. A second one is national defense and the provision of law and order, where economies of scale are critical. A third one is the implementation of projects for which separate regions acting alone cannot internalize externalities. Beyond these important tasks everything else could, in principle, be delegated to subnational levels of governments, or "regions." The regions themselves can also choose to delegate various functions to subregional levels of governments, say, municipalities. The motivation for this system of delegation is that the smaller the size of a jurisdiction, the more tailored to individual preference policies can be, at least in principle.

There are, however, limits to how small a jurisdiction can be because of economies of scale in the production of public goods. For instance, a streetlight serves only a small area of a street. So it would be costly and inefficient to provide streetlights in communities with only a few houses. Thus, in reality, economies of scale and administrative costs dictate how small a jurisdiction can be. In a middle-income country with large regional inequalities, like Colombia, local governments (especially those in poor regions) often lack the technical competence to efficiently carry out complicated public works. Corruption at the local level is more widespread than at the national level. Also an imprecise definition of goals and functions has led to multiple agencies doing the same work, adding waste and confusion.

### 6.3.2   Who Should Tax?

Two very different arrangements are feasible and occur in practice. In the first, revenues are collected nationally, distributed through some formula to the regions, and the regions administer the spending. The other arrangement is one in which taxes are collected locally and regions can tax and spend as much as they want. In reality, most arrangements are in between these two extremes.

The first system has the disadvantage that if appropriate rules are not set, the localities do not internalize the fiscal costs of their spending programs, since revenues are raised nationally. This point has been widely discussed in the academic literature, with specific reference to the organization of legislatures.[11] The idea is that locally elected politicians can channel spending toward a geographically specific area, while in the case of taxes that are collected nationally, there is a tendency to overspend. The reason is that a politician with a geographically defined constituency does not fully internalize the costs of a project that benefits only his constituency because taxes are levied nationally. This is an example of the idea of "concentrated benefits/diffuse costs" that leads to suboptimal policy choices. A similar argument applies to regions, if the latter can spend, but do not collect taxes, and it is especially critical (as we discuss below) if localities can run budget deficits. As we described in section 6.2, the Colombian case is very close to this extreme since almost all revenues are collected nationally.

While the first system has the disadvantage of creating skewed incentives toward spending and deficit, the second system has shortcomings too. In particular, it does not allow for explicit cross-regional redistribution. In addition national governments may have a comparative advantage in tax collection and tax administration, particularly in developing countries where poor regions may have very inefficient local administrative units.

### 6.3.3 Simple Rules
In order for the system of vertical transfers to function efficiently, all its underlying rules must be simple and transparent. Rules mandating transfers on the basis of variables that are difficult to measure and/or vary substantially from year to year, are prone to generate arbitrary decisions, distort incentives for regional authorities, and reduce the reliability and fairness of the system. This is even truer for rules based on contingencies that are difficult to verify.

Complicated rules that attempt to use decentralization in order to achieve a multitude of goals are not effective. They are difficult to enforce because they are based on the measurement of too many variables, and therefore often lead to disagreements over implementation. For instance, Colombia's complex set of rules has led to wide ranging differences in per-capita public expenditure in health and education: per-capita expenditure in education in Bolívar, for example, is less than half of that observed in Cundinamarca and about one-fourth of that observed in San Andrés.

### 6.3.4 Should Local Governments Be Allowed to Run Deficits?
Ayala and Perotti (in chapter 7) consider the pros and cons of balanced budget rules for national governments. The arguments against a balanced budget include the necessity of using deficit and surpluses as a "buffer

stock." Therefore, imposing a balanced budget rule at the national level would interfere with the implementation of an intertemporally optimal fiscal policy. On the other hand, a vast literature has emphasized how political incentive may lead politicians toward running excessive deficits.[12] A balanced budget rule, if enforced, may reduce this problem. Thus one would have to trade off the costs of lack of flexibility of fiscal policy with the benefits of lower political distortions.

An argument against balanced budget rules is that they may create incentives to engage in creative accounting practices to circumvent them. In many cases, including Colombia, lack of transparency of the budget is the main problem of fiscal institutions and procedures.[13] If one considers municipalities, additional arguments weigh in favor of balanced budget rules. Localities know that they will be bailed out by the center and that, somehow, the costs of excessive deficits will be spread out over the entire country.

The bottom line is that many of the arguments suggesting that a balanced budget law may not be a good idea for national government, do not apply in the case of local governments. On the contrary, localities have specific incentives (that national governments do not have) to run excessive deficits. For these reasons one should look favorably to laws that prohibit or severely limit the ability of local governments to borrow.

The evidence drawn on countries, which have these types of laws is comforting. Particularly interesting is the US case, where different states have different regulations and laws about whether or not they can run deficits. That is, some states have a stringent balanced budget law, some have a loose law, and others have none. A vast literature has shown that states with stringent balanced budget laws have had a superior fiscal performance in terms of stable finances and no deficits.[14]

## 6.4  Proposals

Our discussion is divided into four issues:

• The amount of resources that ought to be transferred and the rules used to assign a transfer to each regional government.
• The rules that should govern how the transfers are spent by the regional governments.
• The manner in which debt and deficits at the regional level should be regulated.

• The issue of accountability for regional government, in particular, the possibility of reelection of mayors.

### 6.4.1  How Much Should Be Allocated?

The discussion of how far to push decentralization in Colombia is very important. Some commentators argue that decentralization has gone too far, has caused fiscal imbalances, and has delegated complex tasks to localities that do not have the technical expertise to implement them.

A recent government proposal reflects this preoccupation and implies a moderate reduction over time of the share of transfers to localities. In fact, this proposal calls for an increase of 1.5 percent per year in real terms of these transfers, so if real GDP growth is higher than 1.5 percent, the share of transfers over GDP will decline. Especially if growth is high, this change of policy may lead in the medium/long run to a sizable reduction, as a share of GDP, of the amount transferred to localities. This shift in policy is the result of a preoccupation that decentralization has gone too far, and that regional governments are transmitting fiscal stress to the center. The real problem, in our view, is not "how much" it is transferred to localities (e.g., 30 percent of tax revenues rather than 40), but "how" these transfers occur and to what incentives they are associated. That is, more than the *size* of the transfers, we feel that the *way* in which fiscal responsibilities are allocated is the source of the problem. Thus, more than on the size of the programs, we focus on the way they are allocated and spent.

### 6.4.2  How Should Resources Be Allocated?

A good allocation rule should have three goals: (1) must be simple, (2) allow some redistribution from rich to poor regions, and (3) create incentives for efficient local tax collection.

Often these goals may conflict with each other. For instance, a possible system is to link transfers to the performance of localities in terms of their output (i.e., the quality of local public goods). This idea has excellent incentive properties. However, it may be very complicated to implement, even in an OECD country, and even more in a middle income country. How can one verify, say, the quality of education provided in different municipalities? Or the purity of water? Or the health services provided? Difficulties in implementation of output-based rules seem prohibitive. In fact, with the possible exceptions of New Zealand and the United Kingdom, this type of system is almost nonexistent even in OECD countries.

In principle, to try to extend the use of these schemes to today's Colombia is rather unrealistic. So we won't devote a lot of intellectual energy to coming up with the perfect scheme and try to be realistic. For instance, a system of matching grants may be feasible.

A similar point applies to criteria for redistribution. Ideally an interregional redistributive system should take into account a complex set of indicators that identify relative poverty, relative income, and relative use of public services of targeted populations. However, excessively complicated rules can increase abuse of the system, corruption, and lack of transparency.

### Basic Principles

Currently the rules that allocate funds to department and municipalities are different. It is not obvious why that should be the case. We think that uniformity of allocation rules, compiled with flexibility on the spending side may increase transparency and make localities more responsive to local needs.

The rules for allocation of transfers to localities are, overall, quite complex and not transparent, particularly, in the case of MP and R. These rules seem to be trying to achieve a multitude of goals, creating confusion and leading to undesirable outcomes, such as an unjustifiably large regional dispersion of per-capita expenditures. Our proposal would lead to a drastic simplification of the allocation rules. The rules should be based on three simple components:

1. A fixed percentage of the region's contribution to total national government current revenue.
2. A redistributive component, flowing from rich to poor regions, whether relative richness and poverty are measured by income per capita.
3. An efficiency component linking the regional government's taxation effort to transfers.

In our proposal all additional elements currently contemplated, and discussed in section 6.2, are discarded, as is the distinction between MP and P.

Our proposal can be sketched as follows: Define $T$ the total amount transferred to all regions. Currently this amount is equal to 46 percent of current revenue and the governmental proposal would define it as a given real increase over the previous year. Each regional government $(j)$ received transfers equal to $R(j)$ that are a fraction of total transfers:

$R(j) = A(j)T.$

The proposal is that $A(j)$ is the sum of three factors:

1. A fixed percentage of the region's contribution to total national government current revenue $b(j)$.
2. A *redistributive* component.
3. An *efficiency* component linking the regional government's taxation effort $t$ to transfers $d(j)$.

The share that regional government $j$ receives out of the total transfers is thus:

$$A(j) = b(j) + c(j) + d(j).$$

*Fixed Percentage, $b(j)$*

The first part of our proposal consists of establishing the fraction of fiscal revenues collected in each department or municipality. This evaluation delivers the baseline for allocation of fiscal transfer to each department and municipality. In other words, if a region contributes $b$ percent to the total tax revenues, the baseline should be that it receives $b$ percent of the total transfers.

The motivation of this fraction is simple. Suppose that each locality were identical. Then each locality should get back from the government an equal amount, proportional to the (identical) revenues raised in each locality. Obviously, if this were the only component, then each locality might as well collect and use its own revenues. However, this does not quite follow, if the central government has a comparative advantage at raising revenues.

Taxes make up almost 85 percent of government current revenues. There are two ways of calculating the contribution of each region to the national tax pool. One is to look at national data and establish how much of the income taxes and value-added taxes (the overwhelming majority of all tax revenues) are collected in each region. These computations are far from trivial. Consider an exporter operating in a coastal region whose main office is in Bogotá. In which region should his tax revenues be accounted for?

The second approach starts from information about local tax collections. The share of local-level taxes collected in any particular region within total local-level taxes collected is a good proxy for its share in total national-level taxes collected. For instance, suppose that all local taxes collected in the country amount to $100. Then one proxy for each region's contribution to national taxes would be the share of the $100 that is collected by each specific regional government. This would be a mistake because regions differ in the amount of effort that they exercise in collecting taxes. The correction that we introduce is to estimate what the "normal" effort is in each region. To do it, we regress local taxes to local population and assume that "normal" effort is given by the regression line. Explicit calculations are shown in the appendix.

One serious criticism would arise if local taxes reflected the composition of output. Differences in the ratio of each region's local tax to the national total would then be linked not to effort but rather to output composition. Regions where low-tax activities are dominant would exhibit lower ratios. However, since local taxes are essentially property taxes and consumption taxes, we feel that the procedure does not produce results that have this damaging bias. It is true that this system would "punish" regions that are intensive in the production of activities that have low tax rates (e.g., agriculture) and "privilege" the regions intensive in highly taxed activities (e.g., oil). This is the reason why we include the two other criteria, in particular, the redistributive one.

A third and even simpler criterion would be to set $b(j)$ equal to the fraction of the region $j$'s share of total national GDP. Again, the problem is the data: municipal level GDP is not calculated and must be estimated in order to make the scheme operational.

*Redistributive Component, $c(j)$*

Having obtained the fixed proportion allocation, implicitly assigning transfers as a function of the contribution of each region to the national totals, the second task is to redistribute from rich to poor regions.

Our proposal is to define a zero-sum reallocation of resources wherein resources are "taken" from departments in which income per capita is above the median and "given" to regions where income per capita is below the median. A similar system can be applied to municipalities, although the computation for this level of government may be more problematic. The size of this redistribution is a political decision. The point we want to make is that this zero-sum system of redistribution should be transparent.

*Departments*

GDP data for the department is available only until 1995. This is not a big problem, since there is little reason for one to expect sub-

**Table 6.8**
Ratio transfers/local taxes

| Type | 1997 | 1998 | 1999 |
| --- | --- | --- | --- |
| Departments | 51.4% | 58.7% | 62.6% |
| Municipalities | 30% | 27.7% | 24.5% |

Source: Authors' calculations.

stantial change in five years. However, statistical agencies should increase their effort to produce and disseminate more up to date local information.

Table 6.9 shows our calculations. The first column shows the departments. The second and third columns show, respectively, the percentage deviation of the departments' per-capita GDP with respect to the national median for rich and poor regions. Bogotá, for instance, has per-capita income 96 percent higher than the median, while Sucre has per-capita income 58 percent lower than the median. The forth and fifth columns present the following calculation: out of the total deviation from median, how much is explained by the deviation in this particular department? In the case of the rich departments, for instance, the total deviation from median sums 14.2, of which 20 percent are explained by the deviation observed by Amazonas. In the case of poor departments, the sum is 5, of which 33 percent are explained by Cauca, for instance. These calculations, however, do not take into account the size of different departments. The fifth and sixth columns show the percentage of total rich and poor regions GDP, explained by each department. Rich department's output adds up to about 75 percent of total GDP and column 5 shows what percentage of this subtotal is explained by each rich department.

The last two columns are derived in the following manner: In the case of rich regions, we weigh relative richness by size. In practical terms, we multiply column 4 by column 6. In the case of poor regions, we also weigh relative poverty by size, multiplying column 5 by column 7. This gives us a number that levies a larger surcharge for relatively richer regions but also takes into account the fact that there are size differences among regions.

Our proposal is the following: We start from the numbers that we calculated in the previous subsection. Departments are divided into two groups, poor and rich, according to the previous table:

• We add up the total "fixed proportion" $(b(j))$ transfers in the case of the rich regions. This gives us the base upon which we then estimate

**Table 6.9**
Redistribution of transfers: Departments

| Department | Deviation (%) per capita GDP (high) | Deviation (%) per capita GDP (low) | levyplus | levymin | %plusgdp | %mingdp | adjustedp | adjmin |
|---|---|---|---|---|---|---|---|---|
| Amazonas | 2.89 | — | 0.20 | — | 0.45% | | 1.74% | |
| Antioquia | 0.38 | — | 0.03 | — | 19.09% | | 9.76% | |
| Arauca | 0.61 | — | 0.04 | — | 0.48% | | 0.39% | |
| Atlantico | | (0.18) | — | 0.04 | | 14.70% | | 12.73% |
| Bogotá | 0.96 | | 0.07 | | 32.42% | | 41.93% | |
| Bolivar R. | | (0.12) | — | 0.02 | | 12.79% | | 7.17% |
| Boyaca | | (0.09) | — | 0.02 | | 11.36% | | 4.94% |
| Caldas | 0.15 | | 0.01 | — | 3.33% | | 0.68% | |
| Casanare | 4.38 | | 0.31 | — | 3.04% | | 17.92% | |
| Cauca | | (0.33) | — | 0.06 | | 6.38% | | 10.01% |
| Cesar | | (0.27) | — | 0.05 | | 4.63% | | 5.96% |
| Choco | | (0.58) | — | 0.12 | | 1.35% | | 3.79% |
| Cordoba | | (0.46) | — | 0.09 | | 5.94% | | 13.13% |
| Cundinamar Ca | 0.51 | | 0.04 | — | 8.29% | | 5.71% | |
| Guainia | | (0.63) | — | 0.13 | | 0.04% | | 0.13% |
| Huila | | (0.02) | — | 0.00 | | 7.87% | | 0.69% |
| La Guajira | 0.39 | | 0.03 | — | 1.53% | | 0.80% | |
| Magdalena R. | | (0.33) | — | 0.07 | 0.00% | 6.62% | | 10.54% |
| Meta | 0.62 | | 0.04 | — | 2.61% | | 2.16% | |
| Nariño | | (0.46) | — | 0.09 | | 6.04% | | 13.32% |
| Nte Santander | | (0.26) | — | 0.05 | | 6.56% | | 8.19% |
| Putumayo | | (0.39) | — | 0.08 | | 1.04% | | 1.96% |
| Quindio | 0.59 | | 0.04 | — | 2.14% | | 1.71% | |
| Risaralda | 0.12 | | 0.01 | — | 2.75% | | 0.46% | |
| San Andres | 1.56 | | 0.11 | — | 0.03% | | 0.00% | |

| | | | | | | | | |
|---|---|---|---|---|---|---|---|---|
| Santander | 0.12 | — | 0.01 | — | 5.65% | 2.56% | 0.92% | 7.22% |
| Sucre | — | (0.58) | — | 0.12 | | 11.98% | | |
| Tolima | — | — | 0.05 | — | 18.16% | | 15.82% | |
| Valle | 0.65 | (0.34) | — | 0.07 | | 0.14% | | 0.24% |
| Vaupes | — | — | 0.02 | — | 0.04% | | 0.00% | |
| Vichada | 0.23 | — | — | — | | | | |
| | 14.18 | (5.03) | 1.00 | 1.00 | 1.00 | 1.00 | 1.00 | 1.00 |

Source: Authors' calculations.

the total amount of resources that will be redistributed to the poor regions.

• We assign a percentage of total rich region's $a(j)$ transfers, say, 10 percent, to redistribution. This is made up of the sum of all positive deviations from the median. This gives us specific amount of money that will be redistributed. Each rich region contributes to the total fund as a proportion of their transfers. The figures produced in the table correspond to the case where redistributions amount to 10 percent of total transfers to the rich regions.

• We then impute a "levy" on each rich region's fixed proportion transfers according to the calculation above. Rich region $x$ will contribute to the fund that will be redistributed according to its contribution to the sum of all positive deviations from the median. For example, Antioquia would contribute 9.76 percent of the total fund.

• We similarly assign these resources to the poor regions according to their standing, shown in column 6. For instance, Atlántico would get 12.7 percent of the total fund. An interesting and valuable feature of this system is that it makes transparent the amount of redistributions. Changes in how redistributive the system is would be summarized in one parameter, $b$.

*Efficiency Component, $d(j)$*
Transferring a certain percentage of total funds in proportion to the regions own efforts has several desirable features, most prominently:

• It punishes regions that fall behind tax efforts and encourages regions that make advances in this respect.
• It is an incentive for the population to monitor performance and punish bad administrators.

The problem is this: the ratio of transfers to local taxes has been increasing in the departments and falling in the municipalities. While all regional governments have access to the same taxes, this reveals an incentive problem that is not given much weight in the current setting.[15] One could create a fund that allocates a certain amount of transfers in proportion to the fiscal effort of different departments and municipalities:

• Define a desired degree of incentives, as a percentage of $T$. Suppose that this amount is 10 percent of $T$.

• This sum would be collected lump sum, meaning every region would contribute 10 percent of its estimated transfers (after adjusting for redistribution) and a fund would be formed.

• The fund would distribute resources in zero-sum manner. The median "effort," measured as a deviation from the regression that we used above, divides the sample into two groups, and transfers would occur from the fiscally "lazy" to the fiscally "active" regions.

The appendix shows estimates of local effort along with our estimates of "normal" effort. The proposal is to use this data to calculate a zero-sum incentive scheme that rewards regions that are fiscally active and punish regions that are fiscally lazy. For example, each region would contribute 10 percent of its total transfers into the fund and then draw from the fund according to its relative standing in the effort scale. A very active region (the effort measure is positive) could draw more than the 10 percent it contributes, and a very lazy region would be "taxed" and so could conceivably end up not drawing anything from the fund.

### 6.4.3 How Should Expenditure Be Regulated?

The current system tightly regulates how localities can spend the transfer that they receive. Leaving a larger margin of discretion in local allocations may create a better matching of spending to local needs. More discretion may generate more arbitrariness and corruption in the allocation of spending, even in the current system. A larger margin of discretion may allow local politicians the incentive to deliver "good policies," particularly where they are accountable to the voters. An important related point concerns the definition of "poverty" and "needs." We have summarized in one indicator, income per capita, our measure of poverty. Different departments and municipalities will face different needs, depending on characteristics of the populations, geography, economic structure, and so on. Rather than trying to allocate transfers based on these features and then channel spending with rules, we suggest to permit each locality to decide how to spend. Thus simplification of transfer rules go hand in hand with more flexibility of spending. To see this, take two "poor" departments. In one, low enrollment rates and poor quality of education are the problem. In the other, extreme rural poverty is the more pressing issue. The latter may prefer to spend less in education than current rules permit. In contrast, currently localities are bound to spend a very large fraction of their revenues on health and education, and there is evidence that this system is not efficient (Perotti, chapter 9, this volume).

A related problem concerns the allocation of responsibilities on the spending side between central and local governments. As we have mentioned, all levels of governments participate in social expenditure, duplicating functions and making the system nontransparent. There are two polar possibilities that may resolve the problem. Take the case of education. The first possibility is to bypass regional governments altogether and allocate the funds directly at the schools (some 60,000 all over the country). The problem is that monitoring is crucial and not very easy in such a centralized system.

The second possibility is to have the regional governments implement a decentralization of their own by allowing them to design rules that allocate funds to the schools. The amount of transfers that they receive would be based on the rules outlined above, but the decisions as to how to allocate them among different expenditure programs would be their own.

The important thing is that one and only one level of government should be involved in each function, paying teachers, for instance. For this example we should emphasize that to the extent that teachers' salaries are fixed nationally and make up 80 percent of total spending in education, there is little leeway for departments, municipalities, and schools to tailor spending to local needs. (Chapter 9 develops the issue of public employment in more detail.)

### 6.4.4  Should Borrowing Be Allowed?

On balance, the risk of allowing localities to borrow from the markets, and in particular, from banks, outweigh its benefits. Localities should be allowed to run deficits only by borrowing against future transfers from the central government. So, if in one year a locality needs to spend more, it can "borrow" from the central government. The latter will curtail future transfers in the appropriate amount. Obviously localities are free to accumulate surpluses. Localities should not be permitted to borrow from banks or to issue bonds.

*If we had to pick among our proposals the one that we think is the most important, it is control* of excessive borrowing by local governments from private and public banks. The problem is so critical not only in Colombia but in many other Latin American countries that it is worth encouraging the central government to spend political capital to achieve this goal.

For the financing of large investment projects in infrastructures, theoretically, one could think of allowing local governments to borrow from the markets for investment projects. In practice, this is a dangerous idea. First, for the same reasons discussed above, localities may have an incentive to overborrow and overspend in local infrastructures. Second, it is well known that what is defined as "investment" in public budgets is open to strategic manipulations.

Ayala and Perotti (in chapter 7) shows how a disproportionate amount of spending items that should be classified as current are labeled investments. If this strategic mislabeling occurs at the central level, where budget are occasionally scrutinized by international organizations, it is even more likely to occur at the local level. This alone is a good reason why large public investment projects should be decided and implemented by the central government.

### 6.4.5 Should Local Governments Be Reelected?

Two striking features of local politics in Colombia are (1) that mayors and governors cannot be reelected and (2) that they have a very short tenure (three years). The motivation of this rule has to do with avoiding the entrenchment of special interests and corruption of individuals.

An active debate in the US concerns the pros and cons of term limit for governors, precisely on these grounds. While term limits avoid the entrenchment of incumbents, they imply a short-termism attitude of politicians by which they can effectively eschew accountability with respect to the voters. In general, Latin American countries have adopted very stringent and short-term limits for both nationally and locally elected officials. The one-term limit of mayors and governors in Colombia is particularly striking as it is coupled with a short electoral cycle. Within a very short three year horizon, with no possibility of reelection, mayors and governors tend to focus on short-term problems, and not to address reforms and advances that may pertain to the production of results. Lengthening the term of office to four or five years and allowing at least one possibility of reappointment seems reasonable and more in line with international standards.

### 6.5 Conclusions

The decentralization process of the last decade in Colombia is at the center of the political debate for several reasons. Politically it is the battlefield for national versus local interests and political entrepreneurs. As for the efficiency in the delivery of social services, questions have been raised about how successful this process has been. From a macroeconomic point of view, the decentralization process has been a major source of fiscal imbalances.

We have used economic theory and political economy to examine some of the decentralization issues for Colombia and made several concrete proposals. The topic of fiscal federalism is an immense one, and we could not explore every aspect of it. For instance, we did not address the structure of taxation, namely whether reforms in the tax structure may make it more feasible to increase the share of local spending that is covered by local revenues.

We focused on four issues: vertical transfers, allocations of responsibilities in expenditure, issues of local debt and deficits, and accountability

**Table 6.10**
Contributions to national taxes

| Department | Actual | Fitted | Effort |
|---|---|---|---|
| 1 | 20.26 | 20.76 | −0.50 |
| 2 | 25.52 | 24.93 | 0.59 |
| 3 | 21.34 | 21.59 | −0.24 |
| 4 | 24.35 | 24.16 | 0.19 |
| 5 | 26.92 | 25.08 | 1.84 |
| 6 | 23.89 | 23.98 | −0.09 |
| 7 | 24.03 | 23.85 | 0.18 |
| 8 | 23.63 | 23.56 | 0.07 |
| 10 | 22.31 | 22.15 | 0.17 |
| 11 | 23.03 | 23.61 | −0.57 |
| 12 | 22.81 | 23.26 | −0.44 |
| 13 | 23.43 | 23.73 | −0.30 |
| 14 | 25.49 | 24.12 | 1.37 |
| 15 | 22.04 | 22.67 | −0.63 |
| 16 | 19.08 | 19.81 | −0.73 |
| 18 | 23.45 | 23.46 | −0.01 |
| 19 | 21.36 | 22.73 | −1.37 |
| 20 | 23.26 | 23.64 | −0.38 |
| 21 | 23.37 | 23.06 | 0.31 |
| 22 | 23.27 | 23.75 | −0.48 |
| 23 | 22.64 | 23.55 | −0.91 |
| 24 | 21.62 | 22.12 | −0.50 |
| 25 | 22.75 | 22.90 | −0.15 |
| 26 | 23.51 | 23.42 | 0.09 |
| 27 | 22.63 | 18.84 | 3.79 |
| 28 | 24.26 | 24.05 | 0.21 |
| 29 | 22.68 | 23.23 | −0.55 |
| 30 | 23.76 | 23.81 | −0.05 |
| 31 | 25.52 | 24.73 | 0.79 |
| 32 | 18.79 | 20.33 | −1.54 |
| 33 | 19.48 | 19.62 | −0.14 |
| Totals | 710.49 | 710.49 | 0.00 |

of regional authorities. The current system in Colombia is weak in all four fronts, and we have attempted to show ways to improve it.

## Appendix: Calculation of the "Fixed Proportion" of Fiscal Transfers

The first component of transfers from the central government to the regional government $x$ would be linked to region $x$'s contribution to total national taxes, $T$. If the regions contributed equally, they would all get the same transfers.

One way to estimate each region's contribution to national taxes is to use the data on regionally collected taxes. Roughly all regional taxes add up to about 2.8 percent of GDP, and this figure is derived chiefly from consumption and property taxes. Region $x$'s "share" of this 2.8 percent of GDP is our proxy for region $x$'s contribution to national taxes.

We know the regional distribution of these resources. However, region $x$'s share of the 2.8 percent of GDP includes "effort." To filter this out, we estimate the following regression:

$$x = a + b\text{POP} + e,$$

where POP is the region's population. The observed value is made up of two parts: the regression line and the residual. We take the fitted value as the "normal effort" and the residual as the "own effort" estimation. The sum of "own effort" should be equal to zero. Table 6.10 shows the results for departments. Results for municipalities are available upon request.

## Notes

This chapter was written before the Constitutional Reform of December 2001 introduced changes to the decentralization regime in Colombia, so we do not discuss the resulting framework. Nevertheless, we want to note that many changes are in the direction that we propose here. We thank George Borjas, Roberto Perotti, Howard Rosenthal, and several other members of the group meeting in Cartagena, participants in seminars at the National Planning Department (DNP), Universidad de los Andes and *Banca 2000* in Bogotá, for very useful comments. Maria Mercedes Carrasquilla provided extremely helpful organizational support.

1. The economic literature on this point is on the so-called fiscal federalism. For a recent survey, see Bates (1999); for a broad discussion of policy issues, see Ter Minassian (1999).

2. See Tanzi (1996) for some critical views about federalism and Ter Minassian (1999) for a broad overview.

3. For an interesting discussion of public finances in Latin America with a focus on the relationship between central and local governments, see Gavin and Perotti (1997). For an insightful discussion of Argentina, see Jones, Sanguinetti, and Tommasi (2000).

4. The pension system is currently very distorted; it is very generous for a small fraction of the labor force, especially public employees. Among the latter, teachers receive an extremely generous treatment, relative to others. At the time of this writing the government is preparing a reform proposal for the pension system.

5. IADB (1997).

6. Law 60 of 1993 summarizes the state of the art in regard to transfers and consolidates all previous legislation. Previous legislation is made up of two pieces, each dealing with one sub national government (departments and municipalities). These are Law 46, 1971, which introduced the *Situado Fiscal*, or transfers to the departments, and Law 12 of 1986 that regulated the *participation* of municipalities in the value-added tax.

7. For example, Castañeda. T. (2000), Garay (1995), and Wiesner (1997).

8. Echavarría, Rentería, and Steiner (2002).

9. Taken from Echavarría, Rentería, and Steiner (2002).

10. But real transfers should grow 2.5 percent per year between 2002 and 2004, and 2.0 percent between 2004 and 2008.

11. See Weingast, Shepsle, and Johnsen (1981) for an early contribution, Alesina and Perotti (1999) for a survey, and Milesi-Ferreti, Rostagno, and Perotti (2000) for recent empirical evidence.

12. See Alesina and Perotti (1995) for a survey.

13. This point is convincingly made by the chapter on fiscal institutions, Ayala and Perotti (2000).

14. See, for instance, Poterba (1994), Alt and Lowry (1994), and Alesina and Perotti (1999) for a survey.

15. Wiesner, E (1995) emphasizes this problem and calls for the introduction of more incentives.

# References

Alesina, A., and R. Perotti. 1999. Budget deficit and budget institutions. In J. Von Haggen and J. Poterba, eds., *Fiscal Institutions and Fiscal Performance*. Chicago: University of Chicago Press.

Alesina, A., and R. Perotti. 1995. The political economy of budget deficits. IMF Staff Papers.

Alt, J., and R. Lowry. 1995. Divided government, fiscal institutions and budget deficits: Evidence from the states. *American Political Science Review* 88: 811–28.

Arbeláez, M. A., and J. J. Echavarría. 2002. Crédito, liberalización financiera e inversión en Colombia. *Coyuntura Económica* 32(4): 102–41.

Bates, W. 1999. An essay on fiscal federalism. *Journal of Economic Literature* (September): 1120–49.

Castañeda, T. 2000. Problemas estructurales de la descentralización en Colombia. *Economía Colombiana* 277(February): 89–99.

Departamento Nacional de Planeación (DNP). *Boletín Sobre Descentralización* (various issues).

Echavarría, J. J., C. Rentería, and R. Steiner. 2002. Decentralization and bailouts in Colombia. Mimeo.

Garay, L. J. 1995. *Descentralización, Bonanza Petrolera y Estabilización: La Economía colombiana en los años 90*. Bogotá, CEREC, Fescol.

Gavin, M., and R. Perotti. 1999. Fiscal policy in Latin America. *NBER Macroeconomic Annual*. Cambridge: MIT Press.

Inter-American Development Bank. 1997. *Economic and Social Progress in Latin America.* Report. Washington, DC.

Inter-American Development Bank. 1994. *Economic and Social Progress in Latin America.* Special Topic: Fiscal Decentralization. Washington, DC.

Milesi-Ferreti, G. R. Perotti, and M. Rostagno. 2000. Political institutions and fiscal policy. Unpublished.

Poterba, J. 1994. State responses to fiscal crises: A natural experiment. *Journal of Political Economy* 102: 799–821.

Ter Minassian, T. 1999. *Fiscal Federalism.* Washington, DC: International Monetary Fund.

Tanzi, V. 1996. Fiscal federalism and decentralization: A review of some efficiency and macroeconomic aspects. In *Proceedings of the Annual World Bank Conference on Development Economics, 1995.* Washington, DC.

Wiesner, E. 1995. *La Descentralización, el Gasto Social y la Gobernabilidad en Colombia.* Bogotá: Departamento Nacional de Planeación, Asociación Nacional de Instituciones Financieras.

Zapata, J. G., O. L. Acosta, and A. Gonzáles. 2001. Evaluación de la Descentralización Municipal en Colombia. Se consolidó la sostenibilidad fiscal de los municipios colombianos durante los años noventa? *Archivos de Economía.* Departamento Nacional de Planeación, Bogotá.

# 7 The Colombian Budgetary Process

**Ulpiano Ayala and Roberto Perotti**

Ulpiano Ayala passed away in July 2002. Roberto Perotti will always remember fondly a great and impassioned economist and a very warm and friendly person. For helpful conversations and clarifications we thank, without implicating, Sonia Cancino, Fabio Fajardo, María Alejandra Ojeda, Paola Nieto, and Viviana Pérez, all division chiefs at the Public Investment Unit of DNP; Ezequiel Lenis (director) and Diego Jaramillo at the Directorate of the Budget; Olga Lucía Acosta at Fedesarrollo; and all participants at the Cartagena meeting.

## 7.1 Introduction

In recent years the rules that govern the budgetary process have started to be viewed as important determinants of fiscal policy and its potentially important macroeconomic implications. As a consequence improvements in the budgetary process are widely considered to be a preliminary step in maintaining (or regaining) responsible fiscal policy.

A well-structured budgetary process can fulfill an important role in the setting of fiscal policy. We believe that it is important for government to be clear and realistic at the outset about their fiscal responsibility in maintaining the budget. In our view, there is little defense, procedural or otherwise, against a government that is determined to run "bad" budget without opposition from Congress. There are simply no rules that can protect a country in these circumstances. In particular, we believe the rules governing the formation and the dissemination of information on fiscal policy should achieve at least three goals:

• Provide transparency in fiscal policy.
• Adjust fiscal policy in the presence of shocks of moderate to large dimensions.

• Prepare the fiscal policy package in language that allows a person with a moderate knowledge of economics and accounting to understand its main thrust.

This last condition is the most important one. Only the "market" can exert pressure on that government; otherwise, there is no enforcement mechanism to prevent a government from running a "bad" fiscal policy. The market should be able to form an independent idea of the fiscal objective of the government. In the current Colombian situation, this does not seem likely: the average journalist, and even a trained economist, would have difficulties understanding all the various budget documents. The Colombian budgetary process does not lack rules—it just has too many. What it needs is a healthy dose of transparency.

Comisión de Racionalización del Gasto y de las Finanzas Públicas (1997) contains a review of the Colombian budgetary process. The main difference between this review and the points we note above is that the Comisión emphasizes guidelines (or lack thereof), the integration of the budget in an economic plan, and spending control. As will become clear from our discussion, there should be much less emphasis (or none at all) placed on these three points.

## 7.2   Theory and Empirical Evidence

In the last decade a substantial body of theoretical and empirical research has investigated the effects of budgetary institutions on fiscal policy. Much of this literature can be interpreted as investigating the mechanism by which budgetary institutions limit the tendency of executive or legislative bodies to overspend, relative to some benchmark. This is the perspective that we will use in interpreting the literature and evaluating the Colombian budgetary process.

### 7.2.1   Theory
How is fiscal policy affected by budgetary institutions? We provide here a survey of the main arguments, and refer the reader to Alesina and Perotti (1999) and Poterba (1996) for more complete accounts.

#### *Preparation of the Budget*
Schematically, one can think of two polar methods of budget preparation. In one, the minister of finance is in charge from the start; he collects the budget requests from the individual ministries, bargains bilaterally

with each minister, and puts together the totals. At the other extreme, the total budget is arrived at by a process of multilateral bargaining in which all ministries participate at the same time, with the minister of finance as merely the organizer of the process, but with little more power than the other ministers. Velasco (1999) presents a stylized formalization of this aspect of the budget process. In the terminology of Alesina and Perotti (1999), the first method is more hierarchical, the second more collegial. From the point of view of enforcing fiscal discipline, the advantage of a hierarchical method is that it allows the minister of finance to better internalize the effects of the overall budget. Suppose that the government is composed of 10 ministers; for simplicity, assume that the budget is balanced. In a hierarchical system, if each minister spends an extra dollar, the minister of finance, who is in charge of the whole budget, can internalize the costs of raising 10 extra dollars in taxes. In a collegial system, each minister internalizes, at most, the costs of raising "his own" extra dollar; the result is a tendency to spend more, in equilibrium. On the other hand, the costs of a more hierarchical system can be, as always in these cases, a "less democratic" budget process.

### Presentation, Discussion, and Approval of the Budget

A similar trade-off appears once the budget has been introduced to Parliament. In a hierarchical system the government (usually in the person of the Minister of Finance) has considerable agenda-setting power during the discussion phase, and it can have strong veto power on the initiatives of Parliament tending at modifying the total budget or its components. In a collegial system, by contrast, the Parliament can amend the draft budget freely, increase or decrease its spending and revenue items and totals, and set the agenda of the discussion phase. If one accepts the premise that the Parliament, because of its mere size, is likely to be more subject to many narrow interests and more prone to spending, the trade-off between these two polar systems in the discussion phase is similar to that in the preparation phase. Baron and Ferejohn (1989) and Baron (1991) formalize the role of agenda control in the budgetary process.

### Transparency

A budget that is difficult to read and interpret can undermine fiscal discipline for two reasons. First, lack of transparency generates incentives for the government to engage in creative accounting, namely in accounting practices that hide the true size of a spending item.[1] Second, lack of transparency makes it difficult for interested individuals or groups to form an idea of the true size of the fiscal package, thus undermining the possibility of effective control. Transparency is greatly undermined when the budgetary process consists of many documents, almost always with considerable differences in presentation and coverage. The last effect is that there are as many fiscal packages as documents, so that the debate keeps shifting, often without participants realizing it, from one deficit figure to another, from one definition of the budget to another.

### Rules

Budgetary laws and procedures frequently set specific rules that the government must conform to: a typical example is a balanced budget rule, which prohibits budget deficits. Rules are usually meant to enforce fiscal discipline, because they constrain the possible choices of the government and legislators. Yet there is growing recognition that they can be a double-edged sword: for instance, a government determined on running a budget deficit will try to bypass a balanced budget rule by taking several spending items off the budget. The rule is formally satisfied, but at the cost of undermining transparency and even the budget. Thus one should be aware that rules are not a substitute for fiscal responsibility, a view that we will share in our discussion of the Colombian budgetary process.

### Formal Control

After the budget has been approved, its implementation is monitored at several stages. Usually the actual realized revenues and expenditures must be certified by a controlling agency, to make sure they conform to the budget approved by Parliament or to discuss any discrepancy. We do not discuss this phase in this chapter. The role of the controlling agency is usually merely formal, with few or no measures it can take to enforce its rulings. To the extent that the budgetary process has any impact on fiscal outcomes, the four aspect discussed above are much more important than formal control.

### 7.2.2 Empirical Evidence

Having discussed the many theoretical reasons why the budgetary process is important, one should be aware that the empirical evidence on the links between the budgetary process and fiscal outcomes is limited, particularly as concerns sovereign countries. The reason is threefold: it is difficult to measure unambiguously the different aspects of the budget process, there is very little variation over time in budget institutions, and the sample is usually very limited (at most 20 OECD or 20 Latin American countries, depending on the study). Von Hagen (1992) and von Hagen and Harden (1994) rank the budget processes in the 12 countries of the European Community along several dimensions, including the strength of the minister of finance in the preparation phase, the strength of the government in the discussion and approval phase, and the degree of transparency of the budget. They find evidence that more hierarchical and more transparent procedures are associated with lower average budget deficits in the eighties. De Haan, Moessen, and Volkenkirk (1999) find evidence that the role of the minister of finance is important. One limitation of these studies is the extremely small number of observations (12 countries). On a sample of 20 OECD countries, the point estimated in Kontopoulos and Perotti (1999) and Perotti and Kontopoulos (2001) is also consistent with the hypothesis that spending limits or more centralized budgetary processes are more favorable to fiscal responsibility. However, the standard errors are much too wide to allow any inference with a reasonable degree of confidence.

One study of particular interest for Colombia is Alesina et al. (1995). Using responses from questionnaires sent to Ministries of Finance, the authors classify the budget process in 20 Latin American countries. They find econometric evidence that countries with more hierarchical and transparent procedures tend to have lower average budget deficits during the 1980s.

There is more formal evidence on the effects of the budgetary process in US states, as opposed to foreign countries. There is a substantial variation across states in the rules governing the budget process; in particular, several states have balanced budget rules, while others have not. Contrary to sovereign states, balanced budget rules at the state level are much more enforceable, partly because states have a more limited ability to borrow. Von Hagen (1991), Poterba (1996), Alt and Lowry (1994), Bohn and Inman (1995), Alesina and Bayoumi (1996), and Inman (1996), all show that, at the state level, rules do seem to have some impact on fiscal outcomes, in the intended direction. One should be aware that these results might not hold for sovereign countries: their budgets are much more complicated, hence there is much more scope for creative accounting and therefore for rules to impact negatively on transparency and ultimately in fiscal discipline. In addition sovereign countries engage much more actively in countercyclical fiscal policy; hence they have more incentives to circumvent rules.

### 7.3  Budget Process in Colombia

### 7.3.1  Structure and Preparation of the Budget

The budgetary process in Colombia is summarized in figure 7.1. A National Development Plan (Plan Nacional de Desarrollo, PND) is presented to Congress by every incoming administration during the first four months of its mandate. The Plan includes the National Investment Plan (Plan Nacional de Inversiones, PNI), which sets total investment spending over the four year of the administration's mandate.

As the first step in the yearly budgetary process, the Minister of Finance, in consultation with the National Planning Department (Departamento Nacional de Planeacion, DNP), sets the macro guidelines and preliminary revenue and expenditure ceilings. After this, two simultaneous and relatively independent processes take place:

Each planning agency elaborates their budget proposals, which are then discussed with the entities in charge of sector and global coordination: the Ministry of Finance, DNP, Sector Ministries, and the Regional Planning Councils (CORPES).
The Ministry of Finance and DNP prepare a Financial Plan (Plan Financiero, PF), which must be evaluated by the Council of Fiscal Policy (CONFIS), and must be formally approved by the Council of Economic and Social Policy (CONPES).

The Financial Plan establishes the macroeconomic foundation for the budget and determines the compatibility between the public sector deficit and the flow of funds of the rest of the economy. In accordance with the Plan and based on the proposals made by each public agency, DNP prepares a detailed Operative Annual Investment Plan (Plan Operativo Anual de Inversiones, POAI), which must also take into account the framework set by the pluriannual National Development Plan. The POAI must also be approved by the Council of Economic and Social Policy (CONPES), and thereafter submitted to the Directorate of the Budget within the Ministry of Finance, to be included within the project of the National General Budget (Presupuesto General de la Nacion, PGN), possibly after modifications following a reconciliation process with the Ministry of Finance.

The process of preparation of the budget in Colombia is relatively short. At the level of the spending agencies it starts in January and by March 15 the directorate of the budget at the Ministry of Finance must

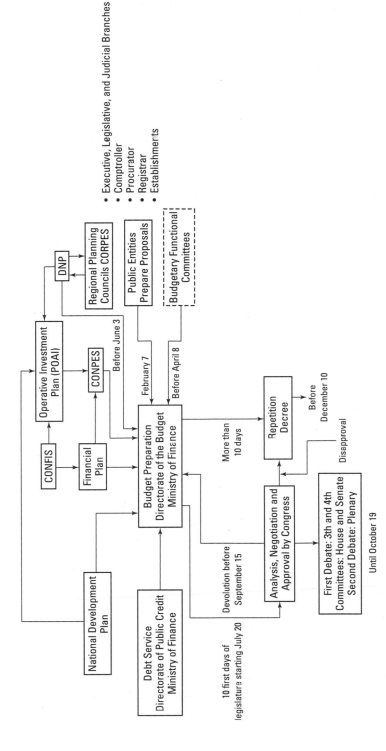

**Figure 7.1**
Budget preparation, negotiation, and approval in Colombia

have received all their proposals. Bilateral functional committees, composed by functionaries of the agencies and the budget management units of the Ministry of Finance and DNP, discuss each agency's budget until April 15.

The investment budget is submitted by DNP to the Ministry of Finance by June 20, and the government presents the whole Project of the National General Budget to Congress within the first ten days of the ordinary session, which starts on July 20.

Meanwhile the Directorate of the Budget collects and reviews the debt plans and requirements of the noncommercial national public agencies (Establecimientos Públicos), to be submitted to the Directorate of Public Credit at the same ministry. This same unit prepares the plan of the whole service of the debt, to be sent by April 30 to the Directorate of the Budget, to be integrated within the project of the national budget. Debt figures in the budget should meet limits established by special and separate laws, the Debt Ceilings Laws, introduced by the government whenever the corresponding authorizations expire or must be increased. These laws do not follow any established schedule related to the budgetary process.

### 7.3.2  Budget Documents

The Financial Plan is a planning and management instrument for the short and medium terms. It is based on the cash operations of all entities with relevant impacts on the fiscal, monetary, and exchange rate positions of the country. The cash deficit is measured and the financial requirements are stated for the central government as well as for the whole nonfinancial public sector, which includes regional governments, the main public enterprises and noncommercial establishments, the social security sector, and the National Coffee Fund. The goal of the Financial Plan is to ensure the compatibility of the Annual Cash Plan (Plan Anual de Caja, PAC) with the external and internal credit resources as well as with the monetary and exchange targets agreed previously with the board of the central bank. The Council for Fiscal Policy, CONFIS, establishes accordingly the disbursement targets for the nonfinancial public sector, and especially for the central government. The Operative Annual Investment Plan (POAI) specifies approved investment projects classified by sectors, and executing agencies. It must comply with the investment limit set by the Financial Plan, as well as with the four-year National Investment Plan in the National Development Plan. In principle, no investment program not included in the National Investment Plan can be included in the annual budget within annual budgets, unless Congress has approved them.

The general budget of the nation comprises an income and capital resources budget, divided into (1) current income revenues, (2) "parafiscal" contributions (mainly payroll taxes, accruing trough specialized public institutions and enterprises), (3) capital revenues, and (4) own-resources of the noncommercial national public enterprises. On the spending side, the Appropriations Law specifies expenditure according to three economic categories: (1) operating expenses ("gastos de funcionamento"), (2) investment expenses, and (3) debt service. The appropriations law establishes total amounts for each of these categories, which cannot be modified except in the cases detailed below. The PGN is followed by a Liquidation Decree (Decreto de Liquidación), which prescribes more detailed allocations; these can be changed within the limits established by the Appropriations Law (i.e., without changing the totals of the three main economic categories), by permission of the directorate of the budget. The Budget Law also includes temporary rules to assure appropriate execution of the PGN.

The Annual Cash Plan establishes the allowable expenditure within the calendar year, according to the Financial Plan, and it also considers the execution of arrears carried over from previous years. In addition the Monthly Cash Plan establishes the monthly resources available through the centralized account of the national treasury, as well as the allowances established for payments financed by resources owned by the noncommercial public entities.

The Organic Statute of the Budget (Estatuto Orgánico del Presupuesto, EOP) is a high rank law that establishes the fundamentals of the budget process. The Statute defines the national general budget as including budgets of the national noncommercial public establishments (Establecimientos Públicos) and the budget of the nation. The latter one involves the executive branch as well as the legislative and judicial branches, the independent control agencies (procuraduría and contraloría), and the electoral agency, but it excludes all sorts of noncommercial decentralized entities (establecimientos públicos), commercial public enterprises, and mixed capital enterprises where the state has invested public resources.

### 7.3.3 CONFIS and CONPES

CONFIS, Consejo Superior de Política Fiscal, is the governmental committee in charge of fiscal policy, and it coordinates the budgeting system.

It is composed by the minister of finance, the director of DNP, the economic adviser to the president, and the vice ministers of finance (technical and general), as well as the directors of the budget, public credit, taxes and customs, and the treasury at the Ministry of Finance. It must approve, modify, and evaluate the Financial Plan, advise on the fiscal effects of the Investment Plan, elaborate the Cash Plan (PAC), and approve the budgets of the commercial enterprises of the state. CONPES, Consejo Nacional de Política Económica y Social, is composed by the minister of finance, seven other ministers, representatives of DNP, and is headed by the president of the Republic. Within the budgeting process CONPES must approve the POAI as well as the Financial Plan prepared by CONFIS.

### 7.3.4   Presentation, Negotiations, and Approval of the Budget

The draft of the national general budget is submitted to Congress accompanied by a macroeconomic program, evaluating the consistency of fiscal policy with the other main policies (monetary and exchange rate), within the growth expectations and the frame of the development plan. There may also be a "complementary (revenue) budget," if there are expenditures lacking financing at the time of the preparation of the basic budget. Once the budget project has been presented, the specialized committees of the two legislative bodies will hear the central bank about the macroeconomic impact of the budget and the level of public expenditure.

The committees of the Senate and the House examine jointly the budget proposal and must reach a conclusion about the level of expenditure by September 15. By the end of the same month the budget draft, as modified by the committee, must be introduced to the floor discussion in each chamber of Congress. The debates can be simultaneous. In case the budget is not approved by October 20, the government proposal will become effective, amended by the modifications approved in the first debate.

In case the budget proposal has not been presented to Congress within the first ten days of the legislative period, or if Congress does not approve it, the executive must issue a decree repeating the budget of the previous year. However, the government may reduce expenditures if there are not sufficient revenues for the next fiscal year.

Once the budget is approved, by December, the government issues a Liquidation Decree, taking into account all the modifications, and incorporating an Annex that details all appropriations for the forthcoming fiscal year. The Liquidation Decree includes general provisions, also to be proposed by the Ministry of Finance, in order to attain adequate execution of that budget. They are temporary and, in principle, should not include substantive rules, introduce new taxes or changing existing ones, or change the Organic Statute of the Budget.

### 7.3.5 Execution of the Budget

The execution of the budget is regulated by a new version of the Financial Plan, issued at the end of the fiscal year prior to the budget year, to be approved by CONFIS. As mentioned before, the Annual Cash Plan must also be specified in monthly terms. The Monthly Cash Plan (1) classifies commitments by functional categories (personal services, transfers, operating expenses, investment, and service of the debt), (2) includes contracts in course of execution or signed during previous fiscal periods, (3) includes all new programmed contracts, and (4) separates all current income collected through the treasury from revenues handled directly by decentralized entities, and it projects all capital income to be received through the fiscal year, differentiating between income of the nation and of the national establishments.

The Ministry of Finance can also arrange budget reallocations within the year. Part of such flexibility results from the inclusion of a "provisions" component, assigned to finance the fiscal cost of laws to be approved within the fiscal year.

### 7.3.6 Control

There are three types of control of the budget:

#### Political Control

To be executed by the Congress, using these instruments: (1) citation of the ministers to plenary or committee sessions, (2) citation of the heads of administrative departments (depending on the presidency), (3) examination of the reports produced by the president, ministers, and heads of the administrative departments, and (4) examination of the report on liquidation of the execution of the budget and the report on the treasury to be presented by the general comptroller (auditor) of the Republic.

#### Financial and Economic Control

To be done by CONFIS, the directorate of the budget at the Ministry of Finance, and DNP, with the purpose of evaluating results and to assess the process of budget management.

*Fiscal Control*

In charge of the Office of the General Comptroller of the Republic, in order inspect the collection of resources and to verify compliance of the existing laws, norms, procedures, and rules.

### 7.3.7 Budget of the Commercial and Industrial Enterprises of the State

CONFIS must also review and approve the budgets of the commercial and industrial enterprises of the state at the national level, which are outside the National General Budget. These are wholly owned by the state, but they have administrative autonomy. Their budgets must follow general directives and comply with coherence requirements of the Financial Plan. Their budgeting procedures follow the general principles stated by the Organic Statute of the Budget (except being subject to embargoes). Their financial surpluses, when they do not have the societary structure, belong to the nation. CONPES determines the amounts to be transferred as capital resources of the national budget, the date of deposit of such deposits in the national treasury. It must leave at least 20 percent of such profits to the generating enterprise. Should the public enterprises adopt the societary form, as in the case of the shares of the nation in enterprises of mixed nature, the corresponding profits are also property of the nation, and the representatives of the Nation in the Boards of such enterprises must follow the instructions of CONPES regarding capitalization and distribution of dividends.

### 7.4 Problems and Proposals

### 7.4.1 Degree of Centralization of the Budget Process

In assessing the degree of centralization, it is useful to distinguish the three phases of preparation, discussion in Congress, and implementation of the budget.

*Discussion and Implementation Phases*

Although the current legislation is less clear than it could be, the Colombian budget process assigns a strong role to the minister of finance in the last two phases. The general framework is provided by Article 60 EOP, according to which:

The Minister of Finance is the organ of communication of the Government with Congress in budget matters. As a consequence, only the Minister can solicit on behalf of the Government the creation of new incomes or other revenues: ...

changes in the tax rates, changes or movements of spending items included by the government in the draft budget law, the consideration of new spending items, and the authorization of new borrowing.

This article is not entirely clear on whether the minister is the only actor who can accomplish all these acts, or whether he is the only actor within the government; but other articles of the EOP and of the Constitution help dispel many of the doubts. During the discussion phase the committees need a written authorization in order to modify a *partida de gasto*; Congress needs a written authorization by the minister of finance[2] to increase a *partida de gasto* or introduce a new one (Article 351 of the Constitution), while it can, with some exceptions, eliminate or reduce *partidas de gasto* by its own initiative (Article 63, EOP, and Article 351, Constitution).[3] Regarding revenues, Congress cannot increase them without a written authorization by the minister (Article 62, EOP), although the EOP is silent on the more important case of a reduction in revenues.

Thus, overall, Congress seems to have little power to increase the deficit relative to the budget project (with the possible exception of decreasing revenues) without the approval of either the minister of finance or the relevant ministers. Overall, we believe the spirit of the budget procedures during the discussion phase is fundamentally sound, but it could and should be stated much more clearly in one article, requiring the Minister of Finance to give written authorization for any increases in spending or decreases of revenues. We do not think that a similar authorization is needed for increases in revenues or decreases in spending; in fact the ability of Congress to decrease spending by its own initiative is a good insurance policy against the case of a spendthrift minister of finance.

The minister has also a strong role in the implementation phase of the budget. By Article 39 of EOP, only the minister can introduce a new operating expenditure. By Article 76 of EOP, the government through the minister of finance can at any moment reduces or postpones a budgetary appropriation under a set of conditions, including a shortfall in revenues or the need to ensure "macroeconomic coherence." The combination of Articles 79, 80, 81, and 88 of EOP implies that the government only, through the minister of finance, can introduce to Congress new spending relative to the approved budget.[4]

The basic allocation of authority in the implementation phase is also, in our view, fundamentally sound. Here too we believe it could be stated in much clearer terms; in particular, the wording of Articles 79, 80, and 81 of EOP does not exclude a role for Congress to introduce new spending; in practice. However, these articles (together with Article 88) are interpreted as reserving this role to the FM.

### Preparation Phase and the Plan Nacional de Desarrollo

The Colombian budget process is much less centralized in the preparation phase. The root of the problem is the emphasis on planning that permeates all economic policy in Colombia, and which manifests itself in the key role attributed to the Plan Nacional de Desarrollo (PND) in the political rhetoric. This has two consequences: it dilutes the powers of the minister of finance, and it decreases the transparency of the whole budgetary process.

As in all plans, investment is the key tool for the implementation of the PND, and like in many countries with a planning tradition, this leads to a separation of the current and the investment budget, the former attributed to the minister, the latter to the planning agency, in the Colombian case DNP. This separation of the current and capital budgets undermines the very reason for centralizing the preparation of the budget in one entity, namely ensuring that someone can internalize the whole budget. The minister of finance has a strong role in the very first phase, since it decides the aggregates for investment and *gasto de funcionamento*, which become part of the June *Plan Financiero*.[5] The two aggregates must then be allocated to ministries, but very little bargaining occurs on operating expenditures, which are mostly set for each ministry incrementally relative to the previous year's figures. Virtually all the bargaining on allocations occurs on investment spending, which implies it is conducted bilaterally by DNP through the *comités funcionales*. As we discuss later, bargaining on appropriations might be of little significance when—as in recent years—arrears amount to about the same size as new appropriations, but even the cash allocations in the PAC are divided between the Ministry of Finance and DNP. In this case DNP has the prominent role, since for obvious reasons most of the cuts in the cash allocations relative to appropriations occurs in investment spending.[6]

Thus the separation of the current and investment budgets imply a considerable dilution of the powers of the Ministry of Finance, and of its ability to direct the process of allocations of spending between ministries. As IMF (1999) emphasizes, this separation of roles could also undermine the intertemporal coherence of fiscal policy, as it can easily generate underprovision of maintenance spending for investment projects, or overprovision of investment given the budgeted level of maintenance expenditure.

But there are even more fundamental reasons why the emphasis on planning undermines the centralization of the budget process. By its nature, the PND itself is a hodgepodge of good intentions, to which virtually all institutions and interest groups in the country contribute with their own preferred investment project. According to the Constitution, the PND is elaborated by the government with the "active participation of the planning authorities, the territorial entities, and the Consejo Superior de la Judicatura." The draft Plan must be submitted to the Consejo Nacional de Planeación, which is formed by "representatives of the territorial entities, and of the economic, social, ecological, community, and cultural sectors" (Article 340 of the Constitution). To all this, one must add the Departmental Planning Councils (Consejos de Planeación Departamental), each of which elaborates their own *plan de desarrollo*.

But the dilution of the centralization of the process goes further. By its very nature, a plan generates a multitude of documents that have to be consistent, at least formally, with each other and with the plan. Each of the other documents is prepared by a different entity, and often must be approved by yet a different one. Table 7.1 summarizes these features of the different budget documents.

The problem is that CONFIS and especially CONPES are collegial bodies, where the minister of finance is at best a *primus inter pares*.[7] One could view this arrangement as a legitimate although flawed in our view—design of the legislator to limit the powers of the minister, but in reality there is little doubt that this arrangement is the result of a planning mentality that feeds on ever more agencies and institutions, and of the uncontrolled growth of claims on the budget process by interest groups

**Table 7.1**
Colombian budget documents

| | PND | PF | POAI | Budget | |
| | | | | Operating expenses | Investment expenses |
| --- | --- | --- | --- | --- | --- |
| Preparation | Govt | MH (DNP)[a] | DNP (MH)[a] | MH | DNP |
| Nonbinding advice | | CONFIS | CONFIS | | |
| Approval | CNP[b] | CONPES | CONPES | CONFIS[c] | |

a. "Coordination."
b. Consejo Nacional de Planeación.
c. CONFIS authorizes obligaciones on future years that do not have appropriation in current budget year (Article 24 of EOP).

within the bureaucracy. The result is, in the best scenario, dilution of the centralization of the process, and in the worst scenario, confusion.

Thus we propose that POAI be abolished and that the PND be treated merely as a political guidelines of a program without any legal or formal implications for the budgetary process. We think that the Office of the Budget at the Ministry of Finance should prepare both the current and the capital budgets. The Plan Financiero could be prepared by the same agency. An implication of our proposal is that the Consejo Nacional de Planeación, the analogous bodies at the departmental level, and CON-FIS, should be eliminated. The branch of DNP that deals with the budget could be incorporated in the Ministry of Finance. We do not see any role for CONPES in the budgetary process.

It is certainly legitimate of the government to collect the concerns and the problems of the country by giving voice to all actors in society. But this should be a political process, not an institutional one, and should not generate an official document with the status of a law, like the PND. The current framework is too unwieldy, and inevitably generates a document where everything is included, thus discouraging rather than encouraging the discussion of the trade-offs that fiscal policy must face. For this reason it ends up with little operational content. But perhaps the most fundamental reason why the PND should have no place in the Colombian budget process is that a plan should have no place in a market economy.

### 7.4.2 Transparency

#### Proliferation of Budget Documents

The second negative effect of the proliferation of budget documents is on transparency. Several budget documents can be useful if they fulfill clearly differentiated functions, and if it is easy to go from one document to the other. Neither condition is satisfied in the Colombian budget process. By Article 13 of EOP, the budget must be consistent with the Plan Nacional de Desarrollo, the Plan Nacional de Inversiones, the Plan Financiero, and the Plan Operativo Anual de Inversiones. Is this consistency requirement satisfied in practice? And how?

Consider first the relation between the budget and the PND. The key feature of the PND is the *Plan de Inversiones*, which specifies the total investment spending, in real terms, of the central administration, the *Establecimientos Especiales*, the departments and municipalities, and the NFPE's, over the four years of the plan. Its link with the yearly budget is the *Plan Operativo Anual de Inversiones*, which specifies the investment

Table 7.2
Investment in PNI and turnout, 1995 to 1998, general budget

|      | PNI | Authorized by budget law | Commitments |
|------|------|------|------|
| 1995 | 3,515 | 3,908 | 3,473 |
| 1996 | 5,123 | 4,610 | 4,336 |
| 1997 | 5,439 | 4,643 | 4,307 |
| 1998 | 5,890 | 3,802 | 1,587 |
| Total | 19,948 | 16,963 | 13,703 |
| % | | 85.0% | 68.7% |

Source: DNP.
Note: In thousands of millions of 1994 pesos. Yearly figures for PNI are internal DNP figures: they do not appear in any official document and do not have any official status.

projects to be included in the budget, and the yearly amounts to be appropriated. The investment figures in the POAI will then be part of the draft Investment Budget (Article 36 of EOP). By Article 8 of EOP, the annual amounts in the POAI and in the budget must be consistent with the figures in the *Plan Nacional de Inversiones*.

But what does this consistency requirement mean in practice? Virtually any investment spending set in the budgets of the first three years of the Plan de Desarrollo can be claimed to be consistent with the PNI, because one could always argue that investment in the fourth year will adjust residually. However, even this is a very loose constraint: we are not aware of any request ever being made that investment in the budget be consistent, over a four-year horizon, with the Plan de Inversiones, nor are we aware of any official analysis ever being made to check this simple adding constraint ex post. But this exercise can easily been done on the four years covered by the 1995–1998 Plan "El Salto Social," as shown in table 7.2.[8]

Thus appropriations and commitments during the last years of "El Salto Social" were only 85 and 69 percent of PNI figures, respectively. The opposite phenomenon will likely occur in the Plan, "Cambio Para Construir la Paz." Its PNI implies an average share of central government investment in GDP of 0.5 percent over the 1999 to 2002 period; because this share was about 2 percent in both 1999 and 2000, the PNI target is guaranteed to be unattainable, and by a large amount. Furthermore, the current size of (one version of) Plan Colombia alone is roughly equal to the total investment in the PNI for the 1999 to 2002 period. All this is hardly surprising: many shocks can occur over a four-year horizon that can change the picture entirely; there is absolutely no reason why a document written in 1998 should bind the actions of the government in the year 2000. And of course it does not, in practice.

**Table 7.3**
Investment in the budget documents

|                              | POAI  | Draft budget | PF, authori-zations | PF, cash, commitments |
| ---------------------------- | ----- | ------------ | ------------------- | --------------------- |
| Total investment             | 5,600 | 6,400        |                     |                       |
| Central administration       | 3,300 | 4,065        | 4,046               | 2,000                 |
| Fondos especiales            | 1,400 | 1,148        |                     |                       |
| Vigencias futuras            | 860   | 1,000        |                     |                       |
| Resto                        | 1,000 |              |                     |                       |
| Formación bruta de capital   |       |              | 2,375               | 2,000                 |
| Reclasificado                |       |              | 663                 |                       |
| Sin situación de fondo       |       |              | 1,010               |                       |
| Establecimientos públicos    | 2,300 | 2,300        |                     |                       |

To complicate things further, it is not even clear what the consistency between the PNI and the yearly investment budget means in theory: by Article 341 of the Constitution, "the annual budget law can increase or decrease the partidas and recursos approved in the PND." Thus the requirement that the annual budgets be consistent with the four-year plan does not have any bite, in practice, and possibly even, in theory, but it introduces a host of totally unnecessary complications in the process.

Consider now the relations between the annual budget document, starting with the investment figures in the POAI, the Plan Financero, and the draft budget, as displayed in table 7.4.

After reading the fine print, one discovers two differences between the POAI and the budget figures for the central administration: the latter includes $517mn of investment by Forex, and about $600mn of *reservas*, the former does not. But these do not explain the difference between the totals for the central administration. Also no table in the budget gives figures for *establecimientos propios*: one has to read attentively the text on page 73 of the Budget Message to get this figure. Although the total appropriations in the budget and the Plan Financiero are closed, note that the presentation and breakdown is very different. Finally, the cash figures in the Annex table of the Plan Financiero include only fixed capital formation, about half of total investment in the appropriation figure of the same document.

Consider next the Plan Financiero. As we know from section 7.3, its main purpose is to set the goals for cash spending by the central government and the NFPS that are compatible with the availability of credit and the macroeconomic developments. Its importance has grown pari passu with the growing importance of budget arrears: if there were no

**Table 7.4**
Revenues: Plan Financiero and draft budget

|  | Plan Financiero, July 1999 | Draft budget, July 1999 |
|---|---|---|
| Ingresos corrientes | 21,110 | 21,305 |
| Recursos de capital | 1,777 | 18,957 |
| Rendimientos financieros | 494 | 494 |
| Excedentes Financieros | 1,065 | 1,065 |
| Privatizations | | 2,489 |
| Crédito total | | 13,874 |
| Otros | 218 | 1,085 |
| Rentas parafiscales | | 640 |
| Fondos especiales | 637 | 2,214 |
| Total | 23,524 | 43,116 |

arrears, the central government figures in the Plan Financiero and in the budget would be identical. It is therefore understandable that a government should aspire to show a good deal of consistency between the total revenues in the Plan Financiero and in the draft budget; a large discrepancy between the two would imply that the budget is overestimating revenues relative to the Plan Financiero.[9] Indeed, the 2000 budget message states that "for the first time, the total figure of the budgeted revenues of the Presupuesto Nacional is the same as that of the Plan Financiero" (p. 10), at $43.1bn.

It is instructive to compare the revenue figures in Plan Financiero and in the draft Budget, both of which were issued in July 1999. Besides differences in individual items like *rentas parafiscales* and *fondos especiales*, the draft budget includes above the line two items, *privatizations* and *crédito total* that are recorded below the line in the *plan financiero*. *Crédito total* is gross of amortizations, meaning it includes both past debt that comes due and new net issue of debt. However, even after including these two items in the Plan Financiero, it still yields a total of $39.987bn, still far from the budget figure. In fact we could find no way to reconcile the two figures, given the information available in the two documents.

Thus either the requirement of consistency does not have any apparent bite, or it is satisfied by resorting to creative accounting practices. Certainly the existence of these multiple documents generates considerable ambiguity regarding the definition of budget items, their amounts, and the aggregate figures for revenues and spending; ultimately this has a large negative impact on the transparency of the budget. Ideally the whole budget process should consist of just one document. But at the moment there are large differences between the semi-accrual figures of the budget and the cash figures imposed by reality, and it would not be realistic to impose a move to an exclusively accrual or cash basis.[10] Hence two documents are required: the budget and a Plan Financiero. The two documents should have exactly the same structure, and should provide a table of reconciliation—essentially the magnitude of budget arrears (see section 7.4.4) in the budget year and the previous year.[11]

### *Accounting Standards and Reporting: Definition of Investment*

As we have seen, investment is a magic word in the Colombian budgetary process (and it becomes even more magical when combined with "social"). This is largely a reflection of the emphasis on planning, of which investment is the key instrument. The assumption underlying all the budget documents is that only investment has any social value, all other expenditures are necessary evils. This, together with the prohibition to cut the share of social investment spending in the budget, is an open invitation to use a very liberal notion of investment, and one that is at odds with any conventional usage of the term in the macroeconomic and accounting professions. Thus the most important notion in the budget process becomes extremely difficult to interpret.

In macroeconomics and accounting, investment is the addition to the stock of physical capital. The room for controversy in this definition is extremely small. But in Colombia several current expenditures that are deemed to contribute to the formation of human capital are included in the figures for investment. Thus, for instance, the Manual de Programación de la Inversion Publica of DNP states that investment is the sum of "those expenditures that are capable of causing income or of being in any way economically productive ... [and] those expenditures with the purpose of creating social infrastructure. The main feature of this expenditure is that it should increase the capacity to produce and the productivity in the fields of physical, economic and social infrastructure" (p. 12). There is very little that could not fit into this definition.

Not surprisingly, in the 2000 budget about 60 percent of expenditure by the Red de Solidaridad Social, all the spending by the (yet to be created) Red de Apoyo Social, and 90 percent of expenditure by SENA and ICBF are considered capital expenditure.[12] It is doubtful whether, under proper accounting rules, any expenditure by these agencies would be considered investment.[13] Most revenues of *fondos especiales* are automatically recorded as investment expenditure on the spending side: thus in the 2000 budget all the revenues of the Fondo de Solidaridad Pen-

**Table 7.5**
Investment in budget, DNP, NIA, and OECD general government, 1998

|  | Budget (1) | DNP (2) | NIA (3) | OECD (4) |
|---|---|---|---|---|
| General government[a] |  | 13.9 | 3.8 | 2.7 |
| Central government | 3.5 | 4.6 |  |  |
| Other public entities |  | 2.0 | 1.7 |  |
| Local governments |  | 7.3 | 2.1 |  |

Sources: (1) Budget Message 2000, from *Dirección General de Presupuesto Nacional*, appropriations; (2) DNP; (3) DANE; (4) OECD.
a. Central government: *Aportes Nación and Recursos Propios*.

sional, FOSYGA, and the Fondo de Solidaridad del Sector Eléctrico are recorded as investment expenditure.

Outside the central government, the definition of investment seems to become even more nonstandard. The budget does not detail the criteria for the computation of public investment by local governments and NFPE, but a large part or even all of the *situado fiscal* is automatically considered investment.[14] In fact, according to the draft budget, in 2000 investment by Territorial Entities will amount to 9.8 percent of GDP, against 3.4 percent by the central administration and *establecimientos públicos*. Of this investment by Territorial Entities, most is social investment according to the budget: Territorial Entities contribute to 74.2 percent of social investment by the NFPS, which in turn represents 50.8 percent of all public investment.[15]

In table 7.5 we compare public investment according to the budget definition of public investment according to the even more liberal DNP definition and to the National Income Accounts definitions, which is in principle the correct one of fixed capital formation; as a comparison we also display the average general government investment spending in OECD countries, all as shares of GDP in 1998. As one can see the budget definition is more than double the national income account figure for capital formation at the central government level; the DNP definition is more than three times the figure at both the central and local government levels, and all are vastly superior to the OECD average.[16]

Why is this latitude in the definition of investment dangerous? First, it prevents an understanding of the budget. Very little of macroeconomic significance can be inferred with the current use of the term "investment" in Colombian budget documents. Second, it undermines the comparability of different figures and budget documents: one is never quite sure what definition a budget document is using, and we have seen above an example of highly different definitions. Third, it invites creative accounting.

There are several reasons why individual's agencies and the Ministry of Finance might want to exploit the latitude in the definition of investment. At a general level, investment "looks good" in the political rhetoric; knowing this, agencies have an incentive to classify as much as possible of their expenditure as investment.[17] Second, only investment projects are entitled to specific external financing. Third, an agency that wants to hire new public servants must go through a very complicated administrative process, which in some cases can last up to one year; the process is much simpler and shorter in the case of investment spending. For instance, when recently the railway system decided to hire some temporary workers, the expenditure was classified entirely as investment.[18] Note that DNP merely records the investment figures submitted by the individual agencies in its Banco de Proyectos; it does not enter into the legitimacy of the definition of investment used by the agency. On the other hand, there is at least one powerful incentive working in the opposite direction: the PAC cash allocations are much more likely to cut investment spending than *gasto de funcionamento*.

We propose that the definition of investment used in the budget, in all other budget documents and by DNP, should conform to the international standards and definitions. How should this proposal be applied? The New Zealand Fiscal Responsibility Act forced the government to conform to GAAP, a set of accounting rules approved by an independent body, the New Zealand Accounting Standard Reviews Board, and applying to both the public and private sector. Colombia needs not to go this far. It could adopt the rules set in the *Government Finance Statistics Manual* (currently under revision). For accrual accounting, the Public Sector Committee of IFAC (the International Federation of Accountants) is developing a standard, and has already issued a draft on *Guidelines for Government Financial Reporting*. In Colombia, the Contador General has recently set accounting standards for public and private sector income and expense accounts, and for balance sheets. They could also provide alternative sources of accounting standards for the budget.

### Accounting Standards and Reporting: Treatment of the Deficit

The problems with the definition of investment are a manifestation of a more general one: the frequent use of nonstandard accounting practices. Particularly troublesome is the inclusion of gross debt issues[19] (both amortization and new) and of proceeds from asset sales and amortization as a "recurso de capital" (Article 31, EOP), hence above the line. That is, the structure of the budget presentation is as follows:

Revenues = Current revenues + New emission of debt
            + Proceeds form asset sales and privatization
            + Other capital spending + Other revenues.

Spending = Current spending + Capital spending + Interest
            + Amortization of debt come due.

This classification hides the deficit. Properly speaking, the most common definition of the deficit is (see IMF 1999)

New emission of debt − Amortization of existing debt
    + Proceeds from asset sales and privatization
    (plus some quasi-fiscal operations, of limited size).

Without a long and detailed analysis of both the revenue and spending sides of the budget, it is impossible to form an idea of the deficit. And without that, it is difficult to form an idea of the budget.

Including new emission of debt in revenues could have some meaning if this amount was predetermined and taken as given by the Ministry of Finance and Congress when deciding on the budget. But this is not the case. The authorization to incur debt that Congress votes periodically is maximum amounts, which are always larger than the new emission of debt (also called *máximo endeudamiento posible*) in the budget. Moreover authorizations to incur debt are voted whenever needed, and their timing is not tied to that of the budget process. Finally, and perhaps most importantly, the *disposiciones generales* in the Budget Law every year authorize the government to issue TES (government bonds) outside the debt authorization law (see Article 60 of 2000 Budget Law).

Of course, having debt issues above the line makes several budgetary rules meaningless. For instance, by Article 347 (Constitution) "if the revenues legally authorized are not enough to cover the projected expenditure ... the Government will propose ... the creation of new rentas or the modification of existing ones ...."; clearly such a rule has no teeth if the deficit is part of *recursos de capital* and one can issue TES at will.

This practice is engrained in the parlance of the budget. Thus the 2000 Budget Message states on page 8 that "the draft budget amounts to $46.6bn, financed as follows: $21.3bn, with current revenues; $19bn, with 'recursos de capital'; $2.8bn, with 'rentas parafiscales' and 'fondos especiales'; and $3.5bn, with recursos proprios of the Establecimientos Públicos." As one can see, there is no way from this wording to infer the size of the deficit, and not even the usual definition of total spending (that is, net of amortization). In fact, except for a line in a summary table, there is no mention of the notion of deficit in the whole chapter 1 of the Budget Message, precisely in the chapter that should summarize the fiscal manoeuvre proposed by the government.

Other items included under *recursos de capital* should also be recorded below the line, such as proceeds from privatizations. As we have seen, the 2000 Plan Financiero is immune from this practice; indeed, under pressure from the IMF, the December 2000 Plan Financiero even includes a reconciliation table to take care of a few smaller remaining differences with the IMF definition.

We believe the budget too should conform to international standards in this area as well. The Colombian budget should also conform to the standard classification of revenues and spending; the latter in particular should be reported broken down according to both the economic (i.e., mainly into government consumption, public investment, transfers, and subsidies) and the functional classifications (i.e., by the function fulfilled by each expenditure: health, defense, and public services). Here too international standards are available: by the IMF for the economic classification and by the United Nations for the functional classification. In fact work is under way to reclassify the budget according to these two classifications. This is a highly commendable enterprise, and one that should be adopted permanently as part of the budget.

### Coverage

The main function of the budget is to provide an idea of the role of the intervention of the state in the economy. To fulfill this role, the budget should have coverage as wide as possible. Ideally one would like to include all the Territorial Entities and the rest of the nonfinancial public sector. There are obvious legal obstacles that prevent this, but unfortunately the Colombia budget does not provide a complete picture even of the central government.

As it is well known, currently pensions are among the most momentous fiscal policy problems, and a whole chapter of the Budget Message is devoted to the implicit liabilities of the pension system. Yet the budget currently covers only a part of the pensions paid by the central government, namely public sector pensions at the central government level: all the pension (and health) expenditure by Instituto de Seguro Social (ISS) (about half of total pension expenditure) is outside the budget. This is so because the ISS is formally a commercial public enterprise, but the legal obstacles for its inclusion in the budget should not be unsurmountable. At a minimum, ISS and all the other pension funds outside the budget should be included in a separate chapter, with an informational role.

The government is doing a good job in the Plan Financiero to cover all the components of the NFPS. This should be extended to the budget. Presently, the budget does include information on the Territorial Entities and nonfinancial public enterprises. But this information should be provided using the same scheme and classification as for the central government, and indicating clearly the flows from and to the central government. This way one can form an opinion of the own operations of TE's and NFPE's, of their financial relations with the central government, and of their deficits.

### Macro Assumptions and Fiscal Forecasts

There is increasing recognition that the yearly fiscal manoeuvre embodied in the budget is not independent of the macroeconomic environment and is part of a longer-term fiscal policy. The practical implication of this recognition is twofold. First, the budget should include forecasts of the macroeconomic developments, namely of variables like GDP growth and inflation; the presentation should include an explanation of how these forecasts are obtained and of how the government believes they will affect and will be affected by fiscal policy. Second, the current budget should include a medium or even a long-term scenario for fiscal policy, so as to be able to set the current manoeuvre in the context of the whole medium-term policy of the government.

We agree entirely with the first implication. Indeed, the recent Budget Message contains a good presentation of the expected macroeconomic developments. But the question remains how reliable these forecasts are. The accusation is frequently made that governments, including the Colombian government, systematically overestimate GDP growth, in order to justify higher revenues than it is reasonable to assume for the budget year. This is indeed the case for the last four years (see table 7.6), which exhibit a vast overprediction of GDP growth, but interestingly, this has not been associated with gross errors in predicting revenues. In the previous four years the opposite pattern emerges: a good record in predicting GDP growth, but a tendency to overpredict revenues.[20] This table illustrates why macroeconomic forecasts are less important in Colombia than in other countries: revenue projections in Colombia are not based on an econometric model but are mostly the result of an empirical approach.

**Table 7.6**
Macroeconomic and budget forecasts and realizations

|              | 1991  | 1992  | 1993  | 1994  | 1995  | 1996   | 1997   | 1998   |
|--------------|-------|-------|-------|-------|-------|--------|--------|--------|
| GDP growth   |       |       |       |       |       |        |        |        |
| PF[a]        | 3.0   | 3.0   | 4.5   | 5.0   | 5.6   | 5.1    | 5.3    | 4.5    |
| Actual       | 2.1   | 3.5   | 5.2   | 5.7   | 5.4   | 2.0    | 3.0    | 0.6    |
| Revenues (bn$) |     |       |       |       |       |        |        |        |
| PF[a][b]     | 3,000 | 3,995 | 5,954 | 7,728 | 9,926 | 12,531 | 14,505 | 18,299 |
| Actual[b]    | 3,164 | 4,207 | 5,908 | 7,700 | 9,524 | 12,049 | 15,283 | 16,958 |

Sources: Planes Financieros and DNP, from Esguerra, Aranguren, and Ayala (2000).
a. December of year $t - 1$.
b. December of year $t + 1$.

Hence the connection between revenue projections and GDP growth is probably not very tight.

Nevertheless, we believe the Budget should provide up-to-standard projections on future macroeconomic developments. In fact we think the budget should take two steps further in this respect, by outsourcing its forecasts to one or more independent entities,[21] in Colombia or outside, and by presenting a table with the recent track record of the budget forecasts of macroeconomic variables and revenues. Outsourcing macro forecasts will do away with any controversy about the strategic incentives of the government to manipulate them, and will thus enhance the credibility of the budget. Still, since revenue projections are not based mechanically on GDP growth projections, nothing can prevent the government from overestimating revenues even in the presence of more realistic GDP growth figures; presenting a table with a comparison of forecasts and outturns can provide some idea about the track record and therefore the credibility of the present budget forecasts.[22]

Concerning the use of a medium-term fiscal outlook, we believe that it can be a double-edged sword. True, this year's fiscal policy is presumably part of a longer term approach on the part of the administration. But no government or entity can predict with any confidence what will happen more than two years from now, and the current government cannot bind its own future policies, let alone those of its successors. Most important, in some circumstances a medium-term fiscal plan would provide the government with a perverse strategic incentive when some fiscal adjustment is needed. The government can always claim that, although it cannot be done this year due to unfavorable macro circumstances, it will be done the next few years, as the medium-term fiscal plan shows.[23] Thus the medium-term fiscal plan can be used as an excuse for postponing needed but unpopular choices, without at the same time losing credibility or appearing fiscally irresponsible. Finally, a medium-term fiscal plan in a country like Colombia would resurrect, albeit in a milder form, the development plan that we have advocated should be eliminated. Thus we are not convinced that a medium-term fiscal plan should be institutionalized in a country like Colombia.

### 7.4.3 Rules

For expositional purposes it is useful to distinguish among *procedural* rules, establishing the procedures for, say, changing budget appropriations; *numerical* rules, establishing numerical values or limits for certain budget magnitudes; and *accounting* rules, establishing how certain items should be recorded.

As we argued in section 7.2, theoretically it is not obvious what the final effect of rules might be. On one hand, they are usually intended to ensure a "sound" fiscal policy and to limit the powers of the executive and the legislator to engage in budget gimmicks. Yet, even the best-intentioned rules can obtain exactly the opposite effect, by inviting creative accounting in order to bypass them. For instance, a prohibition of budget deficits will probably result, sooner or later, in more and more items being placed off the budget. The end result is less, rather than more, transparency.

Thus we take the view that only those rules that are enforceable with a reasonable probability and effort should be imposed. A key prerequisite for enforceability is simplicity: complicated rules lend themselves more easily to budget gimmicks that are difficult to verify. We have dealt with procedural rules in section 7.4.1, where we argued that, although basically sound, they could be stated more clearly. Some numerical rules are best interpreted as enforcing a constitutional mandate or, more generally, some general principle that is the object of wide agreement. Perhaps the best known such rule is the requirement that public social spending as a share of total spending should not decrease from year to year.[24] This provision can only invite budget gimmicks. Indeed, in this particular case bypassing this requirement is a trivial exercise, since the definition of social spending is so loose that virtually anything can fit in it: "any expenditure whose objective is the satisfaction of unsatisfied basic needs in health, education, environment, drinkable water, housing, and those aiming at the general well-being and the improvement of the quality of life of the population" (Article 41, EOP). As in the case of investment, it is difficult to see any operational content in such a definition; in fact it might not be surprising that in the 2000 budget the share of social spending in total spending is 45.4 percent, and this without including pension and health spending by ISS and several off-budget pension funds.

Interestingly, in the 2000 budget the share of social public spending in total spending is 0.2 percentage points higher than in 1999, thus barely satisfying the constitutional requirement. In fact, not only is the definition of social spending very loose, but also nothing ensures its consistency over time. Over time it has included more and more budget items, precisely in order to satisfy the constitutional constraint. Currently it includes items pertaining to culture, recreation, parks, contribution to religious events, concerts, and virtually all expenditure on education and health, including wages (see Perotti 2000).

Other types of numerical rules can best be interpreted as enforcing some principle of "sound" fiscal policy. It is typical of countries that experience fiscal problems to try and solve them by imposing more and more rules. This is understandable, and not always unproductive (see Poterba 1996). But it is difficult to point out a single numerical rule in the Colombian budget process that has not gone unfulfilled from the very beginning, and predictably so. Article 78 of EOP states that the government must reduce the *gasto de funcionamiento* for year $t$ when reserves created in $t - 1$ for year $t$ exceed 2 percent of the *gasto de funcionamiento* in year $t - 1$. A similar procedure (with a 15 percent threshold) holds for investment spending. How would one go about enforcing this rule? The government can always claim that any given level of expenditure is consistent with it. Similarly the rule that does not allow Territorial Entities to increase the *presupuesto de gasto*, in real terms, relative to the previous year is virtually unobservable and unenforceable, and again operates as a powerful incentive to reclassify items as investment expenditure. Moreover, if taken literally, it implies a continuously falling share of *gasto de funcionamiento* of local governments in GDP—most likely not what the legislator had in mind. In any event, to our knowledge this rule is not enforced.

No budget can be made without some accounting rules. But here too it is important to conform to accepted international practices. Some accounting rules in the Colombian budget process simply do not seem to have any apparent rationale. Article 46 of EOP states that if there is a deficit in $t - 1$, there should be a provision in the draft budget for year $t + 1$ for an equal amount. In its absence, the committees can reject the budget outright. If the law prohibited budget deficits in $t + 1$, this rule would amount to a reduction in debt in $t + 1$ equal to the increase in debt in $t - 1$ (notice, however, that this would not stop the accumulation of debt because it does not take into account the interests accrued in the meantime). But since there is no limit on the deficit of year $t + 1$, the government can always claim that a certain part of the year $t + 1$ revenues are to be set against the year $t - 1$ deficit. Notice that in the budget total issues of debt (new and amortization) are recorded above the line; hence this would amount to recording a decrease in new issues or in amortization equal to the year $t - 1$ deficit, and at the same time an increase in new issues by the same amount. The net effect is 0.

It is interesting to follow the destiny of this rule in the 2000 draft budget. The government argues that it took care of the 1998 deficit in the 1999 fiscal year, through the mechanism of budget arrears, so it does not have to have a provision for it in the 2000 budget. As we have seen, this justification is entirely unnecessary, but it is interesting that the committees did not reject the draft budget, even though by law (Article 46, EOP) they were required to do so.

The recent legislation has seen a proliferation of a final type of rules, one that for lack of a better name could be called "seemingly innocuous" rules. These are rules that give only very generic indications, mostly to address a widespread concern or to make a theoretical point, but without providing any clear indication. In the best scenario these rules only clutter the budget legislation, but in many cases they have a more tangible negative effect, reducing the transparency of the budget process.

We make three examples of rules with no teeth, in descending order of legislative rank. By Article 350 of the Constitution, "public social spending will have priority over any other spending." This is yet another manifestation of the Constitutional emphasis on social spending; we doubt that it has ever been invoked, but if this rule can have any practical consequence, it can only be by inviting creative accounting.

According to the principle of *coherencia macroeconómica* of Article 20 of EOP, "the budget must be compatible with the macroeconomic goals" set by the government and the central bank; according to the principle of *homeostasis presupuestal* of Article 21 of EOP, "the increase in real revenues ... must be compatible with the growth of the economy, so as not to generate macroeconomic disequilibrium." Although these are worthy goals, it is difficult to imagine any government that will claim it is deliberately ignoring them; conversely, it is difficult to imagine how to conclusively prove the budget is not fulfilling these principles.

We propose to eliminate all the rules that we have mentioned. They are either irrelevant or counterproductive. In particular, we propose to do away with the constitutional mandate on social spending. Besides being unenforceable and counterproductive, it encourages a culture of rhetorical discussion dissociated from reality.

### 7.4.4  Intertemporal Links

The budget for a given fiscal year must deal with appropriations that, for several reasons, straddle over different fiscal years. In recent years these items have created considered problems to the management of fiscal policy. To understand them and their effects, it is useful to start with a brief description of the process leading from appropriations to cash disbursement and its terminology. This process involves the following steps:

1. Appropriations[25]
2. Commitments. Contracts are signed
3. Obligations. Work is completed, goods and services are delivered, and bills are issued
4. Payment. Treasury issues checks
5. Cash. Checks are cashed

A payment can take place only if its resources are included in the Monthly Cash Plan, in order to meet the financial and macro constraints specified by the Financial Plan.

At the end of the fiscal year, not all work has been completed: the appropriation has generated a commitment, but not an obligation. This type of appropriations are called "appropriation reserves": commitments that have not created obligations. These appropriations remain alive. In other cases, by the end of the year the work might have been completed and the goods and services delivered, but checks have not been issued. This type of appropriations is called "accounts payable": obligations that have not been paid. These appropriations remain alive too. The sum of reserves and accounts payable is the "budgetary arrears."[26] A third type of intertemporal linkage is created by *vigencias futuras*, an authorization to make a commitment extending to the year following the budget year.

PAC restrictions are the main proximate cause of budget arrears.[27] But the underlying cause is usually assumed to be the frequent overestimation of government revenues, leading to inflated appropriations, which in turn have to be cut by PAC during the year. The size of recent and expected arrears is shown in table 7.7. Total arrears transferred from 1999 into 2000 may reach 18 percent of programmed expenditures for the central

**Table 7.7**
Arrears as percentage of GDP, central government

|  | From 1997 to 1998 | From 1998 to 1999 | From 1999 to 2000 | From 2000 to 2001 |
|---|---|---|---|---|
| Funcionamiento | 0.97% | 1.30 | 1.42 | 1.59 |
| Debt | 0.11 | 0.71 | 0.04 | 0 |
| Investment | 1.37 | 1.21 | 1.63 | 1.05 |
| Total with debt | 2.45 | 3.22 | 3.09 | 2.64 |
| Total without debt | 2.34 | 2.51 | 3.05 | 2.64 |

Source: Message from the President and the Minister of Finance, presenting the *Proyecto de Presupuesto* for year 2000.

government, and almost 85 percent in the case of investment. For this type of expenditure there were almost no arrears in 1990.

Arrears may have significant economic effects: since they constitute a "forced credit" to the public sector, they may induce increase in costs, and even bribes and corruption. They reduce transparency: in the presence of substantial arrears, it is more difficult for Congress and the public opinion to appreciate adequately a given year's fiscal maneuver, since much of it is constrained by the need to make room for arrears and *vigencias futuras*. On the other hand, the cash interventions that generate arrears concentrate on investment, thus inducing a strategic classification of expenditures that has nothing to do with their true economic nature.

A transitory rule, incorporated in the Budget Law for year 2000 (Article 33), has been widely interpreted[28] as ordering all appropriations that have not been executed during that year to be incorporated in the budget for year 2001. This will leave room only for arrears from year 2000 budget that arise from accounts payable. By Article 34, if the execution of an appropriation (i.e., the delivery of goods and services) must go beyond the current fiscal year, a *vigencia futura* must be used. This requires the special approval of the director of the budget, which should ensure more control than was possible with reserves.

These two provisions should clean the budget of accumulated arrears due to PAC restrictions and overbudgeting of previous periods. But, if taken literally, they will also imply almost no room for new investments in year 2001; in year 2000 the execution of programmed investment should amount to no more than 15 percent.

While we agree with the intentions of these two articles, we doubt they will provide a lasting solution to the problem of arrears. First, they do not tackle the underlying problem, namely the excessive appropriations relative to reasonable forecasts of revenues. Second, although *vigencias futuras* are, in principle, the proper way to handle activities and projects lasting more than one year, one should be aware that they also create inflexibilities for the future budgets. In addition the process does not have a clear regulation, and the directorate of the budget at the Ministry of Finance has almost unlimited powers in this area. Third, the articles still allow not only for *vigencias futuras* but also for accounts payable; it is then easy to foresee a large strategic use of *vigencias futuras* and accounts payable to overcome controls imposed on reserves. A parallel budget thus arises, based on commitments of *vigencias futuras*, as well as other mechanisms generating accounts payable, in order to assume obligations or make expenditures not allowed by the revenues programmed for each year, or to permit expenditures to be executed through several periods.

There is little doubt that the accrual basis of the Colombian budget, in addition to the common practice of overbudgeting relative to available resources, combine to produce such high levels of arrears and nontransparency. The arrears problem thus seems to arise more from basic budget policy failures than from accounting weaknesses. Still, improvements in accounting may help. The IMF Code of Good Practice on Fiscal Transparency provides accounting procedures to provide reliable information on arrears, in order to improve transparency and to control them. Such data does not result from simple cash accounting, and must be supplemented with modified accrual statements, such as developed by the International Federation of Accountants, IFAC (see IMF 1999, p. 57).

But perhaps the only real defense against arrears is a more rigorous process of forecasting revenues. To this effect our proposal of outsourcing these forecasts, and subjecting them to external control, could go a long way in limiting future arrears.

## 7.5 Conclusions

After making several criticisms of the Colombian budget process, we want to reiterate a point we made at the start of this chapter: better budget institutions will not automatically solve all Colombian fiscal problems. One has to be realistic: any rule and regulation can be circumvented sooner or later. Casual observation and common sense suggest that, if the government and Parliament of a sovereign country were to agree on a given fiscal policy, there are no budget institutions that can effectively constrain them in the long run. But better budget institutions can be important in realizing three conditions:

1. Allow the media, interest groups, members of Parliament, and any interest individual a better understanding of the fiscal policy proposed by the government, and therefore allow a more effective control on fiscal policy.
2. Increase the incentives for fiscal discipline.
3. Create an environment where a fiscally sound government can do its job more effectively, and a fiscally undisciplined government will be subject to a more informed scrutiny.

We believe these three conditions, as limited as they may appear, can greatly enhance the scope for a more effective fiscal policy in Colombia.

## Notes

1. A typical example is when a spending item is placed off the budget in order to limit the budget deficit.
2. More precisely, the law requires a written authorization by the "relevant" minister; this is usually interpreted as being the Minister of Finance.
3. In practice, in the very last days of the discussion in Congress, many additions to spending are passed that do not bear the written authorization of the Minister of Finance. They could be declared void by the Constitutional Court, although in reality this rarely happens.
4. The government need not go to Congress if it just reshuffles spending *within* operating expenses or investment spending; but it must have Congress' approval if it modifies the total appropriations for these two aggregates.
5. Formally, the Plan Financiero must be approved by CONFIS, but historically the Minister of Finance has had a prominent role in setting these aggregates.
6. Cash cuts in *gasto de funcionamiento* would largely imply that the Government is not paying wages.
7. While CONFIS includes mostly Finance Minister officials, CONPES includes seven other ministers and a host of other officials.
8. We thank Maria Alejandra Ojeda Ortiz of DNP for providing us with these data.
9. Recall that, for revenues, there is little difference between accrual and cash figures.
10. As we will see later, some actions are being taken to get closer to an "obligation" budget.
11. In several countries, like New Zealand, the government is required to publish a few months before the budget a document containing the expected macroeconomic developments and the aggregate figures for the coming fiscal maneuver. The goal is to provide all the agents involved in the process a framework for the budget negotiations. We believe that at this stage it would not be wise to apply this model to Colombia as well, because it would reintroduce the multiplicity of documents that we are trying to eliminate.
12. The *Red de Solidaridad Social* is a system of about sixteen different programs on subsidized housing, social assistance pensions, public employment creation, feeding program, and family assistance (see Perotti 2000 for a discussion of the Red). The *Red de Apoyo Social* is the complex of emergency programs (mostly public employment creation and conditional

cash subsidies to families with children) put in place by the administration to cope with the recession. SENA is the agency in charge of training programs. ICBF is the agency in charge of family assistance and all the programs of child care and school restaurants. SENA and ICBF are not part of the central administration budget, but they are part of *establecimientos públicos*. Spending on the *Red de Apoyo Social* is included in the December 1999 revision to the PF, but had not been decided at the time the budget project was published (July 1999).

13. It appears that programs 310 (*Divulgación, Asistencia técnica, y Capacitación del Recurso Humano*) and at least subprograms 1302 (*Bienestar Social a Trabajadores*) and 1501 (*Asistencia Directa a la Comunidad*) of program 320 (*Protección y Bienestar Social del Recurso Humano*) are automatically treated as investment.

14. The *situado fiscal* is the automatic transfer from the CG to the LG, with mandatory destination health and education expenditure, with a small residual item on water and sanitation.

15. This fundamental ambiguity in the definition of investment spending has gone so far that it is occasionally enshrined in the law. Thus Article 2 of Law 358 1997 states that: "To this effect [the determination of the creditworthiness of Territorial Entities], the salaries, honoraria, social security spending and social security contributions are considered as '*gasto de funcionamento*' even when they are budgeted as investment spending."

16. A further difficulty in interpreting the notion of investment in budget documents is the tendency to switch back and forth between the two different notions of capital expenditure and of fixed capital formation. Thus Cuadro 5 in Plan Financiero gives total capital expenditure at $3,844mn, the sum of $2,000mn of fixed capital formation and $1,744mn of other capital spending. The Annex table to the Plan Financiero gives only fixed capital formation for $2,000mn.

17. DNP merely records investment expenditure in the *Banco de Proyectos*; it does not change the classification of spending it receives from the agencies.

18. DNP, personal communication.

19. Only debt with expiration at issue above one year is recorded under *recursos de capital*.

20. These overpredictions of revenues are due mostly to a tendency to overestimate the effects of tax reforms yet to be approved.

21. Canada recently has taken such a step.

22. The IMF Transparency Guidelines (IMF 1999) go further, and recommend that the budget provide an assessment of the macroeconomic and fiscal "risks" surrounding the estimates. We believe this assessment is bound to be controversial and of dubious informative value, and should only be tried in advanced countries with more tested budget processes and more sophisticated forecasting approaches.

23. There is evidence of this behavior in the budgets of some advanced countries, as in Italy and even the United States.

24. Note that this rule is subject to some confusion. Article 41 of EOP states that the share of social *investment* spending cannot decrease from year to year, but it is not clear whether the notion of social investment spending, which appears in other parts of Article 40 of EOP, is to be considered distinct from that of social investment spending. To complicate matters, Article 350 of the Constitution states that the share of investment spending in total spending cannot decrease from year to year: the qualification "social" does not appear there.

25. Appropriations can be modified through the fiscal year: they can be increased, cut, and shifted between items. We deal here with final appropriations.

26. There may also exist revenue arrears—for example, taxes levied but not collected and uncollected loan repayments due to the government. They will not be discussed here.

27. Some accounts payable may be due to ordinary commercial credit and billing practices.

28. Article 33 is an interesting piece of legislation in that it is, by generalized consent, of a remarkable lack of clarity.

# References

Alesina, A., and T. Bayoumi. 1996. The costs and benefits of fiscal rules: Evidence from the U.S. states. NBER Working Paper 5614.

Alesina, A., R. Hausmann, R. Hommes, and E. Stein. 1995. Budget institutions and fiscal performance in Latin America. Inter-American Development Bank. OCE Working Paper 394.

Alesina, A., and R. Perotti. 1999. Budget deficits and budget institutions. In J. Poterba and J. von Hagen, eds., *Fiscal Institutions and Fiscal Performance*. Chicago: University of Chicago Press.

Alt, J., and R. Lowry. 1994. Divided government, fiscal institutions, and budget deficits: Evidence from the states. *American Political Science* Review 88: 811–28.

Baron, D. P. 1991. Majoritarian incentives, pork barrel programs, and procedural control. *American Journal of Political Science* 35(1): 57–90.

Baron, D. P., and J. A. Ferejohn. 1989. Bargaining in legislature. *American Political Science Review* 83(4): 1181–1206.

Bohn, H., and R. Inman. 1995. Constitutional limitations and budget deficits: Evidence from the US states. *Carnegie-Rochester Conference Series on Public Policy* 45: 13–76.

Comisión de Racionalización del Gasto y de las Finanzas Públicas. 1997. Eficiencia, sistema presupuestal, y control del gasto. In *Tema II: Administracion del Estado*. Santa Fe de Bogotá.

de Haan, J., W. Moessen, and B. Volkenkirk. 1999. Budgetary procedures. Aspects and changes: New evidence for some European countries. In J. Poterba and J. von Hagen, eds., *Fiscal Institutions and Fiscal Performance*. Chicago: University of Chicago Press, pp. 265–300.

Esquerra, P., M. Aranguren, and U. Ayala. 2000. La naturaleza del deficit fiscal y su financiamiento en los años noventa. Mimeo. Fedesarrollo.

Inman, R. 1996. Do balanced budget rules work? U.S. experience and possible lessons for the EMU. NBER Working Paper 5838.

International Monetary Fund. 1999. Manual on fiscal transparency. Washington, DC.

Kontopoulos, Y., and R. Perotti. 1999. Government weakness, fragmentation, and fiscal outcomes: Evidence from OECD countries. In J. Poterba and J. Von Hagen, eds., *Fiscal Institutions and Fiscal Performance*. Chicago: Chicago University Press.

Perotti, R. 2000. Public social expenditure in Colombia: Evaluation and proposals. Mimeo. Columbia University.

Perotti, R., and Y. Kontopoulos. 2002. Fragmented fiscal policy. *Journal of Public Economics*, forthcoming.

Poterba, J. 1996. Do budget rules work? NBER Working Paper 5550.

Velasco, A. 1999. A model of endogenous fiscal deficits and delayed fiscal reforms. In J. Poterba and J. Von Hagen, eds., *Fiscal Institutions and Fiscal Performance*. Chicago: University of Chicago Press, pp. 37–58.

von Hagen, J. 1991. A note on the empirical effectiveness of formal fiscal restraints. *Journal of Public Economics* 44: 99–110.

von Hagen, J. 1992. Budgeting procedures and fiscal performance in the European Community. Economic Paper 96. Commission of the European Communities. October.

von Hagen, J., and I. J. Harden. 1994. National budget processes and fiscal performance. *European Economy: Reports and Studies* 3: 311–418.

# 8 Educational Reform in Colombia

George J. Borjas and Olga Lucía Acosta

## 8.1 Introduction

Public education is one of the largest components of the public sector in Colombia, in terms of its size, share of public expenditures, and geographic coverage. In 1997 Colombia had 85 thousand educational establishments, 390 thousand teachers, and 8.6 million students. One out of every five Colombians is currently enrolled in the public education system, and 36 percent of central government tax revenues are allocated to public education. In addition public school teachers and educational staff comprise the highest percentage of public sector employment. During the last half of the 1980s the central government promoted a reorganization that gave municipalities a greater responsibility in financing and administering most public services. However, there has been some confusion as to which level of government is best suited to administer the public education system. Law 29 of 1989 favored the municipalization of public education, but the 1991 Constitution emphasized the role of the departmental level. Similarly Law 60 of 1993, which regulates the system of transfers of central funds to departments and municipalities, enhances the role of municipalities in the administration of public funds for education. In contrast, Law 115 of 1994, the General Education Law, responded to pressure from the teachers' union and assigned a greater role to the departments. In view of this statutory confusion, it is not surprising that there are three different types of public school teachers in Colombia: the central government funds national teachers, departmental governments fund departmental teachers, and municipalities fund municipal teachers.

It is widely recognized that there are serious inefficiencies in the allocation of resources in Colombia's public education system. These inefficiencies include the setting of teachers salaries by the central government, the generosity of the pension systems available to teachers, and the allocation of educational resources to different geographic areas. This chapter examines various aspects of the public education system in Colombia. We begin our analysis with a description of the main institutional features of public education in Colombia. We then evaluate the impact of the education reforms that took place in the early 1990s. Our empirical analysis suggests that with the exception of teacher salaries, which experienced a significant increase after 1994, the trends in several measures of educational outcomes are roughly similar both before and after 1994. It seems unlikely therefore that the education reforms had much impact on Colombia's education system. We conclude by making policy recommendations that could improve the allocation of resources in this large and important sector.

## 8.2   Institutional Characteristics

Table 8.1 reports the trends in public employment in Colombia. In relative terms, public employment peaked in 1980, when it made up 9.3 percent of the occupied population. By 1999, 7.8 percent of the occupied population was employed in the public sector. Teachers make up the largest group of public servants, accounting for 26 percent of public employees in 1999. (The military and police are the next largest group, comprising 18.9 percent of public employment.)

### 8.2.1   Educational Reforms

A key goal of the 1991 Constitution was to offer universal coverage in basic education (nine grades) to Colombia's population. To achieve this

**Table 8.1**
Evolution of public employment in Colombia

| Years | Workers (thousands) | Percentage of all employed | Annual rate of growth |
|-------|---------------------|----------------------------|-----------------------|
| 1970 | 437.8 | 6.5 | |
| 1975 | 608.4 | 8.2 | 6.8 |
| 1980 | 846.0 | 9.3 | 6.8 |
| 1985 | 913.4 | 8.8 | 1.5 |
| 1990 | 986.6 | 8.2 | 1.6 |
| 1995 | 994.0 | 7.2 | 0.1 |
| 1996 | 1,001.3 | 6.8 | 0.7 |
| 1997 | 1,025.5 | 6.8 | 2.4 |
| 1998 | 1,103.5 | 7.2 | 7.6 |
| 1999 | 1,193.6 | 7.8 | 8.2 |

Source: Encuesta Nacional de Hogares, DANE, various years.

goal, the Constitution initiated the process of decentralizing the administration of the public education system. Through these reforms, Colombia hoped to resolve one of the main sources of administrative and labor conflicts in the education system: the vagueness with which responsibilities are allocated to the various levels of government. As we will see, however, the reforms did not completely solve these issues, nor did they address a key source of the chronic financial predicament facing public education: the level of government responsible for providing public education is not the level of government that pays for it.

### Administrative Levels

Colombia has a central government, 1,170 municipalities, 4 special districts, and 32 departments. The central level includes the Ministry of Education and other relatively autonomous agencies addressing issues related to higher education or to science and technology. The departmental level includes the Departmental Secretaries of Education, the Regional Educational Funds created to administer the resources transferred by the central level, and other educational institutions responsible specially for the training. Finally, the municipal level is represented in the big cities by Municipal Secretaries of Education. Table 8.2 summarizes how the jurisdiction in education issues was allocated to the various administrative levels.

There is currently a great deal of confusion and incoherence in the administration of the public education system. Much of this confusion arises because of the ambiguity in the objectives assigned to each of the administrative levels. There are also many instantes where the governmental entities that should administer certain functions do not have the tools

**Table 8.2**
Distribution of educational functions according to the 1991 Constitution, Laws 60 of 1993, and 115 of 1994

| | |
|---|---|
| Nation | To establish technical, curricular, and pedagogical norms to be used by the territorial entities for orientation. |
| Department | To plan, administer, and coordinate teaching services, and to distribute them to municipalities. To assume the functions of technical development at pilot centers. To prepare the curriculum for teachers. To raise funds to maintain the infrastructure and educational investments. |
| Municipalities | To administer the pre-school, primary, middle-school, and secondary services as delegated by the department. To make the necessary investments in infrastructure and educational establishments. To inspect and supervise educational services. |

**Table 8.3**
Public expenditures on education as percent of GDP

| Year | Central government | Local government | Total |
|------|-----------|-----------|-------|
| 1991 | 0.8 | 2.3 | 3.1 |
| 1993 | 1.3 | 2.5 | 3.8 |
| 1994 | 1.0 | 2.5 | 3.6 |
| 1996 | 1.6 | 2.8 | 4.3 |
| 1997 | 1.6 | 2.9 | 4.5 |
| Average, 1970s | 1.1 | 2.0 | 3.1 |
| Average, 1980s | 0.9 | 2.5 | 3.4 |
| Average, 1990s | 1.3 | 2.6 | 3.8 |

Source: Misión Social DNP, based on formulary F-400 of the DANE.

necessary to carry out those functions. For example, the municipalities should have a central role in the administration of the education sector, but they have very limited authority for the management of human resources in that sector. Similarly the existing regulations emphasize the importance of the department in planning educational development, but the departmental level has little access to the financial resources that are required to conduct this job properly.

*Financing*

As table 8.3 shows, public expenditures on education increased rapidly in the 1990s, from 3.1 percent of GDP in 1991 to 4.5 percent in 1997, and expenditures by local governments accounted for a growing part of total expenditures on education. Since the enactment of Law 60 of 1993, the transfers of current incomes from the central government to territorial entities for expenditures in basic public services (e.g., education, health, and basic water and sewerage) have grown by more than 2 percent of GDP. Nearly 65 percent of these transfers have been assigned to the education sector, mainly to improve the wages of teachers. But the geographic distribution of the transfers is inefficient and inequitable. The monetary transfers are based on the number of teachers as of 1993, regardless of changes in underlying conditions. Because of the transfers, the municipalities and departments contribute a relatively small amount (14 percent of the total) to the financing of public education. Table 8.4 reports that 68.4 percent of the teachers are employed in the public sector. About 80 percent of the teachers in the public sector are employed by the central government or are nationalized, while 20 percent work for departments or municipalities.

**Table 8.4**
Number of teachers by educational level in public and private sectors, 1997

| Educational level | Teachers in public sector | Teachers in private sector | Total teachers | Percentage in public sector |
|---|---|---|---|---|
| Pre-school | 20,749 | 22,613 | 43,362 | 47.9 |
| Basic primary | 141,872 | 39,349 | 181,221 | 78.3 |
| Basic middle and secondary | 104,390 | 61,428 | 165,818 | 63.0 |
| Total | 267,011 | 123,390 | 390,401 | 68.4 |

Source: DANE, social indicators.

## 8.2.2   The Teachers' Union and the *Estatuto Docente*

In every Latin American country, teacher unions are the largest organizations of public sector workers, and these unions have been more organized and politically active than other public sector unions (de Cerreno and Pyle 1996). Although the key goal of the Latin American teacher unions has typically been to provide higher wages and better working conditions for their members, recent studies (Maceira and Murillo 2001) argue that these unions have pursued political strategies because of the statutory limits placed on the teachers' right to strike and because of the politicization of appointments to the education sector.

Most of the actions of FECODE, the Colombian Federation of Teachers, suggest that the key goal of the union has been to improve the economic and professional status of teachers. The conflicts between the government and FECODE have typically arisen over financial and administrative matters. The financial conflict arises because of the systematic inadequacy of funds for public education. FECODE supports the nationalization of public expenditure in education because, as Duarte (1996) states, "this will enhance its power as a national intermediary between the central government and the teachers. This also explains the strong opposition of FECODE to the descentralisation...."

The current regulations of the teaching profession in Colombia have their origin in an educational statute (*Estatuto Docente*) promulgated in 1979. This statute specifiees the norms that regulate the recruitment, labor stability, promotion, and retirement of teachers. The statute, and particularly the way it has been administered, have introduced a numer of inefficiencies into public education:

• Too much centralization. Teacher salaries are set by the central government, with little input from the regional government agencies that end up paying the bill.

• Inefficient appointment process. The departments and the municipalities can create temporary teaching positions. The provisions of the *Estatuto Docente* imply that these short-term positions eventually become permanent positions, putting additional pressure on the central government to increase its monetary transfers.

• Ineffective disciplinary regime. The directives (rectors) do not exercise any disciplinary control over the teachers. The *Estatuto Docente* orders that promotions be determined internally within the magistery, using a set of rules that are not always related to teaching activities.

According to the regulations outlined in Law 4 of 1992 and in Law 60 of 1993, the president of the republic must set the remuneration of the teachers who are subject to the relevant regulations in the *Estatuto Docente* in the first ten days of every year. We show below that teacher salaries increased substantially during the 1990s.

### 8.2.3  Teacher Pensions

The average teacher in Colombia is 43 years old. In table 8.5 we compare the pension benefits available to teachers with those established in Law 100 of 1993 (or Law of Social Security Reform) for other workers in Colombia. In general, the pension benefits granted to teachers are extremely generous. First, public teachers do not have to contribute to the funding of the system in order to receive a pension. Most nonteachers contribute 25 percent (13.5 percent is obligatory).

Second, teachers qualify to receive the special pension (pension de gracia) at 50 years of age. Under the pay-as-you-go system set up by Law 100 of 1993 for nonteachers, the retirement age is 55 for women and 60 for men.

Third, a different base salary is used to calculate the the pension for teachers and nonteachers. The special pension is based on the basic monthly salary that the teacher had at the time of retirement, *including* bonuses and other benefits. In addition the teacher's retirement pension is based on the average salary of the last year employed. In contrast, the pension benefits for nonteachers are based on the average salary in the last ten years of the entire career if more than 1,250 weeks have been contributed.

Finally, the pension regime grants teachers the right to receive several of these pensions simultaneously. The generosity of the pension program for teachers has created a substantial liability for the Colombian economy. As table 8.6 shows, the current liability of the pensions for the 303

**Table 8.5**
Pension benefit regimes of the magistery and Law 100 of 1993

| Benefits | Special pension (pensión de gracia) | Retirement pension | Retirement pension by old age | Law 100/93 |
|---|---|---|---|---|
| Beneficiaries | National teachers, nationalized and district, hired before 12–31–80 | National teachers, nationalized and hired by districts, departments, and municipalities | Persons that reach mandatory retirement age and do not have own resources for their subsistence | Affiliated with the pay-as-you-go system |
| Time of service | Typically 20 years | Typically 20 years | Person in active service at time of retirement | 1,000 weeks. Worker saves capital that generates at least one pension equal to 110% of the minimum salary |
| Age | 50 years, both men and women | If hired after 1–1–90, age 50 for women, 55 for men; if hired before 1–1–90, age 50 for men and women | 55 years old | 55 years old for women, 60 years old for men |
| Contribution | Nation in charge | Nation in charge | Nation in charge | 13.5% until 4 minimum wages 14.5% for 4 minimum wages or more; 75% paid by employer and 25% by worker |
| Base salary for calculating pension benefits | Basic monthly compensation, including bonuses and benefits | Average salary during the last year of service | Last monthly salary earned | Average salary in the last 10 years or in the whole work life if contributed more than 1,250 weeks |
| Pension amount | 75% | 75% | 20%, plus 25% for each year of service | 65% with 1,000 weeks of contribution, until 85% with 1,400 weeks. *Individual savings* depend on the capital accumulated on the individual saving account |

Notes: The nation is in charge of the special pension, which is paid by Cajanal and administered by the Fondo de Pensiones Públicas-FOPEP. Retirement pensions that began with the promulgation of Law 91 of 1989 (December 29) are paid by the Fondo Nacional de Prestaciones Sociales of the Magistery. But Cajanal and the Fondo Nacional de Ahorros cover pensions started before the date of that law. For teachers hired after January 1, 1981, there is only one recognized retirement pension paying 75% of the monthly average salary of the last year worked.

**Table 8.6**
Pension liability in 1999

|                                          | Active beneficiaries | Pensioned | Passive liability as percentage of GDP |
|------------------------------------------|----------------------|-----------|----------------------------------------|
| Teachers                                 | 303,000              | 61,848    | 30.0                                   |
| Beneficiaries of the Social Security Institute | 2,300,000      | 435,000   | 40.0                                   |

thousand active teachers is 30 percent of GDP. This compares to a liability of 40 percent of GDP for the 2.3 million nonteachers covered by the *Instituto de Seguros Sociales.*

## 8.3   Evaluating the Impact of Education Policy Reforms

In view of the substantial changes in education policy adopted by the Colombian government during the 1990s, it is worth investigating if the reforms had an observable impact on the educational opportunities faced by school-age children. In this section we examine several related issues. First, how did the reforms affect the economic opportunities available to public school teachers? Second, did the reforms increase the enrollment rate of school-age children? Third, are teacher resources better allocated across localities in the post-reform period (either through increase internal migration of teachers or through increased employment in the localities where teachers were most needed)? And, finally, is there evidence of geographic convergence in the educational opportunities available to Colombian children?

To evaluate the impact of the education policy reforms, we used the *Encuesta Nacional de Hogares* (ENH), a national household survey conducted quarterly by the *Departamento Administrativo Nacional de Estadística* (DANE). The survey covers ten Colombian cities. Although the five largest cities in the country are covered by the survey, the survey also covers medium-sized and smaller cities. One drawback of using the available ENH data for analyzing the impact of the education reforms is that it only covers the urban labor markets of Colombia.

The survey provides information on household characteristics (e.g., place of residence and years since the last migration), and on each respondent's characteristics (e.g., age, sex, educational attainment, marital status, and place of birth). The ENH also provides information on a person's labor market status and, if employed, on the worker's industry and occupation of employment, monthly salary, and hours of work. We use the ENH surveys for June 1991, June 1994, and June 1998.[1] The trends between 1991 and 1994 help us describe what was happening in Colombia's education sector prior to the enactment of the decentralization reforms in Law 60 of 1993. The trends between 1994 and 1998 help us describe the changes that occurred in the postdecentralization period. With the exception of teacher salaries, which experienced a significant increase after 1994, the trends in several measures of educational outcomes are roughly similar both before and after 1994. It seems unlikely therefore that the education reforms had much impact on Colombia's education system.

### 8.3.1 Trends in Teacher Salaries

We use the various ENH surveys to calculate both the adjusted and unadjusted wage differential between teachers and nonteachers in the Colombian labor market. We calculate these wage differentials for two types of teachers: public school and private school teachers. A worker is a public school teacher if he or she reports an occupation of "teacher" in the ENH and works in the public sector. A worker is a private school teacher if he or she reports an occupation of teacher and works in the private sector.

We estimate the following earnings function separately in each of the ENH surveys:

$$\log w_i = X_i\beta + \alpha_1 PU_i + a_2 PR_i + \varepsilon_i, \tag{1}$$

where $w_i$ gives the (monthly) monetary income of worker $i$; $X$ is a vector of socioeconomic characteristics (described below); $PU_i$ is a dummy variable set to unity if the worker is a public school teacher; and $PR_i$ is a dummy variable set to unity if the worker is a private school teacher. The regression model is estimated in the sample of workers aged 18 to 64. Initially we do not include any variables in the standardizing vector $X$. The coefficients $\alpha_1$ and $\alpha_2$ then measure the unadjusted wage differentials among the various types of workers in the Colombian labor market. The coefficients reported in the first column of table 8.7 indicate that public school teachers earn more than private school teachers and earn far more than the rest of the workers in the Colombian labor market. In 1994 the log wage differential between public school teachers and nonteachers was 0.540, which translates to an approximate 71.6 percent wage differential between the two groups.[2] Similarly the log wage differential between

**Table 8.7**
Salary differentials between teachers and nonteachers, 1991 to 1998

| Variable | Regression models estimated in 1991 ENH | | | Regression models estimated in 1994 ENH | | | Regression models estimated in 1998 ENH | | |
|---|---|---|---|---|---|---|---|---|---|
| | (1) | (2) | (3) | (1) | (2) | (3) | (1) | (2) | (3) |
| Private school teachers | 0.181 | 0.301 | 0.267 | 0.276 | 0.357 | −0.216 | 0.559 | 0.642 | −0.039 |
| | (0.039) | (0.037) | (0.031) | (0.039) | (0.038) | (0.034) | (0.035) | (0.034) | (0.030) |
| Public school teachers | 0.589 | 0.595 | 0.007 | 0.540 | 0.548 | −0.051 | 0.854 | 0.866 | 0.107 |
| | (0.035) | (0.033) | (0.028) | (0.037) | (0.035) | (0.032) | (0.035) | (0.034) | (0.030) |
| Controls for: | | | | | | | | | |
| Age, sex | No | Yes | Yes | No | Yes | Yes | No | Yes | Yes |
| Education | No | No | Yes | No | No | Yes | No | No | Yes |

Notes: Standard errors are reported in parentheses. Regressions are estimated from a sample of workers aged 18 to 64. Regressions in the 1991 sample have 29,112 observations. Regressions in the 1994 sample have 28,532 observations. Regressions in the 1998 sample have 29,436 observations.

public school and private school teachers was 0.276, which translates to an approximate 31.8 percent wage differential between the two groups.

The regression coefficients reported in table 8.7 reveal that much of the wage advantage accruing to public school teachers can be accounted for by differences in observable socioeconomic characteristics, particularly differences in educational attainment. The wage differentials between teachers and nonteachers fall dramatically when the vector $X$ is expanded to include the worker's educational attainment.[3] In 1994, for example, the 0.540 log wage advantaged enjoyed by public school teachers plummets to a $-0.051$ log wage *disadvantage* once the regression is controlled for educational attainment, while the 0.276 log wage advantaged enjoyed by private sector teachers becomes a $-0.216$ log wage disadvantage. In other words, although teachers earn more than the typical worker in the Colombian labor market, they earn less than comparably skilled nonteachers.

The data also show that the reforms in educational attainment increased the average pay of *both* public school and private school teachers. The relative salary of teachers was relatively stable between 1991 and 1994, but increased substantially between 1994 and 1998. For example, the unadjusted percent wage gap between public school teachers and nonteachers fell slightly from 80 to 72 percent between 1991 and 1994 but rose from 72 to 135 percent between 1994 and 1998. Similarly the unadjusted percent wage gap between private school teachers and nonteachers rose from 20 to 32 percent between 1991 and 1994, but rose between 32 to 75 percent between 1994 and 1998.

The fact that the educational reforms increased the mean wage of *all* teachers by roughly the same amount implies that the wage gap between public school and private school teachers remained relatively constant over the period. In both 1994 and 1998 public school teachers earn about 15 percent more than comparably skilled private school teachers. The educational reforms enacted in the 1990s therefore do not seem to have altered the relative incentives of teachers to enter the public and private sectors. Nevertheless, the increased pay of teachers should, in the end, provide additional incentives for more workers to enter the teaching profession in Colombia.

### 8.3.2  Trends in Enrollment Rates

An explicit goal of the educational reforms undertaken by the Colombian government in the 1990s was to provide better educational opportunities for the country's children. Table 8.8 summarizes some of the key

**Table 8.8**
Enrollment rates of children aged 5 to 16, 1991 to 1998

| Age group | 1991 | 1994 | 1998 |
|-----------|------|------|------|
| 5–6 | 76.2 | 83.9 | 87.3 |
| 7–8 | 95.8 | 96.6 | 95.4 |
| 10–13 | 95.1 | 95.8 | 93.7 |
| 14–16 | 80.3 | 82.2 | 81.9 |
| All ages | 88.6 | 90.6 | 90.1 |

descriptive trends in school enrollment rates in the population of children aged 5 to 16. Perhaps the most striking result is that even though enrollment rates were increasing prior to 1994, there was a slight *decline* in enrollment rates between 1994 and 1998. The fraction of children aged 5 to 16 enrolled in school rose from 88.6 to 90.6 percent between 1991 and 1994, but declined from 90.6 to 90.1 percent between 1994 and 1998.

There are dramatic variations around this general trend across various age groups. For example, the enrollment rate increased substantially in the postreform period from 83.9 to 87.3 percent for the youngest children (aged 5 and 6), but declined for all other age groups. Therefore, although the overall evidence shows that enrollment rates declined between 1994 and 1998, the youngest children—the children who are probably the most likely to be affected by the additional teaching resources—did experience a substantial increase in their enrollment rates. Note, however, that the enrollment rate of this group was rising rapidly even *before* the education reforms. Between 1991 and 1994 the enrollment rate of children aged 5 to 6 increased from 76.2 to 83.9 percent. It is difficult therefore to attribute much of the 1991 to 1994 enrollment increase among the youngest children in Colombia to the decentralization reforms.

There is also significant variation in the school enrollment trends across households belonging to different socioeconomic strata.[4] As table 8.9 shows, there are substantial differences in enrollment rates among children in the different socioeconomic classes, with the lower socioeconomic classes having substantially lower enrollment rates at any given age. For instance, in 1998 the enrollment rate of children aged 10 to 13 who come from the low socioeconomic class was 90.2 percent, the rate for children who come from the middle class was 95.7 percent, and the rate for children who come from the high socioeconomic class was 96.0 percent. Not surprisingly, the household's socioeconomic class is an important determinant of whether the children in that household are enrolled in school.

**Table 8.9**
Enrollment rates, by socioeconomic strata

| Age group | Low 1991 | 1994 | 1998 | Middle 1991 | 1994 | 1998 | High 1991 | 1994 | 1998 |
|-----------|------|------|------|------|------|------|------|------|------|
| 5–6 | 66.4 | 76.7 | 80.9 | 81.2 | 87.8 | 90.5 | 92.7 | 96.9 | 98.2 |
| 7–8 | 93.5 | 94.5 | 92.2 | 97.1 | 97.9 | 97.3 | 99.4 | 98.2 | 97.3 |
| 10–13 | 92.6 | 93.5 | 90.2 | 96.4 | 97.0 | 95.7 | 98.3 | 97.6 | 96.0 |
| 14–16 | 70.2 | 73.8 | 73.1 | 85.4 | 86.5 | 86.9 | 84.3 | 89.6 | 85.6 |
| All ages | 83.4 | 86.2 | 85.0 | 91.4 | 93.0 | 93.0 | 93.9 | 95.1 | 94.0 |

However, the evidence also shows that the enrollment rate increased most for the youngest children who come from the lower socioeconomic classes. For instance, the enrollment rate of children aged 5 to 6 who come from low socioeconomic class households increased by about 10 percent points in 1991 to 1994 (before the education reforms), and by an additional 4 percentage points, from 76.7 to 80.9 percent in 1994 to 1998. Again, it is difficult to infer from the data that the education reforms had much beneficial impact on the enrollment rates of disadvantaged young children in Colombia.

### 8.3.3   Internal Migration of Teachers

The debate over the performance of the public education sector in Colombia often assumes that there is a misallocation of teachers across geographic areas. There are "too many" teachers in some locations, and "too few" in others. This misallocation of teachers can generate a substantial amount of inefficiency in the provision of public education to Colombia's children. In effect, teachers are relatively scarce in those areas where they are most needed, and relatively abundant in less crucial localities.

This type of discussion effectively assumes that teachers—and public school teachers, in particular—exhibit a type of "job lock." Because of political, social, or economic reasons, teachers resist moving across localities once they obtain a teaching position. We now examine the validity of the hypothesis that teachers are particularly immobile in the Colombian labor market.

The ENH surveys report the number of years that they have resided in their current location. We define a worker to be a migrant if he or she has resided in the current city for two years or less. We restrict our study of internal migration to the sample of persons who are working at the time of the survey and who are 18 to 60 years old.

The first three columns of table 8.10 summarize the descriptive evidence on migration rates available in the ENH. The data clearly show that teachers, regardless of whether they teach in public or private schools, have substantially lower migration rates than nonteachers. For instance, the migration rate for nonteachers is 6.7 percent in the 1998 ENH survey, indicating that 6.7 percent of nonteachers had moved across localities in the two-year period prior to the survey (i.e., between 1996 and 1998). The mobility rate of workers in the teaching profession is far lower. In 1998, for example, only 4.3 percent of private school teachers and 3.4 percent of public school teachers had moved across cities in the prior two years. In short, teachers have substantially lower internal migration rates than nonteachers—and public school teachers seem to have particularly low migration rates. It is also worth noting that there was a marked *decline* in internal migration rates of public school teachers both between 1991 and 1994, and between 1994 and 1998. The migration rates for these teachers fell from 5.1 to 4.8 percent between 1991 and 1994, and from 4.8 to 3.4 percent between 1994 and 1998. If anything, the inefficiencies implied by job lock among public school teachers increased during the period of the education reforms.

Much of the gap in internal migration rates between teachers and nonteachers disappears once we adjust for differences in socioeconomic characteristics among the various groups, particularly their age. Consider the regression model:

$$m_i = X_i\beta + \alpha_1 PU_i + \alpha_2 PR_i + \varepsilon_i, \tag{2}$$

where $m_i$ is a dummy variable set to unity if worker $i$ moved across cities in the two-year period prior to the survey. As before, $X$ is a vector of socioeconomic characteristics, $PU_i$ is a dummy variable set to unity if the worker is a public school teacher, and $PR_i$ is a dummy variable set to unity if the worker is a private school teacher. We estimated equation (2) separately in the 1994 and 1998 surveys, and used the sample of workers who are 18 to 60 years old.

The last six columns of table 8.10 report the differences in migration rates between teachers and nonteachers (i.e., the coefficients $\alpha_1$ and $\alpha_2$) after controlling for various sets of socioeconomic characteristics. In 1998 the unadjusted difference in the probability of migration between public school teachers and nonteachers is 3.4 percentage points. Table 8.10 shows that this unadjusted gap drops to 1.4 percentage points (and is not statistically significant) when the regression specification is expanded to include the worker's age as a regressor, and drops further to 0.4 per-

**Table 8.10**
Differences in migration rates between teachers and nonteachers

| | Probability of migration | | | Adjusted differences, 1994 | | | Adjusted differences, 1998 | | |
|---|---|---|---|---|---|---|---|---|---|
| | 1991 | 1994 | 1998 | (1) | (2) | (3) | (1) | (2) | (3) |
| Public school teachers | 0.051 | 0.048 | 0.034 | -0.026 (0.011) | -0.006 (0.011) | 0.017 (0.012) | -0.034 (0.009) | -0.014 (0.009) | 0.004 (0.010) |
| Private school teachers | 0.056 | 0.050 | 0.043 | -0.024 (0.012) | -0.021 (0.012) | -0.001 (0.012) | -0.024 (0.009) | -0.026 (0.009) | -0.010 (0.009) |
| All other workers | 0.067 | 0.074 | 0.067 | — | — | — | — | — | — |

Notes: Standard errors are reported in parentheses. Regressions are estimated in a sample of workers aged 18 to 60. Regressions in the 1994 sample have 30,560 observations. Regressions in the 1998 sample have 32,714 observations.

centage points when the regression also includes the worker's educational attainment.

It should not be surprising that a large part of the unadjusted migration rate differential between public school teachers and nonteachers can be attributed to differences in socioeconomic characteristics between the groups, particularly differences in their age distribution. After all, it is well known that migration rates decline with age in many countries (Greenwood 1997). Labor economists typically explain this empirical pattern by arguing that the economic payoff to internal migration, like the economic payoff to all human capital investments, decline as workers get older (since older workers have fewer years in which to recoup the costs of making the move to their new location).

Public school teachers in Colombia are, on average, much older than other workers. In 1998, for example, the typical public school teacher was 42.0 years old, as compared to 34.7 years old for private school teachers, and 35.1 years old for nonteachers. This sizable difference in the mean age between public school teachers and other workers is the key factor responsible for the relative immobility of teachers in the Colombian labor market. In other words, Colombian public school teachers are relatively less mobile not because of factors that are specific to the teaching profession, but because public school teachers are substantially older and internal migration rates tend to decline with age.

This simple fact may have important implications for future discussions of education policy and teacher mobility in Colombia. After all, it is probably desirable to reduce the inefficiency created in the education sector by the job lock of teachers attached to particular regions. Ideally, teaching resources would be fluid across localities, responding to market needs. One obvious incentive system that would motivate teachers to move across areas would be to institute a system of regional differences in teacher pay, with the financial rewards being greater in those areas where teaching resources are most needed. The fact that teachers tend to be relatively older, however, implies that the regional wage differentials required to induce teachers to migrate to the targeted cities might have to be substantial. As a result it may be relatively expensive to reduce inefficiencies in the education sector in Colombia by encouraging more internal migration of public school teachers.

### 8.3.4 Determinants of the Increase in the Number of Teachers
Because teachers are relatively immobile across cities in Colombia, the government could improve access to educational opportunities in "dis-

advantaged" areas by hiring relatively more teachers in those cities where the school-going population is growing rapidly or where there is a relative shortage of teachers relative to the size of the school-going population. There was in fact a substantial increase in the number of teachers— employed in both private and public schools—between 1991 and 1998. In 1991 there were 220.127 public sector teachers and 77.500 private teachers. In 1994 there were 231.992 public-sector teachers and 98.615 private-sector teachers. By 1998 there were 303.225 public-sector teachers and around 125,000 private-sector teachers.

It is well known that there are long-standing structural differences in access to publicly provided educational opportunities across regions and cities in Colombia. Hence it is of interest to investigate if the teaching resources provided by the additional hires were allocated in ways that cater to the needs of the school-going population. In particular, did teacher employment grow fastest in the areas where the teachers would seem to be most needed?

We aggregated the ENH household data to the city level, and calculated measures of teacher employment and educational activities for each of the 30 cities that can be matched in the 1994 and 1998 ENH surveys. Table 8.11 summarizes some of the aggregate statistics that can be calculated from the ENH at the city level. It is evident that the number of public school teachers rose at a substantially faster rate in some areas. The number of public school teachers, for example, rose by 0.586 log points in Barranquilla, by 0.460 log points in Bogotá, and by 0.125 log points in Medellín. The table also illustrates significant regional differences in the educational resources available to students. In 1994, for example, there were 23.3 school-age children per teacher in Barranquilla, 17.4 in Bogotá, and 28.6 in Soledad.

To examine the question of whether the increase in the number of teachers between 1994 and 1998 occurred in those cities where they would seem to be most needed, we estimated a number of regression models with the generic specification:

$$g_j = \alpha + \beta \log \frac{C_j}{T_j} + \text{other variables} + \varepsilon_j, \tag{3}$$

where $g_j$ gives the rate of growth in the number of public school teachers employed in city $j$ (defined as the log of the ratio of the number of public school teachers employed in 1998 to the number employed in 1994), $C_j$ gives the size of the school-age population in the city (defined as the

**Table 8.11**
Regional differences in the education sector for selected cities

| City | Rate of growth | | School-age children | Children per teacher (in 1994) | Students per teacher (in 1994) | Number of observations |
|---|---|---|---|---|---|---|
| | Private school teachers | Public school teachers | | | | |
| Barranquilla | 0.315 | 0.586 | 0.060 | 23.3 | 21.5 | 9,837 |
| Bello | 1.013 | −0.744 | 0.101 | 23.4 | 21.7 | 1,020 |
| Bogotá | 0.657 | 0.460 | 0.109 | 17.4 | 16.1 | 9,694 |
| Bucaramanga | 0.427 | 0.288 | 0.179 | 19.4 | 17.0 | 4,928 |
| Cali | 0.375 | 0.527 | 0.136 | 22.6 | 19.7 | 8,826 |
| Cucuta | 0.260 | −0.280 | 0.198 | 15.0 | 12.8 | 5,855 |
| Dosquebradas | 0.586 | 0.378 | 0.119 | 18.8 | 17.0 | 2,096 |
| Floridablanca | 1.061 | 0.721 | 0.277 | 21.9 | 20.1 | 2,227 |
| Manizales | 0.747 | −0.069 | 0.029 | 11.8 | 11.0 | 7,206 |
| Medellin | 0.420 | 0.125 | 0.211 | 18.7 | 16.5 | 9,801 |
| Pasto | 0.061 | 0.176 | 0.197 | 8.7 | 7.6 | 7,600 |
| Pereira | 0.389 | 0.173 | 0.106 | 19.1 | 16.9 | 4,600 |
| Soledad | 0.724 | 0.821 | 0.074 | 28.6 | 27.1 | 2,492 |
| Villavicencio | −0.020 | 0.840 | 0.097 | 32.1 | 28.1 | 7,141 |

number of children aged 5 to 16 in 1994), and $T_j$ gives the total number of teachers employed in the city as of 1994. The ratio $C_j/T_j$ therefore gives the number of school-age children per available teacher in 1994. If the new hires were allocated to those cities where they are most needed (in terms of their presumed educational impact), one would expect the coefficient $\beta$ to be positive, as the teacher employment growth should have occurred in those cities where there are the most potential students per available teacher. To determine if the impact of the number of school-age children per available teacher on the growth in the employment of public school teachers was affected by the education reforms, we also estimated equation (3) using the respective data from the 1991 to 1994 period. The comparison of the two regressions would allow us to determine if the trends are similar pre- and postdecentralization. Finally, we estimated the various regression models using an alternative dependent variable: the growth rate in the number of teachers employed in private schools in city $j$.

The key results of the regression analysis are reported in table 8.12. It is evident that the 1994 to 1998 percentage increase in the number of public school teachers was greatest in those areas that had the largest number of potential students per available teacher as of 1994. This correlation moreover is statistically significant and numerically important since the elasticity is nearly one. The regression results for 1991 to 1994 also indicate that the point estimate of the coefficient $\beta$ is positive. Note, however, that it is not statistically significant. The allocative efficiency associated with putting new teaching resources in the areas with the greatest need therefore seems to be greater in the postreform period.

The regressions suggest a number of additional interesting findings. For example, although there is a strong correlation between the employment growth of public school teachers and the initial number of school-age children per available teacher, no such correlation exists for private school teachers in 1994 to 1998. In other words, the "need for teachers" helps explain the regional dispersion in the employment growth of public school teachers but does not help explain the regional dispersion in the employment growth of private school teachers.

Second, the regressions also show that the correlation measured by the coefficient $\beta$ in equation (3) remains even after we control for additional factors that might generate an increase in the number of public school teachers employed in a particular locality. For example, the regressions included a measure of the increase in income in the locality.[5] It is likely that localities where incomes are rising faster might "spend"

**Table 8.12**
Determinants of rate of growth in the employment of teachers

| | Teachers in public schools | | | | Teachers in private schools | | | |
| | 1991–1994 | | 1994–1998 | | 1991–1994 | | 1994–1998 | |
| Variable | (1) | (2) | (3) | (4) | (1) | (2) | (3) | (4) |
|---|---|---|---|---|---|---|---|---|
| Log (number of children per teacher in 1994) | 0.145 (0.267) | 0.196 (0.267) | 0.757 (0.259) | 0.834 (0.272) | 0.657 (0.376) | 0.722 (0.334) | 0.292 (0.410) | 0.424 (0.449) |
| Rate of growth in city's average income | — | 2.156 (1.166) | — | 1.863 (0.716) | — | 1.987 (1.534) | — | 1.744 (1.241) |
| Rate of growth in number of school-age children | — | −0.172 (0.902) | — | 0.206 (0.864) | — | −1.624 (1.306) | — | 0.301 (1.561) |
| Log (number of public school teachers in 1994) | — | −0.023 (0.047) | — | — | — | 0.096 (0.053) | — | — |
| Log (number of private school teachers in 1994) | — | — | — | −0.047 (0.059) | — | — | — | −0.052 (0.073) |
| $R^2$ | 0.014 | 0.186 | 0.271 | 0.460 | 0.122 | 0.410 | 0.026 | 0.133 |
| Sample size | 23 | 23 | 25 | 25 | 24 | 24 | 21 | 21 |

Notes: Standard errors are reported in parentheses.

some of the additional wealth on additional teachers. In fact there is a strong positive correlation between fast-rising incomes and the increasing employment of public and private school teachers, but it remains the case that the number of public school teachers rose most in the cities where there many potential students per available teacher.

### 8.3.5 Geographic Convergence in Educational Opportunities

An important goal of the educational reforms enacted during the 1991s was to equalize the educational opportunities available across localities in Colombia. Our empirical analysis is designed to estimate the extent to which educational opportunities converge across localities over a particular time period. One possible variable of interest is the relative number of school-age children per teacher in the locality. The generic regression model has the form:

$$\Delta \log \frac{C_{jt}}{T_{jt}} = \alpha + \alpha \log \frac{C_{j,t-1}}{T_{j,t-1}} + \varepsilon_{jt}, \tag{4}$$

where $C_{jt}$ gives the number of school-age children (aged 5 to 16) in city $j$ at time $t$, and $T_{jt}$ gives the total number of teachers in the city at time $t$. The dependent variable therefore gives the log change in the number of school-age children per teacher between 1991 and 1994 or between 1994 and 1998. The independent variable gives the level of this variable as of 1991 or as of 1994, depending on the regression specification.

The regression model in equation (4) resembles the typical convergence models estimated in the cross-country growth literature (Barro 1991; Mankiw, Romer, and Weil 1992). The coefficient $\delta$ is the convergence parameter. This coefficient measures the extent to which educational opportunities (as measured by the number of school-age children per teacher) were equalized across localities over a particular time period. The coefficient $\delta$ for the regression estimated over the 1994 to 1998 period would be negative if the policy changes implemented in that time period helped equalize educational opportunities across cities. If $\delta$ were positive, it would imply divergence in educational opportunities, for the cities where there were many children per teacher in 1994 were also the cities that experienced the highest increase in this variable during the 1994 to 1998 period.

Table 8.13 summarizes some of the evidence from our convergence regressions for both the 1991–1994 and 1994–1998 periods. The top panel of the table shows that the estimated convergence coefficient $\delta$ is

**Table 8.13**
Convergence regressions

| Dependent variable | Sample period 1991–1994 | | Sample period 1994–1998 | |
|---|---|---|---|---|
| | (1) | (2) | (1) | (2) |
| *A. Change in log (number of school-age children per teacher)* | | | | |
| Log (number of school-age children per teacher at beginning of sample period) | −0.516 (0.183) | −0.514 (0.170) | −0.473 (0.235) | −0.754 (0.186) |
| Change in log incomes over sample period | — | −1.753 (0.758) | — | −2.102 (0.467) |
| *B. Change in log (enrollment rate)* | | | | |
| Log (enrollment rate at beginning of sample period) | −0.200 (0.117) | −0.217 (0.116) | −0.433 (0.150) | −0.401 (0.149) |
| Change in log incomes over sample period | — | 0.101 (0.072) | — | −0.004 (0.048) |
| *C. Change in log (number of students per teacher)* | | | | |
| Log (number of students per teacher at beginning of sample period) | −0.524 (0.177) | −0.517 (0.166) | −0.588 (0.234) | −0.791 (0.178) |
| Change in log incomes over sample period | — | −1.631 (0.760) | — | −2.052 (0.447) |

Notes: Standard errors are reported in parentheses. The 1991–94 convergence regressions have 29 observations. The sample sizes for the 1994–98 convergence regressions are as follows: regressions for the number of school-age children per teacher have 26 observations; regressions for the enrollment rate have 29 observations; and regressions for the number of students per teacher have 26 observations. All regressions are weighted by the sample size of the cell used for calculating the dependent variable.

consistently negative in all the specifications, indicating that there was indeed a *narrowing* of differences in the number of school-age children per teacher across the 30 Colombian cities in the ENH data both between 1991 and 1994 and between 1994 and 1998. In the 1991 to 1994 period, the estimate of $\delta$ is −0.516, with a standard error of 0.183. In the 1994 to 1998 period, the estimate of $\delta$ is −0.473, with a standard error of 0.235. In other words, the change in the number of school-age children per teacher was smallest (i.e., most negative) in those cities that had the most school-age children per teacher at the beginning of the period. The regression analysis therefore implies that the rate of convergence in the number of school-age children per teacher was not affected by the education reforms.

The remaining panels of the table attempt to determine if there was convergence in other measures of educational output. The middle panel of the table, for example, shows that there was also a great deal of convergence in the enrollment rate across cities (where the enrollment rate is defined as the fraction of the school-age population that is enrolled in school). As before, the convergence coefficient is negative and significant in both time periods. Finally, the bottom panel of the table examines the degree of convergence that took place in the pupil/teacher ratio, a commonly used measure of educational quality in the literature. The evidence again indicates that there was a great deal of convergence in the pupil/teacher ratio in the both the 1991–1994 and 1994–1998 periods.

Overall, we find strong evidence of equalization of educational opportunities across Colombia's localities throughout the 1990s. The evidence does not suggest that much of this convergence can be attributed to the educational reforms because the rate of convergence is roughly constant throughout the decade.

It is important to note that we do not know if the convergence found across the 30 cities surveyed in the ENH also applies to the wider differences in educational access that exist between the rural and urban sectors.

## 8.4  Policy Implications

In this chapter, we have identified a number of problems in the administration of the education system in Colombia, and we assessed the extent to which the educational reforms adopted in the early 1990s have changed teacher salaries and educational opportunities for Colombia's children. Overall, our empirical results do not suggest that the educational reforms adopted in Law 60 of 1993 had much impact on the education system. Therefore many issues remain to be addressed to improve efficiency in the education system. These include less centralization, allowances for regional wage differentials, reforms of teacher pensions, the *Escuela Nueva*, and other reforms.

### 8.4.1  Less Centralization

There remains a great deal of confusion in the civil service system facing teachers. Much of this confusion arises because the local jurisdictions that hire teachers have little say over how teacher pay is determined. At the present, teachers can be hired by authorities in the central government, in the departments, or in the municipalities. Teacher salaries and pension benefits, however, are centrally determined. Moreover temporary teaching jobs are created by localities, but they often ignore the fact that because of the provisons of the *Estatuto Docente*, these temporary positions often evolve into permanent positions.

The efficiency of the education system would be greatly enhanced if the hiring and salary decisions were made by the same government jurisdictions. This simple change in the "rules" would encourage those who make the decision of hiring a teacher to pay attention to the cost of the decision, as well as encourage those who set teacher salaries to pay more attention to the factors that determine how many and which teachers are employed. This simple reform of the system would introduce much-needed accountability into the civil service for teachers. The teachers union, FECODE, would likely be opposed to this reform because it would decentralize the labor market for teachers.

### 8.4.2  Regional Wage Differentials Allowances
The central setting of teacher salaries creates serious inequities in *real* pay across geographic regions of Colombia. Obviously there are cost of living differentials and differences in amenities across the various areas of Colombia. By setting a constant nominal salary for teachers throughout the whole country, the central authorities are effectively creating differences in economic opportunities that make working in some areas more valuable than working in other areas. Given these differences in real wages, it should not surprising that teaching resources are not optimally allocated across Colombia's geographic regions in the present system.

A simple—though inevitably controversial—change in the pay-setting rules would help remove much of this inefficiency. The government should allow nominal differences in pay across regions in Colombia, so that the real wage would be roughly constant across Colombia's geographic regions. A constant real wage implies that all geographic areas would be equally remunerative, so that teachers would not necessarily prefer to work in one area over another. In short, local labor market conditions, rather than a central mandate of nominal pay equality for all teachers, would determine the salaries of teachers in Colombia. If there were a shortage in the supply of teachers to a particular locality, salaries in that region would rise—relative to the salary in the other regions—and thereby attract more teachers.

### 8.4.3  Teacher Pension Reforms
The teachers were excluded from the last round of pension reform. At the present time teachers do not make any financial contribution to their pension programs. Furthermore the fund created by the government to cover the pension payments that will eventually have to be made to

teachers has a huge liability, amounting to 30 percent of GDP. In its agreement with the International Monetary Fund, the Colombian government agreed to extend the pensions reforms of 1994. Reforming the teacher pension program should be a central aspect of any pension reform that is undertaken in the future.

Currently teachers can retire when they reach the age of 50. Many teachers in fact do not retire at that age but collect one of the pension benefits available to them while still working in the teaching profession. We conclude that any pension reform for teachers should incorporate two key changes. First, it should increase the age of retirement. Second, it should discourage "double-dipping" and "triple-dipping" from the various teacher pensions.

Our data indicate that teachers are relatively older than other workers, so that a large number of teachers will be retiring within the next decade. The huge expenditure that will be necessary to meet the pension liability at that time can be somewhat reduced by making teachers eligible for pensions at the same time as all other workers in Colombia (i.e., age 55 for women and 60 for men). The government could also reduce the costs by imposing taxes on teacher pension benefits if the teacher remains employed after "retirement." In the long run the pension reform should strive to consolidate the various retirement programs available to teachers into a single program, thus reducing the chances that teachers—unlike other workers in Colombia—can receive two or three pension benefits in their retirement years.

### 8.4.4 The *Escuela Nueva* and Other Reforms

Our discussion has focused on ways to improve the administrative efficiency of the education system. It is clear that there is an equally pressing need to improve the quality of education provided in Colombia's public schools. Only 20 percent of the children who enter first grade finish the program of basic education. Moreover only about a third of those who complete their basic education do not repeat a school year.

The *Escuela Nueva*, a school program that has been widely adopted in Colombia's rural sector, seems to have had significant success in improving education opportunities available in that area. Under this program, teachers have much greater flexibility in making their own decisions regarding the education process in their classroom. The curriculum is also more independently targeted to different students and stresses practical problem solving, so that it more easily engages the students. Parents are also involved through increased participation in school activities. It would be worthwhile to examine whether this type of program could be expanded to cover Colombia's public schools in urban areas.

The recent reforms adopted by Bogotá and Antioquia also show the promise of decentralization and choosing different institutional frameworks in urban settings. In Bogotá, the local administration increased the number of "places" for students by 140,000, with slightly over half (80,000) obtained by making better use of existing resources, and the remainder by granting funds to private schools to build new schools in the poorest areas. The new administrators received "vouchers" equal to what it would cost to educate a child in one of the purely public schools. These administrators take all responsibility over the recruiting of teachers and the administration of the school. The evidence suggests that parents prefer these "mixed" private-public schools, both because of the quality of the school administration and because of the absence of labor conflict that has been a hallmark of Colombia's public schools in the past.

## Notes

1. The ENH uses a random stratified sampling approach. We use the sampling weights provided by the ENH throughout the analysis.

2. The approximate percent wage differential is given by $(e^{0.540} - 1) \times 100$.

3. We control for the worker's educational attainment by including a vector of dummy variables indicating if the worker has no education, primary education, secondary education, or higher education.

4. The definitions are as follows: the "low" socioeconomic group has values of "low-low" or "low" in the stratum variable contained in the ENH; the "middle" group has values of "medium-low" or "medium"; and the "high" group has values of "medium-high" or "high."

5. This variable is given by the change in the city's mean log income between 1991 and 1994, or between 1994 and 1998.

## References

Ayala, U., C. Soto, and L. Hernández. 1999. *La remuneración y el mercado de trabajo de los maestros públicos en Bogotá*. In *Coyuntura Social* 20: 83–122.

Barro, R. J. 1991. Economic growth in a cross-section of countries. *Quarterly Journal of Economics* 106: 407–33.

Comisión de Racionalización del Gasto y de las Finanzas Públicas, CRGP. 1997. Informe Final. El Saneamiento Fiscal un Compromiso de la Sociedad. Tema III. Descentralización. Capítulo Gasto Público en Educación Básica.

Coyuntura Social. 1999. Análisis Coyuntural: Cómo vá la descentralización en el país? 20: 59–80.

De Cerreno, A., and C. A. Pyle. 1996. *Educational Reform in Latin America*. Council on Foreign Relations.

Departamento Nacional de Planeación. 1999. *Gasto Social 1980–1997*. Colombia: Quebecor/Impreandes Colombia S.A. Publicación Seriada 21.

Departamento Nacional de Planeación, DNP. 1998. Primer Seminario Internacional de Análisis y de Diseño Institucional. Hacia el Rediseño del Estado.

Departamento Nacional de Planeación. 1999. *La Educación en Cifras*. Colombia: Quebecor/ Impreandes Colombia S.A. Publicación Seriada 19.

Departamento Nacional de Planeación. 2000. *Indicadores de Coyuntura Social*. Colombia: Quebecor/Impreandes Colombia S.A. Publicación Seriada 24.

Duarte-Agudelo, J. 1995. State education and clientelism in Colombia: The politics of state education administration and of implementation of educational investment projects in two Colombian regions. PhD thesis. University of Oxford.

Duarte-Agudelo, J. 1996. La Debilidad del Ministerio de Educación y la politización de la educación: dos problemas a enfrentar en el Plan Decenal. *Fedesarrollo. Coyuntura Económica* 14: 145–67.

Fedesarrollo. Proyecto Agenda Colombia. 1998. *Sector Educativo: Diagnóstico y Recomendaciones*.

Gómez Buendia, H., and R. Losada-Lora. 1984. *Organización y Conflicto: La educación primaria oficial en Colombia*.

Gómez Buendia, H., R. Londoño, and G. Perry. 1986. *Sindicalismo y Política Economica*. Fedesarrollo Cerec.

González, J. I., A. Sarmiento, et al. 1998. *Estructura, evolución y determinantes del salario en el sector público*. Mimeo. Misión Social del Departamento Nacional de Planeación, Departamento Administrativo de la Función Pública y Ministerio de trabajo.

Greenwood, M. J. 1997. Internal migration in developed countries. In M. R. Rosenzweig and O. Stark, eds., *Handbook of Population and Family Economics*, vol. 1B. Amsterdam: Elsevier, pp. 647–720.

Informe de la Misión de Empleo, o Informe Chenery. 1986. El problema laboral Colombiano: Diagnóstico, perspectivas y políticas. Agosto September.

Maceira, D., and V. Murillo. 2001. Social sector reform in Latin America and the role of unions. Working Paper 456. Washington, DC: Inter-American Bank Desarrollo.

Mankiw, N. G., D. Romer, and D. N. Weil. 1992. A contribution to the empirics of economic growth. *Quarterly Journal of Economics* 107: 407–38.

Molina, A. 1998. Servicio Civil. Mimeo. División Especial de Evaluación. Departamento Nacional de Planeación.

Mora, H., U. Ayala, C. Gutierrez, and A. Velasco. 2000. Financiamiento de la educación: Evaluación de la viabilidad del sistema de capitalización. Foro convocado por la Fundación Corona y El Tiempo. Proyecto de Reforma Pensional.

Sanchez, F., et al. 1999. Quién se Benefició del Gasto Social en los Noventa? En *Coyuntura Social* No 20. Fedesarrollo.

Sarmiento, A., and B. Caro. 1997. El avance de la Educación en Colombia: lento, insuficiente e inequitativo. *Planeación y Desarrollo* 28: 11–24.

Sarmiento, A. 1999. La educación en el Plan Nacional de Desarrollo: Cambio para Construir la Paz 1998–2002. *Debates de Coyuntura Social* 12: 90–98.

Younes, M. D. 1992. Las reformas del Estado y la Administración Pública. Editorial Temis.

World Bank. 1994. Civil service reform in Latin America and the Caribbean. In S. A. Chaudhry, G. J. Reid, and W. H. Malik, eds., *Proceedings*.

World Bank. 1995. *Making Decentralization Work*. Washington, DC.

# 9 Public Spending on Social Protection in Colombia: Analysis and Proposals

Roberto Perotti

## 9.1 Introduction

Traditionally health and education expenditure have played the lion's share both in the theoretical discussions and in the allocation of social spending in Colombia. This reflects the widespread view that social policy should be aimed at eradicating the causes of poverty rather than its manifestations. I argue in this chapter that this view has little theoretical content; more important, it might be responsible for an attitude that downplays all those social programs geared to the poor that do not contribute, in some way or another, to building human capital. I argue instead that these programs should have full citizenship in a country at the level of development of Colombia.

However, even within the existing nonhealth and noneducation social spending, the current allocation is very skewed toward programs that do not benefit the poor or often do so only marginally. In particular, pensions take up an inordinate share of social spending and are paid almost exclusively to the top two quintiles of the distribution. This leaves very little room for other programs—mostly programs toward children, families, and labor markets. These programs in turn suffer from problems of their own, in particular, an almost complete lack of any usable evaluation, an excessive fragmentation into many agencies and subprograms, and—an almost unavoidable consequence—lack of clarity on their goals.

## 9.2 A Theoretical Framework for Social Spending

What is public social spending? For expository purposes, it is useful to follow a standard classification (e.g., see World Bank 1997a) and distinguish between social services (e.g., education and health), social insurance (e.g., old age and invalidity pensions and unemployment insurance),

social assistance (cash transfers to the poor, family assistance benefits, maternity benefits, in-kind transfers) and employment generating
programs.

Most industrialized countries have built their social protection systems
around social insurance, leaving social assistance to pick up the uninsured
who fall through the cracks and to subsidize large families and maternal
leaves. There are three reasons why Latin American countries cannot
aspire to the same structure of social protection. First, Latin American
countries can rely only on much smaller revenues.[1] Second, because of
the widespread rates of informality and of technical problems, it is difficult to keep track of the work and contributory history of individuals; in
any case, few workers would have unbroken records of contributions.
Third, for many poor individuals it is simply rational to stay out of
an insurance system, even if subsidized: poorer individuals have much
shorter life expectancies, and they put a high premium on liquidity (see
James 1999).

On the other hand, the experience of industrialized and developing
countries alike has shown that universal, untargeted social assistance
programs can quickly become very costly. This option too is therefore
closed to Colombia.

This leaves two more options: targeted social assistance, or social service spending. So far Colombia has clearly chosen the latter. A very popular view, in Colombia as well as in the rest of Latin America and in
international organizations, is that social expenditure should eliminate
the *causes* of poverty rather than its *manifestation*: in other words, it
should have an impact on the *ability to earn* rather than merely on the
*current consumption* of an individual. While, as we will see, theoretically
this distinction is not entirely clear, its practical implication *is* clear: public education and other spending promoting human capital are a superior
form of social expenditure than social assistance programs.

This view has recently found new life under the "asset approach" to
poverty (e.g., see Attanasio and Szekely 1999; Birsdall and Londono
1997; Flórez et al. 1999). When credit markets are imperfect, individuals
with few assets cannot diversify properly, and remain more vulnerable to
negative shocks. This in turn perpetuates their low-asset ownership. The
key policy issue is therefore the removal of market distortions that impede asset accumulation by the poor. Social assistance transfers aimed at
smoothing consumption have three main problems according to this view
(e.g., see Attanasio and Skezely 1999): they are temporary, and therefore
cannot have long-term effects on asset stocks; they induce distortions; and

they can have general equilibrium effects that damage the poor rather than benefiting them. A more productive approach is to remove those market distortions that impede a proper diversification in the first place—chiefly imperfections in credit markets; alternatively, social expenditure should be aimed at promoting directly the accumulation of human capital by spending on education and health.

At one level, it is difficult to disagree with this view. All incomes are returns to some type of assets; hence poverty must be associated with low-asset ownership. The correlation between income and education is extremely high; and one can easily think of a variety of reasons why removing credit constraints could enhance the accumulation of physical and human capital. The role of credit constraints in the accumulation of wealth and the dynamics of wealth distribution is indeed the subject of a lively theoretical (and some empirical) research of the 1990s. Among the main contributions, see Galor and Zeira (1993) and Aghion and Bolton (1992, 1997); De Gregorio (1996), Jappelli and Pagano (1994), and Perotti (1996) provide some preliminary empirical evidence on the issue.

But removing credit constraints, if it can ever be achieved, can take a very long time, and it is also easy to think of myriad other market failures that can impede asset accumulation by the poor even with smoothly functioning credit markets. Indeed, most European countries have free access to education and health, large social insurance systems, and often some of the best-developed credit markets in the world. Yet they still have large social assistance systems that pick up those individuals who are not fully insured or that, for a variety of reasons, fall through the cracks of the social insurance system.

It is also incorrect to state that temporary transfers (i.e., poverty or bad health transfers that are paid out as long as an individual-specific occurrence lasts) cannot have permanent effects on asset accumulation by the poor. Precisely because individuals are credit constrained even a temporary recession can have a permanent effect on the asset stock of the poor. For instance, in Colombia secondary school enrollment by the poor fell dramatically during the recession of the late 1990s, possibly with long-term effects on their asset accumulation. By increasing income when the marginal utility of current consumption is very high, even a temporary transfer can prevent these long-term effects, as some recent theoretical literature has pointed out (e.g., see Galor and Zeira 1993; Perotti 1993). In fact criticism of the temporariness (from an individual standpoint) of transfers is often confused with a different notion, namely the policy uncertainty on the transfer. If for political or other reasons the transfer is in place intermittently, and with large changes in eligibility and amounts, then its income smoothing properties will be diminished, and so will its positive effects on accumulation.

A second frequent criticism of temporary transfers refers to their distortionary effects; yet it is difficult to think of *any* social policy, including public spending on education, that does not have some type of distortionary side effect.

The reality of life is that while waiting for the removal of all barriers to asset accumulation, every society selects categories of individuals who, for a variety of reasons, it deems appropriate to provide with some form of protection against permanent negative shocks or events, and with some form of consumption smoothing. This is so even though these individuals cannot break away from their dependency or do not accumulate human capital while smoothing consumption, as in the case of the elderly poor, the disabled, and the unemployed. Asset accumulation alone (unless its meaning is so wide that it becomes virtually meaningless) cannot be a justification for the welfare state.

In the past two decades Colombia has made great progress in education and health. It is not clear that increasing spending on these two functions, and particularly on education, will achieve better outcomes. As the recent debate has emphasized, the problem with the Colombian education system might be less its spending per child than the way it is run (see chapter 8). The time has come for government to think seriously about setting up a permanent social assistance system, though not everything and everyone can or should be covered.

But what theoretical guidance is there for this choice? Very little. We do not have a coherent, practical model to guide us in evaluating the trade-offs between the many possible programs, nor do we have a usable social utility function. We must recognize that ultimately the set of individuals, risks, and events that Colombia wants to cover will be mostly the result of a moral and political choice.

And what empirical guidance is there? Again, very little. Theoretically, the incentive and disincentive effects of each program are well known (e.g., see Besley and Coate 1994; Blank, Card, and Robins 1999; Moffit 1996; Pencavel 1986; Saez 2000), but empirically, our knowledge is much more limited, even in industrialized countries. For many Colombian programs even basic data on the number of beneficiaries and their characteristics are sorely lacking.

Thus the reality is that in assessing the Colombian social expenditure system, one must do with a theoretical framework, an amount of information, and a set of feasible alternatives that are orders of magnitude below the ideal ones and those available in industrialized countries. In the absence of a full-fledged, comprehensive theoretical framework, it is important to be explicit about the guidelines that will be followed in this contribution:

1. While, theoretically, untargeted social assistance tends to be less distortionary, untargeted programs tend to be extremely costly, as the Negative Income Tax experiments in the United States in the 1960s and 1970s have made it abundantly clear (see Atkinson 1995 for a survey of the theoretical arguments and of the empirical evidence on the Negative Income Tax experiments). Consequently a widespread application of untargeted programs would require enormous fiscal resources, which is politically unfeasible in the current climate. In addition, in general equilibrium the higher tax revenues needed for large untargeted programs might make the latter *more* distortionary than targeted programs. Not surprisingly, even industrialized countries are moving away from universal benefits and towards more targeted programs.[2] A fortiori, because of its limited fiscal resources, Colombia just does not have any alternative to targeting.

2. The goals of both the social insurance system (excluding fully funded pension systems) and the social assistance system should be to protect against the risk of extreme poverty. I find it difficult to think of a tenable social utility function that rationalizes the many Colombian programs currently aimed at the middle class or the poor, but not the very poor (except in those cases where insurmountable technical or administrative problems prevent reaching the latter).

3. To maximize the impact on poverty with the limited resources available, four key factors should be kept in mind in assessing a social assistance program:

• Distributional incidence. Other things equal, the same objective in terms of poverty reduction and income smoothing can be achieved with fewer fiscal resources if the program is targeted to the poor.[3]

• Overlap with other programs in terms of individuals and risks covered.

• Organizational simplicity. Many good programs on paper are unmanageable by local governments or agencies with limited organizational resources or information.

• Sustainability. The long-run costs of a program, when it reaches full membership, may be much higher than the initial costs. An underestimate or neglect of the steady-state costs seems to be the cause of the failure of several well-intentioned programs in Colombia.

4. How well a given amount of fiscal resources can reach this goal depends on the whole structure of fiscal policy. If public spending is concentrated mostly on the remuneration of civil servants, and on programs that benefit them and a minority of formal sector workers, there will be little left for efficient social assistance programs. This is the case, I will argue, of the current Colombian fiscal structure. Thus social spending has to be evaluated in the broader context of the entire fiscal policy of the government.

5. Just because we know very little about the disincentive effects of social programs, we should not dismiss them lightly. Several industrialized countries, pioneered by the United States and the United Kingdom, have recently moved toward systems of phased tax credit for individuals who get off social assistance, thus mitigating the distortionary effects of these programs (see Blank, Card, and Robbins 1999 and Pearson and Scarpetta 2000 for surveys). Such move is precluded in a country like Colombia, where the income tax plays a very marginal role for most individuals, and where the informal sector is large. But no conceivable program is entirely new. Between them, Latin American countries have accumulated an enormous experience in all types of programs one would want to start. There is nothing wrong with making use of the experience accumulated by other countries and by practitioners in international organizations. In very recent years there have been some experimental studies of a few social programs in a handful of Latin American countries, particularly *Progresa* in Mexico (see Hoddinot and Skoufias 2000 and Schultz 1999 for preliminary evidence; Orazio Attanasio at the University College London has recent set up a network of scholars to pursue empirical research on these experimental programs). This evidence should be considered in designing changes to the Colombian welfare state.

6. One of the most important developments in thinking about social spending in the last two decades has been the notion of "community involvement" in social assistance and employment generating programs. This view has been very influential in Colombia—where it has been one of the defining features of the Red de Solidaridad Social—and in other Latin American countries. It has taken various forms: local residents should initiate and even control the implementation of certain local services (e.g., child care centers in Colombia). They should present the menu of projects for employment and housing programs, and they should help locate the beneficiaries of targeted programs. Unfortunately, it is often the case that programs relying heavily on community involvement rarely reach the very poor. The reason is simple: the very poor are exactly those that, for a variety of reasons, do not have the ability or the incentives to

**Table 9.1**
Fiscal policy in Colombia and Europe

| | Shares of GDP | | Shares of primary expenditures | |
|---|---|---|---|---|
| | Colombia | Europe-15 | Colombia | Europe-15 |
| Primary expenditures | 19.9 | 47.9 | | |
| Purchase of goods and services | 16.5 | 21.6 | 82.9 | 45.1 |
| Capital expenditures | 5.9 | 2.4 | 29.6 | 5.0 |
| Wage expenditures | 6.5 | 12.6 | 32.7 | 26.3 |
| Wage expenditures** | 6.9 | | 34.7 | |
| Non-wage contributions | 4.1 | 7.6 | 20.6 | 15.9 |

Sources: Colombia: Gavin and Perotti (1997) dataset and DNP (1997), except line **, from Comisión de Racionalización de Gasto (1997a) Europe: EUROSTAT (1999).

participate in the community initiatives. For instance, they do not have the financial means and the technical skills required to initiate and develop projects for local public employment programs, or they do not have the human capital to participate effectively in local debates and assemblies.

## 9.3 Fiscal Policy and Social Spending in Colombia

### 9.3.1 Social Spending in the Broader Context of Fiscal Policy
A discussion of social expenditure cannot start without placing it in the broader context of the whole government expenditure. Table 9.1 shows that Colombia has, as expected, a much lower incidence of general government primary spending in GDP than advanced European countries: about 20 percent against almost 50 percent. Of this expenditure, it devotes more than 80 percent to total purchases of goods and services, against about 45 percent of European countries.[4] Most important, it devotes a considerably higher share to the payment of government wages, between 32.7 and 34.7 percent of total primary spending, against a European average of 26.3 percent.

In 1995 there were about 935,000 general government employees in Colombia (excluding those employed in the municipalities not capital of departments); their average wage was about $5.22mn, or 3.7 times the minimum wage and 2.82 times GDP per capita. In the same year there were about 45,000 employees in the Establecimientos Públicos (SENA, Incora, etc.) and 56,000 employees in the Empresas Comerciales y Industriales del Estado (ISS, Ecopetrol, Telecom, etc.), with average salaries of $6.91mn and $10.53mn, respectively.[5] By 1999, total public sector employment had grown to 1,194,000 individuals, about 7.8 percent of total employment (see Acosta 2000). This share is much lower than in many European countries; yet as we have seen, the share of public spending on wages in GDP is only about half of that in European countries. The result is a much higher relative average public sector wage (and this in a country that has already a much higher income inequality).

Is this just the reflection of a different composition of public than private employment? Using household survey data, and after controlling for education and experience, Panizza and Qiang (2000) show that Colombia has consistently the highest public sector wage premium among Latin American countries, typically between 15 and 20 percent.[6] Perfetti (1997) also shows that after controlling for education and experience, in 1994 the public sector premium ranged from 16 to 50 percent, depending on the size of the private establishment (it is higher for smaller establishments). In addition government employees enjoy many other benefits, from job security to high pensions with little or no contributions. In fact Colombia devotes an inordinate share of total pension expenditure to public sector employees: about 60 percent, against a typical 20 percent in advanced economies (see section 9.4.1 for more details).[7]

This allocation of resources among the different types of government expenditure has an important implication: it is an ineffective way of combating poverty. If the average general government employee were the only income earner in his family, this would put his family at about the 65th percentile in the distribution of household income. But because, on average, other members of the family also earn income, it is likely that the household of the average employee of the general government is at least at the 70th to 75th percentile in the distribution of income by households. Table 9.2, from the 1993 CASEN survey, shows that government

**Table 9.2**
Government employees in the distribution of income

|          | Urban | Rural |
|----------|-------|-------|
| Q1       | 4.0   | 2.1   |
| Q2       | 5.9   | 3.4   |
| Q3       | 8.7   | 4.6   |
| Q4       | 10.8  | 5.9   |
| Q5       | 14.9  | 7.9   |
| Poor     | 5.0   | 2.5   |
| Non-poor | 11.9  | 5.7   |

Source: Leibovich and Nuñez (1999), based on Encuesta Calidad de Vida (1993). Distribution of income is by families. Definition of "government employee" is not specified.

employees tend to be overwhelmingly represented in the higher quintiles of the distribution of spending. Finally, Ayala, Soto, and Hernandez (1998) found that in 1998 in Bogotá 83 percent of households with a public sector teacher were in the upper three deciles of the population. Only 10.5 percent of households with public sector teachers were in the lower 50 percent of the distribution. It is likely that these figures would be even more extreme for the country as a whole, because wages of public sector teachers vary less than household income across the country.

The conclusion is that Colombia is facing a hard choice: simply put, it is devoting an extraordinary amount of resources to a pampered government sector, and to a few private workers in the formal sector who have access to the pension system.

### 9.3.2  Social Conditions in Colombia

*Evolution of Poverty in the 1990s*
This section sketches the main elements of the evolution of poverty in the 1990s (for the previous period, see World Bank 1994). There are two basic definitions of poverty in Colombia: that based on the DANE poverty line calculated annually from the Encuesta Nacional de Hogares,[8] and that based on the index of Unmet Basic Needs, also calculated by DANE on the basis of census data in census years and the ENH in non-census years.[9]

*DANE Poverty and Indigence Lines*[10]
Table 9.3 shows that after increasing sharply in 1992 (the year of the agrarian crisis), poverty fell steadily until 1997, getting back to the 1991 level. However, this pattern masks a marked difference between urban

**Table 9.3**
Percentage of population below DANE poverty and indigence lines

|      | Poverty line | | | Indigence line | | |
|------|----------|-------|-------|----------|-------|-------|
|      | National | Urban | Rural | National | Urban | Rural |
| 1991 | 57.7 | 47.3 | 68.4 | 23.6 | 13.8 | 35.2 |
| 1993 | 56.4 | 43.6 | 70.7 | 23.3 | 11.6 | 37.7 |
| 1996 | 52.8 | 42.8 | 77.4 | 18.7 | 9.9 | 40.3 |
| 1997 | 50.3 | 39.1 | 78.9 | 18.1 | 8.3 | 42.9 |
| 1998 | 51.5 | 39.1 | 75.8 | 17.8 | 8.3 | 37.4 |
| 1999 | 55.0 | 45.2 | 79.7 | 20.9 | 11.0 | 45.9 |

Sources: DNP-UDS-DIOGS, in DNP (2000), based on ENH, various years.

and rural areas; in the former, the reduction in poverty after 1992 was substantial so that poverty in 1997 was below its 1991 level. In the latter, poverty increased after 1992 so that poverty in 1997 was higher than in 1991. In both urban and rural areas, poverty increased sharply in 1999, the worst recession in the last thirty years, so that in urban areas it is back nearly to its 1991 level. The evolution of indigence displays a similar pattern.[11]

CEPAL (1998), using a similar definition of the poverty and indigence line but based on its own elaboration of the available household surveys in Latin America, presents a slightly different view: poverty and indigence increased throughout the 1990s in both the rural and the urban sectors.

Despite these differences, there is a common message: rural poverty has not declined, and it has even increased in the 1990s. In fact CEPAL (1998) shows that Colombia and Venezuela are the only two countries that have not been able to reduce rural poverty during the 1990s.

The causes of the increase in rural poverty are not entirely clear. As I show below, unemployment started increasing only in 1997, and rural wages increased in the early 1990s. It would also be important to assess whether the increase in rural poverty in the 1990s was caused by displaced populations in areas affected by the guerrilla or by more fundamental economic developments; policy implications would be very different in the two cases. Note also that in many Latin American and industrialized countries, poverty has increased mostly among female-headed single-parent families. This does not appear to be the case in Colombia.

*NBI Indexes of Poverty and Misery*
The picture changes substantially if one uses the NBI index (table 9.4). This shows a large and steady fall in both urban and rural poverty and

**Table 9.4**
Percentage of population in poverty and misery according to NBI index

|      | Poverty |       |       | Misery |       |       |
|------|----------|-------|-------|----------|-------|-------|
|      | National | Urban | Rural | National | Urban | Rural |
| 1985 | 45.6     | 32.3  | 72.6  | 22.8     | 12.6  | 44.4  |
| 1993 | 37.2     | 26.8  | 62.5  | 14.9     | 9.0   | 30.3  |
| 1996 | 26.0     | 16.9  | 48.6  | 8.9      | 4.1   | 20.7  |
| 1997 | 25.9     | 17.8  | 46.5  | 8.6      | 4.5   | 19.1  |
| 1998 | 26.0     | 17.4  | 47.8  | 8.2      | 4.1   | 18.6  |

Sources: DNP-UDS-DIOGS, in DNP (2000), based on ENH, various years.

misery between 1993 and 1996 or 1997, even larger than the fall between 1985 and 1993. Rural poverty increases slightly in 1998, but misery keeps falling.

One should bear in mind that the NBI index has been widely criticized (e.g., see the World Bank 1990 and 1994) for being heavily biased toward housing, and therefore against rural areas: for instance, in rural areas lack of electricity need not indicate poverty. In addition the correlation between the NBI index and the income of households is not high: in 1991 in urban areas the NBI index would miss about 66 percent of indigent individuals, and conversely, 80 percent of those classified as poor according to the NBI index are above the indigence line. In fact in 1991 the average income of the NBI poor households was about three times the average income of households below the indigence line (see World Bank 1994).

### Comparison with Latin America

International comparisons of poverty are extremely difficult to make; it is therefore not surprising that different sources give somewhat contrasting answers on the extent of poverty in Colombia relative to other Latin American countries.

According to the World Bank headcount of poverty (defined as the share of population with income below $2 per day, PPP adjusted), Colombia is doing quite well relative to the other Latin American countries; on the other hand, the ratio of rural to urban poverty is the highest in Latin America. However, CEPAL (1998), based on national household surveys, gives almost the opposite picture: poverty in Colombia is quite high, but the ratio of rural to urban poverty is not an outlier by Latin American standards (table 9.5).

Because of the discordant pictures from these two international comparisons, it is difficult to assess how serious the incidence of rural poverty is in Colombia relative to other Latin American countries. But there are indications that the World Bank view might be more correct.[12] For instance, the percentage of households with access to safe water in Colombia is higher than the Latin American average in urban areas, but lower in rural areas (table 9.6).[13]

### Participation Rates, Employment and Unemployment

#### Participation Rates

After being flat between 1990 and 1997, the participation rate of women increased substantially starting in 1997. Among the likely reasons are the

**Table 9.5**
CEPAL: Poverty in Latin America

|                    | Year | National | Urban | Rural |
|--------------------|------|----------|-------|-------|
| Argentina          | 1997 |          | 13    |       |
| Bolivia            | 1997 |          | 47    |       |
| Brazil             | 1996 | 29       | 25    | 46    |
| Chile              | 1996 | 20       | 19    | 26    |
| Colombia           | 1997 | 45       | 39    | 54    |
| Costa Rica         | 1997 | 20       | 17    | 23    |
| Ecuador            | 1997 |          | 50    |       |
| El Salvador        | 1997 | 48       | 39    | 62    |
| Guatemala          | 1990 |          |       | 72    |
| Honduras           | 1997 | 74       | 67    | 80    |
| Mexico             | 1996 | 43       | 38    | 53    |
| Nicaragua          | 1997 |          | 66    |       |
| Panama             | 1997 | 27       | 25    | 34    |
| Paraguay           | 1996 |          | 40    |       |
| Peru               | 1997 | 37       | 25    | 61    |
| Republic Dominican | 1997 | 32       | 32    | 34    |
| Uruguay            | 1997 |          | 6     |       |
| Venezuela          | 1994 | 42       | 41    | 48    |
| Latin America      | 1997 | 36       | 30    | 54    |

Source: Panorama Social de America Latina, 1998.

**Table 9.6**
Households with access to safe water, 1992 to 1997 (latest year)

|         | National | | | Urban | | | Rural | | |
|---------|----------|------|------|-------|------|------|-------|------|------|
|         | 1970–75  | 1980–85 | 1992–97 | 1970–75 | 1980–85 | 1992–97 | 1970–75 | 1980–85 | 1992–97 |
| Colombia | 64 | 91 | 75 | 86 | 100 | 90 | 33 | 76 | 32 |
| Latin America | — | — | 36 | — | — | 83 | — | — | 36 |

Source: World Development Indicators, 1999.

declining incomes, urban migration, and the phenomenon of displaced families. In contrast, the participation rate of men increased very little after 1997, and it is now lower than in 1996 or 1991.

*Employment*
Employment of women increased, at a rate of 4.1 percent in 1991 to 1995 and 2.5 percent in 1995 to 1999. Employment of men initially kept pace with female employment, increasing at a rate of 3.6 percent in 1991 to 1995, but then it decreased at a rate of −0.9 percent in 1995 and 1999.[14]

*Employment Rates*
Hence, despite the increase in the participation rate, the employment rate of women did not increase over the 1990s, except briefly in 1998. The employment rate of men did decrease substantially, by almost 10 percentage points, between 1995 and 1999.

*Unemployment Rates*
As a consequence of the developments in the participation and employment rates, the unemployment rates of both women and men have started increasing after 1995, but for different reasons. Unemployment among women increased because participation rates increased more than employment; unemployment among men increased because participation rates did not change much, but employment rates fell.

*Composition of Employment Changes*
Almost all the difference in the dynamics of male and female employment between 1995 and 1999 can be explained by two types: "empleo domestico" and "self-employment." Using an alternative disaggregation, by sectors rather than by functions, the key difference between male and female employment was in two sectors: "comercio" and "servicios comunales, sociales y personales." Overall, 64 percent of employment growth in 1991 to 1999 was in "self-employment," and 65 percent was in "comercio" and "servicios comunales, sociales y personales." These figures are important because high levels of informality characterize all these sectors.

*Age Structure of Unemployment*
It is important to note that the unemployment age structure is different from that of most industrialized countries. Unemployment is highly concentrated among the very young, 15 to 19 years, followed by 20 to 29 years, and it falls steadily as age increases, reaching a low 4.4 percent among individuals over 60. These figures might imply that well designed training programs could be effective in reducing unemployment, for two reasons: they reduce the participation rate of individuals with the highest unemployment rate, and build human capital in individuals most affected by unemployment. Two important caveats: it is not clear whether there are a lot of discouraged workers in the older cohorts, and whether unemployment figures have any meaning in an economy with very high rates of informal employment.

*Unemployment by Income Levels*
Unemployment is mostly concentrated among the poor: it is much higher, and has increased much more, in the first quintile. One possible reason is that a considerable part of the recent unemployment is due to the crisis in the construction sector.

### 9.3.3 Tools for Targeting Social Expenditure
As argued in section 9.2, Colombia has no alternative to targeting its social expenditure. A key determinant of the effectiveness of social expenditure is thus the effectiveness of the targeting tools currently in use.

#### Geographic and Individual Targeting
For programs like infrastructure, public utilities, water, and sanitation, geographic targeting works well in identifying the areas to subsidize. In Colombia, the most widespread such index is the "index of socioeconomic stratification," mostly based on housing characteristics. In urban areas it allows identification of blocks or rooms (*manzanas* or *cuartos*), in rural areas and small towns, of individual housings. Those in levels 1 or 2 are usually classified as poor. In principle, by December 1994 all urban municipalities and by May 1995 all rural municipalities should have adopted this stratification (Decreto 2220, November 5, 1993). Fifty to 60 percent of municipalities in 1994 had a socioeconomic stratification, obtained through various methodologies, and mostly to be used by public utilities. Municipalities with more than 40,000 inhabitants could also use the Mapa de Pobreza based on the NBI index.[15] Other municipalities could use different indexes, such as those prepared by ICBF or by utility companies. In practice, the NBI index is still widely used, particularly in allocating program funds across municipalities or departments. Recently a new index has been developed, the ICV index, based on the results of the 1997 Encuesta de Calidad de Vida (see Sarmiento and Gonzalez 1998 and Cortes, Gamboa, and Gonzalez 1999 for a description). It is a standard of living index based on 12 categories, and structurally similar to SISBEN, to which I turn next.

In the last decade Colombia has developed a system of classification of households patterned after Chile's CASBEN. The SISBEN system is a proxy-means test based on the results of the 1993 CASEN survey of 25,000 households. Information on 15 household characteristics—mostly ownership and characteristics of assets and durables[16]—are collected in a host interview to fill the Ficha de Caracterización Socioeconómica; a simple software then transforms the 15 scores, one for each category, into an aggregate score.[17] The households are then classified into 6 strata (each social program has different cutoff points); levels 1 and 2 are usually considered poor. In a first round, the municipality takes a survey, trying to target the areas that are most likely to have the most needy persons. In a second round, the survey can be initiated by the community, NGO's, or individual households who believe they might be classified in the first three levels of SISBEN but who have been overlooked in the first round. Usually rural municipalities survey more marginalized areas first.

As of June 1997, 98 percent of municipalities were using SISBEN, with 6,200,000 persons surveyed in the urban sector and 6,500,000 in the rural sector, corresponding to about 38 percent of the population.[18] By 1996, SISBEN was used mostly to determine eligibility in the Regimen Subsidiado de Seguridad Social en Salud (82 percent of municipalities with SISBEN)[19] and eligibility for programs in the Red (62 percent of municipalities with SISBEN), in particular, for REVIVIR. Only 17 and 16 percent of municipalities were using SISBEN for eligibility in education and nutrition subsidies, respectively (see DNP-PNUD 1996).

However, there is a large variance in the degree of coverage of the population by SISBEN; in 1996 the share of population covered by SISBEN ranged from 16.3 percent in Cundinamarca, 20.1 percent in Cauca, 25.6 percent in Cesar, 33.2 percent in Magdalena, to 65.7 percent in Huila, 67.7 percent in San Andres, and 72.2 percent in Casanare. If there is a negative correlation between the average income of a municipality and SISBEN coverage, this might introduce a perverse mechanism whereby the poorest municipalities have a higher tendency to undersample the poor.

Unfortunately, very little information is available on the percentage of poor individuals who have not been sampled by SISBEN. One might worry that the very poor are also the least informed about SISBEN. But even at the village level there are usually either local organizations of citizens or informational networks that advise families initially forgotten by SISBEN to request an evaluation.[20] On the other hand, of the 47 percent municipalities that contracted out the SISBEN evaluation, 35 percent stated that they had problems with coverage, because not all marginalized areas had been covered (see DNP-PNUD 1996).

Some suggestive evidence can be gathered by comparing SISBEN results with evidence from surveys, like ENH. In Cali, SISBEN covered 41.1 percent of urban areas and 98.7 percent of rural areas. The percentage of individuals in SISBEN levels 1 and 2 was 28.3 percent in urban and 23.7 percent in rural areas. Using the NBI index, in 1993 estimates of the poverty rate were 20.3 percent in urban and 32.4 percent in rural areas (see Zarta 1998). This comparison should obviously be taken with great caution, because the main reason for developing SISBEN was precisely the alleged inadequacy of NBI to capture the notion of poverty. Yet, because the discrepancy between urban and rural areas is so large, it suggests that a higher percentage of poor was not sampled in rural compared to that in urban areas.[21]

### Evaluation and Proposals

SISBEN is an inexpensive instrument[22] to target social spending properly. It has been argued for a long time that income and the NBI index are inadequate instruments for targeting; the former because it can be highly seasonal and is prone to be misrepresented, the latter because it does not capture adequately the difference urban and rural areas.[23] SISBEN overcomes these difficulties, and is a very advanced tool, such as few Latin American countries currently possess.[24]

The key issue is why, despite its low cost and good properties, the use of SISBEN is so erratic outside the Health Ministry. All existing array of targeting tools is currently used: socioeconomic stratification, NBI, ICV, and other local indexes. In Chile the use of CASBEN for education and health subsidies was discontinued because the administering agencies did not have ready access to CASBEN classification in municipalities. This mistake should be easily avoided in Colombia, where municipalities hold the SISBEN scores and there is an obligation for the latter to make them readily available to interested agencies.

But SISBEN suffers from three different problems. First, there is often mistrust on the part of agencies regarding the possible manipulation of SISBEN scores by municipalities. For instance, there is anecdotal evidence that some RED programs avoided using SISBEN because they feared some municipalities had inflated the ranks of levels 1 and 2. Conversely, there are accusations that some programs avoided SISBEN in order to be able to allocate funds more freely to their political clientele. Both these claims might well be true to some extent, but a quantification of their incidence is currently impossible.

The second problem is that SISBEN lacks a centralized system for keeping tracks of the scores. For instance, an agreement was signed recently between the Cajas de Compensacion Familiar and ICBF to use some funds from the former in order to revamp HCB (Hoqares Comunitarios de Bienestar) in Bogotá and its department. Use of SISBEN to allocate the funds between the capital city and the rest of the department proved unfeasible because it was impossible to determine how many SISBEN 1 and 2 individuals were present in the two areas, and again, it was feared that self-reporting by the different localities would be subject to strategic misrepresentation.

The third problem is more speculative in nature. Some programs might have avoided using SISBEN in some areas because they feared that not all poor individuals had been evaluated.

To make SISBEN fully operational, a centralized information system keeping track of SISBEN scores in the different municipalities seems essential. Due to the high mobility of the poorer population in some areas, such a system should use cross-checks to follow migrant families.[25] A nationwide system should also be used to prevent abuse of SISBEN, whereby some families ask to be evaluated in more than one municipality in order to increase the probability of being given a score of 1 or 2. Although such abuse is known to exist, at present there is no estimate of how widespread it is.[26] A nationwide system is also a prerequisite for the use of SISBEN to allocate resources of a program within departments and across departments. Finally, it is essential to form a clear idea of the reliability of SISBEN, particularly in rural areas, in terms of coverage of all poor individuals.

The alternatives to SISBEN involve using other tools for individual targeting, like income, or to resort to geographic targeting, like using the NBI index or the socioeconomic stratification. Both alternatives are costly. In particular, geographic targeting always implies some leakage of resources to individuals who are not the prime target of a program.

A debate has arisen recently on the relative merits of SISBEN and ICV. Both are proxy-means tests, and conceptually very similar, with ICV including a few less variables than the current version of SISBEN. This debate seems to reflect to a large extent both a highly theoretical view[27] and some institutional partisanship, with DNP seemingly supporting ICV against SISBEN.

It is important to be clear about the different properties of the two indexes. ICV is based on a survey, therefore it cannot be used for individual targeting; by contrast, in principle SISBEN covers all individuals who belong to its levels 1 or 2.[28] Thus ICV covers the whole country, while SISBEN could be used for geographic targeting only by exclusion (i.e., if all households that are not in levels 1 or 2 are excluded from the subsidy in question). Besides this, the two indexes are very similar, and much of the superiority of ICV is academic. SISBEN has proved to be an excellent tool, and for individual targeting it has no alternative. It is much more appropriate to devote intellectual and financial resources to make it fully operational, than to continue an endless and highly academic debate.

### 9.3.4 Social Expenditure in Colombia

Social expenditure plays a key role in the Colombian Constitution and in the policy debate. Article 350 of the Constitution states that "public social spending will have priority over any other spending." But what is social expenditure? In Article 41 of the Estatuto Organico de Presupuesto, this is defined as "any expenditure whose objective is the satisfaction of unsatisfied basic needs in health, education, environment, drinkable water, housing, and those aiming at the general well-being and the improvement of the quality of life of the population." Thus Colombia combines a very loose definition of social expenditure with a very strong constitutional mandate to protect it. The result is, inevitably, confusion. In fact there are currently at least three different definitions of social expenditure circulating in Colombia (see Restrepo 1998), in addition to the many definitions used by individual researchers: the Budget, DNP, and Plan Nacional de Desarrollo definitions.[29]

Given this, it should come as no surprise that they generate widely different estimates of the size of social expenditure in GDP (see table 9.7). Depending on what definition one uses, in 1997 social expenditure ranged from a minimum of 7.8 percent of GDP to a maximum of 15 percent (under the DNP definition).

Clearly, one definition is as good as any other, as long as they are explicit. But as a result of the current confusion it is often difficult to know what someone is referring to when using the notion of social expenditure. This is not without practical consequences, given the overwhelming importance attached to the notion of social spending in the Colombian policy debate. International comparisons become of little value when social

**Table 9.7**
Alternative definitions of social expenditures

|        | 1995 | 1996 | 1997 | 1998   |
|--------|------|------|------|--------|
| DNP    | 13.7 | 15.5 | 15.0 | 15.9[a] |
| Budget | 10.6 | 12.6 | 13.1 | 13.3[a] |
| PND    | 7.0  | 8.0  | 7.8  | 7.5[a]  |
| IMF    | 6.1  | 7.6  | 7.8  | 7.9    |

Sources: CGR (1997) and IMF (2000).
a. Budgeted.

expenditure is defined so loosely.[30] In addition, in many ways the current definitions are misleading. By its nature, the budget definition can only cover spending by the central government; therefore it has only a limited coverage of pension spending because ISS is outside the budget. Items like "sport, recreation and culture" or "environment," which do not belong in any reasonable definition of social spending, appear in all definitions only because they are cited in the Constitution. Presumably for a similar reason the most comprehensive definition, by DNP, includes items like "contributions to trade unions and religious events," "public parks and botanic gardens," and so on. Because the Colombian Constitution does not allow the share of public social spending in total spending to fall from one year to the next, over time the Budget definition of social spending has included more and more items only in order to satisfy this constitutional mandate (see chapter 7). This fact, however, is never recognized in policy debates, which routinely make time series comparisons of this definition of public social spending.

To organize the discussion around a well-tested scheme, I will use the classification that EUROSTAT has applied for several decades to European countries.[31] It consists of the following items: (1) sickness/health care, (2) disability, (3) old age, (4) survivors, (5) family/children, (6) unemployment, (7) housing, and (8) other spending on social exclusion not elsewhere classified. This classification has two advantages. First, it distinguishes explicitly the different functions, each obeying a clear economic rationale (the nature of the risk or event covered). Second, it allows meaningful international comparisons, not so much with Latin American countries but also with industrialized countries. Even though in the short run a country like Colombia cannot afford the same level of social spending as the typical European country, it is still useful to compare the composition of its social spending to that of a group of countries whose mature welfare states cover more or less all risks and event.

To reflect data availability, I combine some categories in the EUROSTAT classification and end up with the following classification of social expenditure: (1) policies toward the elderly and the disabled, (2) families, children, and other social exclusion,[32] (3) unemployment and employment generation programs, (4) housing, and (5) health.

Note that the EUROSTAT definition excludes expenditure on education, on water and sanitation, and on rural programs. The latter are fairly small programs in Colombia, although they can have substantial redistributive power. I will also have very little to say on health expenditure, a

sector that, together with education, has received more attention in Colombia than all the other sectors combined; I believe it is important to
redress the imbalance.

## 9.4   Sectoral Social Policies in Colombia

### 9.4.1   Policies toward the Elderly and the Disabled

*Institutional Features and Distribution of Pension Spending*
The institutional features of the Colombian pension system, its problems,
and reform proposals have been the subject of a large literature (see
Acosta and Ayala 1998; Ayala 1999; and Comisión de Racionalización
de Gasto 1997b for surveys). For this reason, here I will focus mainly on
distributive issues, and on the role of pension spending in the context of
public social expenditure.

Schematically Colombia now has a three-pillar policy toward the
elderly. The first is the state-run, defined benefit pension scheme (or Prima
Media). The second is the private sector, defined contribution system of
AFPs, Chilean-style. In contrast to other countries, like Argentina, these
two pillars are mutually exclusive for an individual. Together they make
up the "social insurance" component of the policies toward the elderly.
The third pillar is a purely redistributive scheme for the elderly poor that
are not entitled to a social insurance pension. At present this pillar is
represented by a small program, REVIVIR, and by many small programs
run by municipalities. This is the "social assistance" component of the
policies toward the elderly.

There has been a lively debate recently about the financial viability (or
lack thereof) of the first pillar. Estimates of the unfunded pension liabilities vary widely but tend to be invariably staggering, especially given the
limited tax base.[33] A related problem, but a much less discussed one, is
that of the annual pension spending. Exact figures are hard to come by,
but the best estimate is that in 1998 Colombia spent between 4.5 and 5
percent of GDP in pensions, against a European average of 14.5 percent
of GDP (see table 9.8).

However, the underlying demographics are very different (see table
9.9): the European dependency ratio (the ratio of population older than
60) is about three times as high as that of Colombia, 20.6 percent against
6.5 percent. And while pension coverage of individuals above 60 is almost
universal in most industrialized countries, in Colombia only about 30
percent of individuals above 60 perceive a pension. As a consequence

**Table 9.8**
Share of pensions in GDP, 1998

| | |
|---|---|
| *ISS* | 1.38 |
| *Teachers' fund* | 0.19 |
| *Other entities* | 1.36 |
| Cajanal | 0.00 |
| Caprecom | 0.17 |
| Military | 0.27 |
| Police | 0.32 |
| Ferrocarriles | 0.09 |
| Colpuertos | 0.44 |
| Fonprenor | 0.00 |
| Congress | 0.07 |
| CAPRESUB | 0.00 |
| *Law 100 funds* | 1.13 |
| Public pension fund (FOPEP) | 0.81 |
| FSP | 0.05 |
| Fondo prestacion salud | 0.04 |
| REVIVIR | 0.03 |
| Other institutions | 0.20 |
| *Telecom* | 0.05 |
| *Ecopetrol* | 0.05 |
| *Funds of territorial entities* | 0.30 |
| Total | 4.46 |

Source: Ayala and Acosta (1998), except last three lines that are rough estimates of the author.

**Table 9.9**
Pensions in Colombia and Europe

| | Colombia | Europe |
|---|---|---|
| Pensions | About 800,000 | |
| Population > 60/population | 6.5% | 20.6% |
| Pensioners/population > 60 | 31.7% | about 80% (Ger, US, UK) |
| Pensioners/population | 2.1% | about 16.5% |
| Pensioners/active population | 48.1% | |
| Public pension expenditures/total pension expenditures | 50% | 25% (US) 17% (Ger) |

Source: IADB (1997), World Bank (1995), and author's calculations.

only about 2 percent of the population perceives a pension in Colombia, against about 16.5 percent in European countries. The result is an extremely high average pension in Colombia: in 1997, about 2.7 times the minimum salary, that is, about twice the GDP per capita.

Thus, controlling for demographics, Colombia has a European style pension system but with much lower total tax revenues and a much higher rate of informality. The result is a much higher share of pension spending in total spending (controlling for the different dependency ratios), and a much higher concentration of pension spending on a few individuals.

### Redistribution to the Higher End of the Distribution of Income
As emphasized above, it is important to set out clearly what are the redistributions involved in the Colombian pension system. I am not aware of studies that have quantified these flows; but the main qualitative features seem clear. In this section, I begin with those flows that favor individuals already in the upper end of the distribution of income.

#### Redistribution to All Prima Media Participants
For virtually all participants, the Prima Media system is more than actuarially fair. It is hard to argue that this serves any redistributive purpose: as in all Latin American countries the system is mostly intended for public sector workers and urban workers in the formal sector. The resulting distribution of pension spending is highly skewed. It is impossible to obtain precise figures, but a (crude) proxy can be obtained by looking at the distribution of ISS contributors in 1995 (likely to be an underestimate, because it excludes many public sector workers, who earned on average 3.69 the minimum wage in 1995 and had replacement rates close to 100 percent of the last salary). Only 10 percent of individuals who contributed to ISS in 1995 earned less than one minimum wage. Because the latter was equal to about 93 percent of per capita GDP in 1995, and because the poorer workers are unlikely to contribute for long enough to qualify for a pension, it is safe to assume that very few individuals in the first three quintiles of the distribution of income earn any pension at all. As a comparison, it is useful to look at the distribution of (equivalized) per-capita pension spending by quintiles in Europe (table 9.10). As one can see, the first three quintiles perceive a higher pension, as a share of their pre-pension income, than the upper quintiles. There are countries, like Denmark, where the absolute amount received as pensions are higher in the lower quintiles. A skewed pension spending is actually a common feature to all Latin American countries. But Colombia's re-

**Table 9.10**
Distribution of pensions in Colombia, Europe, and Denmark, 1994

| | Colombia | | Europe | | Denmark | |
|---|---|---|---|---|---|---|
| | Values | Percentage of income | Values | Percentage of income | Values | Percentage of income |
| Q1 | ~0 | ~0 | 1,113 | 51.6 | 2,117 | 97.7 |
| Q2 | ~0 | ~0 | 1,946 | 42.0 | 1,642 | 27.2 |
| Q3 | ~0 | ~0 | 2,107 | 29.1 | 933 | 10.1 |
| Q4 | >0 | >0 | 2,050 | 18.9 | 1,043 | 8.7 |
| Q5 | >0 | >0 | 3,159 | 16.6 | 1,841 | 10.0 |

Source: EUROSTAT (1999), table C1.0E.
Note: Figures are in thousands of Purchasing Power Standards.

placement rates, and the resulting actuarial imbalances, are very high by international standards. For instance, the replacement rate for a person who has worked for at least 28 years is at least 85 percent of the average of the last 10 years of salaries. Given an expected lifetime of 15 years for men at 60, and assuming a return on reserves of 5 percent, the social security tax that would make this profile actuarially fair is 16.5 percent, far above the current 13.5 percent (see Ayala 1999).

Moreover the replacement rates are particularly generous for three categories of individuals: men (women) who were under 40 (35) in 1994 or who had contributed for at least 15 years in 1994, because they can use the pre-1993 reform rules; public sector workers, who contribute little or nothing at all; and poor workers with income close to the minimum wage, who benefit from the minimum pension guarantee and the supplements of the Fondo de Solidaridad Pensional.

Thus, the system has built in an adverse selection mechanism, whereby all the young individuals with a long contributory life ahead are better off in the fully funded system, while individuals with low or no contributions are better off in the Prima Media system.

*Redistribution to Public Sector Workers*
A second distinctive feature of the Colombian pension system is that it is highly geared toward public sector employees: probably about 60 percent of total pension spending in Colombia accrues to former public sector employees, against 17 percent in Germany and 25 percent in the United States. In addition in 1996 about 483,000 workers, or about 52 percent of the 935,000 general government employees (see section 9.3.1), belonged to the system of unreformed funds (i.e., those funds not affected by the

1993 reform) and had benefits even more generous relative to contributions. In what follows, I try to give an idea of the types of redistribution to several types of public sector workers via the pension system.

*Teachers*  The usual justification for the exemption of teachers from the 1993 reform is that the more generous system of pensions and *cesantias* (severance payments) can be interpreted as a compensation for lower salaries. But there is no evidence of a wage penalty for teachers. Using data from Bogotá, Ayala, Soto, and Hernandez (1999) found that in 1994 public sector teachers earned considerably less than private sector teachers and other public and private sector professionals with the same characteristics in terms of education, age, and sex. Focusing on the "other private sector professional," as the comparison group, in 1998 the gap between male public sector teachers and other male private sector professionals with same years of education was reduced to 10 percent for 25-year-old individuals, and 5 percent for 40-year-old individuals. The gap for women was still at about 30 percent.

However, the estimated gap refers to monthly salaries, and do not take into account differences in hours worked. For instance, a survey by Fecode in 1994 showed that teachers are in school for 27.3 hours a week and prepare classes for 9 hours, thus working about 75 percent of the contractual 48 hours. After adjusting for this factor, Ayala, Soto, and Hernandez find that male and female public sector teachers earn more (and males considerably so) than other comparable private sector professionals. A similar picture emerges in Liang (1999), who also allows for interesting international comparisons. After controlling for shorter hours (according to this source, in Colombia teachers work for an average of 36.8 hours a week, against 50.3 hours for nonteachers), the hourly wage premium of Colombian teachers is 20 percent, the second highest in Latin America. If one also controls for longer vacations, the premium rises to 35 percent.[34] Without controlling for shorter hours, Acosta and Borjas (2000) found that in 1998 public sector teachers earned about the same monthly salary as private professionals with the same characteristics. If one controlled for shorter hours, public sector teachers would show a considerable (about 25 percent) premium.

An exact quantification of the compensation of teachers via the pension system is impossible, but the main features are clear. These are some of the special features of the teachers' pension system (see Acosta and Borjas 2000 for more details):

1. The social security tax on teachers is 3 percent, against 13.5 percent in the reformed social security system.

2. Primary school teachers who started working before 1980 are entitled to a *pension de gracia* equal to 75 percent of their salary. In 1999, 74,500 teachers out of a total of 298,000 active teachers were entitled to a pension de gracia; their average age was 48 years (Acosta 1999).

3. Teachers are entitled to a *pensión ordinaria de jubilación*, between their 50th and 60th year of age, depending on their gender and regime; this pension is compatible with the pension de gracia and teachers do not have to stop working. In 1999 there were 31,136 active teachers with a pension of the Fondo del Magisterio; 26,171 active teachers with a pension de gracia and a pension of the Fondo del Magisterio; and 252 retired teachers with two pensions of the Fondo del Magisterio and a pension de gracia (Acosta 1999).

4. When they retire, all their pensions are redefined based on the salary of their last year of work.

*ECOPETROL Workers*   The average pension of ECOPETROL workers is very high, at 6.9 minimum salaries in 1996. Yet ECOPEPROL workers are entirely exempted from any contribution. This extremely large redistribution via the pension system accrues to workers who in 1995 earned, on average, $17.32mn, or 12.2 times the minimum wage and 9.36 times per-capita GDP (source: Comisión de Racionalización de Gasto 1997a).

*Military and Police*   While the exemption of public sector teachers and of ECOPETROL from the 1993 reform appears difficult to justify, the political arguments for an exemption of the police and the military can be more compelling: in the present political situation, no government can afford to alienate these two categories. Indeed, while Colombia is alone in Latin America in granting a total exemption to public sector teachers from the pension system, exemption of the military is a common feature of many Latin American countries.

Still, there is one area where the government can intervene, and possibly at small political costs. Currently the pensions of the military and the police are indexed to the wages of active armed forces. This is very expensive, and unjustified. In the past few years several OECD countries have taken the step of indexing pensions to the CPI, rather than wages, and this has often been the single most effective measure to slow down the increase in pension expenditure. In addition this indexing has often been much less contentious than expected, possibly because the issue appears to be a mere technicality. But its compounded effect over the years can be very large.

*Local Public Sector Workers* A fourth pattern of "perverse redistribution" concerns public sector employees in the reformed sector. For them, the *prima media* system is still very generous: many did not contribute at all, others contributed much less than their benefits in present discounted value terms; in 1996 about 250,000—between active and passive members—belonged to the system of local *cajas*, which provided generous benefits with minimal or no contributions. But unfortunately very little is known of the aggregate pension expenditure and obligations of these cajas. One piece of information is revealing, however; the average pension in the 222 cajas that had been liquidated and transferred to ISS (111,000 workers) and to the Fondo Pensiones Territoriales (62,000 pensioners) was 3.4 minimum salaries in 1996 (Gestion Fiscal 1998).

### Redistribution to the Lower End of Income: Within the Social Insurance System

A second, more standard pattern of redistribution is toward the lower end of the spectrum. It is both toward individuals within the system and toward elderly individuals outside the system, in the form of social assistance pensions. Both programs are currently extremely small (about 0.03 and 0.05 percent of GDP, respectively); hence they are interesting not so much for their effects in the present arrangements but rather for the lessons they can provide in the case the Colombian pension system reorients itself away from the upper end of the distribution and toward the more needy individuals.

Consider first redistribution within the system. Both the Prima Media and the AFP systems redistribute resources toward contributors close to the minimum wage, in two ways. Ley 100 establishes a lower floor on all old-age pensions. Second, the Fondo de Solidaridad Pensional supplements contributions to the Prima Media system by individuals who cannot temporarily contribute.

#### The Minimum Pension Guarantee

There are at least two trade-offs in a minimum pension guarantee. The higher the minimum pension, the higher are the incentives to contribute for those who expect to qualify for the minimum pension only but also the higher is the burden on the budget. Further, the higher the guaranteed minimum pension, the smaller is the step increase in the pension for any additional year after the minimum length of contributions for the minimum pension. Hence a higher minimum pension increases the incentives to contribute for the minimum required number of years, and to stop contributing thereafter (see James 1999).

As with most trade-offs, it is not obvious what is the optimal point. But, at a minimum, one should be aware that in most respects, Colombia has made widely different choices from most other Latin American countries that have recently reformed their social security systems.

The minimum guaranteed pension in Colombia is equal to the minimum wage at the moment it starts, and afterward it increases by the greater of the ICP inflation rate or the increase in the minimum wage. But the minimum wage is extremely high in Colombia. In 1994, it was about 72 percent of the average salary of a worker in the seven main cities, hence an even larger share of the average salary in the country (see Ferné and Nupia 1996). In the same year it was equal to 68 percent of the average urban income, 160 percent of the urban poverty line, 123 percent of the average rural income, and 190 percent of the rural poverty line (DNP 1998a). In addition the minimum pension requires only 10 years of contribution, after which there is little incentive to continue contributing for low-wage workers who cannot realistically expect to ever get anything more than the minimum pension.

Most other Latin American countries have made different choices:[35]

*Chile.* The minimum guaranteed pension is 20 percent of the average of the last 10 years of wages or 75 percent of the minimum wage, whichever is greater. It requires 20 years of contributions. The government supplements the accumulation to bring the payout from the private pension funds to the minimum guaranteed level. The government's supplement is paid out of general revenues. Currently about 50 percent of workers are likely to qualify for the minimum pension. The payment of this pension is not automatic: most municipalities have long queues of individuals who are entitled to the pension.

*Mexico.* The minimum guaranteed pension is about 40 percent of the average wage, and will decline to 25 percent when the first cohort of new workers retires.

*Argentina.* The basic pension in the first pillar, which is a universal pension and therefore similar to a guaranteed pension, is 27.5 percent of the covered average wage. It requires 30 years of contributions.

There is also an old age pension for those workers who do not qualify for regular benefits. It is currently at 10 percent of the average wage, and it is paid after the worker reaches age 70. It requires 10 years of contributions, a criterion met by many women and informal sector workers. *Brazil.* The "age" pension pays 70 percent of the wage base to men (women) over 65 (60) in the urban sector and over 60 (55) in the rural sector. It requires 5 years of contributions. The typical pension is about 30 percent of the average wage. As this type of social pension has become a heavy burden on the budget, the government is gradually increasing the contribution requirement to 15 years.

## The Fondo de Solidaridad Pensional

The goal of the Fondo de Solidaridad Pensional (FSP) is to subsidize the contributions to the Regimen General de Pensiones (RGP) of certain poor workers who cannot temporarily contribute, in order to avoid breaks in their record of contributions. Specifically, the target population is those workers who earn less than a minimum salary (1.5 minimum salaries if self-employed) and also belong to one of the following categories (see DNP-UDS 1996): (1) workers in informal urban and rural sector, (2) community mothers, (3) disabled workers, and (4) workers of cooperatives.

The program is cross-subsidized by a surcharge of 1 percentage point on the contributions of workers who earn more than 4 minimum salaries, up to 20 minimum salaries. The eligibility criteria have changed little since the inception of the program. Besides decreasing the age at which the subsidization becomes available for some workers, the main changes are the increase in the rate of subsidization for rural workers from 70 to 90 percent, starting in 1998, and the abolition of the requirement of 500 weeks of contributions for urban workers, starting in 1997, as it was quickly realized that virtually no worker in the informal sector would satisfy this criterion.

It should be noted that the target population excluded individuals earning less than two-thirds of the minimum wage (except community mothers), or belonging to SISBEN 1, as it was felt that they would not have enough resources to complement the FSP contribution (see Flórez, Moreno, and Barrios 1994). The problem has suffered from low membership, relative to its target. Membership in 1997 was 242,480 individuals, with the following breakdown: 25 percent community mothers, 40 percent workers in urban informal sector, 33 percent rural workers, and 2 percent disabled workers. This figure is still short of the pool of potential members. Among the reasons for the low membership are the following:

1. It appears that many workers were not aware of the existence of the program, despite an advertisement budget of $880mn. For instance, only about 3 percent of the all-rural workers earning less than the minimum salary were affiliated, and only 62 percent of community mothers.
2. There has been some confusion about eligibility.[36]
3. Rural workers also have low membership, for two reasons. First, in rural areas, campesinos often cannot pay the contributions because of the limited network of ISS offices; as a consequence, in 1996, 7.5 percent of members could not contribute for two or more months in a row, which automatically caused their elimination form the rosters (see DNP-UDS 1997). Second, some argue that many potential rural clients of the program still had problems paying their 30 percent share of the contribution, partly because of the seasonality of their earnings. From 1998, the rate of subsidization for rural workers increased at 90 percent; in addition CONPES recommended that the organizations of campesinos be allowed to pay contributions in lump sum, anticipated, to ISS. But it was not clear whether ISS would allow this.

It is not clear whether these problems have been successfully addressed. CONPES has stopped publishing its yearly review of the Fondo de Solidaridad Pensional after 1998, possibly indicating diminished interest in this program.

The program has also suffered from a number of administrative problems. In 1997, 67 percent of individuals were at least two months late in their payments, and according to Ley 100 they should have been dropped from the benefits of the FSP. There appears to be three main reasons for this situation:

1. Many individuals had difficulty paying their contributions, because as of December 1997 only BCH branches would accept payments, but BCH had a limited network of branches (see DNP-UDS 1997). CONPES decided that from 1998 on, an individual would be dropped from the list of beneficiaries if he was four or more months late in the payments. No information has been provided on whether this measure has had any effect.
2. There was a juridical debate on the cumulability of contributions to Regimen contributivo and Regimen subsidiado. ISS would not accept the

cumulability (see DNP-UDS 1997). There is no information on the outcome of this debate.

3. Still in 1997, many of the entities that exact the 1 percent surcharge on behalf of FSP (pension funds, AFP's, ISS, Fondo del Magisterio, etc.) failed to turn over the proceeds regularly to the FSP. Because the FSP has currently a large surplus, this does not seem a major problem at the moment. It will become more serious when and if FSP gets into its steady state.

### Redistribution to Lower End of Income: Outside the Social Insurance System (Social Assistance)

Redistribution to elderly individuals outside the Prima Media system is accomplished essentially by one program, REVIVIR, which is part of the Red de Solidaridad Social. REVIVIR was established by Ley 100 of 1993 to pay up to 50 percent of minimum salary to indigent elderly individuals older than 65 (50 if handicapped). Decree 1135 of 1994 issued the provisions to operationalize the program, determined the cofinancing by territorial entities, and established a pilot program for 1994 and 1995.

To qualify, an elderly individual must belong to level 1 of SISBEN, or have at least two unmet basic needs; additional requirements are (see DNP-UDS 1996):

1. A monthly income below the amount of the subsidy;
2. The individual must live in families with household income below the minimum salary, or
3. Live in institutions or not be attached to any household.

Priority had to be given to this last category. The requirements for a municipality to participate in the program were as follows:

1. Use of SISBEN.
2. Existence of some program for elderly people.
3. Cofinancing of at least 50 percent of expenditure.

The program is administered by FOSES, while municipalities identify the beneficiaries. It is part of the RED de SOLIDARIDAD. The monthly subsidy is equal to the difference between poverty and indigence line according to DANE. It appears that the subsidy can be given in any combination of cash and provision of goods and services. In 1997 the breakdown of the assisted population was "Abuelos en la calle" 6 percent, "Abuelos in ancianatos" 11 percent, "Abuelos que viven solos" 29 percent, and "Abuelos que viven en familia" 54 percent.

While CIDER (1998) argues that this breakdown is evidence of insufficient targeting, the sum of the first three categories is 46 percent, not necessarily a bad targeting outcome for social programs. But clearly a more rigorous evaluation of the program is needed.

In a survey of 115 municipalities, the alcaldes ranked it above the other main RED programs, namely the two-vivienda programs, the employment program, and the apoyo alimentario.

Like the FSP, REVIVIR suffers from low membership. In 1999 its coverage was 90,310 individuals, little changed since 1997. But a DANE survey in 1993 had located a pool of potential beneficiaries of 320,638 elderly in SISBEN 1, of whom 98,658 are disabled individuals over 50 and 221,980 are indigent individuals over 65.

Also like FSP, REVIVIR has suffered from administrative problems: 53 percent of the 675 interviewed participants report interruptions in the subsidy. It is not clear how serious this problem is.

### Evaluation and Proposals

The key problem of the current pension system is clear: it spends too much on too few people. For a country like Colombia, with limited fiscal resources, pensions must be used to protect elderly individuals from poverty, not to ensure the continuation—or the improvement, as in the case of teachers—of their living standards into old age.

A second, related problem is the remarkable complication of the current system with its large numbers of special regimes, each obtained by small groups bargaining for special treatment. A consequence of this fragmentation is that the system is to a large extent unable to keep track of contributors and pensioners. No effective reform can be achieved without this type of information.

The pension reform proposal that was due to be discussed by Congress in April 2000 went in the right direction, compatibly with the many vetoes engrained in the system.[37] The proposal was far-reaching, and covered many more issues than discussed here. The discussion that follows is not meant to be exhaustive of the issue; rather, it concentrates mostly on a few salient distributive aspects.

The FSP and the social assistance components of the pension system are small, and usually attract very limited attention. Yet a by-product of reducing spending on standard pensions should be freeing up resources for other social programs. Social assistance old age pensions and a well-thought FSP should be two of them. The experience of industrialized countries shows that the eradication of old-age poverty has been probably the most remarkable achievement of their social security systems in the postwar era. But, besides their limited size, the implementation of these components in Colombia has so far been flawed.

The key problem is that the minimum wage is too high in Colombia, and legally and politically it is difficult for the government to pay less than the minimum wage. Thus both the minimum wage guarantee and the FSP pay too high a pension, equal at least to the minimum wage.

The Fondo de Solidaridad Pensional also has gone beyond its initial purpose. As emphasized by Ayala (1999), the FSP has subsidized the contribution of individuals with very little or no incentives of their own to enter the system. This was not meant to be the original mission of the FSP, which should have taken care of temporary situations to ensure a continuing record of contributions. In other words, the current operation of FSP creates little or no incentives for individuals to contribute their share, and could create an adverse selection problem with individuals in search of an invalidity or survivors pension. This is likely to be the case, for instance, with community mothers, 95 percent of whom in 1993 earned less than two-thirds of minimum salary (see Flórez, Moreno, and Barrios 1994).

It is well known that in Latin America there are powerful incentives for poor individuals to stay outside the formal pension system (see Holzman, Packard, and Questa 1999; and James 1999). But the requirement that FSP be linked to affiliation to the Regimen General de Seguridad Social en Salud has clearly exacerbated the problem. It is not clear what is the rationale for this requirement.

But what should one do with those individuals who are not covered by the FSP, namely the poorest individuals? Colombia should start thinking about a well-devised social assistance program. REVIVIR was just a half-hearted attempt, with too limited financial and organizational resources to be effective. But it also had some design flaws.

Its heavy emphasis on decentralization and municipal cofinancing defies the purpose of a redistributive program directed precisely to the poorest: presumably the poorest municipalities are also those with the highest incidence of elderly indigent. In general, a decentralizing social assistance program might make sense in countries, like the United States, where local governments have a sufficient tax base and a sufficiently diversified population to be able to sustain and administer the program by themselves. It makes much less sense in countries where local government varies enormously in their tax bases and administrative capabilities.

The pension component of REVIVIR does not need flexibility. A social pension is the same everywhere, and it can be managed nationally. Other services to indigent elderly should be adaptable to local needs. But at the same time it is clear that many municipalities do not have the technical or the financial ability to run this program by themselves. Perhaps the program should be run by a nationwide agency with good local ramification and flexibility.[38] Of course, such a step should be undertaken only after making sure that it will not strain the operations of the agency.

Related to this last point, it does not seem appropriate to link participation in this program to the fulfillment of the requirement that a municipality should have a program for the elderly indigent of its own. There is probably a high correlation between the technical capabilities of a municipality and the level of poverty in that municipality, including old-age poverty. Therefore REVIVIR might miss the target population exactly in the areas where it is needed the most. Making this program part of the Red de Solidaridad Social, with little organization of its own, has further exacerbated the problem: according to CIDER (1998), in only 38 percent of the municipalities is REVIVIR run by an agency that also runs similar programs.

Decentralization also impinges on the sustainability of the program: only 32 percent of the municipalities claim to be able to financially support the program if financing from the RED is discontinued. In fact, in 1998 the share of municipal financing in total REVIVIR spending was only 25 percent, half the statutory share.

The targeting effectiveness of REVIVIR is also a matter of dispute. According to CIDER (1998), based on interviews to 675 elderly participants in the program, REVIVIR enrolled 67 percent of participants into the Regimen Subsidiado en Salud, gave access to health services to 33 percent, obtained "visual and mobility aids" for 16 percent, and promoted the "institutional attention" for 11 percent. However, these claims are mostly qualitative, thus hard to evaluate.

There remain two key, connected issues: the financial sustainability of the program and its disincentive effects. It is hard to know what a far-reaching program would cost: a rigorous quantitative evaluation of REVIVIR does not exist, even though in 1998 CONPES had instructed an evaluation to be made. But a back of the envelope calculation is relatively easy. Based on current costs and enrollment, it would take about 0.2 percent of GDP to pay the current level of benefits to the 321,000 individuals that qualify for REVIVIR according to DANE.

Second, a social assistance pension could certainly have effects on the saving propensity and labor market attachments of the poor, via a wealth effect. While this effect should not be dismissed off hand, we must recognize that we have absolutely no idea about its possible magnitude.

### 9.4.2   Policies toward Families and Children

*The Institutional Framework*
At present, policies toward families and children are run mostly by ICBF, a central government agency with a 1998 total budget equal to about 0.5 percent of GDP (0.6 percent with municipal participation), and funded with the proceeds of a 3 percent payroll tax. The RED de Solidaridad Social, often in coordination with ICBF, runs a few programs. The present system contains elements of several different types of programs:

* Day care
* Food distribution and nutrition help
* School feeding
* Help for mothers heads of families
* Preventive and health care
* In-kind support for children in school age
* Various programs for adolescents and minors

Table 9.11 describes all the programs and their budgets.

*Programs for Preschoolers, Infants, Pregnant and Lactating Women: Theory*
Why are programs for preschoolers so important in developing countries? There are several reasons. First, malnutrition and health problems among preschoolers are a higher risk in these countries. Second, these programs could help foster the personal development of a child. According to studies of the US Perry Preschool Program for disadvantaged children, former participants in the program have earnings at 27 that are higher by up to 60 percent than nonparticipants, much higher rates of high-school graduation, and lower delinquency and teen age pregnancy rates (see Barnett 1992, 1993). A Rand study estimates large net social benefits from these programs.

However, this and other types of evidence come from sophisticated programs in the richest countries in the world. In essence, we do not have reliable estimates of the long-run benefits on development for developing

**Table 9.11**
ICBF and RED programs for families and children, 1998 (million pesos)

|  | Budget | Beneficiaries |
|---|---|---|
| *Children under 7* |  |  |
| Atencion al menor de 7 anos | 81,312 | 406,623 |
| CAIP—tradicional |  | 130,892 |
| CAIP—no convencional |  | 4,444 |
| Lactantes y preescolares |  | 20,363 |
| Jardines comunitarios |  | 4,607 |
| Intervencion nutricional materno infantil |  |  |
| Hogares comunitarios de Bienestar | 259,776 | 1,380,40 |
| HCB |  | 916,725 |
| FAMI |  | 463,725 |
| Apoyo alimentario (RED) | 55,293 | 916,725 |
| Bono alimentario para ninos en edad preescolar no cubiertos en HBI—area rural (RED) | 6,414 | 85,069 |
| *Minors between 7 and 18* |  |  |
| Restaurantes escolares |  | 2,537,327 |
| Asistencia nutricional al escolar y adolescente | 69,309 | 2,473,977 |
| Atencion complementaria al escolar y adolesc. | 11,382 | 63,350 |
| Subsidio escolar (RED) | 9,196 | 149,984 |
| Clubes juveniles | 3,775 | 42,003 |
| Menor autor de infracion penal | 21,409 | 27,487 |
| Protecion menor de 18 anos | 22,781 | 191,687 |
| Menor abandonado en peligro | 49,920 | 62,692 |
| Protecion menor y famlia | 1,676 |  |
| Protecion de la familia | 10,250 | 1,030,292 |
| Talentos deportivos (RED) | 1,202 | 3,030 |
| Compra y distribucion de alimentos | 28,026 |  |
| Formacion, administracion, informacion | 9,558 |  |

countries.[39] However, it may well be that in these countries pre-school programs could work mainly via more basic effects on nutrition and health. A variety of experiences in Latin American countries suggest that well-designed programs, linking childcare to nutrition and health, might be very effective in fostering the health of small children (see Deutsch 1999; Myers 1999). I will return to these effects later.

A third effect of pre-school programs might consist in freeing up the time of parents attached to the labor force. A study on data from the favelas of Rio de Janeiro found that earnings of poor mothers with access to childcare facilities increased by up to 20 percent. Like most other studies in this field, this study too was however plagued by endogeneity problems.

There is a fourth potentially important effect of preschool programs that is almost always neglected. These programs typically provide an implicit subsidy to families, via their nutrition component and in some cases by implicitly subsidizing the work effort of mothers. In a recession, in the typical Latin American country the participation rates of women increase via a negative wealth effect. This has been the case during the current recession in Colombia, where the participation rate of women increased from 46.9 in 1997 to 53.3 in 1999. Thus pre-school programs could provide a countercyclical social policy since the value of their subsidy increases in times of recessions.

Last, pre-school programs tend to have good self-targeting properties in developing countries, where poor families tend to have a much larger size than rich families.

Using this surrogate theoretical framework, I will now turn to assess the Colombian system of pre-school programs and their effectiveness.

### Programs for Preschoolers, Infants, Pregnant and Lactating Women: Institutions

Programs for pre-schoolers are run mostly by ICBF. The historical mission of ICBF is to run child-care centers. There are three basic types of child-care centers: CAIP, the older one, HCB (Hogares Comunitarios de Bienestar), and Jardines Comunitarios de Bienestar; in 1997 the former represented 12.5 percent of all spending by ICBF, HCB 41 percent, and Jardines Comunitarios a small 0.1 percent.

CAIP has two "modalities": traditional and Nonconventional. Traditional CAIPs are standard child-care centers, run by professional staff, in ICBF premises (if more than 90 children) or community premises (if less than 90 children). A CAIP provides day-care, supplemental feeding, health care, and pre-school education for children under 7. Nonconventional CAIPs are run by trained community personnel, and are characterized by more flexible hours than Traditional CAIPs; the community determines their schedules and locations.

There are two "modalities" of HCB: the original type, with child-care centers for children between 0 and 7 years, started in 1987, and FAMI (Familia, Mujer e Infancia), started in 1991. HCB is the largest program of ICBF. It covered about 900,000 children in 1998 and 1999. An HCB consists of a day-care center for children under 7, run by a "community mother," a person chosen by the community who need not have any qualification (except having completed nine grades of school, a requirement that is often not enforced; see below). She receives some rudimentary training by ICBF in childcare and nutrition. ICBF also helps community mothers obtain subsidized loans to upgrade their facilities, and pays a her a monthly salary: as we have seen, 95 percent of community mothers earn less than two-thirds of the minimum wage. In addition ICBF provides 80 percent of the daily nutritional requirements by distributing directly a nutritional supplement, called Bienestarina.

Another defining feature of HCBs is that they are meant to involve heavily the community. In principle, each family must "cooperate" with the community mother at least once every 15 days.

A HCB serves a maximum of 15 children. Priority is given to marginal neighborhood, and to children under 7 with at least two unsatisfied basic needs (NBI). The budget of an HCB is executed by Asociaciones de Padres de Familia. Each Association administers between 15 and 20 HCBs, and each operates a Junta de Padres de Familia. The bulk of the funds come directly from ICBF; in addition each family is required to pay a monthly fee equal to 25 percent of a daily minimum salary—in 1992 this was equal to 7 percent of the monthly cost per child.

After 1991, ICBF slowed down the expansion of standard HCBs in order to improve quality. It started a new "modality" of HCB, FAMI, with as target population pregnant women, lactating mothers and children under 2 in extreme poverty. The home is still run by a "community mother" elected by the Asociación of Hogares Comunitarios; she supervises two groups of 15 women, in two daily sessions, giving advice on nutrition and health and making home visits.

The third type of child-care center, Jardines Comunitarios, was created with the goal of involving the community more closely. Its target are children between 2 and 5 years of age who have at least one parent with little or no labor force attachment. Each Jardín Comunitario is composed of 120 children divided into two groups of 60 children who attend every other day. A professional educator heads each Jardin; each group is run by a community mother, and further subdivided into 4 groups of 15 children, each under the supervision of a volunteer parent.

Besides child-care centers there are other programs directed to preschool children, financed by the RED and usually managed by or in close cooperation with ICBF. (1) *Apoyo alimentario a niños de edad preescolar*. Part of the RED, but administered by ICBF with cofinancing from municipalities. Its goal is to improve the nutrition of children in HCBs by taking their rations from 60 to 73 percent of daily calories need. It covers automatically all children in HCBs only. (2) *Bono alimentario a niños de edad preescolar no cubiertos por HCB (área rural)*. Also part of the RED, but administered by ICBF with cofinancing from territorial entities. It distributes high-calories food to poor children in rural areas using the network of suppliers organized by ICBF. The coverage in 1998 was 85,000 children. This program has always been very small, and it seems to be one of the programs that the RED is about to discontinue: it does not appear in the accounts of ICBF after 1997. (3) *Programa de Atencion Materna Infantil (PAMI)*. This program, part of the RED, had two components: build or rehabilitate health centers, especially in the 11 departments with infant mortality rates above average, and attach to the Regimen Subsidiado women and children under 1. The Ministry of Health executed it, with cofinancing from municipalities; the Red de Solidaridad Social also had a role, consisting in locating needy women in poorest areas, and in promoting the program. By the end of 1995, in its first component, it had built 140 health posts in 128 municipalities; in the second component, it had affiliated to Regimen Subsidiado de Seguridad Social 82,000 mothers and 64,000 children under 1 (82 percent of plan). There are no signs of this program in recent years. Finally, there are two ICBF programs on which no information is available: (4) *Asistencia al menor en recuperación nutricional*; (5) *Intervención nutricional materno infantil*.[40]

### Child-care Programs for Preschoolers: Costs and Usage

From this point on, I will focus on the child-care components of ICBF, HCB, and CAIP, the only programs on which information is available. By universal agreement, the quality of care offered by CAIPs is much higher than that of HCBs. Yet in the last decade the government has made a conscious effort to redirect resources away from CAIP and toward HCB. There are two reasons for this change in policy. First, and mostly under the influence of UNICEF, HCB was perceived as a more community-oriented program, involving the active participation of parents; CAIPs, by contrast, were viewed as typical "charity," with no involvement of parents or the community. Under the prevailing ideology of the time, this perceived feature of CAIP was a considerable handicap. The second reason was that CAIP was perceived as a rather costly program, directed mostly at the urban middle class.

To evaluate this policy, and its possible alternatives, one needs at least three pieces of information: (1) what are the effects of CAIP over those of HCB, (2) what are their relative costs, and (3) who uses the two programs.

#### Effects of CAIP and HCB

There is virtually no information on this issue. The last comparison of the two programs was made in 1993 (Flórez and Méndez 1993). Although very careful, it was not meant to contain any experimental evidence, and it focused mostly on issues of usage and costs rather than on their effects. A nonexperimental attempt at evaluating some effects of HCB was made in 1996 (ICBF 1997), but it covered only HCB. In fact, since 1993, there is virtually no information—besides program appropriations and payments, and number of beneficiaries—on *any* ICBF program other than HCB. Still, from anecdotal evidence and from conversations with experts in the field, it is safe to assume that the quality of care provided by CAIP is considerably higher than that of HCB.

*Relative Costs of CAIP and HCB*
Costs per child depend crucially on actual enrollment, a controversial figure. Official data on enrollment are obtained by multiplying the number of HCBs by 15, the maximum number of children per establishment. Yet, as Flórez and Méndez (1993) showed, actual enrollment is likely to be on average less than 13 children per HCB, and from survey data, the actual HCB enrollment could have been as low as 50 percent of the official enrollment. Based on official enrollment, in 1999 the cost per child of CAIP was about 170 percent that of HBI.[41] Yet World Bank (1997b) shows that while in 1987 the cost per child at CAIP was 2.6 times that at an HBI home, in 1996 the same ratio was only 1.2.

If this last figure is correct, there seems to be little doubt that the policy of promoting HCB against CAIP is misguided, given their widely different qualities. But any progress on this fundamental issue will always be impossible unless the question is settled once and for all. This should not be difficult: it does not take a lot of resources to sample 100 HCBs and 100 CAIPs in rural and urban areas.

*Usage of CAIP and HCB*
Who uses CAIP and HCB? It is not possible to answer this question for recent years. But a detailed answer is possible based on the 1992 ENH survey.[42] The conventional wisdom is that HCB and especially CAIP are mostly urban programs. Yet data on usage are not entirely consistent with this view. Table 9.12 shows that usage of HCB was more frequent in rural areas, where 12.4 percent of families with children aged 2 to 6 used HCB, against 6.3 percent in large cities, 10.5 percent in intermediate cities, and 11.3 percent in small cities. In contrast, CAIPs were used slightly more in large cities, by 9 percent of households with children aged 2 to 6, than in rural areas, by 7.1 percent of the same type of households. But the 1993 CASEN survey gives a much higher relative usage of HCB in both rural and urban areas.[43]

**Table 9.12**
Usage of CAIP and HCB by households: Colombia, urban and rural

|  | Colombia | Large cities | Medium-size cities | Small cities | Rural |
|---|---|---|---|---|---|
| ENH |  |  |  |  |  |
| HCB | 10.0 | 6.1 | 10.5 | 11.3 | 12.4 |
| CAIP | 7.8 | 9.0 | 4.9 | 8.6 | 7.1 |
| CASEN |  |  |  |  |  |
| HCB |  | 18.6 |  |  | 25.4 |
| CAIP |  | 6.3 |  |  | 2.9 |

Notes: ENH: Flórez and Méndez (1993), Cuadro 2.11, based on 1992 ENH; universe is families with children 2 to 6. "CASEN": Leibovitch and Nuñez (1999), based on 1993 CASEN; universe is all households.

**Table 9.13**
Use of CAIP and HCB by households with children aged 2 to 6 in urban and rural areas

|  | Colombia | | Urban[a] | | Rural | |
|---|---|---|---|---|---|---|
|  | CAIP | HCB | CAIP | HCB | CAIP | HCB |
| D1 | 6.8 | 17.5 | 12.0 | 9.5 | 5.5 | 18.7 |
| D2 | 9.2 | 10.4 | 8.5 | 7.6 | 6.5 | 16.6 |
| D3 | 7.1 | 11.1 | 8.9 | 8.9 | 8.7 | 12.8 |
| D5 | 7.6 | 8.2 | 10.5 | 12.6 | 6.9 | 10.7 |
| D10 | 5.8 | 2.2 | 4.9 | 2.2 | 9.7 | 11.4 |
| Total | 7.8 | 10.3 | 9.0 | 6.1 | 7.1 | 12.4 |

Source: Flórez and Méndez (1993), Cuadro 2.11, based on ENH 1992.
Note: Percentages are of each decile of households with children between 2 and 6 whose children are enrolled in CAIP or HCB.
a. Urban: major cities.

Users of HCB do tend to be of lower socioeconomic standing than users of CAIP. But the difference is mostly visible in rural areas. Table 9.13 shows that among families with children aged 2 to 6, in urban areas the first three deciles were about equally likely to send their children to CAIPs as to HCBs, but in rural areas the first three deciles used HCBs much more frequently than CAIPs, with the difference tapering off at higher deciles. In both areas, however, richer individuals are more likely to send their children to CAIPs than to HCBs. Because the average income in rural areas is much lower than in urban areas, the first three deciles encompass most poor in urban areas but only part of the poor in rural areas. Another perspective on the same issue can be gained by looking at the usage of HCB and CAIP by poor individuals (defined as those with income below 2 US dollars per day, in PPP at 1985 prices) in

**Table 9.14**
Use of CAIP and HCB by poor and non-poor in urban and rural areas

|  | Urban | | Rural | |
|---|---|---|---|---|
|  | CAIP | HCB | CAIP | HCB |
| Poor | 6.2 | 30.8 | 2.3 | 27.3 |
| Non-poor | 6.3 | 15.6 | 3.7 | 23.0 |
| All | 6.3 | 18.6 | 2.9 | 25.4 |

Source: Leibovitch and Nuñez (1999), based on Encuesta CASEN 1993. Percentages are of poor or non-poor households that have enrolled their children in HCB or CAIP. "Poor": households with less than US$2 per capita in PPP, 1985 prices.

**Table 9.15**
Use of CAIP and HCB by poor and non-poor in urban and rural areas

|  | Urban | | Rural | |
|---|---|---|---|---|
|  | CAIP | HCB | CAIP | HCB |
| ENH |  |  |  |  |
| Poor | 38.2 | 47.3 | 69.7 | 84.4 |
| Non-poor | 61.8 | 52.7 | 30.3 | 15.6 |
| CASEN |  |  |  |  |
| Poor | 19.7 | 33.0 | 48.2 | 64.0 |
| Non-poor | 80.3 | 67.0 | 51.8 | 36.0 |

Notes: "ENH": assumed first 2 deciles in urban and first 6 deciles in rural are poor (from distribution of all households in CASEN survey). "CASEN": computed from table 9.14. Percentages are of enrollment in HCB or CAIP attributable to "poor" or "non-poor" households. "Poor": households with less than US$2 per capita in PPP, 1985 prices.

urban and rural areas (see the 1993 CASEN survey results in table 9.14). As in the previous table, poor individuals do tend to use HCB much more than CAIP in rural areas; but now this is true also in urban areas.

What is the actual breakdown by income of users of HCB and CAIP? Table 9.15 shows that the poor are the largest users of HCB in rural areas (where they make up about 60 percent of the households), but their proportion in CAIPs is only marginally smaller. Table 9.16 shows that this difference is accounted for mostly by the first decile; from the third decile on usage of HCB and CAIP in rural areas is similar.

*Child-care Programs for Preschoolers: Incidence*
Who benefits from HCB and CAIP spending? I will focus here on the only program whose incidence has been studied, HCB. Based on the 1992 ENH, in urban areas, the net subsidy[44] of HCB represented a negligible share of the income of all families with children aged 2 to 6, at most 1

**Table 9.16**
Share of CAIP and HCB enrollment by deciles in urban and rural areas

|       | Colombia |       | Urban[a] |       | Rural |       |
|-------|----------|-------|----------|-------|-------|-------|
|       | CAIP     | HCB   | CAIP     | HCB   | CAIP  | HCB   |
| D1    | 14.2     | 27.5  | 23.6     | 27.7  | 9.7   | 18.8  |
| D2    | 18.6     | 15.9  | 14.6     | 19.4  | 14.5  | 20.9  |
| D3    | 12.1     | 14.6  | 13.0     | 19.3  | 17.0  | 14.2  |
| D5    | 10.0     | 8.1   | 12.3     | 4.5   | 10.6  | 9.7   |
| D10   | 3.1      | 0.9   | 2.4      | 1.6   | 4.5   | 3.0   |
| Total | 100.0    | 100.0 | 100.0    | 100.0 | 100.0 | 100.0 |

Source: Flórez and Méndez (1993), Cuadro 2.13, based on ENH 1992.
a. Major cities.

percent for the first decile of the distribution of household income. But in rural areas, the HCB net subsidy is equal to 6.3 percent of the income of the first decile of all households, and 2.9 percent of the second decile. Thus HCB has good targeting properties; unfortunately, no information of this sort is available for the other programs.

### Child-care Programs for Preschoolers: Evaluation
How well do programs for preschoolers fulfill the tasks briefly set out in section 9.2.4? In the absence of experimental evidence and longitudinal data, it is difficult to make a rigorous assessment. But one can attempt an informed guess from the available evidence.

The quality of the care provided by community mothers is obviously questionable. From the 1996 survey, 57 percent did not take the standard measurements of children upon enrollment, and less than 10 percent could interpret the individual and collective growth curves. Fifty-five percent of HCBs in rural areas did not have teaching material; 58 percent did not have toys.

A second potential benefit of HCBs, we have seen, is the implicit subsidization of the mother's work. But 58 percent of spouses of household heads who use HCBs were not attached to the labor force in 1993 (Flórez and Méndez 1993). However, this percentage is much higher in rural areas, 64 percent, than in large cities, 47 percent; and it is higher among the poor (e.g., it is 81 percent in the first decile of the rural distribution) than among the rich. The case of CAIP might be different, as they were designed in part to satisfy the needs of working parents. They require less (or no) involvement, and tend to have more flexible hours, partly because in many cases they are contracted out by ICBF. Yet the extra flexibility

Table 9.17
Reasons for not using HCB in urban and rural areas

|  | Large cities | Medium-size cities | Small cities | Rural | Colombia |
|---|---|---|---|---|---|
| Using HCB | 6.1 | 10.5 | 11.2 | 12.6 | 10.4 |
| Reasons for not using HCB: |  |  |  |  |  |
| No facility nearby | 2.7 | 3.1 | 3.6 | 36.6 | 18.8 |
| No space | 6.0 | 6.4 | 7.0 | 5.0 | 5.8 |
| Too costly | 8.0 | 7.8 | 6.2 | 3.6 | 5.6 |
| Other | 37.8 | 41.7 | 49.6 | 30.0 | 36.7 |
| Total | 100 | 100 | 100 | 100 | 100 |

Sources: Flórez and Méndez (1993); Cuadro 2.11.

of CAIP might not be enough: except for the last decile, on average, the rate of inactivity of households spouses that use CAIP is very similar to that of HCB users. Several studies have argued that hours flexibility is the key to the effectiveness of childcare centers in increasing the income of users, and that often private child care centers outperform public ones exactly for this reason. Hence flexibility might be one of the key directions for reform of childcare policy.

In summary, HCB and CAIP do not seem to have an important role in freeing up working time for mothers. As we have seen, the use of HCBs is more common among the poor and in rural areas, where there is evidence that limited supply constrains usage further (see table 9.17). Yet the poor in rural areas are exactly those who have more time available. Why then do these families send their children to HCBs? Not for their educational role, nor—to a large extent—because they have to go to work. The remaining possibility is the implicit food subsidy they provide.[45] If this is the case one should think of more efficient ways of conveying the food subsidy to families, an issue that we will take up again later.[46]

The nutritional aspect of child-care programs is particularly important for children under 2 because malnutrition is particularly severe in this age group, and because there is evidence (mostly anecdotal) that the returns to intervention by 2 years of age are high (see Deutsch 1998). In 1996, only 12.2 percent of children enrolled in HCB were in this age group, but this number per se does not indicate whether there was an unmet demand for the services to children under 2, and how effective the current level of service is. The specific program targeted at this age group and their mothers, FAMI, by 1998 had about 465,000, half the official users of HCBs. FAMI was intended mostly for poor families. However, results from the 1993 CASEN survey show that in rural areas poor and nonpoor families were about equally likely to use FAMI. Usage at that time was very limited. It might be that numbers have changed by now, but no recent information is available on this program.

### Child-care Programs for Preschoolers: Proposals

To summarize, the evidence shows that HCBs are heavily used in rural areas as well, where there are also indications of high unmet demand; the educational functions of HCB are limited, and the quality of care provided is inferior to that of CAIP. There are concerns about the effectiveness of ICBF programs for children 0 to 2, and flexibility is the key for child care to be of use to working mothers.

Based on this (admittedly tentative) evidence, the following is a possible set of proposals:

1. ICBF should think about moving back to the CAIP model. If costs are a problem, it should think about more cost recovery, with fees on a sliding scale, such as based on the SISBEN classification.
2. Despite lack of any evaluation, there are concerns that FAMI is not doing a good job in addressing the need of pregnant and lactating women and their children under 2, mostly because FAMI community mothers are not sufficiently well trained. ICBF should consider shutting down FAMI (subject to some evaluation of the program).
3. All existing programs by the ICBF or RED that duplicate efforts, such as PAMI, should be scrapped entirely, and similarly for programs with minuscule clientele, like Jardines Comunitarios.
4. ICBF should enhance the flexibility of its programs, particularly of HCBs. World Bank (1990) already observed that in 1990 ICBF was administering directly 97 percent of HCB's, and "no agency can single handedly manage between 30,000 and 60,000 day care centers (depending on estimates)." In dispersed areas, where as we have seen HCB might have a natural market, the ideal size of an HCB is much smaller than 15. There are currently two obstacles to increase flexibility. First, the high degree of centralization of ICBF. By all accounts, ICBF is run in Bogotá, where even the departmental managers are appointed. ICBF needs decentralization. However, this has to be done carefully, in order not to provide the wrong incentives to local administrations. Complete decentralization, meaning local financing of welfare programs, would penalize poorer localities. But centralized financing with decentralized decision on the allocation of funds would produce fiscal irresponsibility. The second

obstacle to increase flexibility is the increasing bargaining power of community mothers. By many accounts, community mothers are now a well-organized, unionized force, with many high-ranking political supporters. Although no quantitative evidence can be obtained on this point, many actors in the field acknowledge that community mothers are increasingly a factor of rigidity.

5. Community mothers pose problems in other respects as well. As we have seen, their training is often extremely inadequate. There is also continuing concern about the effectiveness of the home-improvement loans for furniture and equipment. Twenty-eight percent of the community mothers used these subsidized loans for purposes other than in the ICBF guidelines.[47] In addition the turnover rate of community mothers is high (the average tenure is 2 years). When a community mother leaves, she keeps the equipment and furniture, leaving the community to pick up the costs. World Bank (1994) recommended that ICBF should pick up these costs, or find ways to recover the material, but not much has been done so far.

6. If, as I have argued, child-care programs largely fulfill a nutrition subsidization role, there are more efficient ways of conveying food subsidies to the poor. Colombia should consider a system of food stamps, which has been used successfully in Honduras and Jamaica (see Ezemeneri and Subbarao 1998). Delivery of food stamps should be linked to the use of health care facilities by pregnant and lactating women and their children under 2. This would automatically address health problems in this population by providing strong incentives for poor mothers to use health facilities. The experience has shown that nutritional training classes for pregnant and lactating women will not be well attended without further incentives (during a strike of food distributors in Jamaica, attendance in preventive care classes dropped to 30 percent). A few administrative issues to be considered carefully are as follows:

• By itself, the feeding program in clinics is not preventive in nature. To contain some preventive element, it must be combined with some form of targeting based on health risk. As in Chile's PNAC, the programs could select women according to health and nutritional status, in addition to SISBEN.

• Operationally the experience of several countries has shown that when clinics have been put in charge of food stamp programs, the demand for some of their services (baby weighing, health checkups, in general) can increase up to five times (as in Honduras). This has put a strain on their normal operations; more important, doctors and nurses have resisted acting as distributors of food stamps (Jamaica). The solution adopted in Chile was to weigh babies at risk every month, and the other babies every three months. This should be adopted in Colombia as well, although one should be aware that this system would impose stronger organizational and record-keeping requirements.

• Where should eligible pregnant women collect food stamps? A practical solution could be to have clinic perform only pre- and postnatal care, weigh babies, and distribute high micronutrients food, as in Mexico's PROGRESA. Indigent women would still collect food stamps in other government offices. This also has the advantage that it does not burden the clinic with excessive duties, and provide extra help for pregnant and lactating women. In addition it keeps the incentive to use health clinics.[48]

Food stamps should also be extended to the rest of the pre-school population belonging to, say, SISBEN levels 1 and 2. They should be usable in HCBs and, as in Jamaica, they should also be used by other vulnerable groups, such as the elderly indigents.

Food stamps have several advantages besides providing incentives for usage of other services. They tend to enjoy considerable support, because they are perceived as targeted to the poor.[49] Contrary to cash transfers, they do not require an extensive network of rural banks to be cashed—a big advantage in a country like Colombia, with large rural areas that are not served by banks.[50] On the other hand, they have two problems. They pose security concerns, since food stamps are not personalized. And they can generate rents for retailers, who might refuse to accept them at face value. In Jamaica, making food stamps cashable by retailers at no discount in a bank has mitigated this problem; still the problem might persist if a local store is a near monopolist in the area.[51]

### Non-child-care Programs for Preschoolers, Infants, and Pregnant and Lactating Women

Of the five other programs directed at preschoolers, no information is available on the first two: *Asistencia al menor en recuperación nutricional* and *Intervención nutricional materno infantil*. *Apoyo alimentario* is closely linked to HCB, since it is essentially a subsidy from the RED to each child enrolled in HCBs but not in CAIPs. *Apoyo alimentario* and *PAMI* seem to have disappeared from the RED and ICBF accounts. Hence it is practically impossible to evaluate these programs as well.

Table 9.18
Use of restaurantes escolares by poor and non-poor

| Urban | | Rural | |
|-------|----------|------|----------|
| Poor | Non-poor | Poor | Non-poor |
| 3.46 | 2.87 | 3.74 | 8.04 |

Source: Leibovich and Nunez (1999), from Encuesta CASEN 1993.
Note: Percentages are of poor or non-poor households that have used restaurantes esco-lares.

### Other Programs for Minors and Families

As table 9.11 shows, ICBF and the RED administer a large number of other programs, amounting to about 50 percent of the ICBF budget. The two largest groups of programs are school feeding programs (*Restaurantes escolares*) and programs to support minors with legal problems (*Menor autor de infracion penal*). It should be noted that these programs, like most others, include a plethora of subprograms. The other programs range from a school subsidy to buy uniforms and books to children of female-headed households (*Subsidio escolar*, run by the RED), to a program to subsidize young sport talents without means (*Talentos deportivos*), to a small program for pregnant adolescents (a subprogram of *Menores abandonados en peligro*).

The only evidence available, and a limited one, is one school feeding program, Restaurantes Escolares. Table 9.18 shows that the nonpoor tend to use it much more frequently than the poor, particularly in rural areas. This pattern confirms well-known properties of school feeding programs, namely that they are much less targeted than food stamps or well-designed programs for pre-schoolers (see Ezemeneri and Jubbarao 1998); they are also less cost effective because malnutrition is typically more widespread among children aged less than 5. Virtually no other information of scientific use is available on any of these programs. For instance, in evaluating the programs of the RED in this sector during the 1994 to 1998 period, DNP (1998) writes only: "Regarding the program Subsidio Escolar, we suggest an evaluation of its impact, as well as increasing the value of the subsidy to students. The Bono Alimentario program must improve the administrative programs and contracting with mayors, in order to guarantee the execution of appropriations and the achievement of its objectives. The Bono Alimentario program must continue improving the nutritional level of the population attended by HCBs" (p. 35).

*Other Programs for Minors and Families: Evaluation and Proposals*
ICBF and the RED are clearly involved in too many programs in this sector. Some of them, like Talentos Deportivos, have a minuscule constituency. There is also little doubt that some programs are just the result of an ideological commitment to the notion of community involvement. This is the case, for instance, of Jardines Comunitarios, which as we have seen are predicated on a utopistic degree of involvement of parents. The notion of community involvement is also in high fashion in international organizations. But from the point of view of incidence it is a dangerous one, because the very poor are also those who, for cultural and economic reasons, are least able to organize themselves. Note that HCB itself is potentially subject to this problem: ICBF merely ratifies the existence of an Association of Parents; without the latter, no HCB can be established.

Other programs are the result of a well-intentioned desire to cover urgent needs. But there is no question that this has led to excessive fragmentation. The most frequently cited problem in the 1999 Evaluación de Gestión was "The large number of programs and low operating capacity." An important consequence of this fragmentation is that especially for the minor programs, it impedes the development of specific expertise as a limited amount of human resources must be spread thinly over many different programs.

In principle, the large number of programs could be the optimal response to different demands in different parts of the country. But in this case it would be better to decentralize the operations of ICBF, and great care would have to be exercised in order to provide the right incentives to the territorial entities.

A second consequence of this fragmentation is the host of administrative problems that ICBF has suffered in the past, such as long delays in acting on the caseload. Much publicity has been given to the establishment of the Sistema de Evaluación Gerencial, funded in part by the World Bank. There are several other programs, including the Evaluación de Gestión y Resultados, the Sistema de Control Interno, and the Sistema de Evaluación de Gestión. This latter program was meant to give an idea about the performance of the main regional agencies in 5 ICBF programs (HBI, Menor abandonado, adoptions, Menor infractor, and Extrajudicial), by ranking regional offices according to 16 indicators of performance. Unfortunately, the practical usefulness of this program seems limited. The choice of the 5 programs does not seem to respond to any rationale (adoption is an extremely limited program, with less than 5,000 beneficiaries, while FAMI, CAIP, Restaurantes escolares, and other important programs are left out). More important, a regional office is considered "problematic" according to a given indicator if its performance in that indicator is below the average. In general, however, all regional offices, or none, could be problematic, and this "absolute" evaluation would be more useful. In addition not all the indicators are helpful in guiding policy; for instance, only two indicators refer to the largest program of all, HCB, and they measure the fraction of children attended out of the target population, and the fraction of associations with "pago oportuno." Thus I make the following proposals:

1. ICBF should drop most of its programs for minors above 7, and concentrate on a core of key programs. If there is a need for some of the programs it currently runs, it could provide cofinancing and technical advice for interested municipalities.
2. It should consider a nationwide program of food stamps (or cash grants) for families of primary and secondary school students, where disbursement of the subsidy is conditional on the children remaining in school. Like the previous proposal for pre-schoolers, this program has the advantage of combining a targeted subsidy with incentives to build human capital. This program would be patterned after the PROGRESA program in Mexico, which is being established on a large scale and is among the few existing programs whose participation has been randomized and can therefore be evaluated experimentally.[52] PROGRESA seems to have good targeting properties in terms of food consumption (see Hoddinot and Skoufias 2000), and possibly some effect on enrollment rates: Schultz (1999) estimates that it increased primary enrollment rates by 2.2 percentage points, and secondary enrollment rates among the poor by perhaps up to 6 percentage points.
3. Except for HCB and, in part, CAIP, there is virtually no usable public information available on ICBF. It is significant that in the last ten years only two evaluations have been attempted, and both on HCB. It is simply unacceptable that an agency that manages 0.6 percent of GDP does not have any ground on which to base its choices. Thus external evaluation of all major ICBF programs and the surviving RED programs should be a high priority.

### 9.4.3 Employment and Unemployment Policies
Colombia does not have formal unemployment insurance. Because of the high rate of informality and the difficulties in keeping records of the work history of individuals, a formal well-working unemployment insurance

system is virtually impossible in a country like Colombia. In fact few Latin American countries have one, and it is almost invariably limited to very few individuals (e.g., little more than 100,000 in Argentina). Furthermore, as Mazza (1999) shows, they are typically geared toward young individuals at the top of the wage distribution. Thus, for the time being, Colombia should continue without a formal unemployment insurance system. This leaves two other types of programs: training and employment generation programs.

### Training Programs

Training in Colombia is the realm of SENA, the state training agencies patterned after Brasil's SENAI. SENA is a large organization, with a budget in 1998 equal to about 0.3 percent of GDP. It provides training both for youths entering the labor force and for displaced workers.

The only available evidence is on the distribution of attendance by quintile, from the 1993 CASEN survey. SENA training is highly geared toward the upper quintiles. This is not just a reflection of the fact that it is mostly an urban program: even among urban individuals, the poor enrolled in SENA are less frequently than the nonpoor. The emergency training program of the RED, also managed by SENA, was concentrated in the top decile of the distribution of municipalities by revenue per capita; in fact it concentrated in just 18 municipalities (see Alarcon 1997; CIDER 1998).

Training programs can be of long or short duration. The former effectively replace technical schools that in much of Latin America are in dire straits. The latter are mostly used as countercyclical policies in times of high or rising unemployment. Since the last evaluation of SENA seems to have been made in 1980, little information is available on its longer training programs; hence in what follows I will focus on the shorter programs.

Unemployment in Colombia is highly concentrated among the youths: for instance, the unemployment rate among individuals in the 18 to 24 age group is 25.7 percent, against 6 percent in the 50 to 59 group. As emphasized by Marquez (1999), training programs tend to be effective exactly in situations of high youth unemployment rate. A large body of evidence shows that training of displaced adult workers very rarely provides the necessary skills to return to the labor market, while short training programs might provide young adults entering the labor force with usable job search skills provided they are geared toward a quick return to the labor market rather than toward long and generic training (e.g., see

Fay 1996; Martin and Grubb 2001). It is also important to combine these programs with stringent work tests and good job search assistance, as in the recent British New Deal program (see Blundell et al. 2001) and serious sanctions and controls (see Grubb 2000). Thus designing and operating effective training programs requires considerable knowledge and administrative capacity.

However, there is a growing consensus that SENA, like most training agencies in Latin America, is a highly rigid institution, very reluctant to change and to adapt to the changing labor market. Programs like *Chile Joven* in Chile essentially outsource training programs, inviting bids from private providers and from the national training institution. This puts pressure on the national training institution to adapt to the market demand for its services. *Chile Joven* typically provides scholarships to its students and an internship period in a private firm. The first feature, like the conditional grants proposed in section 9.4.2 for mothers and school children, provides a cash incentive for a human-capital enhancing activity.[53]

### *Employment Creation Programs: Theory and Latin American Experience*
Latin America has a long experience with employment creation programs. Starting with the famous Bolivian Social Investment Fund in the early 1980s, virtually every Latin American country has had at least one in the after the debt crisis.

Opinions on the performance of the first wave vary. The available evidence suggests that in many cases they did not reach the very poor, for two main reasons: they were not always labor intensive, and they paid high wages. The recent consensus in international organizations is built around three pillars: employment generation programs should pay much less than the minimum wage, in order to build in a self-targeting mechanism; they should employ highly labor-intensive technologies; and they should be demand driven, meaning local communities and NGOs should propose the menu of projects to implement (e.g., see Ravallion 1998).

Two problems that have plagued Social Investment Funds since their inception are the sustainability of projects and the political use of these programs. Because investment by Social Investment Funds is, by their very nature, of an emergency nature, they rarely budget enough for maintenance, which is typically assumed to be the task of local governments. The result is that a large fraction of projects financed by employment creation programs decay at a very quick rate and are not maintained.

There is little doubt that employment programs are used for political purposes, in Latin America and elsewhere. Some evidence on Peru shows that Social Investment Fund spending was heavily concentrated on marginal electoral districts. It is interesting to note that two of the countries that pioneered public employment programs in the past, Chile and Peru, have not had any such program for a while.

### Colombia's Experience with Employment Creation Programs

Colombia has had a limited experience with employment generation programs in the recent past, in the form of two programs administered by the RED, one for urban areas and one for rural areas. The urban employment program (*Empleo Urbano*)[54] is one of the few RED programs that has been the object of some quantitative evaluation (see Caro 1998; Contraloria General de la Republica 1997; REUNIRSE 1998). It had a limited size, generating the equivalent of 8,700 full-time employments in 1996, roughly equivalent to 0.73 percent of total unemployment in urban areas.

A striking characteristic of this program was the extremely high wage it paid: in infrastructure projects, on average in 1997 it was about 170 percent of that offered in the private construction sector; in services, it was about 150 percent of that offered in the communal service sector. The program also privileged infrastructure projects against service projects,[55] on the premise that infrastructure projects are more useful to the community. However, this premise is unproved, because many emergency projects are undertaken only in order to dispense money in times of unemployment. Moreover service projects have a lower wage, making them more self-targeting,[56] generate more employment, and, according to many participants, allow participation by less organized individuals and even teach them some useful labor market skills.[57]

Like all programs that are part of the RED, *Empleo Urbano* emphasized community participation and initiative. One of the most heralded innovations of the RED was its reliance on the Mesas de Solidaridad, meetings at the municipal and departmental level where citizens, their grassroot organizations and NGOs were invited to provide the criteria for selections of the process, developed by the same actors. As discussed above, this feature reflects a highly ideological position, both within the administration and in international organizations, with a highly populistic tone. But the reality is that this attitude can easily prove counterproductive, because very poor individuals do not have the skills to participate in these processes. In fact all evidence on participation at the Mesas is highly disappointing (see Jaramillo 1999; Cárdenas et al. 1999): according to REUNIRSE (1998), in 1996 only 35 percent of all beneficiaries stated that someone represented them in the Mesas, and only 5 percent participated directly (this percentage rose to 30 percent in 1997).

Perhaps not coincidentally, *Empleo Urbano* was highly concentrated in the richer municipalities. The top two deciles of municipalities in terms of own revenues per NBI person received almost 45 percent of total *Empleo Urbano* funds, against 16 percent of the bottom three deciles (see Alarcón 1997). One could argue that the distribution of spending on a well-designed employment creation program should be related to the number of unemployed individuals. This has not been the case with *Empleo Urbano*.[58] The completion rate in the 234 projects in departmental capitals surveyed by the Contaloría General in 1998 was disappointing: for instance, in Bogotá it was 55 percent.

These numbers confirm that the rhetoric of public employment programs creating useful and needed infrastructure projects can be misplaced. Especially if hastily arranged, they often amount to little more than pure subsidization of unemployment, by another name.

### Employment Creation Programs: Evaluation and Proposals

The employment generation programs of the RED have been widely criticized for being merely conjunctural and not tackling the underlying structural causes of unemployment (e.g., see Caro 1998). This criticism—a manifestation of the asset approach to social spending—misses the whole point of employment creation programs. They are (or should be) an emergency antipoverty device, designed to provide some relief to unemployment in countries that, for technical or other reasons, cannot afford a formal unemployment program.

Still, as discussed above, the small employment creation programs of the RED were liable to a number of different criticisms. In fact, in most respects they were almost the opposite of what current conventional thinking on employment creation programs would prescribe: they paid relatively high wages, and did not focus on labor-intensive projects. This is probably the result of political concessions to populistic pressures, which eventually undermined the usefulness itself of the program as an emergency antipoverty device.

The third component of the Red de Apoyo Social (see sections 9.4.2 and 9.4.3 for the first two components) is a relatively small program (about 0.1 percent of GDP) of public employment in infrastructure, with two subcomponents. The first is called *Mano a la Obra* (about $300mn in three years, two-thirds of which from the central government and one-third form the local governments), directed at poor individuals in SIS-BEN levels 1 and 2, and concentrated in the 78 largest municipalities. The second is called *Vias para la Paz* (about $210mn over three years) that was aimed mostly at building roads in the poorest rural areas. In the urban program each project will be funded by FIP (Fondo de Inversion para la Paz) based on a contract between FIP and the entity that will propose and manage the project (local governments, NGOs, community organizations). The central government will fund labor costs and materials in poor municipalities, contributing about $180,000 per month for each nonqualified person (the minimum wage is currently $260,000 per month). However, local governments will be free to subsidize this contribution, hence the actual wage paid might be higher than $180,000. Like *Empleo Urbano*, *Mano a la Obra* and *Vias para la Paz* place a heavy emphasis on infrastructures, which are unlikely to be maintained properly. In fact the Red de Apoyo Social explicitly prohibits the use of its funds for maintenance purposes.

In addition the target seems unrealistic. *Mano a la Obra* should fund 250,000 five-month spells of employment with a budget of $290mn. As a comparison, in 1996 *Empleo Urbano* generated about 8,200 full employment yearly jobs (at 260 working days per year, about 19,700 five-month spells) with a budget of about $33mn of that year. Based on *Empleo Urbano* costs, one would need about $650mn (current pesos) to generate 250,000 five-month spells in 2000. Even allowing for a slightly lower wage, the target of *Mano a la Obra* seems unrealistic.

In times of emergency with rising unemployment, it might be difficult to resist political pressure for some public employment programs. But at least one should consider carefully whether the emphasis on infrastructure projects that are unlikely to be maintained is well placed, or whether more emphasis on labor intensive services would not be more appropriate for the purpose.

## 9.5 Conclusions

Rather than summarizing the main proposals, it might be useful to focus on three typical features of social policy-making in Colombia: its fragmentation, its "fire-fighting" approach, and its frequent resort to pomposity.

### 9.5.1   The Fragmented Approach to Social Policy

The Red de Solidaridad Social is perhaps the best example of the fragmented approach to social policy. Although it existed before (under a
different name) it was given a decisive push under the Samper administration. In its intentions it should have been the main tool for reaching
the very poor, largely through a heavy emphasis on the notion of community involvement discussed above. As it is typical of social investment
funds, it was not subject to the authority of line ministers, and placed instead directly under the presidency; this should have enhanced its flexibility. But it dispersed its intervention on too many programs (16 at some
point), some of which with a minuscule target population, and others
with a target population that would have been difficult to characterize as
top priority under any reasonable approach to poverty reduction. Eventually, under the new administration, it lost political support, and funding
for many programs has been cut drastically recently. Thus, while its programs have now mostly an historical interest, the Red with its fragmented
approach to a social safety net still offers important lessons.

1. It is important to build a constituency for social programs; devolving
them to an independent agency directly under the presidency, in the style of
social investment funds, might not be an effective way of achieving this.
2. Fragmentation leads to a substantial overlap between programs, with
potential waste of resources, and to confusion. It also becomes impossible
to form an idea of what the government is doing and what needs to be
done. In turn, this makes it difficult to have an idea of the trade-offs
involved.
3. Fragmentation also leads to little accountability, as many programs
are hidden and not known to the media, or discussed only occasionally.
4. Too many agencies are involved, leading to lack of coordination,
waste of organizational resources, and again lack of accountability since
often it is not clear who is responsible for each program.
5. Another consequence of the fragmentation of the social safety net is a
fundamental ambiguity inherent in many programs: in principle, they are
usually open-ended, but in practice, they are based on a queuing mechanism, as funding is insufficient and often erratic. Not only is queuing
against the principle of horizontal equity; it also implies that some individuals with "higher priority" will not receive subsidy, while other individuals with "lower priority" will receive another subsidy. This situation
is partly an unavoidable consequence of limited resources, but also of too
many fragmented programs that compete for these limited resources.

### 9.5.2 The "Fire-fighting" Approach to Social Policy

The Red de Apoyo Social, the new package of emergency social policies recently unveiled by the administration as part of the Plan Colombia, exemplifies the "fire-fighting" approach to social policy-making.

Two of the three programs it contains (conditional grants to families and youth training programs) would make perfect sense as components of a well-thought permanent safety net. However, the package is designed not to build a permanent social safety net but rather to cope with the (hopefully) temporary recession.[59] Partly because of this, and partly because they have been arranged hastily, these programs represent little more than Keynesian money thrown in a recessionary economy.

Institutionally, the Red de Apoyo Social is very similar to the Red de Solidaridad Social. It is inscribed to the presidency, and it has its own, very complex, bureaucracy. But the Red de Apoyo Social does not replace the Red de Solidaridad Social and its programs: it merely adds on to them. Interestingly all three programs of the Red de Apoyo Social, training, public employment, and conditional family grants, were also present, in more or less similar form, in the Red de Solidaridad Social, and formally survive there. In this fashion, programs accumulate, with the old programs receiving less and less funding but remaining formally alive, together with their bureaucracy. The accumulated cobweb of programs becomes nearly inextricable. As the recession ends and the sense of urgency disappears, many programs fall into oblivion, but again without disappearing entirely.

### 9.5.3 Pomposity

Although data on most social programs are sorely lacking, there is no shortage of words. Indeed, the attitude toward social expenditure fully reflects the "planning" attitude that permeates fiscal policy-making in Colombia (see the chapter on the budget process in this book) and privileges grand discourses over hard facts. A typical example, among the many possible, is Pacto por la Infancia, a national guide for similar pacts that should have been signed by territorial entities (Conpes 2917). By end of 1997, 32 departments and 3 cities had signed "Pactos" por la Infancia to coordinate actions on children between different agencies. To accomplish this, 1,600 persons were detached with supervision tasks, together with a network of 1,300 functionaries of ministries, agencies, and territorial entities to watch over the realization of the "Pactos" (CONPES 3002). It is not clear what the concrete goals and the achievements of these "Pactos" have been; in any case no mention of Pactos por la

Infancia can be found in recent documents. It is likely that progress is hampered, rather than furthered, by this attitude toward pomposity and endless coordination of more and more agencies.

## Notes

For helpful conversations and bibliographical indications, I thank, without implicating, O. L. Acosta, U. Ayala, G. Carletto, E. Castano, C. E. Florez, G. Marquez, S. Morris, Z. Partow, F. Pérez, M. Perfetti, L. Rawlings, M. Salazar, A. Sarmiento, E. Skoufias, M. Szekely, C. E. Vélez, J. G. Zapata, M. T. Zarta, and all participants at the Cartagena meeting. M. L. Henao and J. G. Zapata generously provided some data. M. M. Carrasquilla provided invaluable organizational support.

1. On average, in the early 1990s general government revenues were about 20 percent of GDP, in OECD countries about 50 percent.

2. Among Latin American countries, Bolivia recently tried to introduce an almost universal pension, set at a very low 11 percent of the average wage, but it had to quickly abandon the experiment once it became evident that it was financially unsustainable.

3. The classic study on the distributional incidence of social spending in Colombia is Velez (1996).

4. While Colombia devotes a higher share of expenditure to all components of purchases of goods and services, the real difference is in capital expenditure. Note that capital expenditure as a share of GDP is more than twice the European average, and about six times as a share of primary spending. This difference is clearly implausible, and mostly reflects the generalized tendency in Latin American countries to classify many current expenditures as capital expenditures (see the chapter on the budget process in this book).

5. Source: Comisión de Racionalización de Gasto (1997a), Cuadros 5, 6, 10, and 11.

6. In addition to education and experience, Panizza and Qiang control for rural/urban employment, and sector classification for private sector employees.

7. Cross-country data on the share of pensions accruing to government employees are available only for a few countries.

8. The indigence line is defined as the cost of a food basket that satisfies the minimum nutritional requirements of a household. It was first measured in 1984 for 13 cities and the rural areas. The poverty line is defined as twice the indigence line in urban areas and 2.3 times the indigence line in rural areas. The indigence line is updated yearly using some price index, usually a food price index (but one should keep in mind that estimates of the CPI for rural areas do not exist).

9. According to this definition, a household is poor if it meets one of the following criteria:

- Inadequate housing (e.g., dirt floor in urban areas)
- Housing without basic services
- Crowded housing (i.e., with more than three people per room)
- High economic dependence (more than three persons per earner)
- At least one school-aged child (between 7 and 11) not attending school

   A household is in "misery" if it meets two or more of these criteria.

10. Different studies provide different answers on the extent and evolution of indigence and poverty because they use different methodologies to update the indigence line, and because they have different approaches toward correcting the sampling problems of the ENH (chiefly the underreporting of income and the truncation problem; see Sánchez and Nuñez 1999a).

11. According to Sánchez and Nuñez (1999b), there was a diverging evolution of indigence and poverty in rural areas. Rural indigence has decreased substantially between 1991 and 1995, even if rural poverty has not. The reason is that agricultural salaries and income have

increased during this period mostly in the lowest quintile, the relevant one for the indigence line. It will be important to bear in mind this difference between the poverty and indigence lines when discussing social policies in the rural sector.

12. There are likely to be some problems with the CEPAL measurements. Notice, for instance, that this publication gives an incidence of poverty in Brazil of only 29 percent, much lower than in Colombia, and close to the Costa Rican value of 20 percent. Echavarria (1996) uses its own elaboration of the household surveys for Brazil, Chile, Costa Roca, Ecuador, El Salvador, Mexico, Nicaragua, Paraguay, Peru, and Venzuela, and the CEPAL numbers for the other countries; while it is still true that Colombia has a higher overall poverty rate than the average, now it has a ratio of rural to urban poverty above the average.

13. López and Valdez (1996) also argue that access to education, health, and credit in rural areas are below those of similar countries.

14. The data on employment refer to the seven main cities.

15. DANE publishes "La Pobreza en Colombia," which gives the NBI index for every municipality; it allows the identification of the poorer areas in the cities with more than 40,000 inhabitants and in metropolitan areas.

16. Thus SISBEN overcomes an important limitation with several income-based measures of poverty: the seasonality of income. Income is still present in SISBEN, but probably it will be dropped in the next version, mainly because its reporting is subject to considerable misrepresentation.

17. See Sarmiento, Gonzalez, and Rodriguez (1999) for a description of SISBEN and an evaluation and Vélez, Castaño, and Deutsch (1999) for an economic interpretation.

18. See DNP-UDS (1997).

19. By law, levels 1, 2, and 3 should be enrolled in the Regimen Subsidiado. Lack of funding has so far prevented full coverage of level 3.

20. Personal conversation with Maria Teresa Zarta.

21. A similar exercise consists in estimating how often individuals who are poor according to another classification are not considered poor by SISBEN. Sarmiento, Gonzalez, and Rodriguez (1999) have performed such an exercise, using data from the 1997 Encuesta de Calidad de Vida to estimate both the number of individuals in SISBEN levels 1, 2, and 3 and the number of poor individuals according to the alternative definition of poverty. Thus, define the "PL poor" all individuals below the DANE poverty line, and the "SISBEN poor" all individuals in levels 1, 2, or 3 of SISBEN. Then in 1997 the PL poor who were not considered SISBEN poor were about 15 percent of all the PL poor. Similarly, define the "decile poor" as those individuals below the 5th decile of the distribution of income; then the decile poor who were not considered SISBEN poor were about 19 percent of all decile poor.

Note that this exercise has two limitations. The first is conceptual: SISBEN captures a different notion from the poverty line or income. Therefore one should not expect a close correspondence between the two. The second limitation is empirical: the results above are based on calculations from the Encuesta Calidad de Vida 1997; hence they are based on a limited sample.

22. SISBEN is very cheap: it costs about $2.25 in 1996 dollars per questionnaire, or about 0.5 on average per person. This is equivalent to about 0.5 percent of total Regimen Subsidiado spending; unit costs would be even lower if it were used more effectively for other programs.

23. On this last point, see World Bank (1994), which several years ago argued against the use of the NBI index and in favor of its replacement with SISBEN.

24. Chile is the only country that has a similar system already operating; Argentina, Ecuador, and Venezuela are in the process of establishing one.

25. Currently SISBEN does not cover *desplazados*, and all individuals living in *hogares colectivos*, such as prisons, ancianatos, and orphanages.

26. Some municipalities now have a system to detect *duplicaciones de censamiento*.

27. Vélez, Castaño, and Deutsch (1998) argue that SISBEN is an index of utility, while Sarmiento and Gonzalez (1998) and Cortes, Gamboa, and Gonzalez (1999) argue that it is an index of standard of living. The latter also argue that, as an index of standard of living, the ICV index is superior.

28. Theoretically, SISBEN should cover level 3 also, but lack of funding has so far prevented an extension of its coverage.

29. The PND definition refers to El Salto Social.

30. For instance, using the widest definition of social expenditure DNP has argued that Colombia belongs to the group of Latin American countries with the highest share of public social spending in GDP. It is not clear what to make of a comparison that shows Peru as having a 2 percent share of public social spending in GDP in 1990, clearly an implausible number.

31. The OECD uses a similar classification.

32. I combine "other social exclusion" (e.g., drug rehabilitation and policies toward minors with criminal offenses) with policies toward "children and families" because in Colombia they are all carried out mostly by the same agency, ICBF, and are mostly geared to minors.

33. According to estimates by the Finance Ministry, the net debt position of the pension system was 140 percent of GDP in 1997.

34. These numbers are obtained as the coefficient of the teacher dummy variable in wage regressions that control for gender, schooling, experience, private sector, rural/urban employment, and unionization.

35. The rest of this subsection is based mostly on James (1999) and Ayala (1995).

36. According to Article 26 of ley 100 1993, the beneficiaries of FSP must be affiliated to the Regimen General de Seguridad Social en Salud (RGSSS). But a self-employed individual who earns a minimum salary or less does not have enough resources to be affiliated to an EPS, and therefore can only be affiliated to the Regimen Subsidiado. But the latter was not properly set up in 1996; hence according to CONPES the affiliation to RGSSS would be considered accomplished if a person was entitled to the benefits of that regimen according to SISBEN. It is not clear whether this decision has actually been implemented.

37. Unfortunately, its discussion has been delayed, and at this stage it is not clear what the fate of the proposal will be.

38. CIDER (1998) proposes ICBF; however, as discussed in section 9.4.2, ICBF itself has problems of excessive centralization.

39. Van der Gaag and Tag (1998), using data from Bolivia, estimate social returns ranging from 1.4 to 2.1. But the data and the empirical methodology are questionable.

40. This program is listed as having 155,147 children beneficiaries, but 0 budget allocation for 1999.

41. These figures are obtained by dividing the allocation for 1999 by the official number of beneficiaries. It is likely that the overestimate of the official figure of beneficiaries is higher for HCB than for CAIP; hence the relative cost of CAIP per children is likely to be lower than 170 percent.

42. Since then, relative attendance probably has changed, reflecting the gradual phasing out of CAIP. But the figures that follow are still useful to understand the patterns of demand for the two types of childcare when both programs were still supported by ICBF.

43. The CASEN survey also gives much higher rates of usage of both HCB and CAIP. This is probably due to the fact that the survey asked if the household used the services of these two programs at some point in the past.

44. The net subsidy is computed by Flórez and Méndez (1993) as total costs per child minus the small flat fee minus the 3 percent payroll tax, under various assumptions about its incidence.

45. A leading academic expert on HCBs supported this possibility in a private conversation.

46. A prominent nutritional role for HCB does not mean that there are no problems with its performance in this area. In the First Evaluation Survey of 1996, malnutrition was found to be marginally higher among children who attend HCB, even after controlling for socioeconomic level. This seems to be due to the fact that parents think their children get the full ration, while they get at HCB only 50 to 70 percent of the daily ration. Another reason could be that only about 10 percent of the HBIs complied with the ICBF diet requirements in 1996 (World Bank 1997b). However, the difference in malnutrition levels was not statistically significant.

47. The size of the loan fund in 1996 was about US $10m.

48. Note that in Jamaica, handicapped, elderly, and indigent individuals pick up food stamps at the post office and other government offices; pregnant and lactating women pick up stamps at clinics. But it would seem that an indigent woman can pick up stamps twice, unless there is a sophisticated system of record keeping in place.

49. However, history can teach interesting and contrasting lessons on this point. Between 1975 and the early 1980s Colombia had a food stamp program (PAN) that, by all accounts, was considered successful (although we do not know of any evaluation of costs and incidence). It was discontinued because the new Betancour administration shifted its emphasis toward food production and increased income level in the countryside. In addition it was operated by the Ministry of Agriculture, whose constituency and interests lie elsewhere (mainly in food production). Although they can be popular, food stamp programs need the support of the administration to survive.

A second, more recent experiment is a pilot program called Plan DIA, started experimentally in 1994 in some areas. The program used health centers to distribute food stamps to 75,000 poor pregnant and lactating women and to children under 5. It was run jointly by the Ministry of Agriculture and Health. Since this program was so close to the one advocated here, any evaluation of its outcome would be extremely helpful; unfortunately, it has not been possible to find one.

50. Thus, in the recent government proposal of the Red de Apoyo Social, the two requirements for the conditional cash grant were that the municipality should have a bank branch and a rate of immunization higher than 85 percent. This reduced the number of eligible municipalities to 450 out of 1,070.

51. Concerns about rents and corruption are the motivation for the government opting to use cash grants in the conditional grant proposal of the Red de Apoyo Social.

52. A program of conditional grants with similar characteristics is part of the emergency package included in the Red de Apoyo Social. However, it is explicitly intended to last only for three years; it excludes the poorest municipalities (all those without a bank branch and with immunization rates below 85 percent), and it amounts to less than 0.1 percent of GDP per year.

53. The second component of the Red de Apoyo Social is a training program for youths (the first component is the conditional grant mentioned in section 9.4.2). However, this component too is very small (less than 0.1 percent of GDP) and limited to a maximum of three years.

54. *Empleo Urbano* has three components: employment generation proper, training, and support for microenterprises. The last one was extremely small—less than 1 percent of the budget, covering only 56 projects in 26 municipalities—and will be ignored. Training received about 13 percent of the budget in 1996, and has been discussed in section 9.4.3. The remaining 86 percent of the budget was spent on employment creation programs.

55. Service projects are defined as maintenance of infrastructure, parks and "green areas," protection of areas at environmental risk, and collection and treatment of garbage and waste.

56. In 1996 the percentage of MONC (Mano de Obra No Calificada) was 58 percent in services and 38 percent in Infrastructure.

57. According to REUNIRSE (1998), 69 percent of participants in service projects attended a course or received some form of training during the execution of the project, against 31 percent for infrastructure projects.

58. In 1995 the three departments with the largest number of urban unemployed were Bogotá, Valle, and Antioquia, with 290,000, 223,000, and 216,000 unemployed, respectively; the three departments with the lowest number were Sucre, Caquetá, and Choco, with about 7,000, 9,000, and 10,000, respectively. In the same year Empleo Urbano spending in the first three departments was 1,524, 1,928, and 1,068 million pesos, in the latter three departments it was 645, 529, and 277 millions (see Contraloria General de la Republica 1998).

59. It explicitly relies on temporary labor contracts outside the Government in order not to generate permanent labor relationships.

# References

Acosta, O. L. 2000. Servicio publico y burocracia. Mimeo. FEDESARROLLO.

Acosta, O. L., and U. Ayala. 1998. Ajuste del sistema pensional del sector publico en Colombia. FEDESARROLLO, Santaféde Bogotá.

Acosta, O. L., and G. Borjas. 2000. Civil service and bureaucracy. Mimeo.

Agion, P., and P. Bolton. 1997. A theory of trickle-down growth and development. *Review of Economic Studies* 44: 151–72.

Aghion, P., and P. Bolton. 1992. Distribution and growth in model of imperfect capital markets. *European Economic Review* 36.

Alarcón, A. R. 1997. Red de Solidaridad Social: Paliativo Conyuntural de la Pobreza, Olvidandoi el Desarrollo Regional de Largo Plazo. *Informe Financiero*, Contraloría General de la Republica, May, pp. 21–48.

Attanasio, O., and M. Szekely. 1999. An asset-based approach to the analysis of poverty in Latin America. Inter-American Development Bank. OCE Working Paper R-376.

Atkinson, A. 1995. *Public Economics in Action: The Basic Income—Flat Tax Proposal*. Oxford: Oxford University Press.

Ayala, U. 1995. Qué se ha aprendido de las Reformas Pensionales en Argentina, Colombia, Chile y Perú? Inter-American Development Bank. OCE Working Paper 330.

Ayala, U. 1999. Nuevas Reformas al Sistema de Pensiones. *Economia Colombiana* (November): 79–93.

Ayala, U., and R. Perotti. 2000. The Colombian budget process: Analysis and proposals. Mimeo. FEDESARROLLO.

Ayala, U., C. Soto, and L. Hernández. 1999. La Remuneración y el Mercado de Trabajo de los Maestros Públicos en Bogotá. *Coyuntura Social* (May): 83–122.

Barnett, W. S. 1992. Benefits of compensatory preschool education. *Journal of Human Resources* 27(2).

Barnett, W. S. 1993. Benefit-cost analysis of preschool education: Findings from a 25-year follow-up. *American Journal of Orthopsychiatry* 63(4).

Besley, T., and S. Coate. 1994. The design of income maintenance programmes. *Review of Economic Studies* 62: 187–221.

Blank, R. M., D. Card, and P. K. Robins. 1999. Financial incentives for increasing work and income among low-income families. NBER Working Paper 6998.

Birsdall, N., and J. L. Londono. 1997. Asset inequality matters: An assessment of the World Bank's approach to poverty reduction. *American Economic Review* 87(2): 32–37.

Blundell, R., M. Costas Dias, C. Meghir, and J. Van Reenen. 2001. Evaluating the employment impact of mandatory job search assistance programs. Institute for Financial Studies Working Paper WP01/20.

Cárdenas, M., and R. Bernal. 1999. Changes in the distribution of income and the new economic model in Colombia. Series Reformas Económica 36. CEPAL.

Cardenas, M., et al. 1999. *Pobreza y Vivienda de Interés Social en Colombia: Los Programas de Vivienda Urbana de la Red de Solidaridad Social.* Universidad de los Andes/CIDER/ REUNIRSE.

Caro, M. V. 1998. Evaluación del impacto del programa de empleo urbano de la Red de Solidaridad Social. REUNIRSE/CIDER.

CEPAL. 1998. Panorama social de America Latina.

CIDER. 1998. Pobreza, gobierles locales y Redde Solidaridad Social. Universidad de los Andes, Bogotá.

Comisión de Racionalización de Gasto. 1997a. Empleo y salarios del sector público Colombiano, 1985–1995. Santafé de Bogotá.

Contraloría General de la Republica. 1997. La situación de las finanzas del estado 1997. Santafé de Bogotá.

Cortes, D., L. F. Gamboa, and J. I. Gonzalez. 1999. ICV: Hacia una Medida de Estandar de Vida. *Conyuntura Social* 21, November, pp. 159–78.

De Gregorio, J. 1996. Savings, growth and capital market imperfections: The case of borrowing constraints. *Journal of Monetary Economics* 39.

Deutsch, R. 1998. How early childhood interventions can reduce inequality: An overview of recent findings. Inter-American Development Bank, POV-105.

DNP. 1998. Evaluación de la política social, cuatrienio 1994–1998. Santafé de Bogotá.

DNP. 2000. *Indicadores de Coyuntura Social.* Santafé de Bogotá.

DNP-Mision Social. 1999. Gasto social 1980–1997. Santafé de Bogotá.

DNP-PNUD. 1996. Evaluación de la etapa de Implantación del sistema de selección de beneficiarios para programas sociales—SISBEN. Documento CONPES, Santafé de Bogotá.

DNP-UDS. 1996. El Fondo de Solidaridad Pensional. Documento CONPES 2833.

DNP-UDS. 1997. Focalización del Gasto Social. Documento CONPES, Santafé de Bogotá.

EUROSTAT. 1999. *Social Protection, Expenditure, and Receipts: European Union, Iceland, and Norway.* Luxembourg.

Ezemeneri, K., and K. Subbarao. 1998. Jamaica's food stamp program: Impacts on poverty and welfare. World Bank.

Farné, S., and O. A. Nupia. 1996. Reforma laboral, empleo e ingresos de los trabajadores temporales en Colombia. *Coyuntura Social* (November): 155–72.

Fay, R. 1996. Enhancing the effects of active labor market policies. OECD Labor Market and Social Policy Occasional Papers 18. Paris.

Flórez, C. E., and R. Méndez. 1993. Hogares comunitarios de bienestar: Quién se beneficia? DNP. September.

Flórez, C. E., et al. 1999. Riesgos sociales y oportunidades de las familias Colombianas: Bases para el análisis. Mimeo. DNP-Misión Social. December.

Flórez, C. E., H. Moreno, and L. Barrios. 1994. Fondo de solidaridad pensional: Caracterización de la población objetivo. DNP-Misión Social.

Galor, O., and J. Zeira. 1993. Income distribution and macroeconomics. *Review of Economic Studies* 60: 35–52.

Gavin, M., and R. Perotti. 1997. Fiscal policy in Latin America. In B. Bernanke and J. Rotemberg, eds., *NBER Macroeconomics Annual 1997*. Cambridge: MIT Press.

Grubb, D. 2000. Eligibility criteria for unemployment benefits. *OECD Economic Studies* 31: 147–84.

Hoddinot, J., and E. Skoufias. 2000. Preliminary evidence of the impact of progress on consumption. International Food Policy Research Institute, Washington DC.

Holzman, R., T. Packard, and J. Cuesta. 1999. Extending coverage in multi-pillar systems: Constraints and hypotheses, preliminary evidence and future research agenda. World Bank.

IADB. 1997. Informe de Progreso Económico y Social de *América Latina y el Caribe*. Washington, DC.

ICBF. 1997. *Evaluación del Impacto de los HCB 0–6 Años*. Santafé de Bogotá.

International Monetary Fund. 1999. Colombia: Staff report for the 1999 Article IV consultations. Washington DC, December.

Jappelli, T., and M. Pagano. 1994. Savings, growth and liquidity constraints. *Quarterly Journal of Economics* 109: 83–110.

Jaramillo, D. O. 1999. *Balance del Programa Vivir Mejor*. Universidad de los Andes/ CIDER/REUNIRSE.

James, E. 1999. Coverage under old age security programs and protection for the uninsured —What are the issues? Working paper. World Bank.

Leibovich, J., and J. Nuñez. 1999. Los activos y recursos de la población pobre en Colombia. IADB OCE WP R-359.

Liang, X. 1999. Teacher pay in 12 Latin American countries. World Bank.

Marquez, G. 1999. Unemployment insurance and emergency employment programs in Latin America and the Caribbean: An overview. Paper presented at the "Conference on Social Protection and Policy," February 5. Inter-American Development Bank.

Martin, J. P., and D. Grubb. 2001. What works and for whom: A review of OECD countries' experience with active labor market policies. IFAU—Office of Labor Market Policy Evaluation Working Paper 2001-14.

Mazza, J. 1999. Unemployment insurance: Case studies and lessons for the Latin American and Caribbean region. Technical Study RE2/SO2. Inter-American Development Bank.

Moffitt, R. 1996. Incentive effects of the U.S. welfare system: A review. *Journal of Economic Literature* 30: 1–61.

Myers, R. 1995. *The Twelve Who Survive: Strenghtnening Programmes of Early Childhood Development in the Third World*. Michigan: High/Scope Press.

Panizza, U., and Z. Qiang. 2000. Spoiled bureaucrats and exploited women? Public sector premium and gender gap in Latin America. Mimeo. Inter-American Development Bank.

Pearson, M., and S. Scarpetta. 2000. An overview: What do we know about policies to make work pay? *OECD Economic Studies* 31: 11–24.

Pencavel, J. 1986. Labor supply of men. In O. Ashenfelter and R. Layard, eds., *Handbook of Labor Economics*. Amsterdam: North-Holland, pp. 3–102.

Perfetti, M. 1997. Diferenciales salariales entre trabajadores asalariados hombres del sector público y del sector privado, entre 1984 y 1994, en Colombia. In M. Cardenas and N. Lustig, eds., *Pobreza y Desigualidad en America Latina*. Santafé de Bogotá: Tercer Mundo Editores, pp. 251–83.

Perotti, R. 1993. Political equilibrium, income distribution, and growth. *Review of Economic Studies* (September).

Perotti, R. 1996. Income distribution, democracy, and growth: What the data say. *Journal of Economic Growth* (June).

Ravallion, M. 1998. Appraising workfare programs. Inter-American Development Bank, Working Paper POV-102.

REUNIRSE. 1998. Balance y perspectivas. Santafé de Bogotá.

Saez, E. 2000. Optimal income transfer programs: Intensive versus extensive labor supply responses. NBER Working Paper 7708.

Sánchez, F., and J. Nuñez. 1999a. La medición de la pobreza en Colombia. IADB.

Sánchez, F., and J. Nuñez. 1999b. Decentralización, pobreza y acceso a los servicios sociales. Quién se beneficio del gasto público en los noventa? Documento CEDE 99-04.

Sarmiento, A., and J. I. Gonzalez. 1998. Ajuste social y grupos vulnerables. Misión Social-DNP.

Sarmiento, A., J. I. Gonzalez, and L. A. Rodriguez. 1999. Eficiencia horizontal y eficiencia vertical del sistema de selección de beneficiarios (SISBEN). *Conyuntura Social* 21 (November): 107–26.

Schultz, T. P. 1999. Preliminary evidence of the impact of progress on school enrollments from 1997 to 1998. International Food Policy Research Institute, Washington DC.

Van der Gaag, J., and J. Tag. 1998. *The Benefits of Early Child Development Programs: An Economic Analysis.* Washington: World Bank.

Vélez, C. E. 1996. Gasto social y desigualidad: Logros y extravios. DPN-Misión Social, Santafé de Bogotá.

Vélez, C. E., E. Castaño, and R. Deutsch. 1999. Una interpretación económica del sistema de focalización de programas sociales: El Caso del SISBEN en Colombia. *Conyuntura Social* 21 (November): 127–58.

World Bank. 1990. *Colombia: Social Programs for the Alleviation of Poverty.* Washington: World Bank.

World Bank. 1994. *Poverty in Colombia.* Washington: World Bank.

World Bank. 1995. *Averting the Old Age Crisis: Policies to Protect the Old and Promote Growth.* New York: Oxford University Press.

World Bank. 1997a. *Safety Net Programs and Poverty Reduction: Lessons from Cross-Country Experience.* Washington: World Bank.

World Bank. 1997b. Community child and nutrition project: Implementation completion report.

Zarta, M. T. 1998. Análisis de bases de datos SISBEN de Santiago de Cali. DNP, Santafé de Bogotá.

# 10 Toward a Truly Independent Central Bank in Colombia

Alberto Alesina, Alberto Carrasquilla, and Roberto Steiner

## 10.1  Introduction

In the last decade the optimal degree of central bank independence has been an issue receiving the attention of academics and (more important) of policy makers in many OECD and developing countries. The issue of central bank independence is especially important in two emerging situations: the case of countries that have experienced macroeconomic imbalances and are implementing "structural reforms," and the case of the creation of new political entities in need of new monetary institutions, like the European Union and several "reborn" countries regaining their sovereignty around the globe.[1]

The direction of institutional reform has been for the most part toward making central banks independent of political pressure. Recent examples are the United Kingdom, Canada, and New Zealand in the OECD and Chile (1989), El Salvador (1991), Argentina (1992), and Mexico (1993) in Latin America. The new European Central Bank modeled on the German Bundesbank is one of the most autonomous central banks in the world. The motivation of this move is linked to an increased emphasis on price stability as the main, or only, goal of monetary policy after the exceptionally high inflation rates in the 1970s and 1980s around the world.

Colombia had its own central bank reform in 1991. The intention of the legislators was to increase the degree of independence of the central bank, but the reform, which was a compromise of conflicting pressures, has produced an unsavory institutional arrangement. For instance, the presence of the treasury minister on the board of the central bank, the timing and procedures of appointments, and the lack of a clearly specified goal for monetary policy are features that are normally *not* thought of as indicators of independence of the monetary authorities. In addition, as in many other areas of policy, the Colombian Constitution is very detailed in the norms that regulate the central bank. Virtually any major change in the institutional rule governing the central bank requires a constitutional reform.

Our discussion revolves around three issues: changes in the appointment procedures for the board and the governor of the bank, a clearer legislative definition of the mandate of the central bank and the goal of monetary and exchange rate policy, and the definition of the central bank as the supervising entity of the financial sector.

We consider the prospect of making the board of the bank smaller and removing members of the government's executive office from it. Other issues concern introducing an appropriate timing of appointments to create stability in the board, the lengthening of the appointed the governor's tenure as well as that of board members. Together with a staggering of terms, this should reduce the risk that every new executive brings about an entire new board, or at least a new majority in the board of the bank. The idea is to introduce reforms that increase the stability and independence of monetary policy. For the same reason we believe that the central bank should have a clear mandate that sets inflation control as its overarching goal. This is important because the Constitutional Court has already recently become involved in the matter of prioritizing inflation control over other goals and thus contributed to this confusion.[2] Finally, we show that the central bank is the institution well suited to supervise the financial and banking sector. While arguments for and against using the central bank as the financial regulator exist, on balance we conclude that for a middle-income country this is the best solution.

## 10.2   Why Independent Central Banks?

### 10.2.1   The Issues
The rationale for independent central banks is that if politicians (the legislature and/or the executive) have a direct daily control and supervision over monetary policy, they will be tempted to jeopardize long-run monetary stability for short-run benefits. Take these few examples of incentives for such political intervention:

1.   Unanticipated monetary expansions. The expansion may result in temporary reduction in unemployment, through a Phillips curve effect. But market expectations will adjust, and the economy will be trapped in a high-inflation equilibrium.[3] Politicians interested in a short-run burst of growth (and reduction of unemployment) might opt for temporary expansion,

even at the costs of compromising long-term monetary stability. The opposite is monetary tightening, which might be necessary from the point of view of optimal stabilization policy, but government may opt to postpone or water down the monetary restriction.

2. Monetization of deficits. In a period of fiscal imbalance, political pressures might result in monetization of deficits, to the extent that the inflation tax is "hidden" relative to other forms of taxation. Fiscally induced loose monetary policies have been one of the main causes of high inflation episodes in Latin America.

3. Suboptimal election cycles. The incentives to pursue the short-run measures in points 1 and 2 will be particularly high in election years. Thus the creation of suboptimal cycles related to elections.[4]

In a small open economy political incentives make it very difficult, if not impossible, to maintain a fixed exchange rate system. A fixed rate system cannot be maintained without an independent monetary authority firmly committed to price stability. There must be a close link between monetary institutions and exchange rate regimes.

The additional effect of a direct political control of the central bank means that every time a government changes, monetary policy will follow the preferences of the new administration. This feature will add some undesirable unpredictability to monetary policy.[5]

### 10.2.2 How Can an Independent Central Bank Help?

A central bank that is not under the day-to-day control of the president or the legislature can shield monetary policy from the incentives described above, which lead to policies excessively concerned with the short term. It should be clear what is to be expected from laws, as it is, after all, men and women who make monetary policy, and not institutions. Generally, people do not desire dictatorships, although some dictators may provide good policies. So even an objectionable institution can, though rarely, produce good government. However, in general, dictatorships have proved to be in the hands of people who lead to very poor economic outcomes. The argument for promoting "good" institutions is that this helps well-intentioned politicians do "the right things" and creates obstacles for the not so well-intentioned individuals to do the "wrong things."

### *How Can One Measure Political Independence?*

Political independence of central banks around the world has been evaluated in two ways.[6] The first is by examining the laws that regulate the relationship between the bank and the executive and the legislative powers. This concerns the composition of the governing board of the central bank where the presence of members of the government is a sign of low independence. Short-term appointments of board members are also taken as an indication of low independence, since the members are forced into a position of seeking reappointment by pleasing their political sponsors. The power of a president to appoint ex novo an entire board (or most of its members) also reduces continuity and stability in the conduct of monetary policy. A staggered system of appointments in policy committees ensures policy stability and thus policy moderation by avoiding extreme swings in the composition of the committee.[7] Restrictions on who may or may not serve as a board member can further contribute to independence.

In the Colombian case the presence of members of the executive office on the board of the bank is an obvious and clear indicator of low independence by all cross-country indexes. The international evidence on this point is striking. In no OECD country is there any member of the executive branch a voting member on the board of the central bank. In no country in Latin America other than Colombia is there a treasury minister also serving as a member of the board, let alone its president. Therefore the Colombian arrangement, in which the treasury minister is the chairman of the bank's board, is highly unusual.

The second difference has to do with the relationship between government finances and monetary policy. Obviously any rule that requires the central bank to buy government debt reduces the ability of the bank to pursue an independent monetary policy. Rules that regulate the relationship between monetary policy and the fiscal balance vary across countries, and sometimes complicated wordings as hidden rules will make more or less obscure the basic issue of how much the central bank is committed to "help out" with monetization of deficits.

A third area relates to written law on monetary policy. If the constitutional law explicitly imparts to the monetary authority the objective of maintaining price stability, the central bank has the legislative support necessary to deflect political interference.[8] A legislative directive on price stability does not mean that the central bank will follow in every instant a policy of low inflation at all costs, but that a view toward price stability will be pursued *cum grano salis* in the near term. There is, of course, a margin of ambiguity here, but economists generally argue that such ambiguity can be eliminated by a well-defined and relatively narrow target of inflation followed at any instant by the central bank. Others argue for a more flexible approach, according to which a narrowly defined target has to be achieved in the near term, thus allowing for some moderate role for monetary stabilization policies.[9] In effect, whatever the theoretical position, the explicit goal of price stability in the law of the bank demands that it normally take a direction "independent" of the monetary authorities.[10] In other words, an independent central bank may choose once in a while to abandon the goal of price stability, but having an explicit goal of price stability shields the bank from undesired pressures. A vast literature has investigated the pros and cons of inflation targeting in OECD countries.[11] In a recent review of experiences in emerging markets, Mishkin (2000) argues "that although inflation targeting is not a panacea ... it can be a highly useful monetary policy strategy [even for developing countries]." More on this point, below.

### Do Laws "Work"?

An important question is whether the actual degree of central bank independence heavily depends on the laws regulating the institutional position of the bank or whether its de facto behavior is unrelated to those laws and regulations. Research on OECD countries has shown that central bank laws are closely associated with the expected outcomes. More specifically, independent central banks (by law) have been associated with relatively low inflation and macroeconomic stability. Interestingly the benefits of stability have not been associated with the costs of lower average growth or more growth that is variable.[12] Alesina and Summers (1993) point to a strong and negative association between the average level of inflation and the degree of central bank independence in a sample of OECD countries. The same authors show that there is no relationship, however, between central bank independence and variability of GDP growth.

Results for non-OECD countries are less clear-cut. Many central banks that by law should be independent do not behave in ways consistent with this position, and vice versa. In other words, plotting a measure of the legal independence of central banks against measures of inflation will not always show a clear relationship. On the other hand, researchers have found that the frequency of change in the leadership of the central banks has been positively associated with poor monetary management and inflationary pressures. In other words, countries with frequent changes of central bank governors have experienced high and variable inflation.[13] There is, of course, the issue of causality, which often runs both ways.

The point we want to make here, is that "laws" are not always enough to guarantee central bank independence. The actual practice of monetary policy can vary, even across central banks of the same institutional form. However, this observation should not keep the legislator from setting up appropriate institutions that ensure central bank independence. All we want to show is that independent central banks alone do not guarantee monetary stability.

### How about Democratic Control over Monetary Policy?

"Democracy" and delegation are ideas not in conflict with each other. Democratic control over the conduct of monetary policy is achieved by periodic appointments of the board (see below) and by the setting of a goal for monetary policy. For this reason a distinction should be made between goal independence and instrument independence.[14] The former implies that the central bank would choose the goals for monetary policy and the instruments to achieve them. The latter implies that the goals for monetary policy are chosen by the legislature (and/or the executive), and the central bank can independently choose the instruments.

Very few disagree that central banks should have "instrument independence." It would be hard to imagine a legislature debating on the appropriate use of M2 or M3, or about which interest rates to target. However, instrument independence may not be enough. Suppose that a legislature decides that an appropriate goal for monetary policy is to monetize the deficit, a policy that would certainly result in high inflation. The fact that the central bank is free to choose which instruments to use to monetize does not help much.

A standard objection to "goal independence" is that in a democracy elected officials should choose policy goals. Thus, how does one ensure democratic control over monetary policy, insulating the latter from the ebb and flows of politics? Democratic control over monetary policy is achieved in two ways. One is by the appointment procedure, by which there is executive or legislative intervention in the selection of members of the board. The second is by the democratic delegation to the central bank of a goal of inflationary control, which ultimately is the only objective that monetary policy can deliver. An interesting analogy is that of an independent judiciary. No one can argue that an independent judicial system is in conflict with the idea of democracy, although in most democracies justice is in the domain of independent institutions.

Several commentators argue that central banks have to be accountable. One has to be clear on this point. If an accountable central bank is one that has to seek approval for every policy decision, then an accountable central bank is not independent. Independence means that the central bank is accountable in the general sense of inflation control but not in day-to-day policy decisions, however important they might be.

### What about Monetary and Fiscal Policy Coordination?

The one big objection to the idea of central bank independence often voiced is that it makes it difficult to coordinate monetary and fiscal policy. Thus the economy will be led to higher interest rates and experience slower growth than would otherwise be the case. In reality, often the coordination is nothing more than an attempt to loosen the government's budget constraint and open the door for political pressures on the central bank to monetize deficits. In fact, an explicit lack of coordination may signal the fiscal authority to follow more prudent polices. In the past through fiscal adjustments in highly indebted OECD countries, the independence of monetary policy helped reinforce the more prudent fiscal incentives.

Avoiding coordination does not mean that central banks' policies will be oblivious to anything happening in the economy. For example, in banking crises the central bank can choose interventions that will jeopardize in the short run the goal of price stability. However, this is very different from requiring an explicit coordination of monetary and fiscal policy. The insistence on an explicit means of coordination paves the way for governmental control of the monetary/fiscal policy package.

### Monetary Policy Rules and Exchange Rate Policy

In a small open economy exchange rate policies and the exchange rate regime are crucial elements of monetary arrangements. It is hard to envision a central bank in a small open economy trying to achieve monetary stability without being in charge of exchange rate policy.

Even from a political-economic point of view, it makes sense that the central bank be in charge of exchange rate policy. In an economy where import/export constitute a large fraction of GDP, the interests of distinct industries regarding the exchange rate are typically different. The interests of "consumers," namely a large but unorganized group, may be under-represented in a political process heavily influenced by lobbying groups. Political-economic theory suggests that if the benefits of a policy are concentrated and the costs diffuse, the policy may be implemented even if socially inefficient because of the concentrated lobbying effort in favor of the policy. This argument has been raised especially with reference to trade policy. Similar arguments may apply to exchange rate policy, although the exchange rate is much less directly under policy control than, say, tariff rates.[15] The concern for political pressures over exchange rate policies is especially relevant in countries like Colombia, where exporters are concentrated in a few sectors, well organized, and politically influential. In this environment it is appropriate to keep political pressures on the exchange rates at arm's length. A way of doing so is to empower the central bank with the right of choosing the exchange rate regime and exchange rate policies.

The choice of an exchange rate regime and of a monetary policy rule is also clearly linked to the question of maintaining the credibility of the price stability policy of the central bank. At one end of the spectrum of possibilities, one can envision a system of flexible rates accompanied by an inflation target rule for the central bank. In this arrangement, the credibility of the low-inflation policy is with the central bank, and therefore the independence of this institution is essential. The advantage of inflation-targeting rules is that besides the low-inflation guarantee, they allow for short-run stabilization policies. However, nothing but the reputation of the central bank guarantees the administration of these rules. In other words, what prevents the central bank from abandoning the inflation target is fear of damaging its reputation.

Fixed rate regimes have been advocated as a way of anchoring the currency in times of inflation. Nevertheless, as recent experiences of fixed rate regimes (or exchange bands) have shown, they can cause more problems than they solve. Risk premia and the threat of speculative attacks against a fixed rate can seriously disrupt financial transactions with real negative effects. Therefore credibility comes at a high cost and is not easily sustained.

More extreme versions of fixed rates regimes, like currency boards and "dollarization" (i.e., the adoption of a foreign currency), are becoming popular.[16] This is a product of world economic integration and the emphasis on price stability. Such arrangements increase credibility but remove monetary policy from direct domestic control. In other words, in a dollarized regime, threats of speculative attacks or risk premia are less of a problem than in a simple fixed exchange regime, and this is a big advantage. On the other hand, the country that dollarizes delegates monetary policy to another country, and gives up a policy instrument. The country that provides the currency would be in charge of monetary policy. Thus the monetary policy of the anchor country would not respond to the specific needs of the "home country."

**Table 10.1**
Banking supervision worldwide

| | Total countries | Central bank | Treasury | Independent regulator | Mixed |
|---|---|---|---|---|---|
| All sample (% of total) | 106 | 73 (68.9) | 2 (1.9) | 26 (24.5) | 5 (4.8) |
| Non-OECD (% of total) | 77 | 64 (83.1) | 1 (1.3) | 12 (15.6) | 0 |
| Below median income (% of total) | 53 | 46 (86.8) | 0 (0.0) | 7 (13.2) | 0 |
| Latin America excluding Central America (% of total) | 11 | 4 (36.4) | 0 | 7 (63.7) | 0 |
| High income | 29 | 11 | 1 | 13 | 4 |
| Upper middle income | 17 | 13 | 1 | 2 | 1 |
| Lower middle income | 35 | 25 | 0 | 10 | 0 |
| Low income | 24 | 24 | 0 | 1 | 0 |

## Supervision of the Financial Sector

Different countries have different arrangements concerning the supervision of the financial sector. Generally, the supervising body can be the treasury, an independent regulatory body, or the central bank.

Table 10.1 shows that in a vast majority of countries (about 75 percent), the supervision of the financial sector is performed directly by the central bank. This role of the central bank is even more marked in developing countries. In very few countries is the treasury in official and direct control of financial supervision. In most countries where the central bank is not involved in supervision, an independent agency performs this function.

How truly "independent" these agencies are varies from country to country. In Colombia, for instance, the government heavily influences the bank superintendency. First, the president appoints the superintendent and has the power of removing her from office. Additionally on the agency's governing board presides the deputy minister of finance, on delegation from the president. Since this situation is not unique to Colombia, table 10.1 underestimates the role of treasury ministers through their influence over the "independent" agencies. In South America, countries are evenly split among those with central bank supervision and those without. In Argentina, Brazil, Paraguay, and Uruguay, the central bank is the supervisor. In Bolivia, Colombia, Ecuador, Mexico, Peru and Venezuela, it is not. In Chile, the central bank issues bank regulations, although an independent agency performs the supervision.

In theory, the treasury should not be in charge of the supervision of the banking sector because of the conflict of interest, since the public sector will need financing from the banking sector. Clearly, the treasury may be tempted to introduce legislation that favors bank lending to the government, to public institutions, or to local governments. This issue is important if publicly owned banks are a large fraction of the banking sector, as in Colombia, where they hold around 20 percent of total assets. Therefore, keeping the treasury at arm's length from the banking sector can ensure that governmental agencies maintain appropriate finance policies.

The decision to keep banking supervision in the independent central bank is not a simple one to make. Since the central bank is also in charge of monetary policy and acts as the lender of last resort, there may be a bias toward leniency on the banks. The lender of last resort must always exercise subjective judgment when a particular bank is in trouble, as it is frequently unclear whether the problem involves liquidity or solvency. If the perception is that it is liquidity that is at fault, the first best response is to lend. If things come out wrong and the bank turns out to be insolvent, the bank fails and there is an overexpansion of the money supply. On the other hand, if the perception is a solvency problem, the first best response is not to lend. If things come out wrong and it was a liquidity issue, the bank fails and may generate contagion. One could argue that where there is a strict anti-inflation mandate, the central bank, acting as lender of last resort, should bias its decision against lending: there is then risk of an overestimation of insolvency and a bias toward underestimating the banking crisis.

If acting as the bank supervisor, the central bank is judged based on how many banks fail, then each case of banking difficulty poses a policy dilemma. As the lender of last resort, the central bank will be biased against lending, but as a bank supervisor, it will be biased toward lending. For any reasonable sequence of uncertain types of problems (solvency and liquidity) that it faces, it can be expected that a central bank that also acts as bank supervisor will be more inflation-prone than a bank that does not.

An independent regulatory agency runs the risk of being "captured" by the industry it is regulating. The question how truly independent the agency can then be from the executive remains to be seen. If the regulation of the banking sector is delegated to a strong and independent central bank, the risk of regulatory capture is mitigated. There are also informational reasons why it may be appropriate for the central bank to take charge of supervision. After all, detailed information about the banking sector is critical to the conduct of monetary policy.

The degree to which a regulatory agency can be truly independent, effective, and technically competent may vary by country and by level of development. The choice between the central bank and an independent agency may be different for, say, OECD countries and emerging markets. For the latter, our judgment call is that the central bank as the supervising agency is the better choice. More on this point, below.

## 10.3   The Institutional Position of Colombia's Central Bank

### 10.3.1   Background

Before the 1991 Constitution, monetary and exchange rate policies were implemented by the central bank, but conceived within the Monetary Board (Junta Monetaria) created in 1963. The Monetary Board was made up of several ministers and other high-level government officials. This institutional arrangement delivered a remarkable level of macroeconomic stability, if compared with other Latin American countries, but also a persistent level of inflation of about 20 percent. Colombia managed to cope well with moderate (by Latin American standards) levels of inflation in the 1970s and 1980s, thanks to many financial restrictions and regulations.

First, since 1967, extensive capital controls have been in place. Second, there are explicit prohibitions as to the creation of dollar-denominated liabilities (deposits) for the banking system. Third, indexation of selected contracts has solved many of the problems that inflation creates. For example, it was possible to fund long-term mortgage loans with short-term deposits because a monopoly was established wherein all indexed deposits were earmarked to fund them; the labor code introduced wage indexation as early as 1972; the nominal exchange rate was managed through a crawl, which to a large extent attempted to index the rate of nominal depreciation to the rate of inflation.

During the 1980s and (especially) the 1990s many of these institutions were called into question as they were viewed as inconsistent with a more open and competitive economy. In fact the reform of the central bank achieved with the Constitutional reform of 1991 was part of a more comprehensive set of reforms that included, among others, trade liberalization, the elimination of most capital controls, and the elimination of a monopoly, on the part of mortgage banks, for indexed deposits.

Before the reform of 1991 the fact that monetary policy was designed by a board, which included several ministers, was seen in some circles, particularly within the central bank itself, as a bias toward inflation. Relevant to this argument was the debate regarding how to understand the bank's profit and loss account and especially the capital gains stemming from nominal devaluation (*Cuenta Especial de Cambios*). The issue is the following: within an economy in which there is recurrent devaluation, dollar-denominated assets yield profits when expressed in local currency. These profits can be either capitalized or monetized. Traditionally these profits were monetized, largely through credits, which the central bank issued in favor of the government. Around 1984 an intense debate occurred between the government and the central bank on the issue, with several bank officials being against monetization. The outcome of this debate, which was largely won by the government, made it clear to Governor Francisco Ortega and his staff that the monetary board was inflationary.

The tide turned in 1990 when an assembly was called in order to write a new Constitution, which was to substitute the one written in 1886. Very quickly Mr. Ortega and his staff realized that the opportunity for substantive changes in the central bank charter was there. They capitalized on the fact that at the time the economics profession was explicitly dealing with the issue of central bank independence and results were consistent with the idea that independence brings about low and stable inflation, as discussed in section 10.2. It is clear from the documentary evidence that the central bank was the main advocate of independence. A paper entitled "Proposal for a monetary regime in the Constitutional reform" was written by the staff of the bank and circulated to the government in December 1990. This draft was the fundamental proposal, which, by and large, dominated the discussion.

### 10.3.2   The 1991 Reform

The 1991 Constitution radically changed the institutional features of the central bank. Implementation of the constitutional mandate was derived from Law 31 (1992).

As with the rest of the very long and verbose Constitution, the articles that create and bind the operation of the central bank are largely the result of consensus-building between two positions: those who wanted a very independent monetary policy and those who wanted the central bank involved in general economic policy. Lleras (a member of the assembly), in a paper entitled "The Central Banking Regime in the 1991

Constitution: In Search of Consensus," gives a detailed account of how the differing positions converged upon a consensus based text.[17]

One critical point of discussion was the exchange rate. The question was about who should be the exchange authority? If the central bank was not the only institution in charge, what type of rules should be adopted to get the government and/or Congress involved in the set of issues posed by the exchange rate regime? This was an important discussion because traditionally the exchange rate was an instrument by which resources were redistributed across sectors in a rather discretionary manner.

In the end the tension between the central bank autonomy and the politicians' desire to be involved in monetary, and especially in exchange rate policy, was resolved by making the government part of the board. This is the origin of the current odd arrangement whereby the minister of finance serves as the president of the board of an independent central bank. Thus, on the one hand, the constitutional assembly recognized the need for independence, but on the other, because of the critical role of the exchange rate in the economy, the assembly was compelled to "coordinate" the bank with the government. In other words, the bargaining was all about exchange rate polices, and ultimately about inflation and stabilization polices.

### 10.3.3 Consequences

The Constitution established Colombia's central bank as a high-level institution; it is as essential to the constitutional mandate as the Congress, the courts, and the presidency. Very rarely does an independent central bank figure in a nation's Constitution. For example, Argentina's currency board is legal in nature, and not based on a constitutional principle.

The status of the central bank in Colombia implies that relatively large transaction costs (i.e., a constitutional reform) are needed to change relatively minor rules on its regulation. The most important of these rules are as follows:

- The governing board is to be made up of seven members.
- The minister of finance is to be a member and its president.
- The president is to appoint five members. Every four years, a new president must reappoint three of the five, and do so for concurrent four-year periods.
- The board is to appoint the governor of the bank, who is also a member of the board.
- The central bank is to be the lender of last resort (LOLR).

• The central bank cannot lend money to the government, unless it is a unanimous decision by the seven members.
• The central bank cannot lend money to private agents, unless it is (1) in the capacity of LOLR or (2) in the process of intermediation of external credit.
• Twice a year the bank must present a report to Congress, and board members are to routinely attend hearings.

An important point of contention is whether Colombia's "development law" (which every newly appointed government has to submit to Congress six months after coming to office) subordinates the central bank. This is important, especially when the development law conflicts with the objective of price stability. In the recent decision by the Constitutional Court, this subordination point is explicit:

*The Constitution establishes an intermediate regulation as a result of the search for consensus among differing perspectives. In light of this, though the trend that favors recognition of Central Bank autonomy prevailed, and in spite of the fact that its basic objective is the purchasing power of money, the fact remains that very important aspects, proposed by the critics of this scheme were introduced in the Constitutional text. This explains the peculiarity of the Colombian Constitutional design ... the Constitution did not make a choice in favor of either of the two extreme models of a Central Bank, i.e. that in which it is dependent on the government nor that in which it is totally independent.... The subordination to the Development Law (Plan de Desarrollo) is a formal limit to the autonomy of the Central Bank in the exercise of its duty of controlling inflation.* (excerpts of Constitutional Court Sentence C-481-99)

As should be clear, the current position of the Colombian central bank is that it must balance two forces presented in the constitutional text: (1) the idea that monetary and exchange rate policy should be independent from the government, and (2) the opposing idea that monetary policy is too important to be left to technocrats. The result is an ambiguous formal entity, lacking precision in both objective and instrument. Though the explicit objective is to maintain the purchasing power of money, the task is complicated by the also explicit constraint in the sense that this goal must be pursued subject to "general economic policy."

The ambiguity between independence and government control is exemplified by a number of precepts. Consider, for example, the so-called appointed directors. With only one exception the original members (appointed in 1992) came from outside the government, but today only one of the five appointed members comes from outside the government.[18]

The problem fundamentally lies with the procedure used to appoint members. In the main, all five appointed terms expire simultaneously, so compliance with the government elevates the chance of reappointment for any individual member.[19]

In sum, "independentist" rhetoric permeates the Constitution in accepting the importance of a powerful central bank for overseeing monetary (and exchange rate) policy. However, the implementation of an effectively independent monetary policy is greatly diminished by the revealed practices of the government, which reflect a high degree of cautionary intervention.

### 10.3.4 A Few Episodes of Government Intervention

In what follows we argue, using some specific examples, that on occasions the government has been very much involved in setting monetary policy, and that this has been detrimental for monetary stability.

*Monetary Policy in 1997*

At the outset of the Samper administration (1994–1998) the government encountered a board entirely appointed by the previous administration. Quickly the minister of finance expressed his view that the central bank ought to be reformed and, in particular, greater control of the exchange rate regime should be in the hands of the government. This was consistent with the new government's idea that the real exchange rate was over valued, and should be weakened through policy in order to foster growth. In its development plan, the government puts it thus:

*The macroeconomic strategy of the Government will ... correct the unfavorable trends which have been experienced in the last few years by the real exchange rate and private savings.*[20]

The idea was to increase the existing controls to capital inflows and to devalue the nominal exchange rate. The problem was that the institution in charge was the central bank, not the government. The board strengthened the capital controls already in place, but the issue of changing the exchange rate arrangement was more complicated. Internal discussions of the board repeatedly were made public, in particular, in November 1994 when the exchange rate band was shifted upward (appreciated). Any reader of the financial press could conclude that the president of the board and the other members were in disagreement over exchange rate policy.

In 1996 the economy began to experience a sharp downturn and the exchange rate began to appreciate as the fears associated with the ongoing political crisis receded. This time the government had an additional instrument: it was going to exercise its right to appoint two of the members of the board in early 1997. In addition it was able to appoint another member due to the fact that one of the previous appointed members resigned before his term expired.

By the first quarter of 1997 the Samper government had thus appointed three members of the board, all of them recruited from within the ranks of high government—a minister, a deputy minister, and a senior economic advisor to the president. Including the finance minister, this defined a majority. By mid-1997 a new monetary policy based on low interest rates and currency depreciation was in place in order to foster growth. The operational instrument was the monetary base, which increased by 25 percent between December 1997 and December 1998. Apparently, by the end of the year the program was working well for the government. Outstanding loans on the part of the financial system, which had been expanding at a rate of around 25 percent in 1996 and until mid-1997, shot up to over 60 percent by year-end.[21] The deposit interest rate slid from around 28 percent at year-end 1996 to 22 percent in September 1997; the Bogotá stock index increased 35 percent in real terms between June and December 1997, and the real exchange rate depreciated by 14 percent in the same period. In the midst of this expansion, during the fourth quarter of 1997, the economy grew at an annual rate of 4.9 percent.

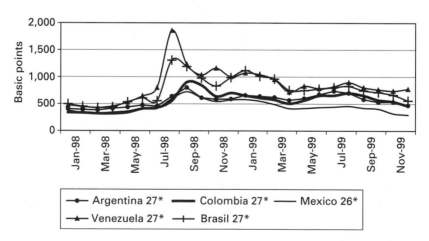

**Figure 10.1**
Latin American debt spreads based on 30-year bonds (Source: JP Morgan)

The heavy expansion induced by the central bank sharply reverted in 1998, and the economy was left with a much more vulnerable financial system, more heavily indebted firms and households, and no fiscal adjustment. In 1998 the economy entered its worst recession in recent history. To be fair, the entire region was in a precarious strait because of the Asian crisis, but the particularly poor performance of the Colombian economy had a clear domestic component. The relative spread on Colombian debt with respect to other Latin American countries increased in 1998 and debt ratings were downgraded by most agencies in 1999 (see figure 10.1 and table 10.2). Our take is that more arm's length between the government and the central bank would have been more prudent monetary policy and reduced the business cycle swing.

### Financial Policies in 2000

Colombia's banking sector has been under stress since at least 1998. At present, nonperforming loans represent about 13 percent of total assets, and the banking system as a whole experienced significant losses in both 1998 and 1999.

Government-owned banks, which hold around 20 percent of total assets, have been capitalized, credit lines have been opened for private banks, and important debt write-offs for mortgage loans have been put in place. Public banks have been experiencing significant and systematic losses for the last two years, notwithstanding all the effort put in place

**Table 10.2**
Colombian sovereign debt ratings

| Agency | Previous rating | New rating |
| --- | --- | --- |
| Moody's | | |
| 1994 | | Ba1 |
| 1995 | Ba1 | Baa3 |
| 11–8–99 | Baa3 | Ba2 |
| Standard & Poor's | | |
| 1994 | | BBB |
| 21–9–99 | BBB− | BB+ |
| 24–5–00 | BBB+ | BB |
| Duff & Phelps | | |
| 1994 | | BBB |
| 08–9–99 | BBB | BBB− |
| 17–3–00 | BBB− | BB+ |

Source: Ministerio de Hacienda.

by the relevant authorities. Since these banks are unable to obtain liquid funds in the market, the central bank has been funding them in a consistent fashion through discount facilities.

The discount mechanism has been supporting a process for which it was not designed. Namely it has shifted from a system designed to deal with temporary liquidity problems to a system where government owned banks have received permanent loans. The public banks receive bonds issued by the government. With the help of these bonds, they are able to meet capital requirements imposed by the superintendency of banks. These banks are therefore considered solvent in accounting terms, though other banks do not think so and do not supply them with liquidity, fearing default. Unable to receive liquidity in the market, the government-owned banks then go to the central bank for cash in return for the same bonds that the government previously issued in order to "capitalize" it. They receive this cash by agreeing to repurchase the bonds they surrender.

The process has been ongoing since 1999 and the stock of paper that the central bank has been rolling over almost daily amounted to some 20 percent of the monetary base in late February 2000. In March 2000 the bank decided to permanently purchase about 30 percent of the stock that it had been previously using in REPO operations.

Under the prevailing arrangements the central bank has no option but to lend to these banks, because they are declared to be "solvent" by the regulatory agency, which is basically a government institution.

## 10.4   Proposals

We focus our proposals on institutional reform of monetary institutions for Colombia in three areas: (1) the system of appointments for the board and the governor of the central bank, (2) the definition of the bank's monetary policy goals, and (3) the definition of the bank's role in financial market regulation.

### 10.4.1   The Appointment System
In order to achieve the goal of independence of the central bank, the following institutional reforms are deemed necessary:

*Composition of the Board*
1. Removal of any member of the executive office from the board of the central bank.

In effect the treasury minister should be removed from the board. Implementation of this reform would involve a constitutional amendment, changing Article 372 of the Constitution.

2. Reduction from the current five members of the board to three plus the chairman. The latter would cast the tie-breaking vote.

The rationale for this reform is twofold. First, it reduces the risk that too many voices "speak" for the bank, creating market uncertainty and confusion. Second, it enables the chairman to have a stronger voice, thus making the conduct of monetary policy more centralized. This proposal would involve a constitutional change.

### Appointment Procedures
3. The involvement of Congress in the appointment procedures.

Currently the executive appoints the governor and the board, without congressional confirmation. This procedure was decided to avoid the risk that Congress may impose candidates who do not have sufficiently strong anti-inflationary credentials. This precaution is legitimate. However, the lack of congressional voice in the appointment procedure has led to the impression that Congress has no role in overseeing the bank. As a result congressional members have attacked the whole idea of central bank independence. Of course, that initiative would worsen the central bank's current status quo.

It is not simple to balance these two considerations. Congressional approval would be required for the governor, on the one hand, as well as approval by the members of the board proposed by the executive. The big question is What happens next if Congress rejects the candidate of the government? Repeated rejections can slow the process and lead to the elimination of many suitable candidates. The government could, on the other hand, propose two candidates for the position of governor and the board members, and Congress would then choose one of the two but not be allowed to reject both.

4. Lengthening the term of office of the governor to seven years, renewable once.

The main advantage of this reform is that, in general, it avoids the coincidence of a new executive, who can immediately choose (under proposal

3 above) a new central bank governor. This reform would require a law modifying Law 32 of 1991 rather than a constitutional amendment. Also considered might be extending the appointments of board members to seven years.

5. Institution of a staggered system of appointment for the board of the bank.

Currently all five appointed members, and the governor, serve concurrent terms. A modification in the appointment procedure would require a constitutional reform.

6. Transitional issues.

So far our proposals considered a board of the bank consisting eventually of four members (including the governor), all appointed for seven-year periods. We think that the transitional procedure should be gradual, and we suggest a phasing-in of the proposed scheme as follows: at the point when the present term of the five appointed members expires, two be released and not replaced; three be re-appointed, one for two years, one for four years, and a third for six years. Upon expiration of their renewed terms, in this scheme each re-appointed member should be replaced according to the procedure outlined above. The same would apply to the governor: when the term in office of the current governor expires, he should be replaced according to the procedure we give above.

7. Restrictions on whom can be appointed in the board and as governor.

The executive should not nominate anyone who currently holds an executive position or has held one in the previous two years.

### 10.4.2  The Goals of Monetary Policy

Stable monetary goals are an important feature of smooth and productive financial markets and ultimately of the economy. It is therefore important to make monetary stability obligatory by law.

In principle, the Constitution leaves to the central bank the goal of maintaining monetary stability. However, by the constitutional sentence C-481-99, the control of inflation is limited by the *Plan de Desarrollo*. A legislative reform is necessary for the central bank to have precedence in making this judgment if the *Plan de Desarrollo* threatens the goal of inflation control in the immediate future.

### 10.4.3  Supervision of the Financial System
We believe that the central bank should assume the role of controller of the financial and banking sectors.

### 10.4.4  Disclosure and Secrecy
We believe that the central bank should adopt a precise and binding procedure to disclose its decisions and minutes of the meetings of the board. Disclosure of information should be strictly according to the procedural rules. The reason for this strict definition of procedure is that market operators need to know how and when to expect updates on monetary policy. Different central banks around the world follow different procedures about disclosures and secrecy. The kind of information withheld is not yet an issue, but the matter of delay in releasing information should be made public. There should be no confusion in the markets' perception that the Central Bank's main goal is inflation stability. Procedures for disclosure of information should be in place and the board should speak as one voice.

## 10.5  Conclusions

The 1991 reform of Colombia's central bank law has produced less than satisfactory institutional arrangements. The intention to establish an independent monetary authority in the conduct of monetary and exchange rate policy has not been completely realized. In our judgment, the institutional arrangement, and the policies of the central bank have accommodated political pressures. At this point we need to consider appropriate institutional reforms to the central bank law.

We have identified three areas of reform. One concerns the procedure for the appointment of the board and the governor of the central bank. Related to this is the issue of restrictions on the profile of who can serve in the board. Another area is the definition of the goals of monetary policy. We suggested an arrangement that seeks to balance the goal of democratic control over monetary policy with that of policy independence. A third area concerns what the central bank should be in charge of. We argued that the bank should take charge of exchange rate policy for two reasons: in a small open economy the exchange rate is a critical variable linked to inflation and monetary policy; second, political pressures concerning exchange rate policies are better kept in check if a strong and independent institution is controlling the exchange rate.

Finally, we think that the central bank should be the institution monitoring the banking and financial sectors for three reasons. The first is that the "capture" of the regulated industry is less likely to occur if supervision is done by the bank rather than by an "independent" regulatory agency. Second, if the central bank, rather than the treasury, performs the supervision and regulation, the incentives for the treasury to "distort" banking practices in its favor are reduced. Last, the informational requirement for the conduct of monetary policy suggests that the central bank can benefit from supervising the banking sector.

Colombia has made an effort in reforming a complex set of monetary institutions, which for over two decades delivered a persistently moderate rate of inflation. The central bank reform—along with the elimination of many indexation practices, the liberalization of financial activity, and the reduction of trade and capital account barriers—can deliver substantial progress. We see these reforms as "second-generation" fine-tuning to correct limitations in the original design that have impeded the bank's accomplishments.

## Notes

When this chapter was written Carrasquilla was with Fedesarrollo and Universidad de los Andes and Steiner with Universidad de los Andes. Carrasquilla is currently Colombia's Finance Minister and Steiner an Alternate Executive Director at the IMF. Opinions expressed in this chapter represent those of the authors', not of the institutions they are affiliated with. We thank Roberto Perotti and participants at the group meeting in Cartagena for comments and Miguel Braun for excellent research assistance. Maria Mercedes Carrasquilla provided outstanding organizational support.

1. In 1946 there were 76 independent countries in the world; there are 193 today.

2. Other chapters in this project have noted how the excessive involvement of courts has created problems in the execution of policy. For a general discussion of the role of the constitutional court in the checks and balances created by the Colombian Constitution, see Kugler and Rosenthal (2000).

3. See Barro and Gordon (1983) for a formalization of this argument.

4. A large literature has discussed these kinds of political business cycles; see Alesina, Roubini and Cohen (1997) for a detailed treatment of this area of research. Shi and Svensson (2000) show that political business cycles are much larger and more prevalent in developing countries than in the OECD.

5. See Alesina, Roubini, and Cohen (1997) on this point.

6. A vast literature has addressed this issue. On the measurement of central bank independence in OECD countries, see Grilli, Masciandaro, and Tabellini (1991) and Alesina and Summers (1993). For developing countries, see Cukierman (1992) and the references cited therein. Most of this literature (especially that on non-OECD countries) is based on data

that ends in the early 1990s. Since the Colombian institutional reform occurred in 1991, the available international comparisons are not relevant.

7. See, for instance, Waller (2000).

8. Normally, "price stability" is defined as a target of inflation, for instance, not more than a 2 percent increase each year.

9. Obviously the medium run allows a bit of flexibility and ambiguity in the operation of the central bank, as it is not clear exactly how long such a period would be.

10. For instance, this is the goal of the European central bank.

11. The reader is referred to Taylor (1999) for a summary of this literature.

12. For results along this line, see Alesina and Summers (1993), Grilli, Masciandaro, and Tabellini (1991), and Cukierman (1992).

13. A case in point is Argentina. Although, by law, the tenure of the governor should be four years, in the 1980s the average tenure was around ten months.

14. See, for instance, Fischer (1995).

15. For discussion of exchange rate politics in Latin America, see Frieden, Ghezzi, and Stein (1999). The case of Colombia is analyzed in Jaramillo, Steiner, and Salazar (1999).

16. For example, Argentina and Hong Kong have a currency board vis à vis the dollar. Bulgaria and Estonia have a currency board with the euro. Ecuador is actively considering full dollarization and Panama is already dollarized. See Alesina and Barro (2002) for a recent discussion of the pros and cons of "currency unions."

17. Lleras (1995).

18. He was the only academic ever appointed to the board of the bank.

19. This point is stressed by Hernandez (1991), then an independent analyst, now a member of the board of the bank.

20. El Salto Social (1994, ch. 3).

21. This is the annualized monthly rate of nominal growth.

# References

Alesina, A., and R. Barro. 2002. Currency unions. *Quarterly Journal of Economics*, 117: 409–30.

Alesina, A., N. Roubini, and G. Cohen. 1997. *Political Cycles and the Macroeconomy*. Cambridge: MIT Press.

Alesina, A., and L. Summers. 1993. Central bank independence and macroeconomic stability. *Journal of Money Credit and Banking* 25: 151–62.

Barro, R., and D. Gordon. 1983. Rules, discretion and reputation in a model of monetary policy. *Journal of Monetary Economics* 12: 101–22.

Cukierman, A. 1992. *Central Bank Strategy, Credibility, and Independence*. Cambridge: MIT Press.

Fischer, S. 1995. The unending search for monetary solution. In *NBER Macroeconomic Annual*. Cambridge: MIT Press.

Frieden, J., P. Ghezzi, and E. Stein. 1999. The political economy of exchange rate policy in Latin America. Mimeo. IADB.

Frieden, J., P. Ghezzi, and E. Stein. 2001. Politics and exchange rates: A cross section approach to Latin America. In J. Frieden and E. Stein, eds., *The Currency Game: Exchange Rate Politics in Latin America*. Baltimore: Johns Hopkins University Press.

Grilli, V., D. Masciandaro, and G. Tabellini. 1991. Political and monetary institutions in the industrial democracies. *Economic Policy* 13: 342–92.

Hernández, A. 1991. La transparente Claridad del Emisor. *Economía Colombiana*, no. 237.

Jaramillo, J. C., R. Steiner, and N. Salazar. 1999. The Political Economy of Exchange Rate Policy in Colombia. Fedesarrollo. Working Paper 11.

Lleras, C. 1995. El régimen de banca central en la Constitución de 1991: Búsqueda del consenso. In R. Steiner, ed., *La Autonomía del Banco de la Republica: Economía Política de la Reforma*. Bogotá: Tercer Mundo Editores.

Mishkin, F. 2000. Inflation targeting in emerging market countries. NBER. Working Paper 7618.

Salto Social. 1994. Plan Nacional de Desarrollo. Departamento Nacional de Planeación. Bogotá.

Shi, M., and J. Svensson. 2000. Political budget cycles in OECD and developing countries. Unpublished manuscript.

Taylor, J. 1999. *Monetary Policy Rules*. Chicago: University of Chicago Press.

Waller, C. 2000. Policy boards and policy smoothing. *Quarterly Journal of Economics* 115.

# Index

Accountability
 of central bank, 342–43
 and civil service for teachers, 268
 and clientelist politics, 84 (see also
  Clientelism)
 under closed list PR systems, 120–21
 and fragmentation of social programs,
  327
 in German-style PR, 120–21
 and nominal (secret) voting, 7, 83, 86, 97,
  98
 and separation of powers, 81
 and voting transparency, 127
Accounting standards and reporting
 and budget, 227, 229, 236–37
 and definition of investment, 228–30
 and transparency lack, 19 20
 treatment of deficit, 230–32
Activist court(s), 84, 90
 Constitutional Court as, 76
AD M-19, 106
Adverse selection, in pension system, 295,
 304
AFPs, 292, 298
Age. See also Elderly
 and internal migration, 260
 and unemployment structure, 285
Agriculture, and violence, 145
Alianza Democrática, 76
Allocation rules
 in decentralization, 193–200, 205
 simplification of, 17
Amazonas, 197
Andean Group, 48
Andean Pact, 43
Annual Cash Plan (Plan Anual de Caja,
 PAC), 216, 217, 218
Antioquia
 educational reforms in, 270
 homicide rates in, 11, 148
Apoyo alimentario a niños de edad
 prescolar, 309, 318

Appropriation reserves, 238
Argentina
 currency board of, 349
 local deficits as problem in, 176
 minimum guaranteed pension in, 299–300
Armed groups. See Guerrillas and guerrilla
 activity; Paramilitary groups; Private
 protection services
Arrears, budget, 228, 238–40
Asistencia al menor en recuperación
 nutricional, 318
Asset approach to poverty, 274–76

Balanced budget, 191–92, 213
Banking system. See also Central bank
 and borrowing by localities, 15, 202
 central bank's capitalization of, 353–54
 central bank as controller of (proposal),
  357, 358
 and regional government debt, 186
 supervision of, 346–47
Barco Vargas, Virgilio, 109
"Best practice institutions," 105
Betancur, Belisario Betancur Cuartas, 109
Bicameralism, separation of power in, 127
Bogotá
 armed groups in, 144
 crime and violence in, 32n.2, 158
 educational reforms in, 270
 evolution of violence in, 168n.34
 murder (homicide) rate in, 59, 134
 per-capita income of, 197
Bolivian Social Investment Fund, 323
Borrowing, local, 15, 16
Brazil
 "age" pension in, 300
 and coffee sector, 42
 GDP growth of, 33, 66–67
 and income distribution, 40
 local deficits as problem in, 176
British New Deal program, 323
Budget documents, 216–17